I asked someone involved with a website releasing the American version how *Nura: Rise of the Yokai Clan* is presented overseas and if people understand what yokai are. Apparently, if you say "yokai yakuza gang boy" in America, everyone is like "Whoa! Cool!" (*laughs*) I see... Rikuo is a "gang boy"...

—HIROSHI SHIIBASHI,
2012

HIROSHI SHIIBASHI debuted in BUSINESS JUMP magazine with *Aratama*. NURA: RISE OF THE YOKAI CLAN is his breakout hit. He was an assistant to manga artist Hirohiko Araki, the creator of *Jojo's Bizarre Adventure*. *Steel Ball Run* by Araki is one of his favorite manga.

NURA: RISE OF THE YOKAI CLAN

NURA: RISE OF THE YOKAI CLAN
VOLUME 21
SHONEN JUMP Manga Edition

Story and Art by HIROSHI SHIIBASHI

Translation – John Werry
Touch-up Art and Lettering – Annaliese Christman
Graphics and Cover Design – Fawn Lau
Editors – Megan Bates, Joel Enos

Printed in Canada

Published by VIZ Media, LLC
P.O. Box 77010
San Francisco, CA 94107

10 9 8 7 6 5 4 3 2 1
First printing, June 2014

www.viz.com www.shonenjump.com

NURA: RISE OF THE YOKAI CLAN

21

GHOST STORY: AOANDON

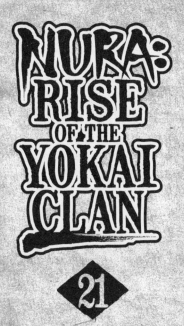

STORY AND ART BY
HIROSHI SHIIBASHI

CHARACTERS

NURARIHYON

Rikuo's grandfather and the Lord of Pandemonium. To prepare for all-out war with Nue, he intends to pass leadership of the Nura clan—a powerful yokai consortium—to Rikuo. He's a mischievous sort.

RIKUO NURA

Though he appears to be a human boy, he's actually the grandson of Nurarihyon, a yokai. His grandfather's blood makes him one-quarter yokai, and he transforms into a yokai at times.

KIYOTSUGU

Rikuo's classmate. He has adored yokai ever since he was saved by Rikuo in his yokai form, leading him to form the Kiyojuji Paranormal Patrol.

KANA IENAGA

Rikuo's classmate and a childhood friend. Even though she hates scary things, she's a member of the Kiyojuji Paranormal Patrol for some reason.

ITAKU

A yokai from the Tohoku yokai village called Tono. For six months, he helped Rikuo acquire a new Fear called Possess. He infuses his blade with Fear before cutting his opponent.

YUKI-ONNA

A yokai of the Nura clan who is in charge of looking after Rikuo. She disguises herself as a human and attends the same school as Rikuo to protect him from danger. When in human form, she goes by the name Tsurara Oikawa. Her mother is Setsura.

YANAGIDA

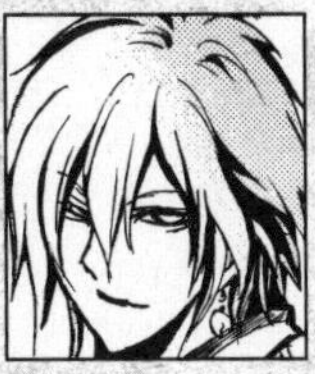

The ayakashi known as Sanmoto's "ears" and one of the Hundred Stories clan's seven leaders. He's held a grudge against the Nura clan since Rihan defeated Sanmoto.

GOROZAEMON SANMOTO

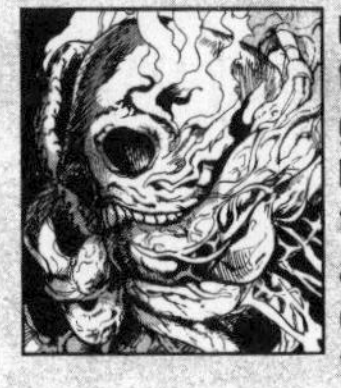

He has a history with Rikuo's father, Rihan, and holds a grudge against the Nura clan. He was originally human but transformed into an ayakashi and separated into seven different body parts. Leader of the Hundred Stories clan.

TAMASABURO

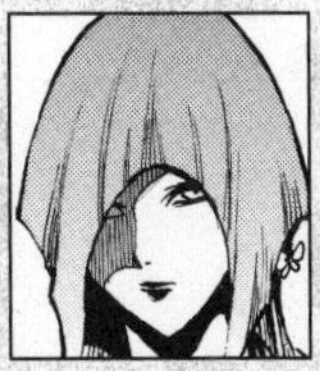

An ayakashi known as Sanmoto's "facial skin" and one of the Hundred Stories clan's seven leaders. He can use the skin of his face to disguise himself as another person.

ENCHO

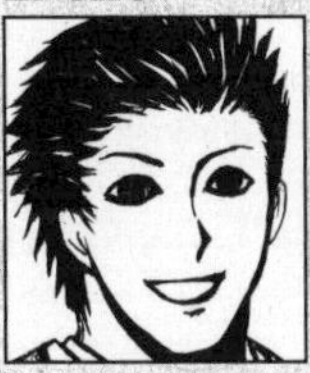

The ayakashi known as Sanmoto's "mouth" and one of the Hundred Stories clan's seven leaders. He has plotted a game of tag in Tokyo for the Nura clan.

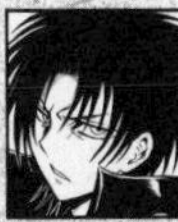

RYUJI

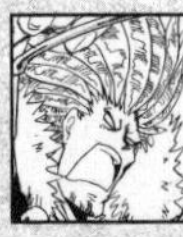

AOTABO

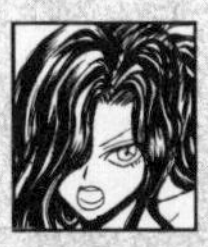

KEJORO

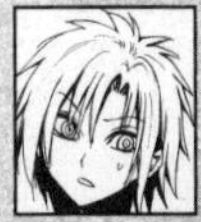

KUBINASHI

STORY SO FAR

Rikuo Nura is a seventh-grader at Ukiyoe Middle School. At a glance, he appears to be just another average, normal boy. But he's actually the grandson of the yokai Overlord Nurarihyon. He's also the Third Heir of the powerful Nura clan. He spends his days in hopes that he will someday become a great clan boss who leads a Night Parade of a Hundred Demons.

Receiving a report that yokai are being born in Shibuya, Rikuo rushes there. He arrives in the nick of time to save Torii and Maki from the Hundred Stories clan leader Kyosai, but Torii gets turned into a yokai again! In the face of this horrible situation, Rikuo exercises the fruits of his training with Itaku. By infusing his blade with Fear to attack only the yokai part of Torii, he is able to make her human again!

Rikuo throws himself into battle against Kyosai, but Kyosai's true goal was to capture Rikuo in one of his pictures. In the midst of battle, he traps Rikuo inside a hideous series of nine paintings called Kusozu. Each time he finishes one, Rikuo's body decays a little more. Though in tremendous pain, Rikuo protects his territory as Third Heir of the Nura clan by delivering Kyosai a final blow!

Meanwhile, Kiyotsugu and Kana scramble to prove Rikuo's innocence!!

TABLE OF CONTENTS

NURA:RISE OF THE YOKAI CLAN

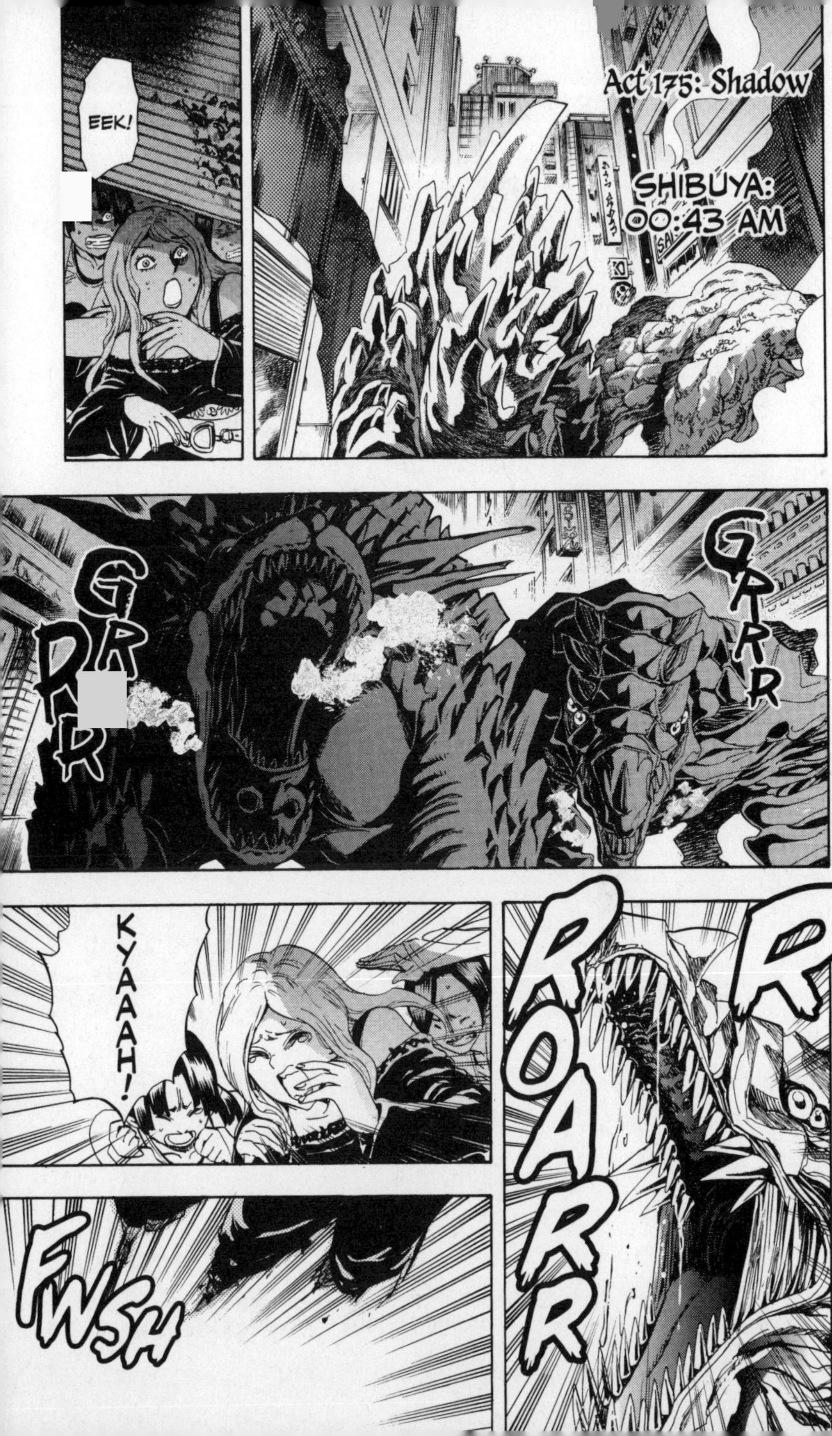
Act 175: Shadow
SHIBUYA: 00:43 AM
EEK!
GRRR
GRRR
R
ROARR
KYAAAH!
FWSH

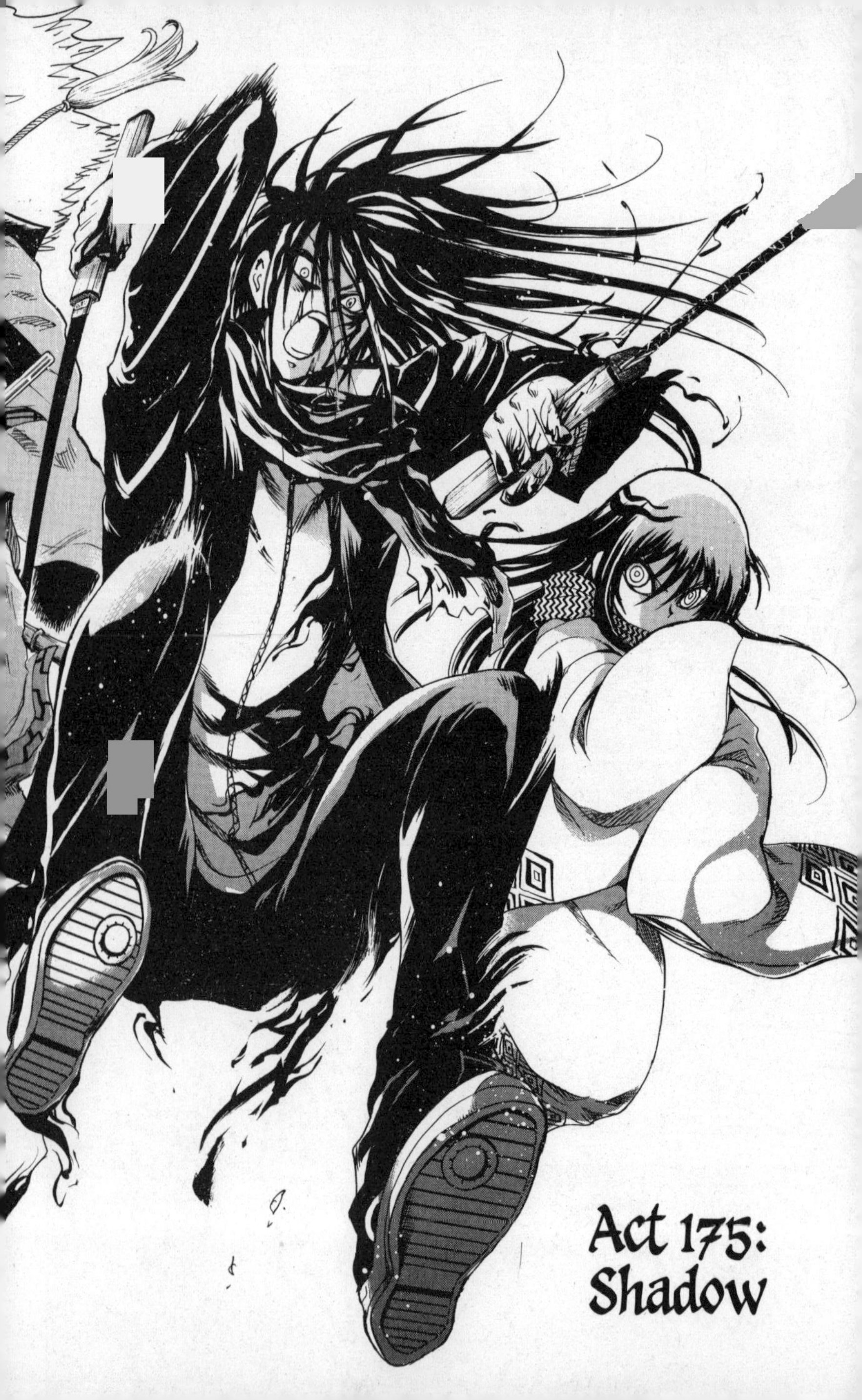
Act 175:
Shadow

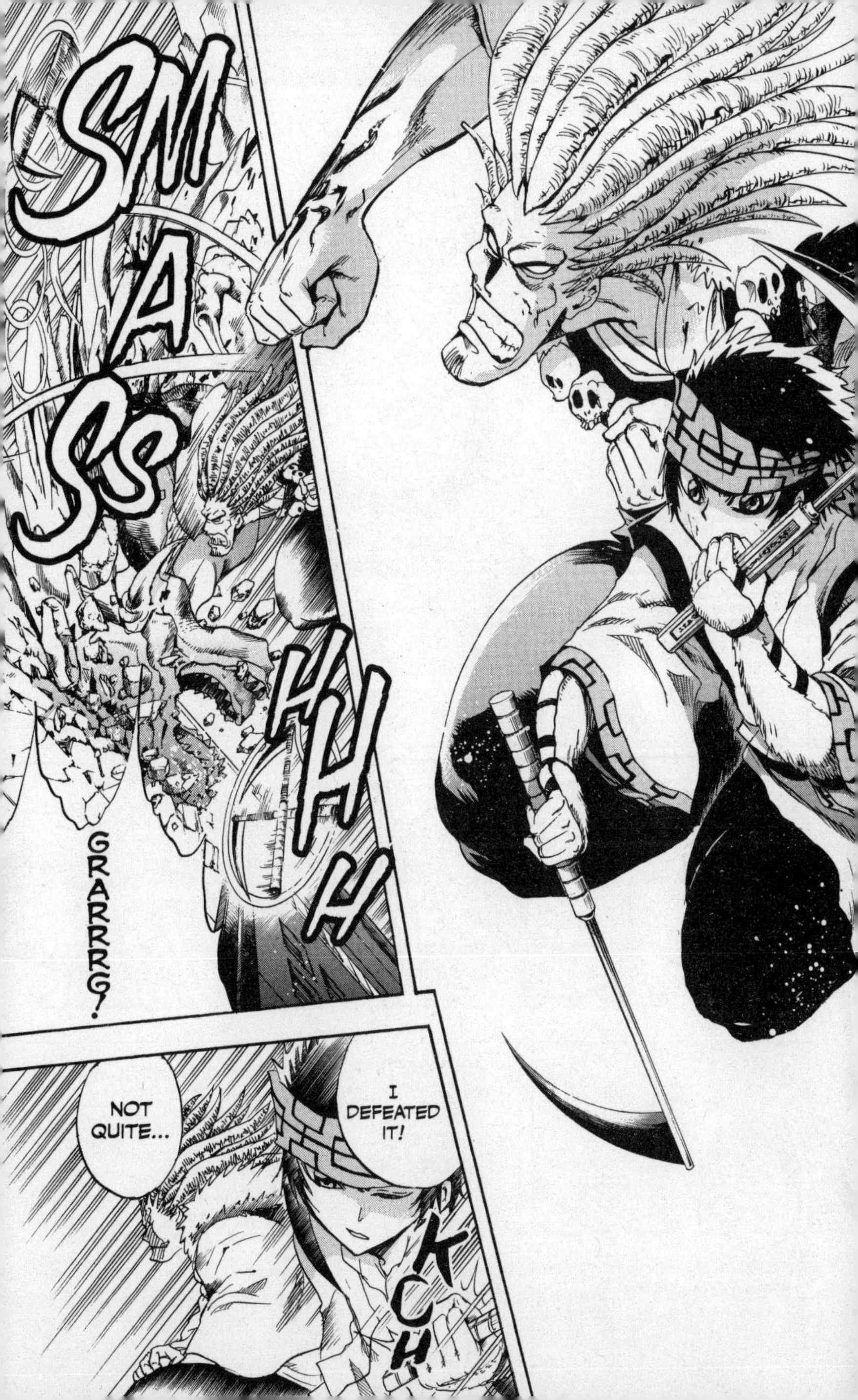
SMASSHHHH
GRARRRG!
I DEFEATED IT!
NOT QUITE...
KCH

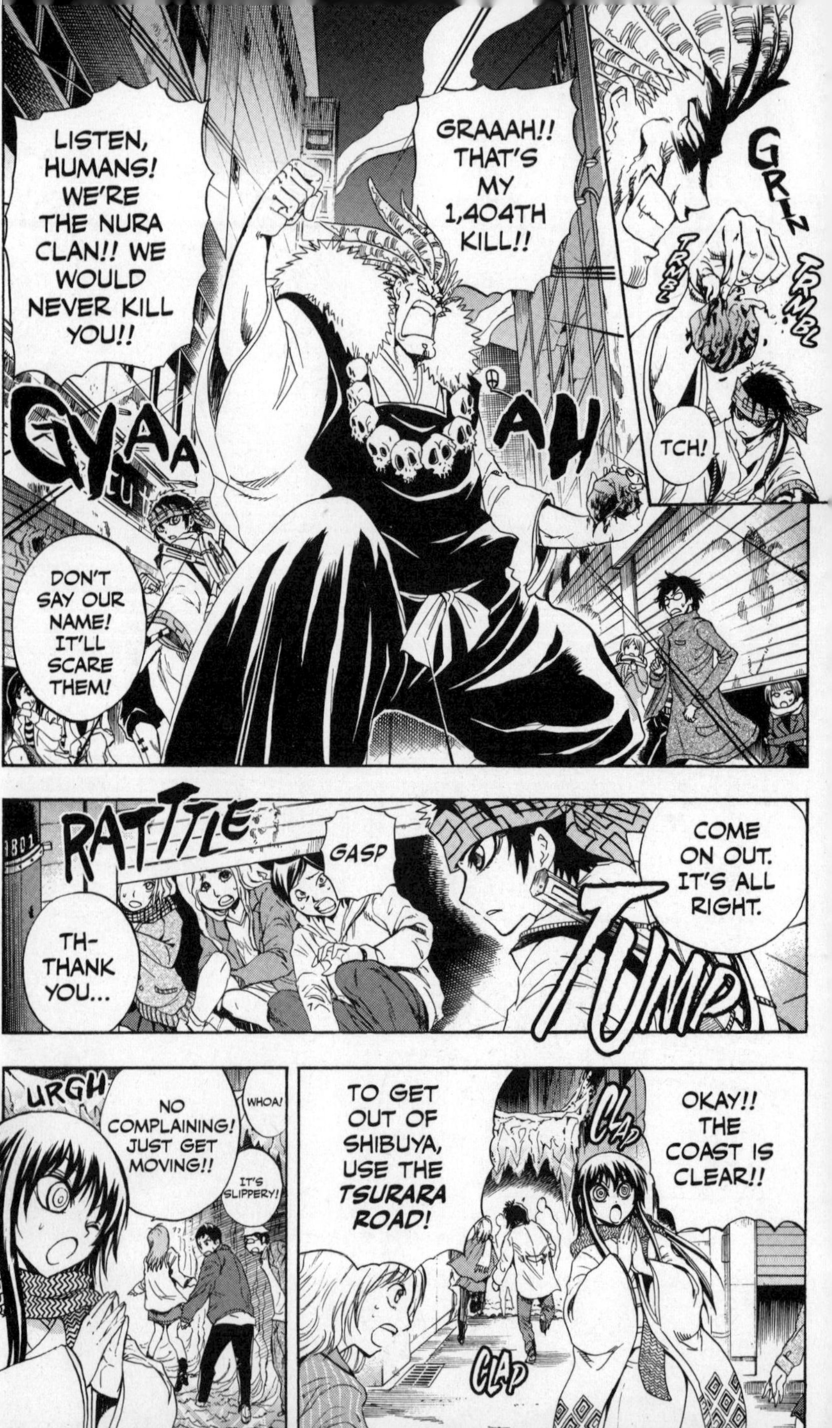
GRIN
TRMBL
TRMBL
TCH!
GRAAAH!! THAT'S MY 1,404TH KILL!!
LISTEN, HUMANS! WE'RE THE NURA CLAN!! WE WOULD NEVER KILL YOU!!
GYAAAH
DON'T SAY OUR NAME! IT'LL SCARE THEM!
COME ON OUT. IT'S ALL RIGHT.
TUMP
GASP
RATTLE
TH-THANK YOU...
OKAY!! THE COAST IS CLEAR!!
CLAP
TO GET OUT OF SHIBUYA, USE THE *TSURARA ROAD*!
CLAP
WHOA!
NO COMPLAINING! JUST GET MOVING!!
URGH
IT'S SLIPPERY!

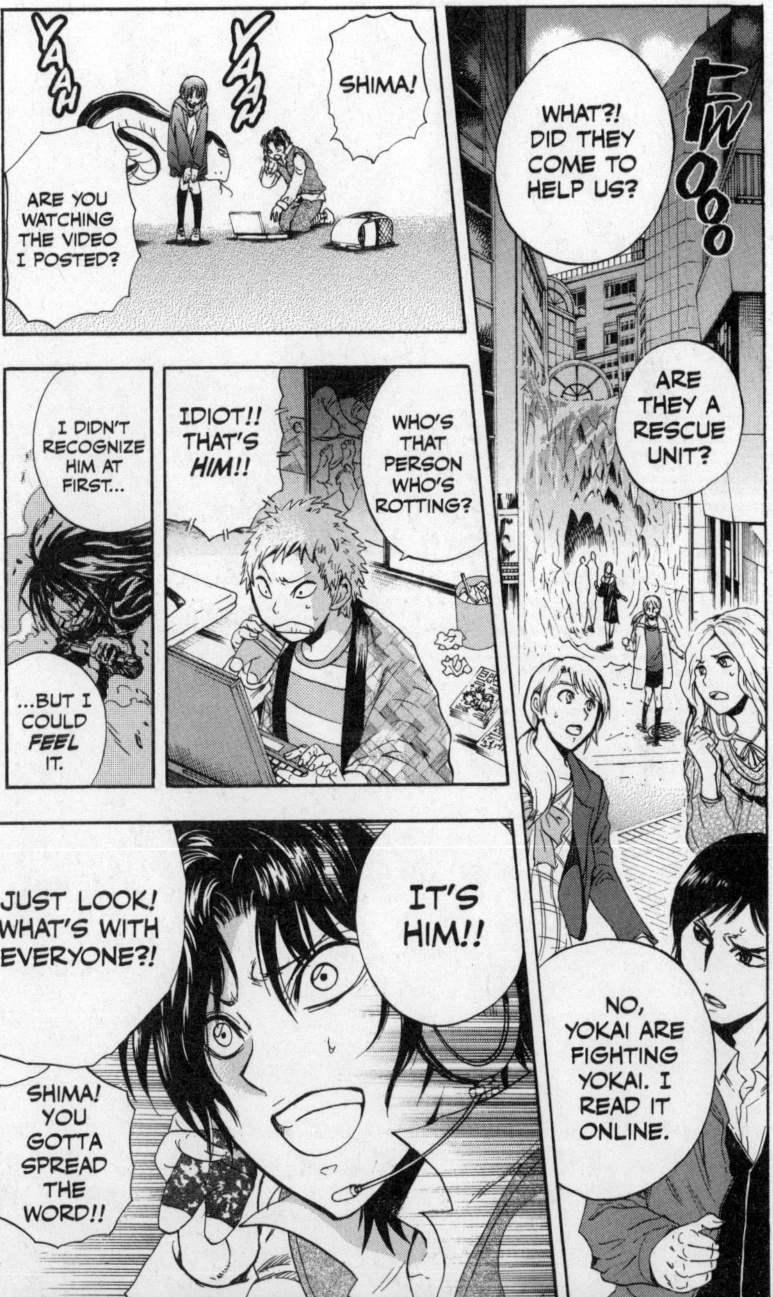
FWOOO
WHAT?! DID THEY COME TO HELP US?
ARE THEY A RESCUE UNIT?
NO, YOKAI ARE FIGHTING YOKAI. I READ IT ONLINE.
SHIMA!
YAAH
YAAH
ARE YOU WATCHING THE VIDEO I POSTED?
WHO'S THAT PERSON WHO'S ROTTING?
IDIOT!! THAT'S *HIM*!!
I DIDN'T RECOGNIZE HIM AT FIRST...
...BUT I COULD *FEEL* IT.
IT'S HIM!!
JUST LOOK! WHAT'S WITH EVERYONE?!
SHIMA! YOU GOTTA SPREAD THE WORD!!

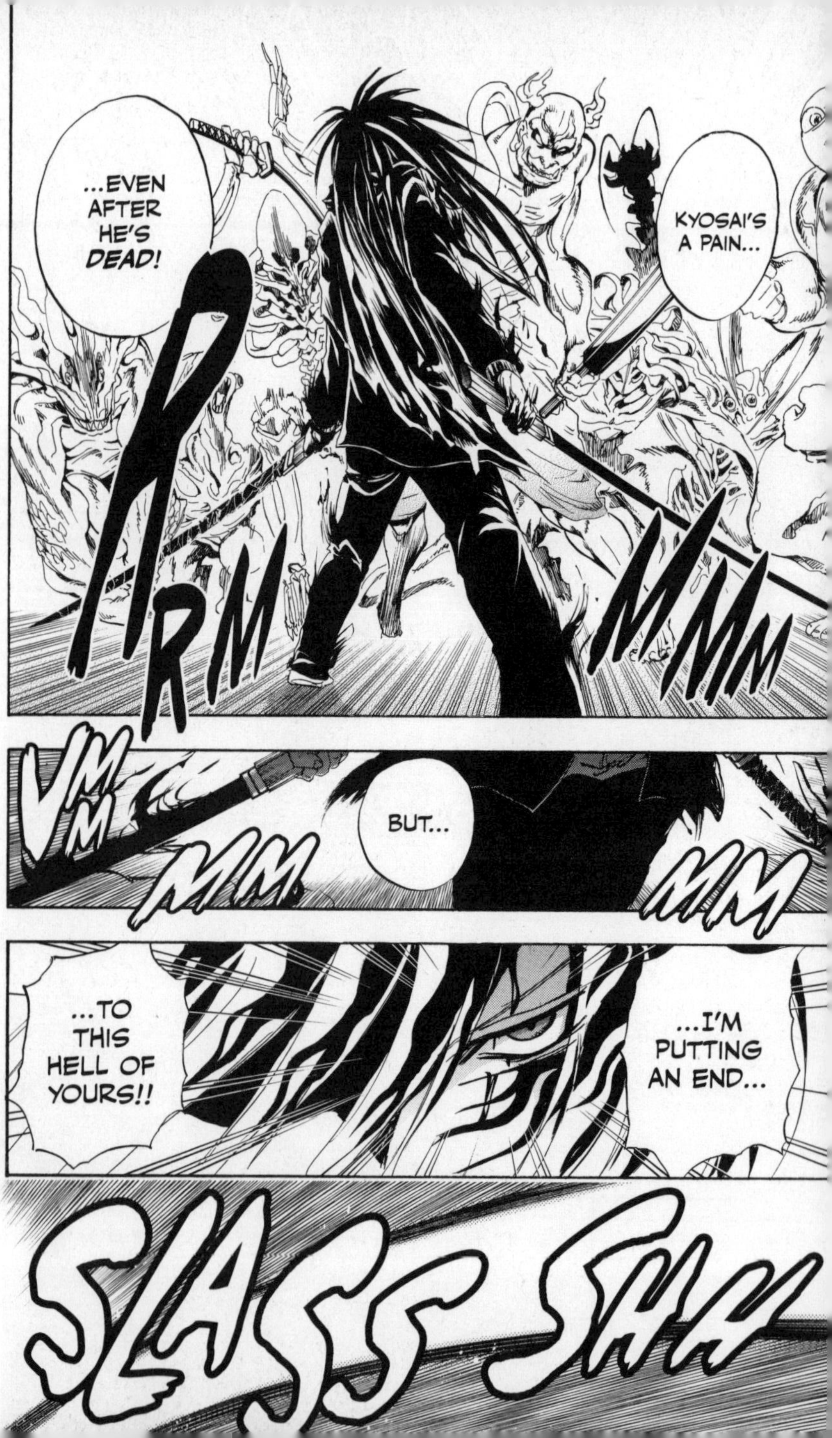
KYOSAI'S A PAIN...
...EVEN AFTER HE'S DEAD!
VRRM
MMMM
VMM
MMM
BUT...
MM
...I'M PUTTING AN END...
...TO THIS HELL OF YOURS!!
SLASS SHH

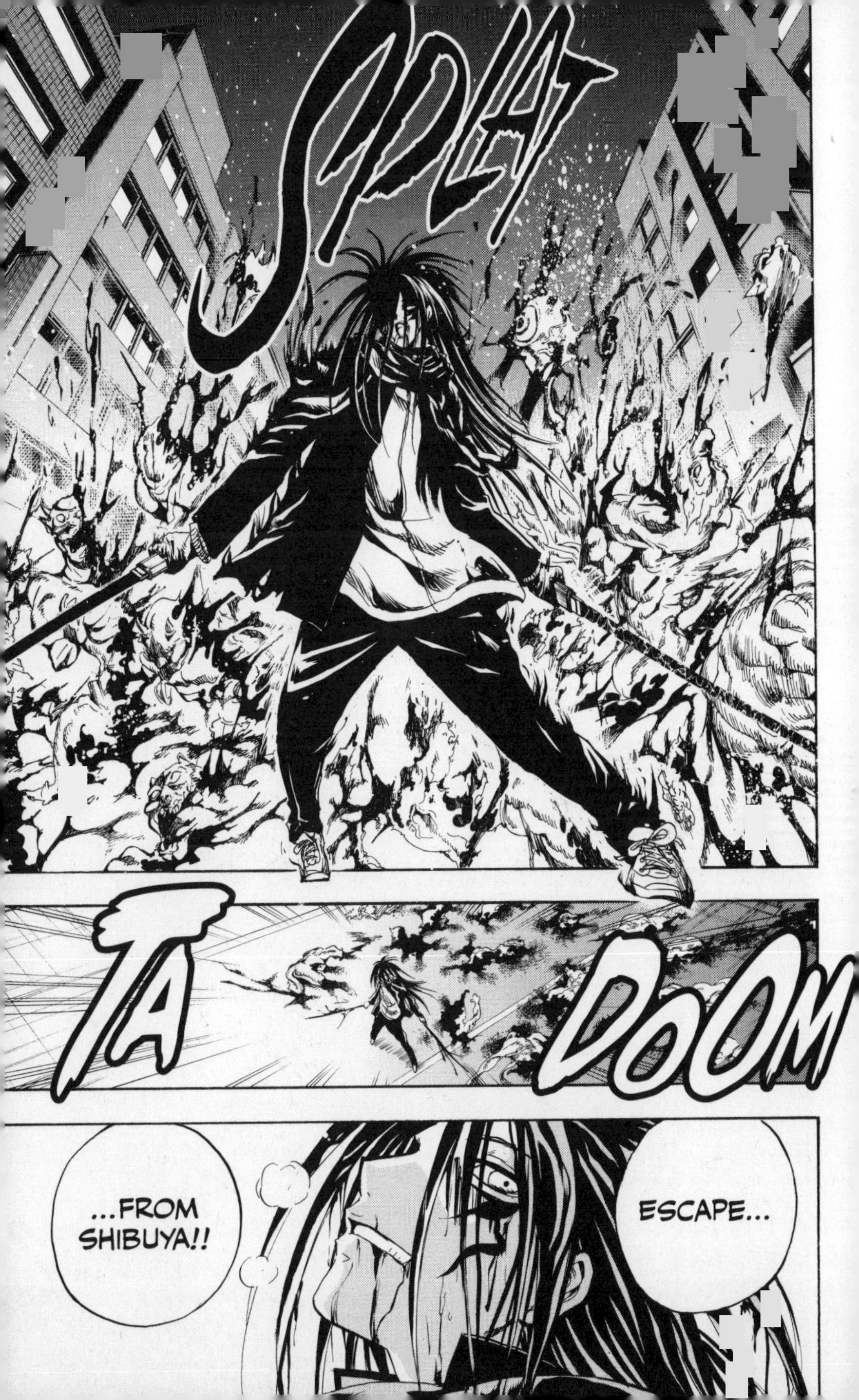
SPLAT
TA
DOOM
ESCAPE...
...FROM SHIBUYA!!

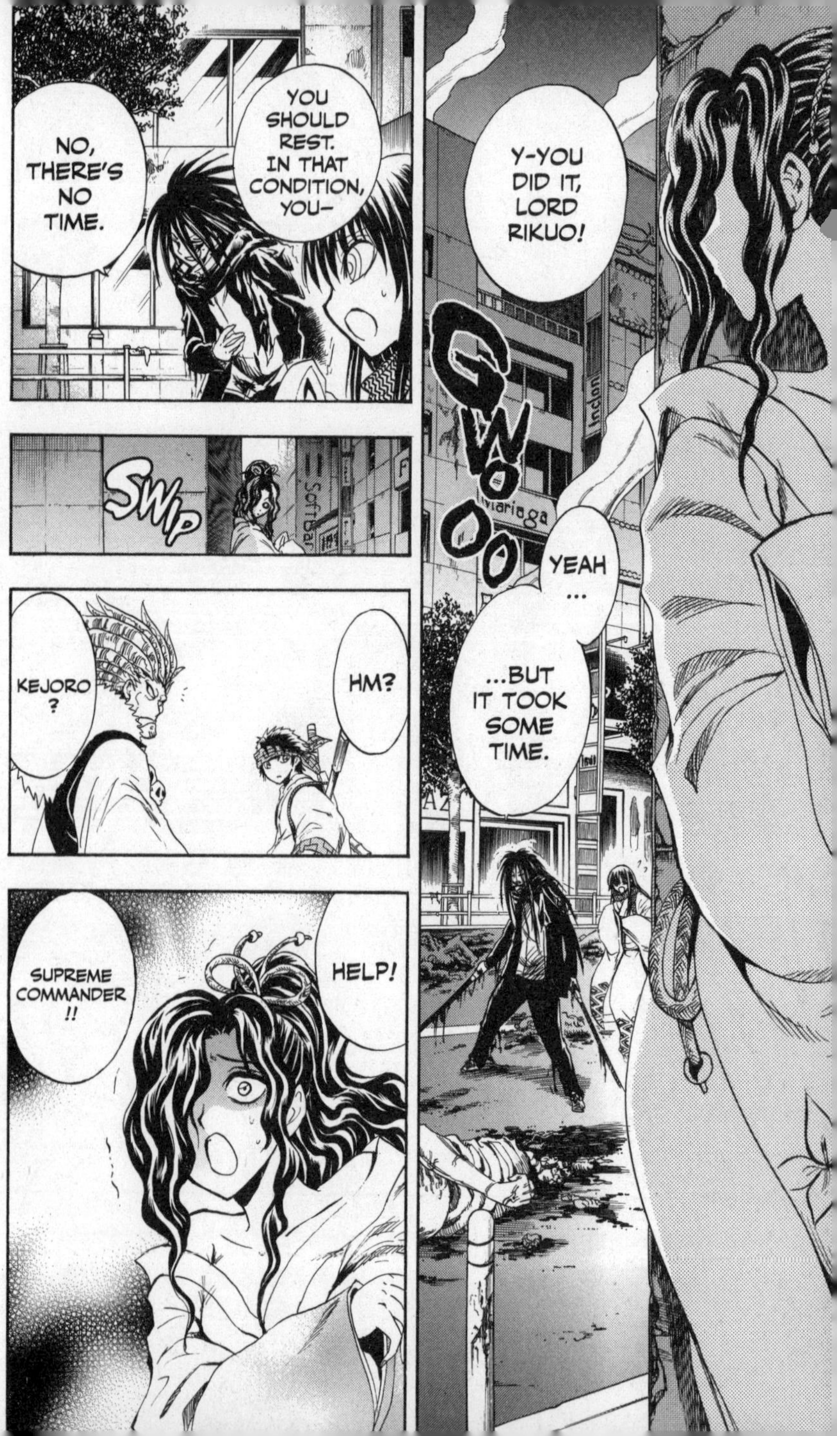
Y-YOU DID IT, LORD RIKUO!
GWOOO
YEAH ...
...BUT IT TOOK SOME TIME.
YOU SHOULD REST. IN THAT CONDITION, YOU-
NO, THERE'S NO TIME.
SWIP
HM?
KEJORO?
HELP!
SUPREME COMMANDER!!

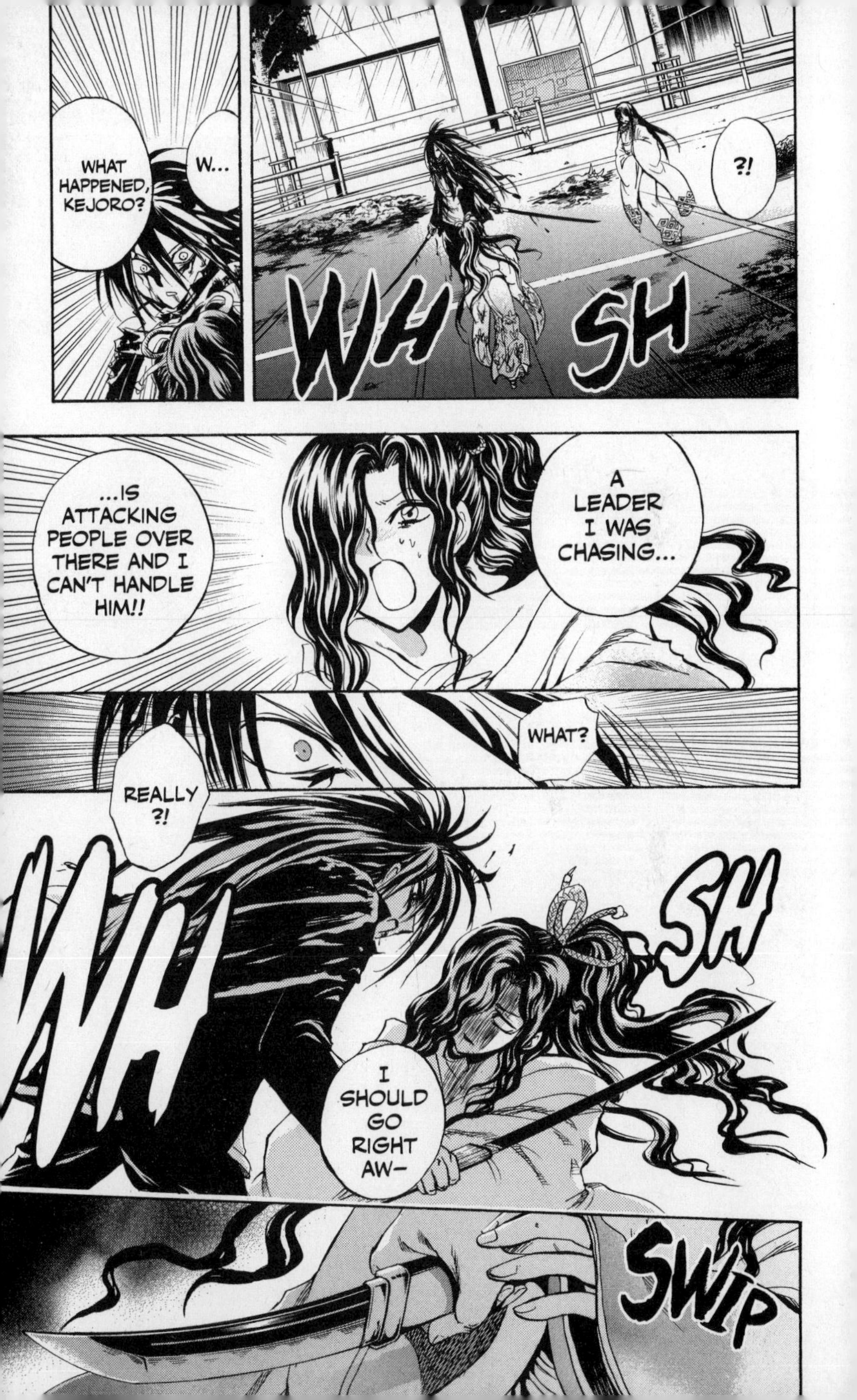
?!
WH SH
W...
WHAT HAPPENED, KEJORO?
A LEADER I WAS CHASING...
...IS ATTACKING PEOPLE OVER THERE AND I CAN'T HANDLE HIM!!
WHAT?
REALLY?!
WH SH
I SHOULD GO RIGHT AW–
SWIP

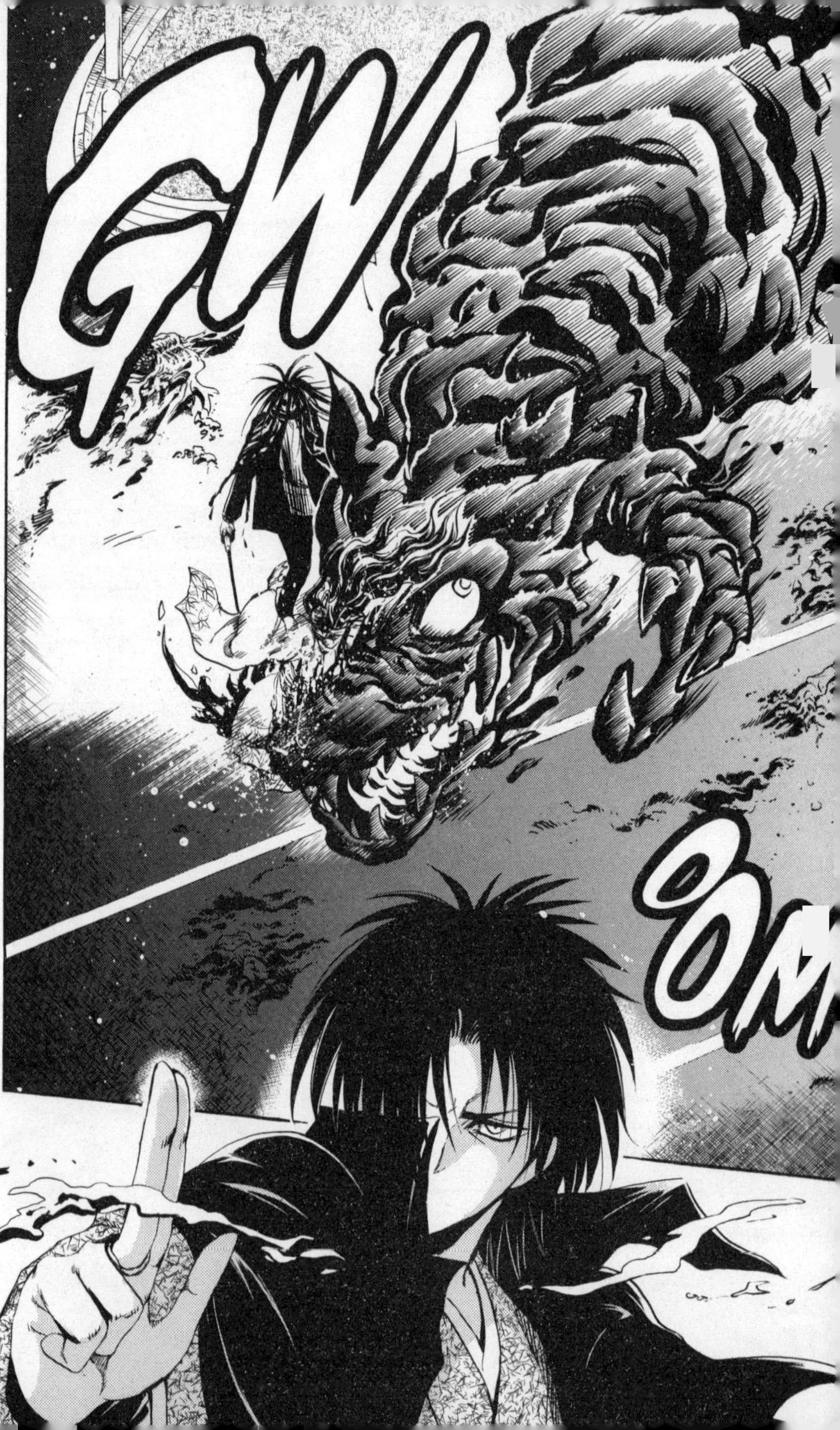

GW
OOM

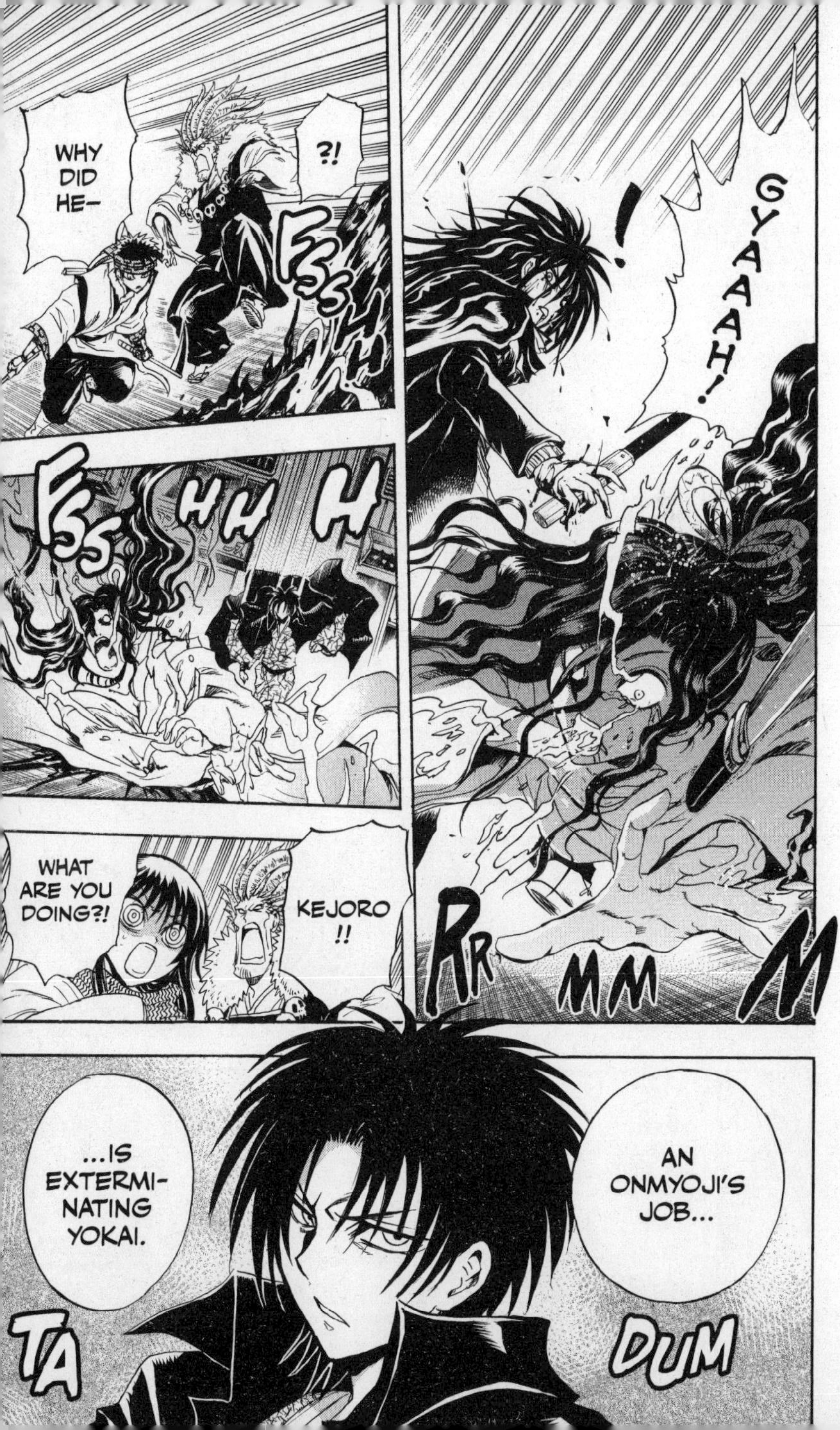
GYAAAH!
!
RRMMM
?!
WHY DID HE-
FSSH
FSSHHH
KEJORO!!
WHAT ARE YOU DOING?!
AN ONMYOJI'S JOB...
...IS EXTERMI-NATING YOKAI.
DUM
TA

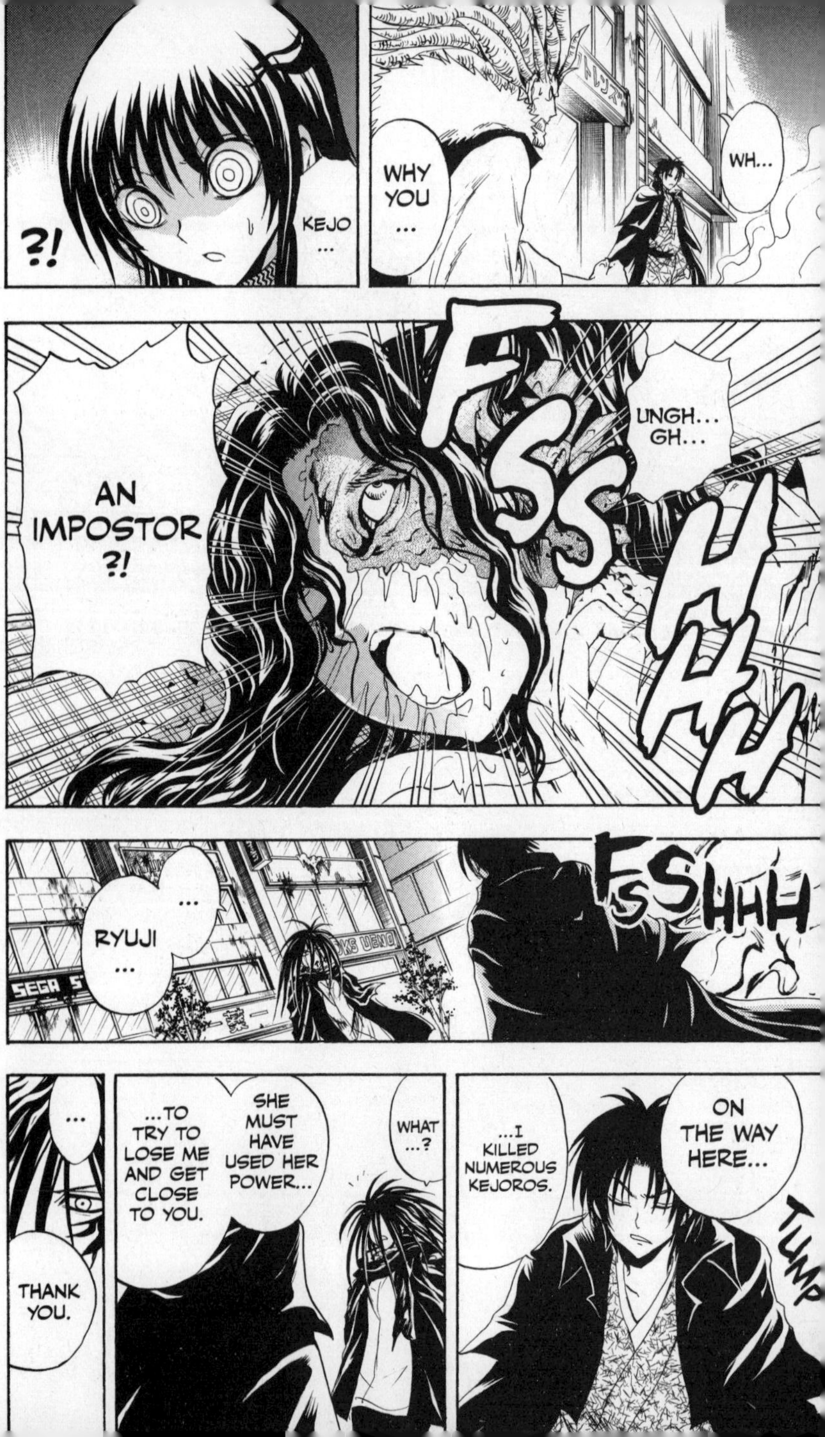
WH...
WHY YOU ...
KEJO ...
?!
UNGH... GH...
FSSHHH
AN IMPOSTOR ?!
FSSHHH
... RYUJI ...
ON THE WAY HERE...
TUMP
...I KILLED NUMEROUS KEJOROS.
WHAT ...?
SHE MUST HAVE USED HER POWER...
...TO TRY TO LOSE ME AND GET CLOSE TO YOU.
...
THANK YOU.

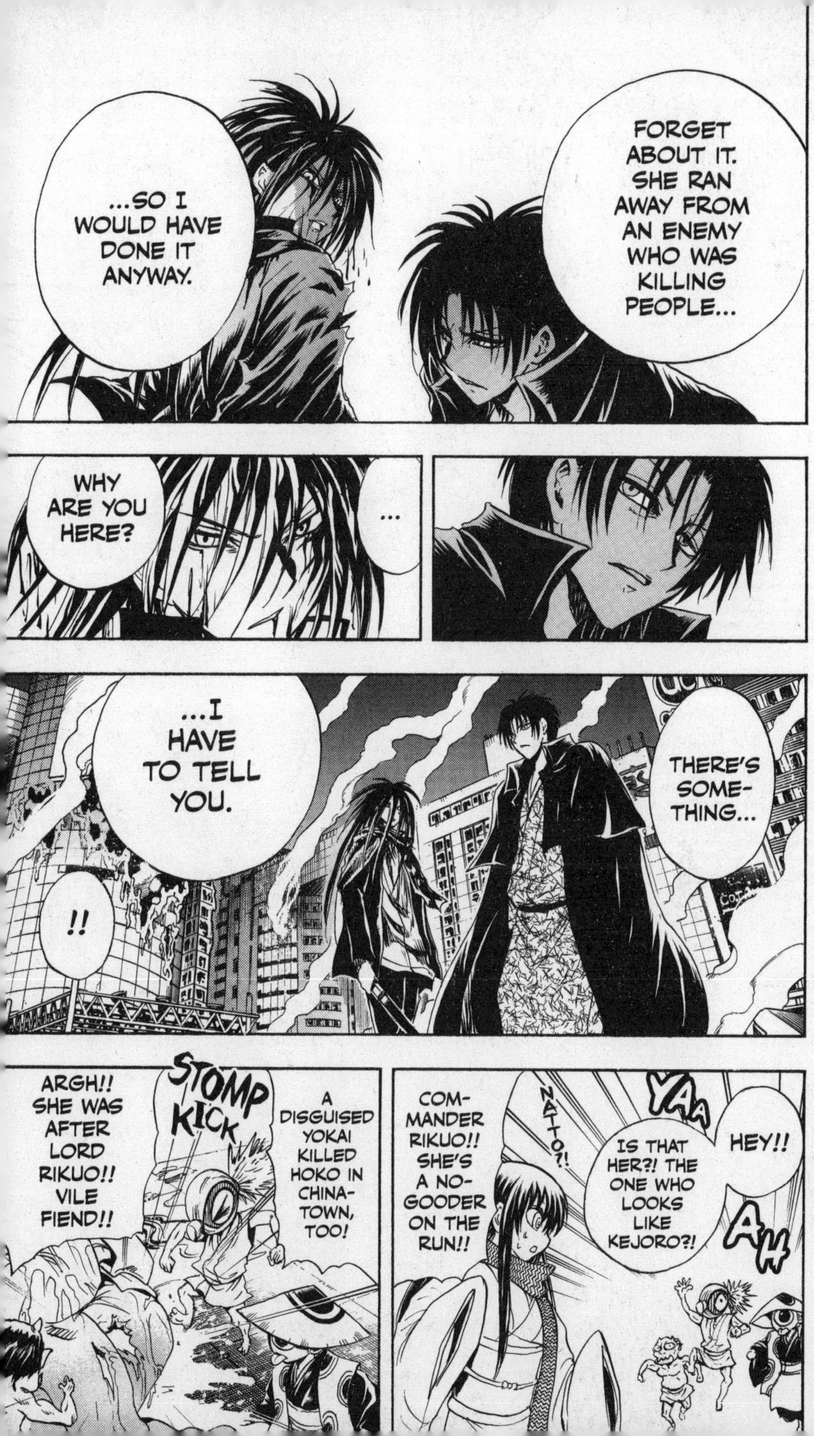
FORGET ABOUT IT. SHE RAN AWAY FROM AN ENEMY WHO WAS KILLING PEOPLE...
...SO I WOULD HAVE DONE IT ANYWAY.
...
WHY ARE YOU HERE?
THERE'S SOME-THING...
...I HAVE TO TELL YOU.
!!
HEY!!
YAA
IS THAT HER?! THE ONE WHO LOOKS LIKE KEJORO?!
AH
NATTO?!
COM-MANDER RIKUO!! SHE'S A NO-GOODER ON THE RUN!!
A DISGUISED YOKAI KILLED HOKO IN CHINA-TOWN, TOO!
STOMP KICK
ARGH!! SHE WAS AFTER LORD RIKUO!! VILE FIEND!!

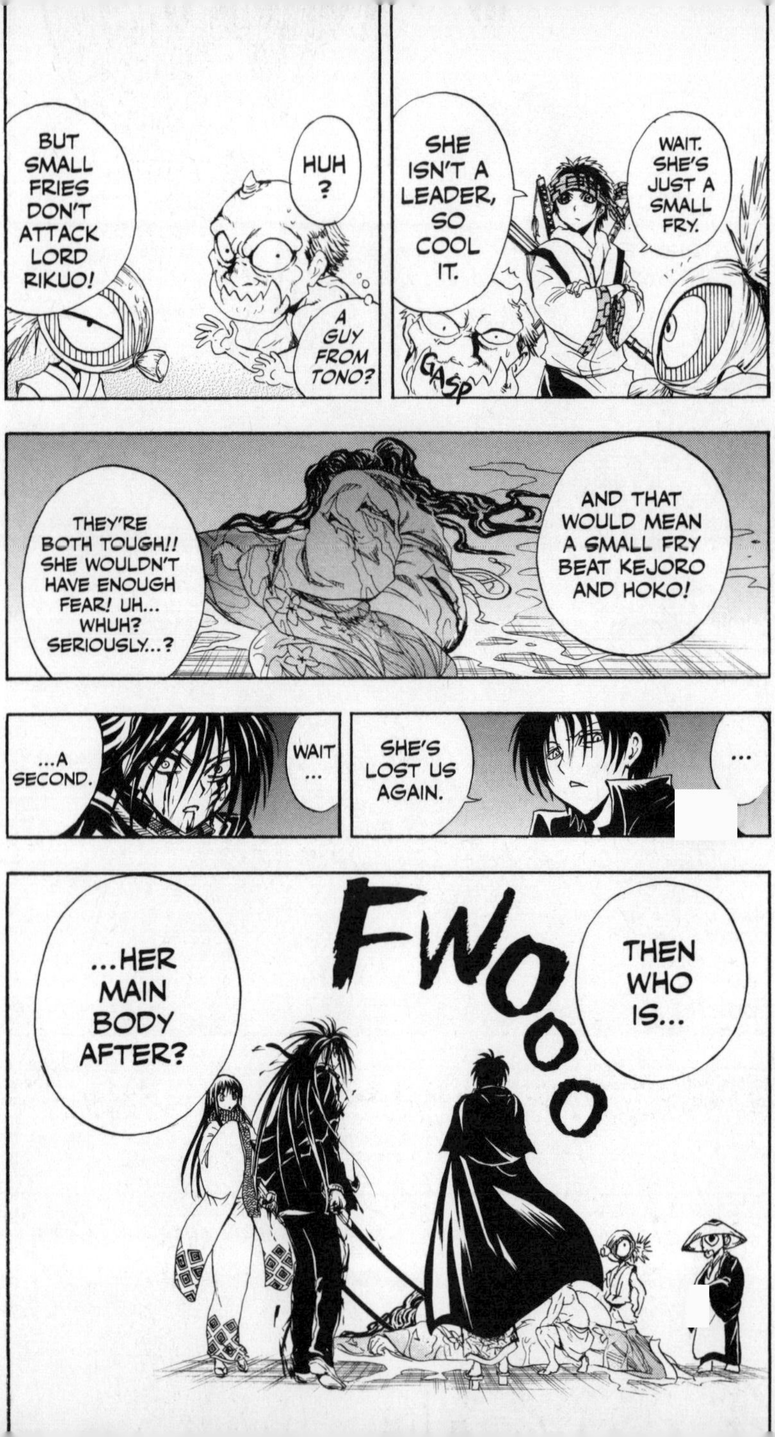
WAIT. SHE'S JUST A SMALL FRY.
SHE ISN'T A LEADER, SO COOL IT.
GASP
HUH ?
A GUY FROM TONO?
BUT SMALL FRIES DON'T ATTACK LORD RIKUO!
AND THAT WOULD MEAN A SMALL FRY BEAT KEJORO AND HOKO!
THEY'RE BOTH TOUGH!! SHE WOULDN'T HAVE ENOUGH FEAR! UH... WHUH? SERIOUSLY...?
...
SHE'S LOST US AGAIN.
WAIT ...
...A SECOND.
THEN WHO IS...
FWOOO
...HER MAIN BODY AFTER?

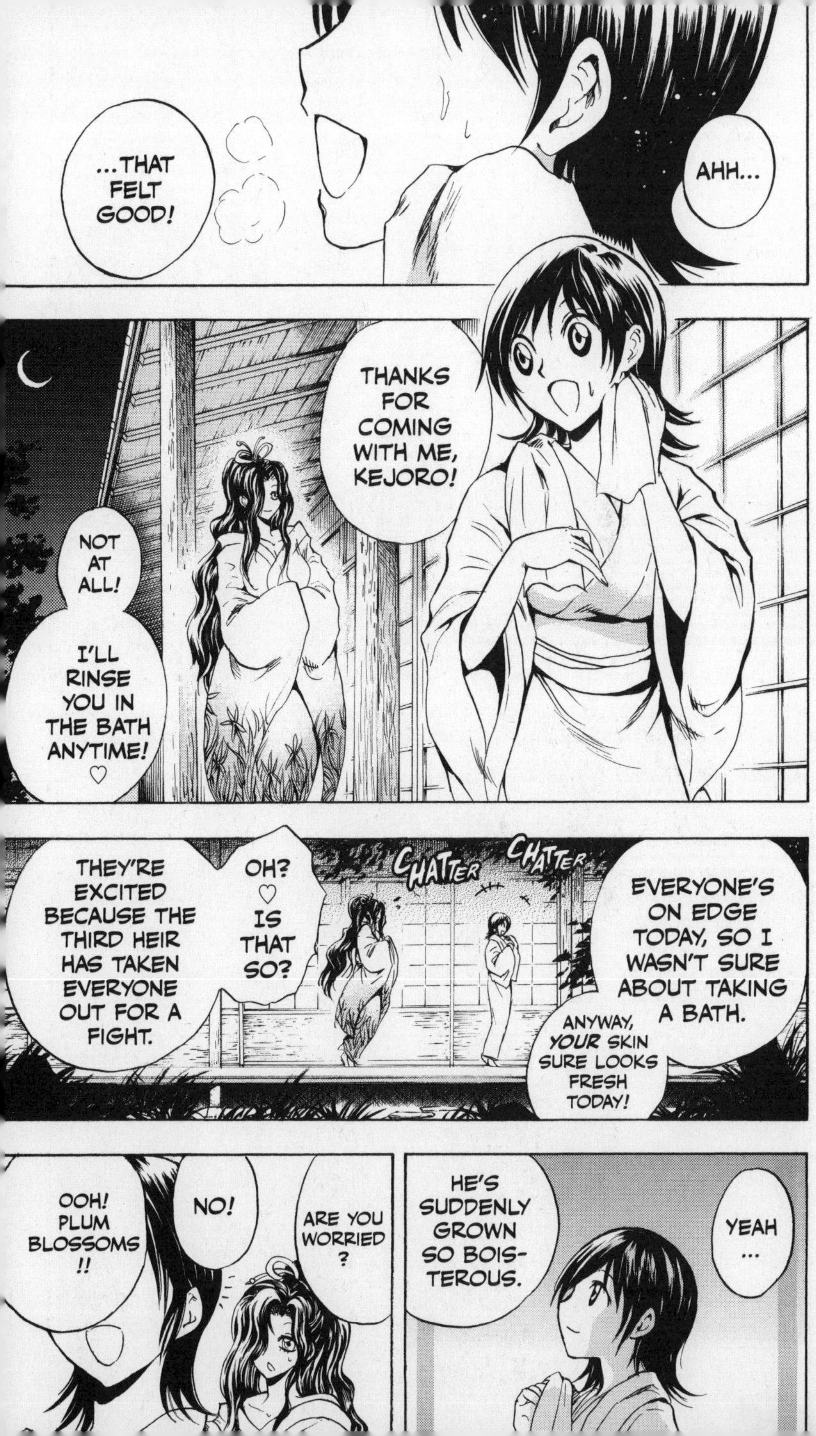
AHH...
...THAT FELT GOOD!
THANKS FOR COMING WITH ME, KEJORO!
NOT AT ALL!
I'LL RINSE YOU IN THE BATH ANYTIME! ♡
CHATTER
CHATTER
EVERYONE'S ON EDGE TODAY, SO I WASN'T SURE ABOUT TAKING A BATH.
ANYWAY, *YOUR* SKIN SURE LOOKS FRESH TODAY!
OH? ♡ IS THAT SO?
THEY'RE EXCITED BECAUSE THE THIRD HEIR HAS TAKEN EVERYONE OUT FOR A FIGHT.
YEAH...
HE'S SUDDENLY GROWN SO BOIS-TEROUS.
ARE YOU WORRIED?
NO!
OOH! PLUM BLOSSOMS!!

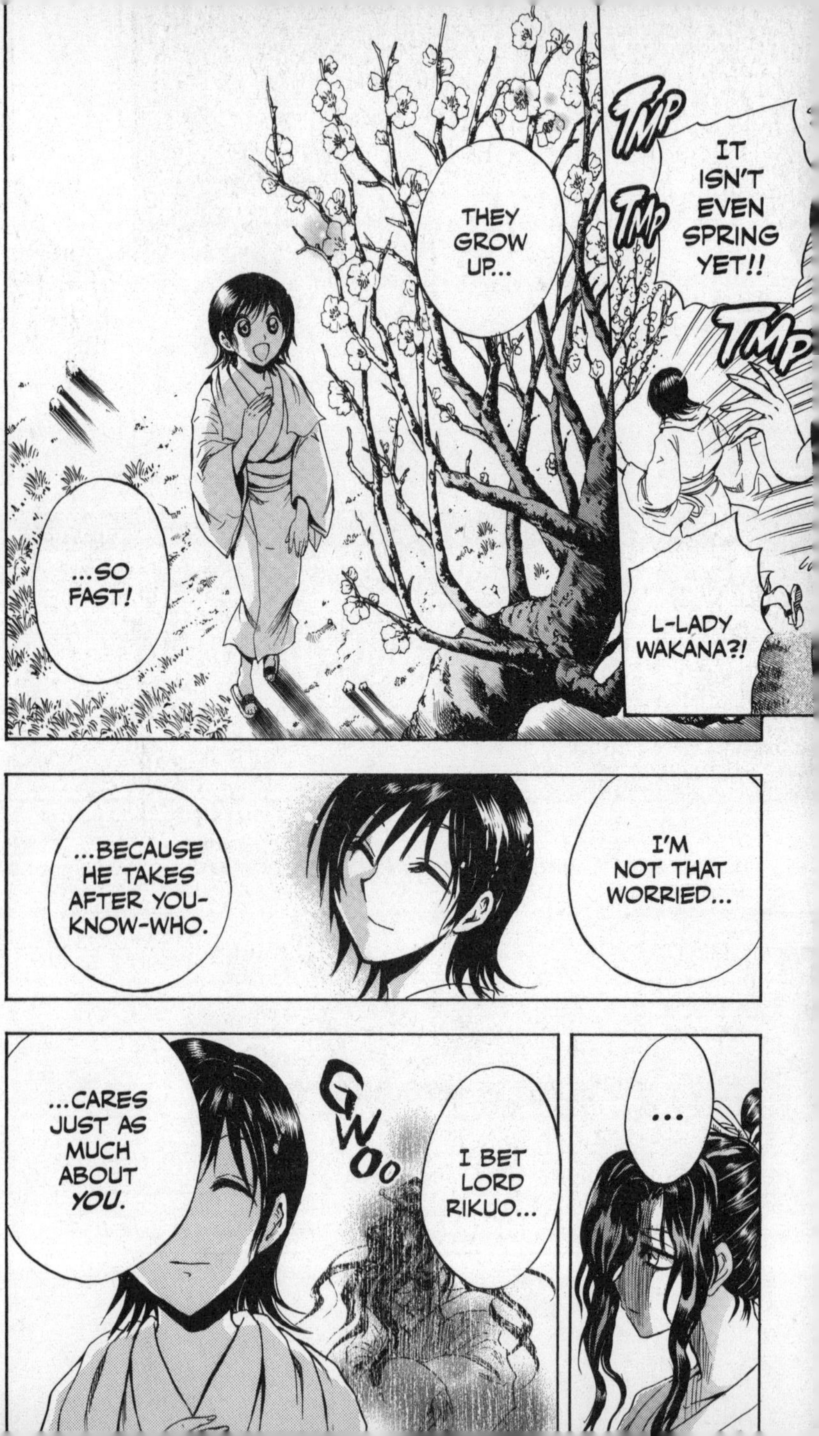
TMP
TMP
IT ISN'T EVEN SPRING YET!!
TMP
L-LADY WAKANA?!
THEY GROW UP...
...SO FAST!
I'M NOT THAT WORRIED...
...BECAUSE HE TAKES AFTER YOU-KNOW-WHO.
...
I BET LORD RIKUO...
GWOO
...CARES JUST AS MUCH ABOUT *YOU*.

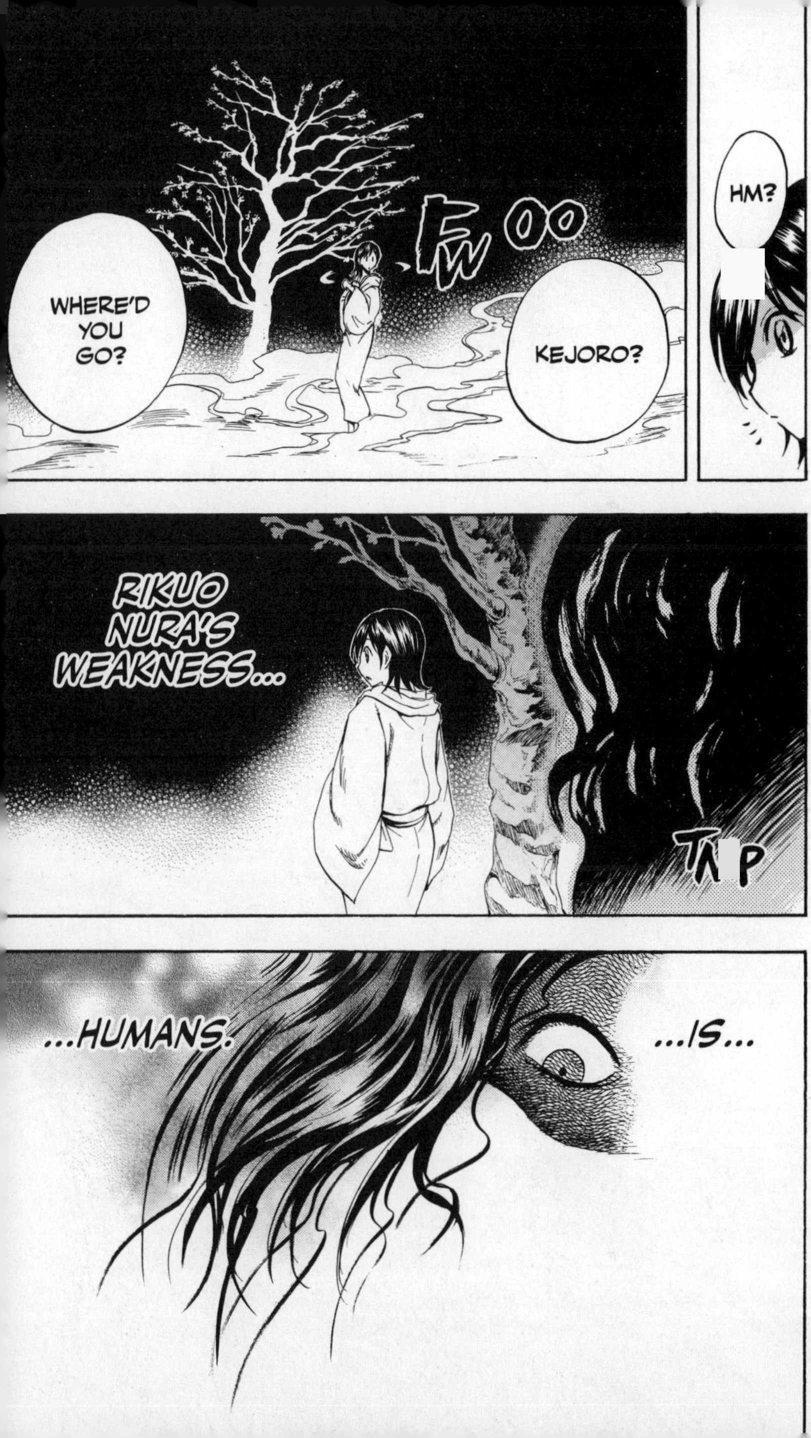
HM?
KEJORO?
FWOO
WHERE'D YOU GO?
RIKUO NURA'S WEAKNESS...
TA P
...IS...
...HUMANS.

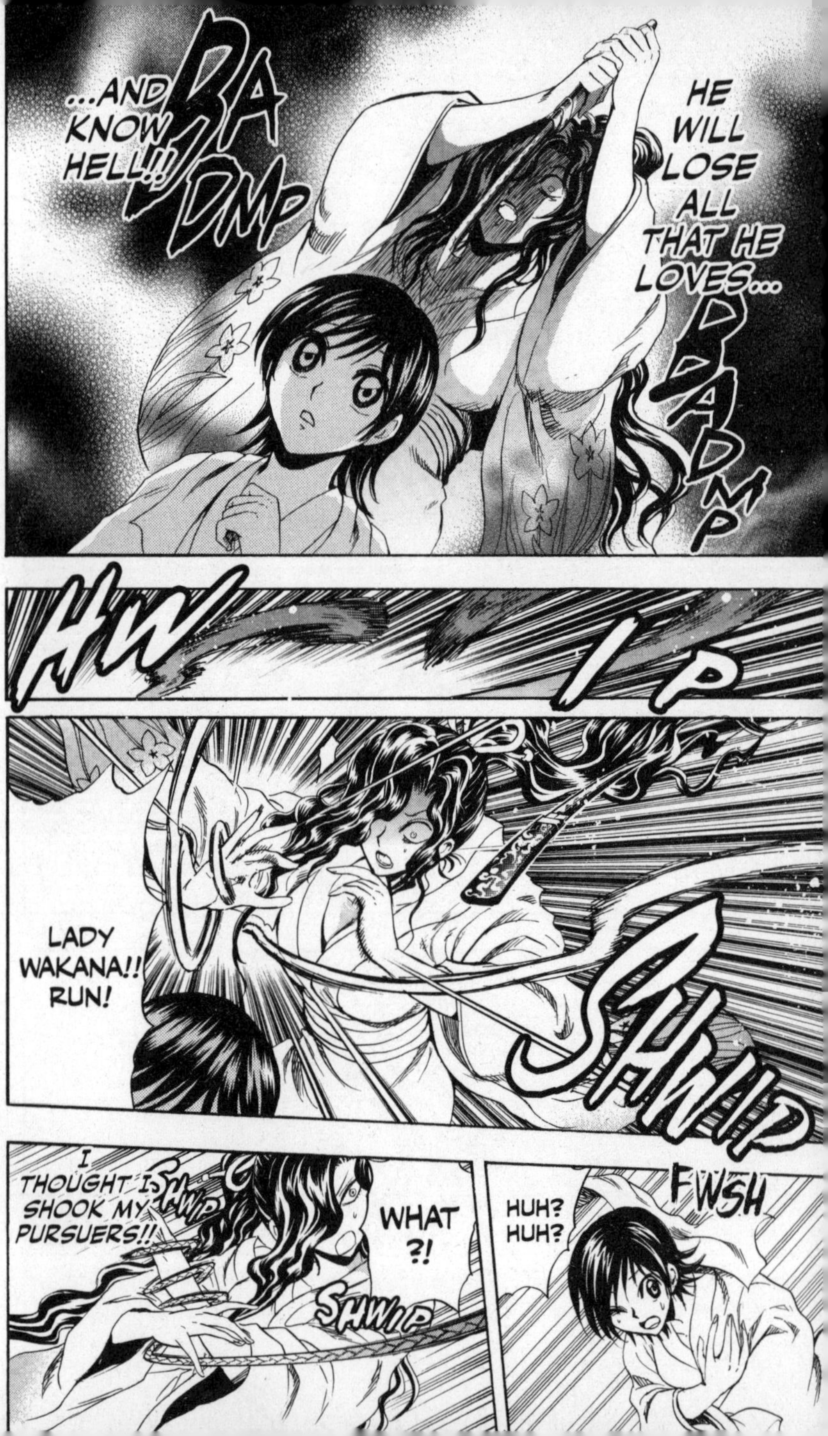
HE WILL LOSE ALL THAT HE LOVES...
DADMP
...AND KNOW HELL!!
BADMP
HWIP
SHWIP
LADY WAKANA!! RUN!
FWSH
HUH? HUH?
WHAT ?!
I THOUGHT I SHOOK MY PURSUERS!!
SHWIP
SHWIP

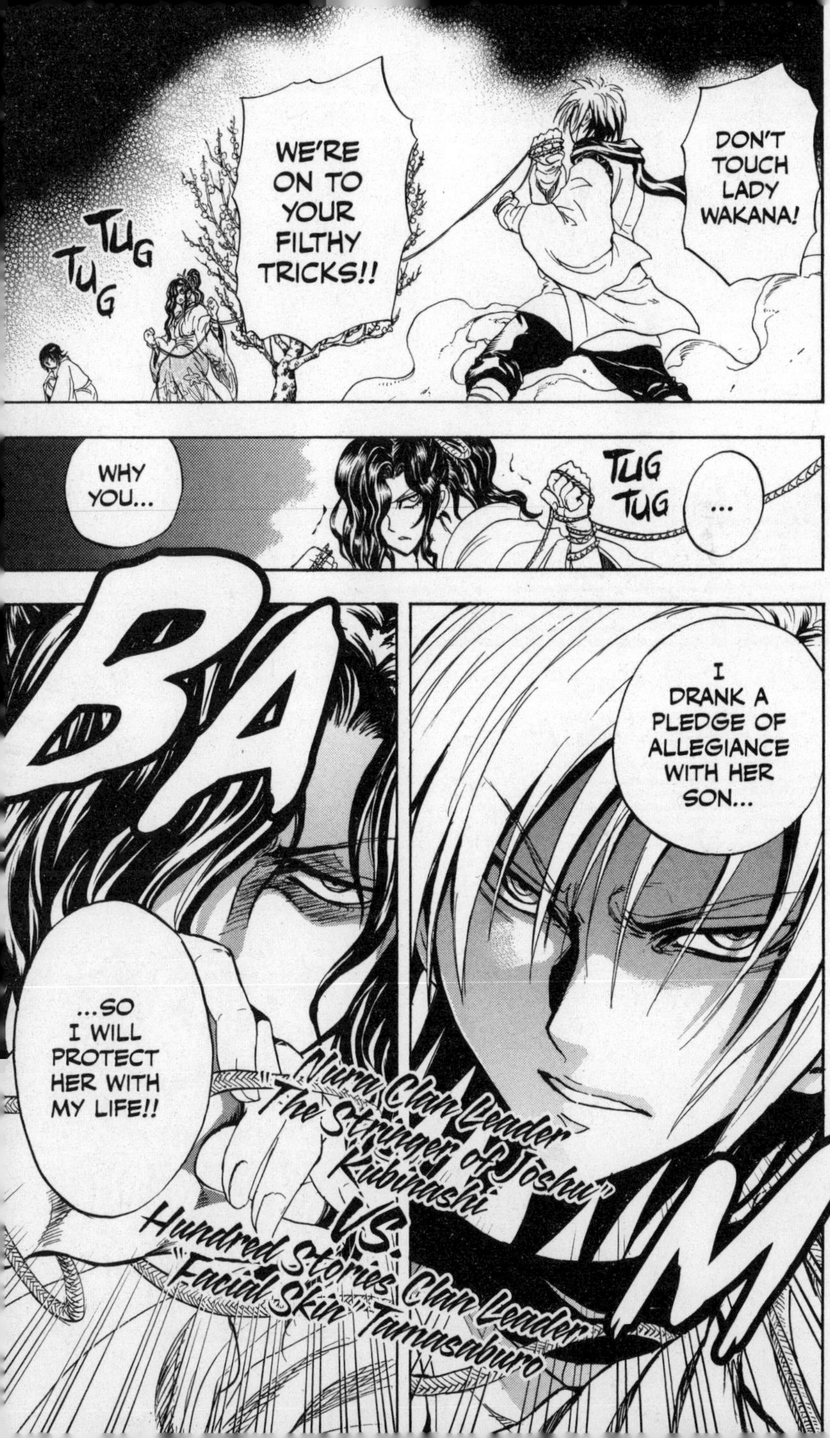
DON'T TOUCH LADY WAKANA!
WE'RE ON TO YOUR FILTHY TRICKS!!
TUG TUG
...
TUG TUG
WHY YOU...
I DRANK A PLEDGE OF ALLEGIANCE WITH HER SON...
...SO I WILL PROTECT HER WITH MY LIFE!!
BAM
Nura Clan Leader "The Stringer of Joshu" Kubinashi
VS.
Hundred Stories Clan Leader "Facial Skin" Tamasaburo

NURA: RISE OF THE YOKAI CLAN

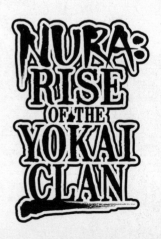

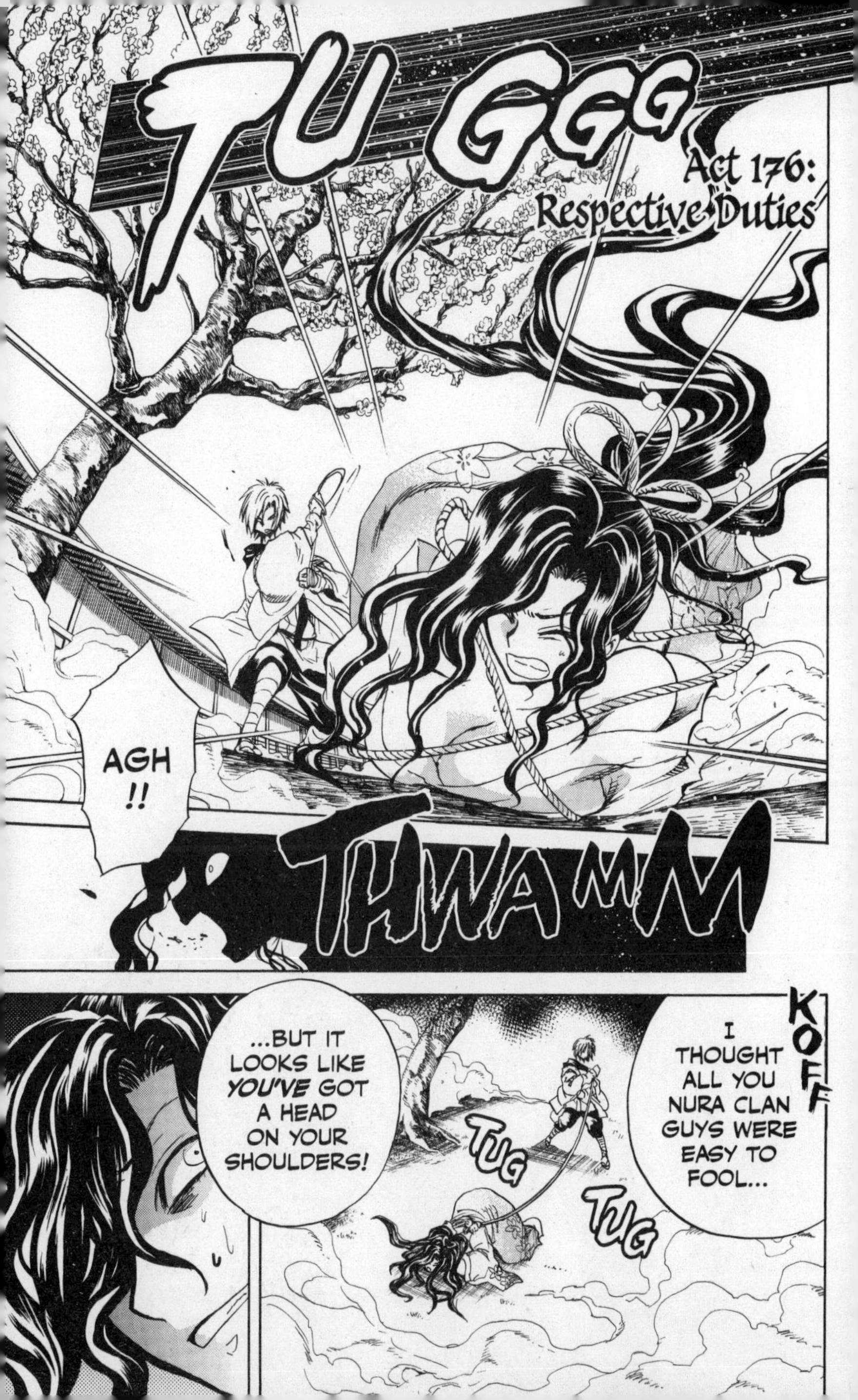
TUGGG
Act 176: Respective Duties
AGH !!
THWAMM
KOFF
I THOUGHT ALL YOU NURA CLAN GUYS WERE EASY TO FOOL...
...BUT IT LOOKS LIKE *YOU'VE* GOT A HEAD ON YOUR SHOULDERS!
TUG
TUG
...

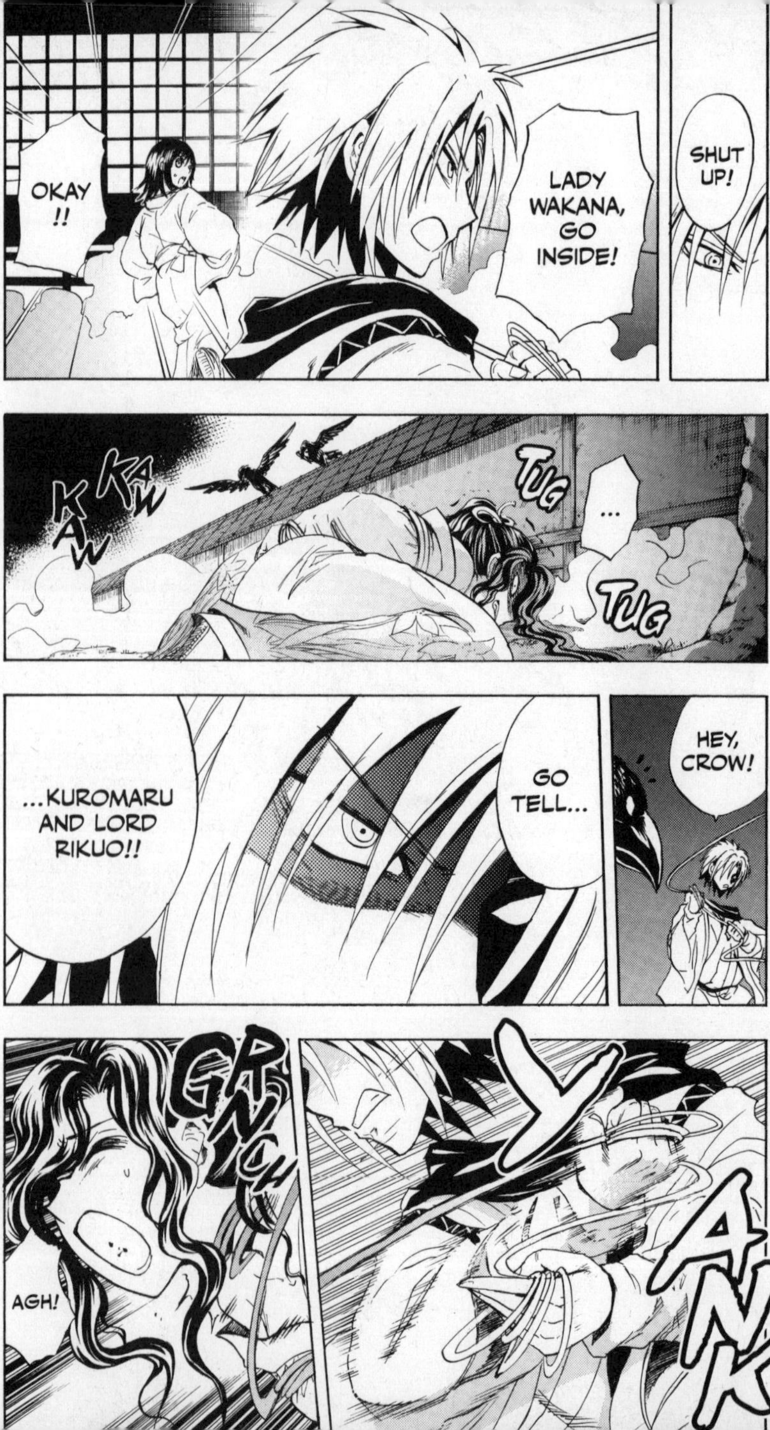
SHUT UP!
LADY WAKANA, GO INSIDE!
OKAY!!
TUG
...
TUG
KAW
KAW
HEY, CROW!
GO TELL...
...KUROMARU AND LORD RIKUO!!
YANK
GRNCH
AGH!

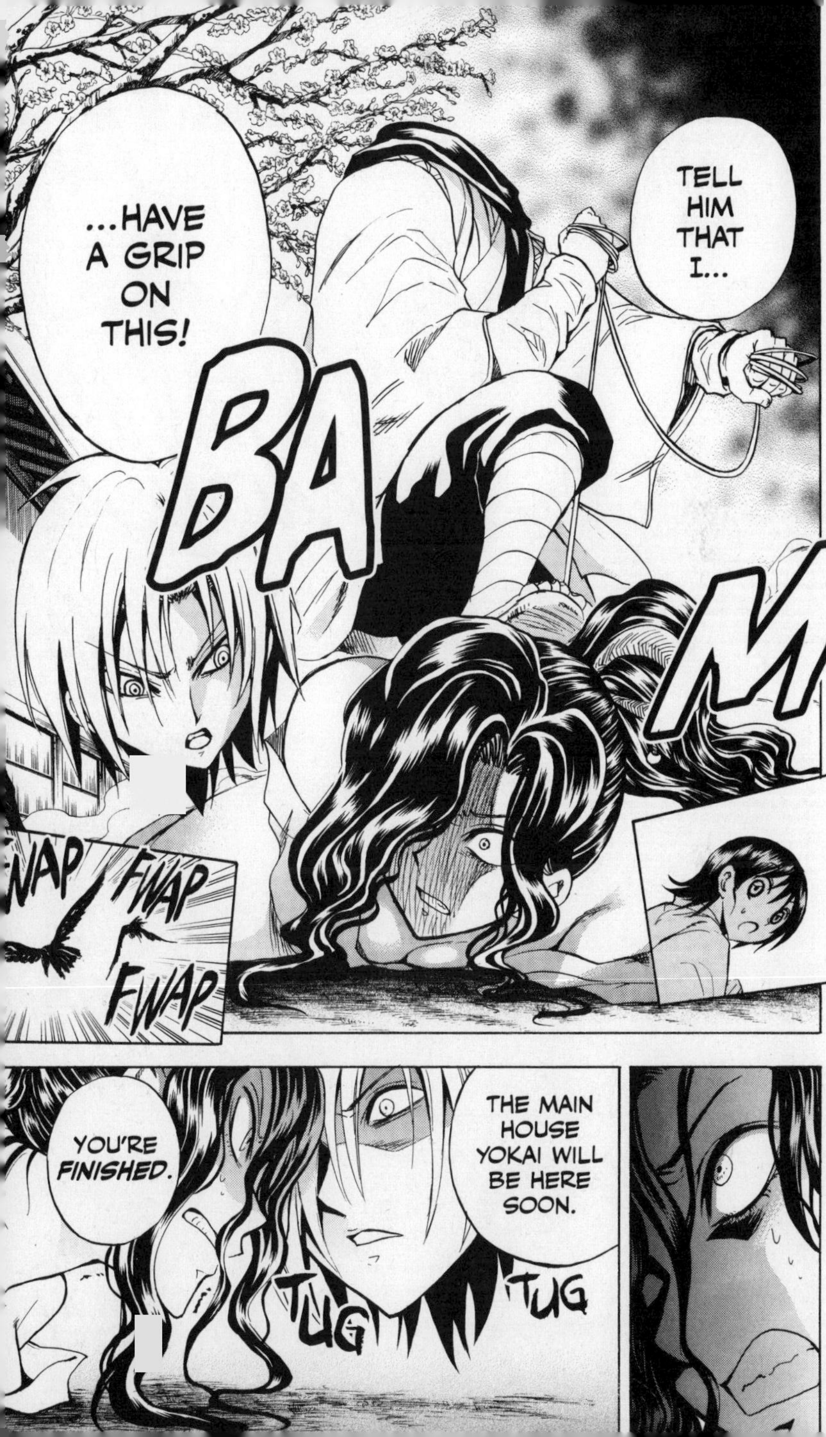
TELL HIM THAT I...
...HAVE A GRIP ON THIS!
BAM
FWAP
FWAP
FWAP
THE MAIN HOUSE YOKAI WILL BE HERE SOON.
YOU'RE FINISHED.
TUG
TUG

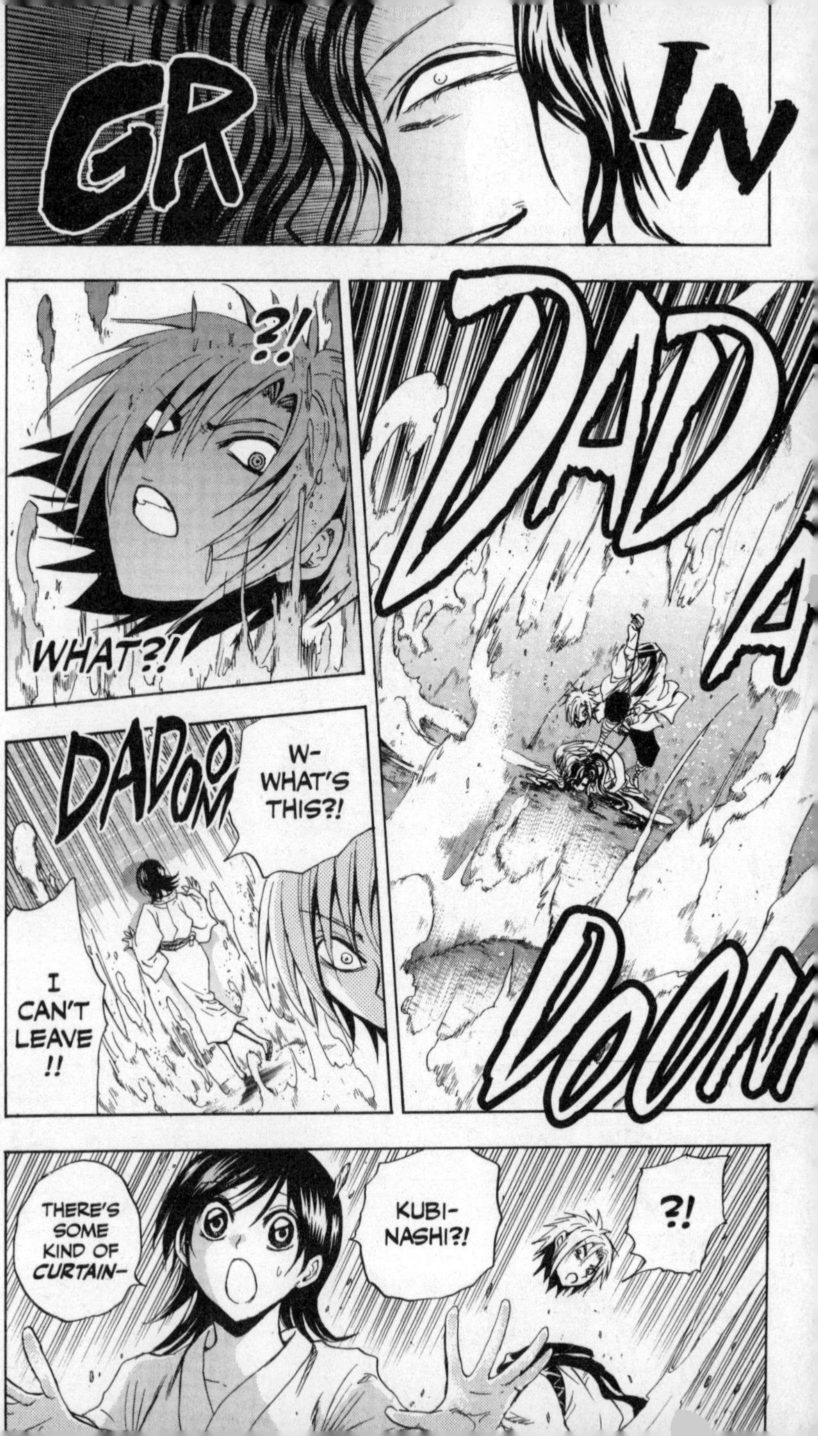
GR
IN
DADA
?!
WHAT?!
DADOOM
W-WHAT'S THIS?!
I CAN'T LEAVE !!
?!
KUBI-NASHI?!
THERE'S SOME KIND OF *CURTAIN*-

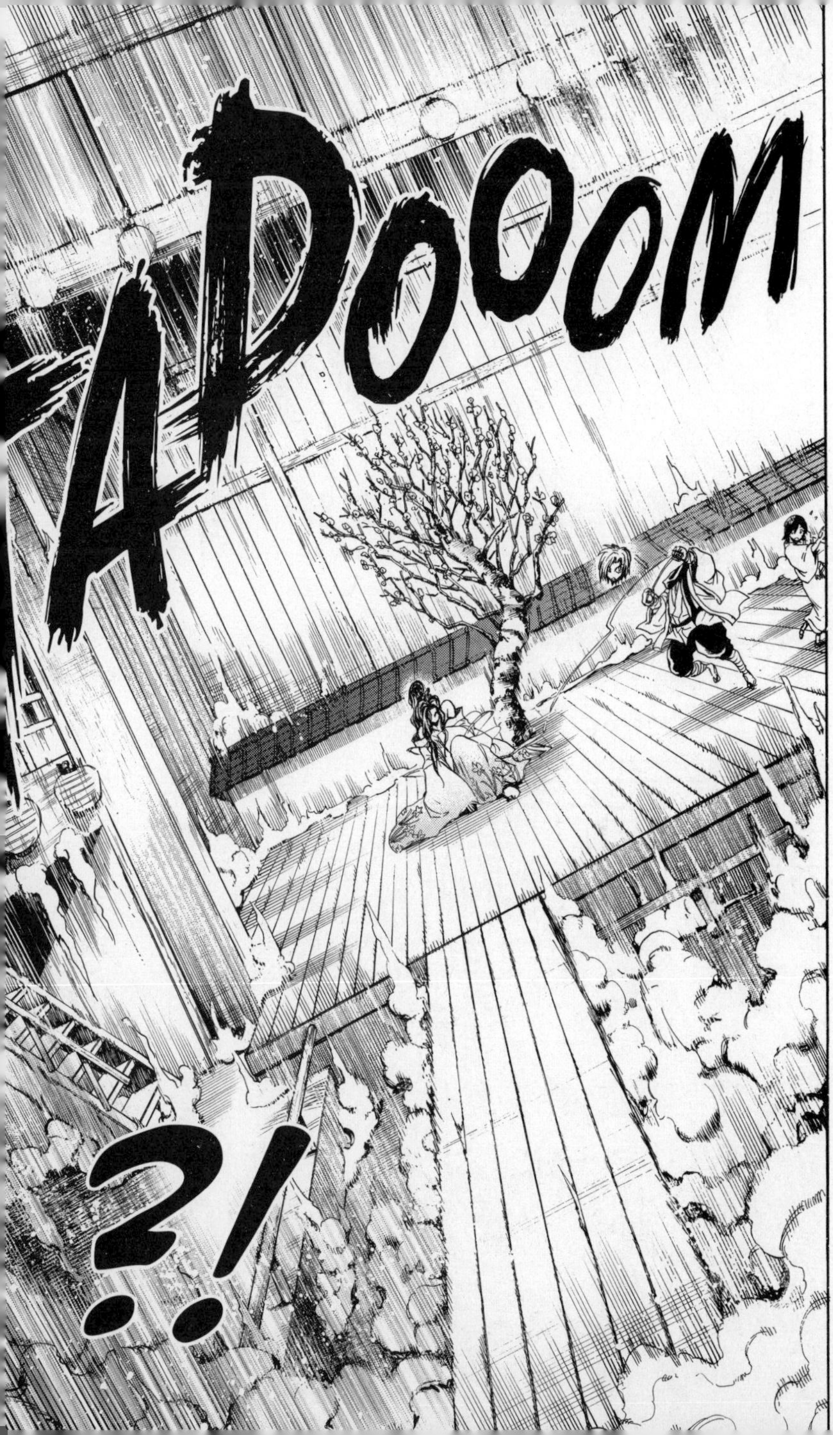
ZDOOOM
?!

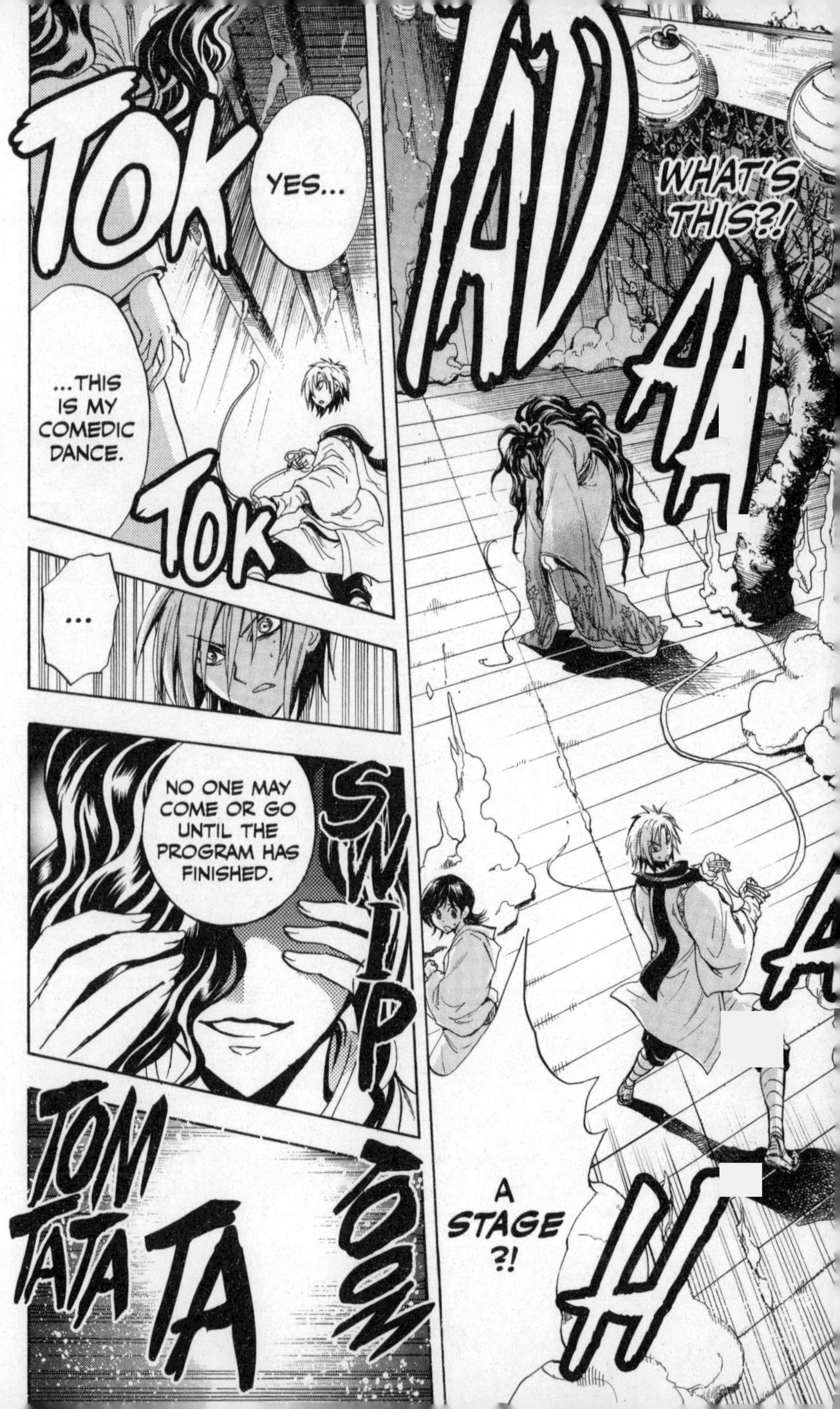
AAAAH
WHAT'S THIS?!
A STAGE ?!
TOK
YES...
...THIS IS MY COMEDIC DANCE.
TOK
...
NO ONE MAY COME OR GO UNTIL THE PROGRAM HAS FINISHED.
SWIP
TOM TATA TA
TOOM

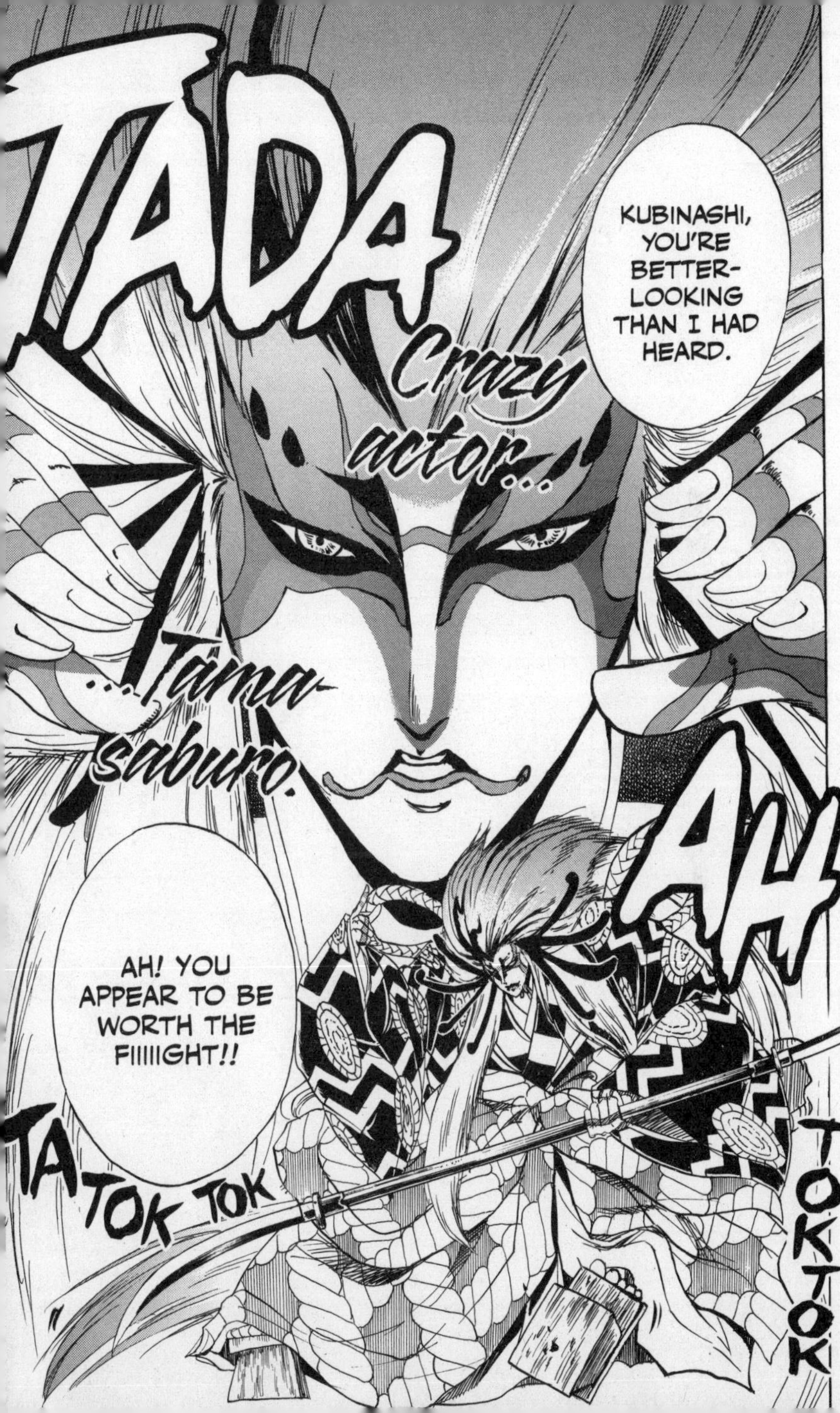
KUBINASHI, YOU'RE BETTER-LOOKING THAN I HAD HEARD.
TADA
Crazy actor...
...Tamasaburo.
AH
TOKTOK
AH! YOU APPEAR TO BE WORTH THE FIIIIIGHT!!
TA TOK TOK

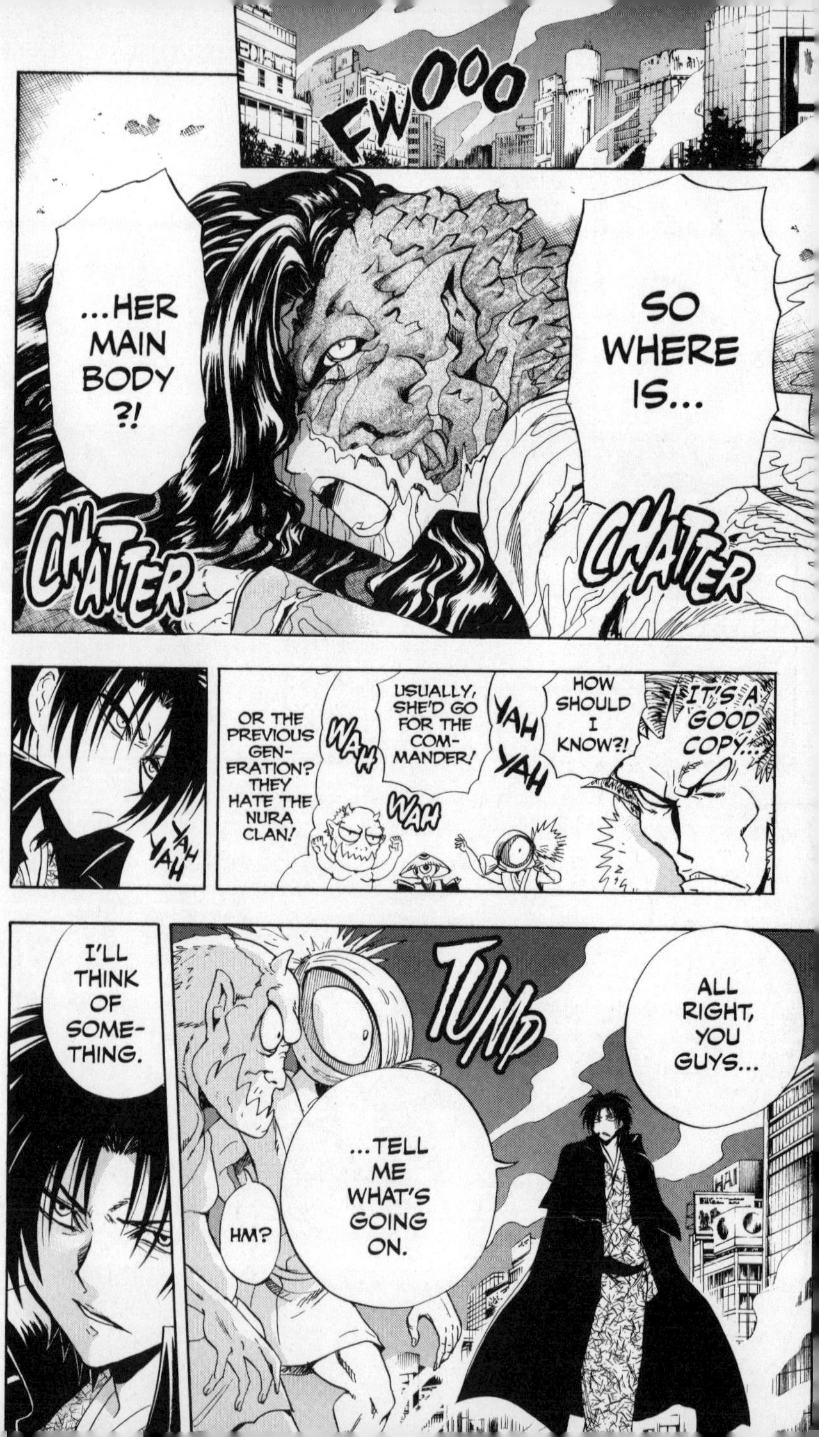
FWOOO
SO WHERE IS...
...HER MAIN BODY?!
CHATTER
CHATTER
IT'S A GOOD COPY...
HOW SHOULD I KNOW?!
YAH YAH
USUALLY, SHE'D GO FOR THE COMMANDER!
WAH
OR THE PREVIOUS GENERATION? THEY HATE THE NURA CLAN!
WAH
YAH YAH
ALL RIGHT, YOU GUYS...
TUMP
...TELL ME WHAT'S GOING ON.
HM?
I'LL THINK OF SOMETHING.

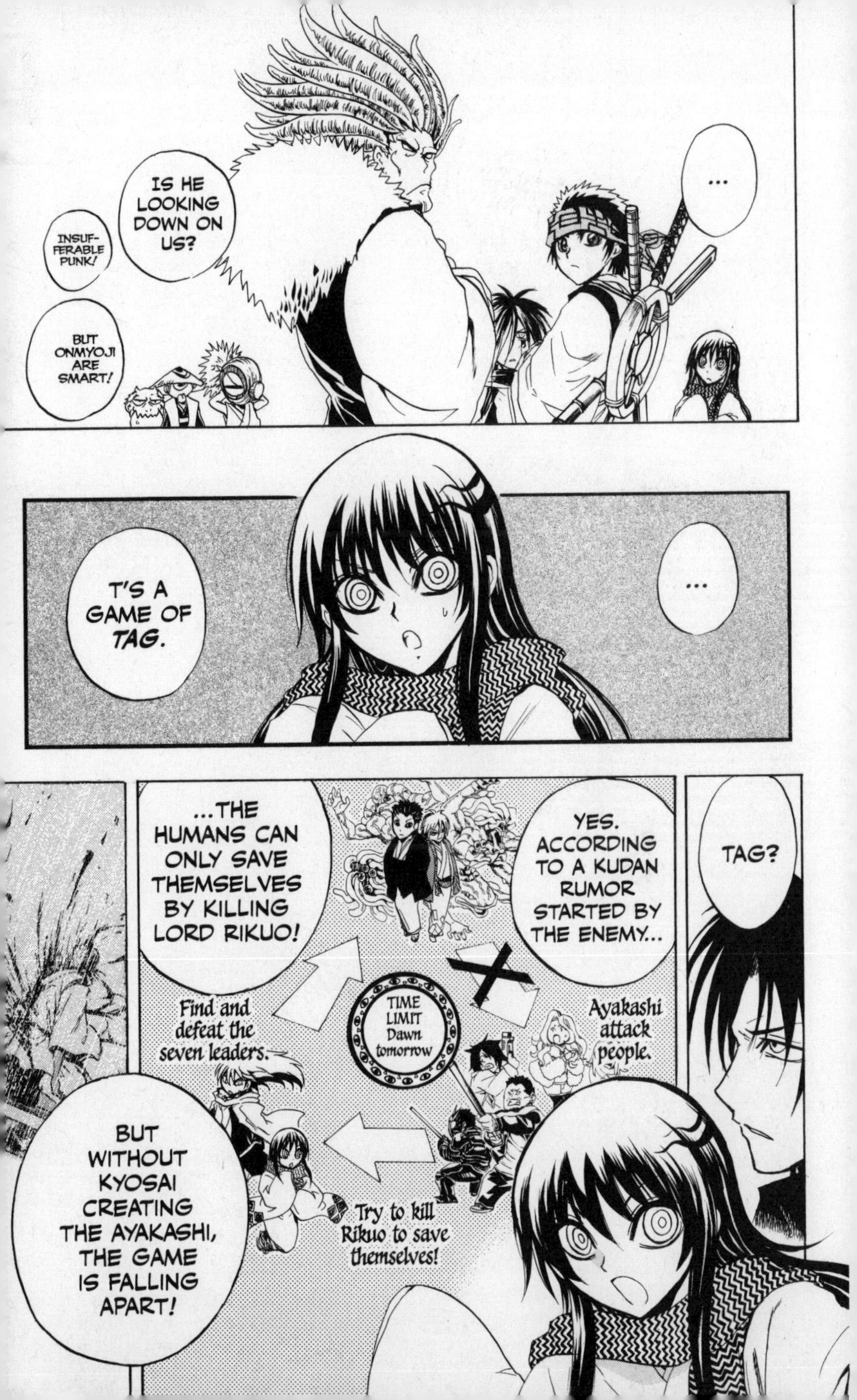
...
IS HE LOOKING DOWN ON US?
INSUF-FERABLE PUNK!
BUT ONMYOJI ARE SMART!
...
T'S A GAME OF TAG.
TAG?
YES. ACCORDING TO A KUDAN RUMOR STARTED BY THE ENEMY...
...THE HUMANS CAN ONLY SAVE THEMSELVES BY KILLING LORD RIKUO!
Ayakashi attack people.
TIME LIMIT Dawn tomorrow
Find and defeat the seven leaders.
Try to kill Rikuo to save themselves!
BUT WITHOUT KYOSAI CREATING THE AYAKASHI, THE GAME IS FALLING APART!

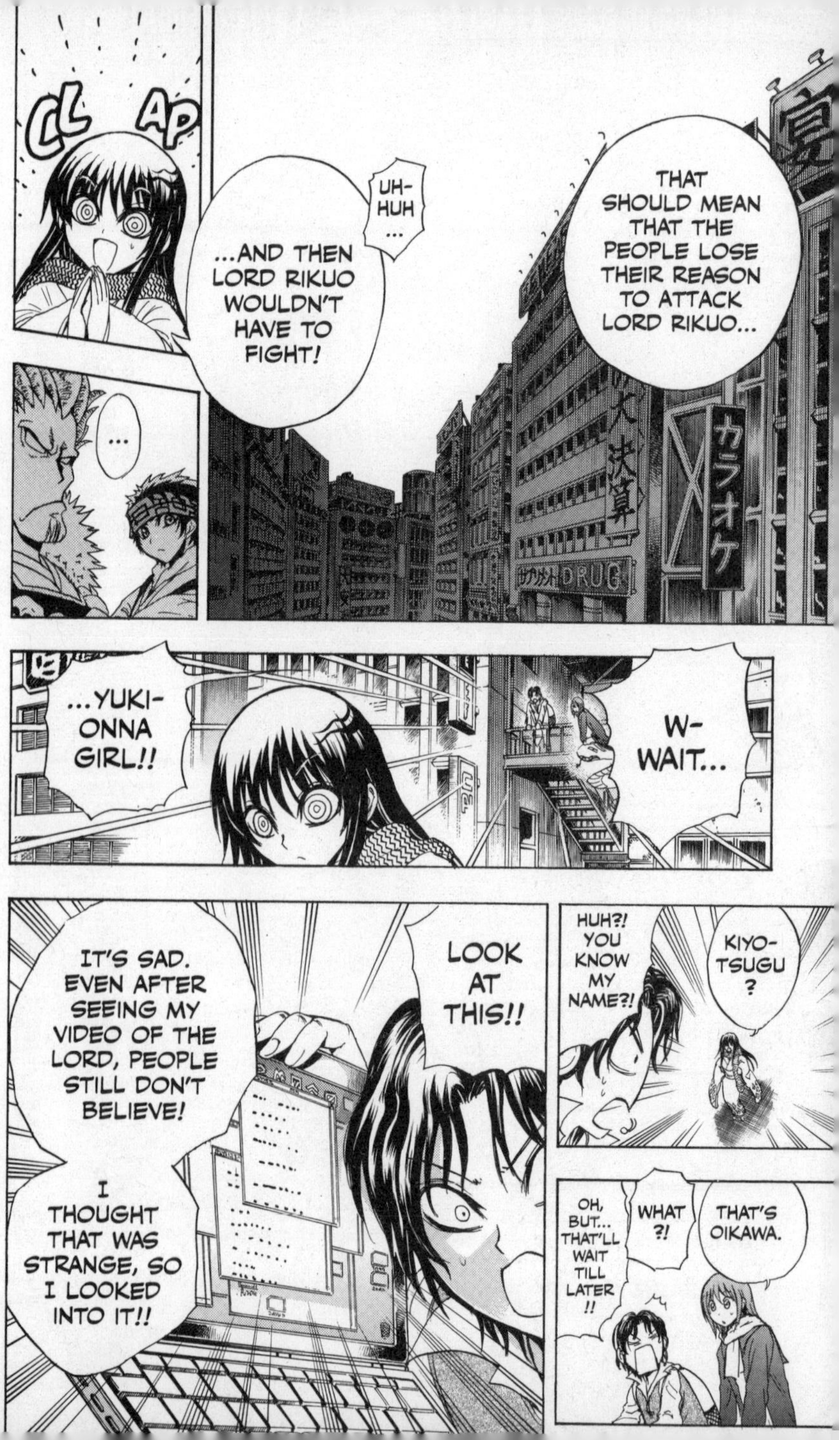
THAT SHOULD MEAN THAT THE PEOPLE LOSE THEIR REASON TO ATTACK LORD RIKUO...
UH-HUH...
カラオケ
大決算
DRUG
CLAP
...AND THEN LORD RIKUO WOULDN'T HAVE TO FIGHT!
...
W-WAIT...
...YUKI-ONNA GIRL!!
KIYO-TSUGU?
HUH?! YOU KNOW MY NAME?!
THAT'S OIKAWA.
WHAT?!
OH, BUT... THAT'LL WAIT TILL LATER!!
LOOK AT THIS!!
IT'S SAD. EVEN AFTER SEEING MY VIDEO OF THE LORD, PEOPLE STILL DON'T BELIEVE!
I THOUGHT THAT WAS STRANGE, SO I LOOKED INTO IT!!

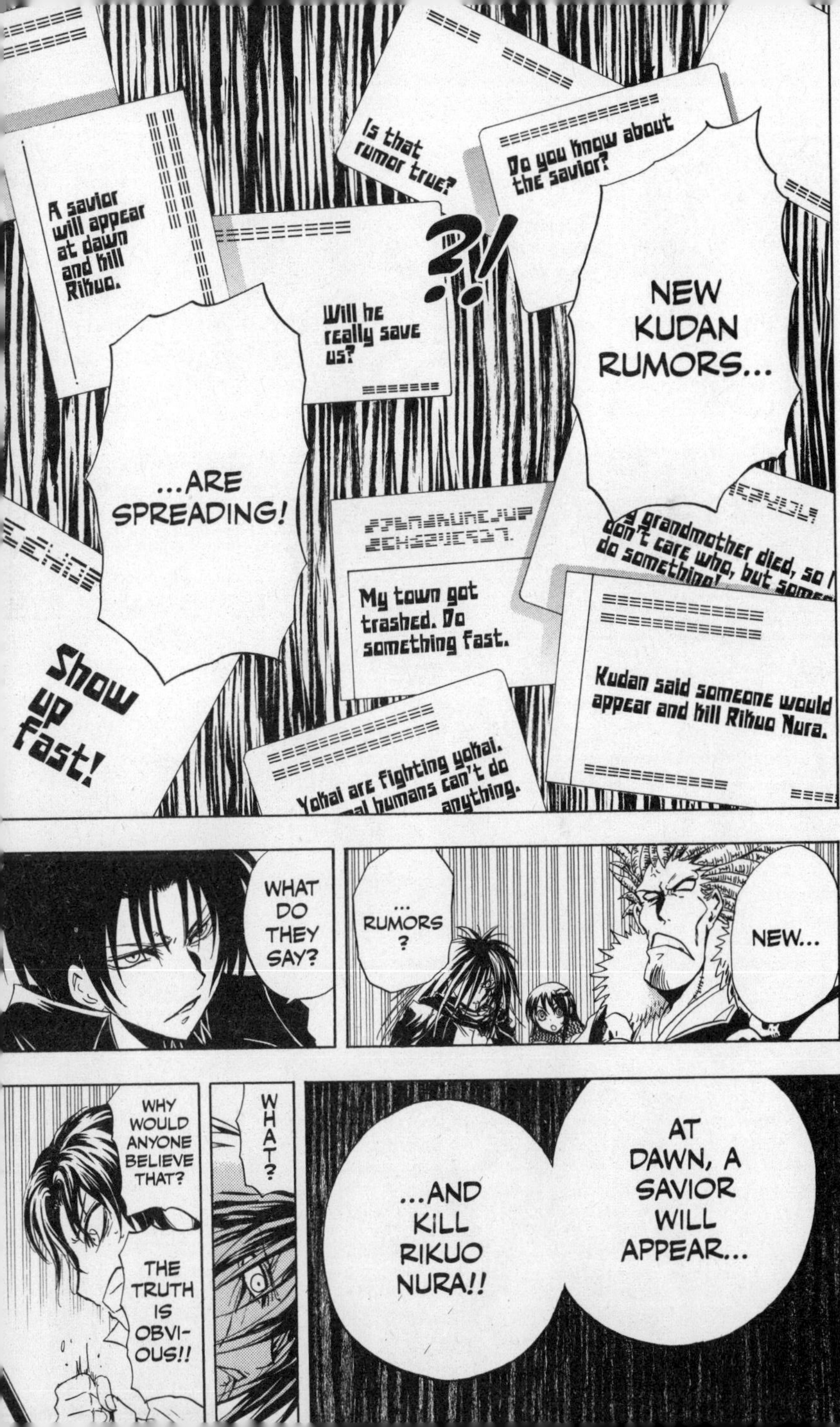

NEW KUDAN RUMORS...
Do you know about the savior?
Is that rumor true?
?!
A savior will appear at dawn and kill Rikuo.
Will he really save us?
...ARE SPREADING!
grandmother died, so I don't care who, but some do something!
Kudan said someone would appear and kill Rikuo Nura.
My town got trashed. Do something fast.
Yokai are fighting yokai. al humans can't do anything.
Show up fast!
NEW...
...RUMORS?
WHAT DO THEY SAY?
AT DAWN, A SAVIOR WILL APPEAR...
...AND KILL RIKUO NURA!!
WHAT?
WHY WOULD ANYONE BELIEVE THAT?
THE TRUTH IS OBVIOUS!!

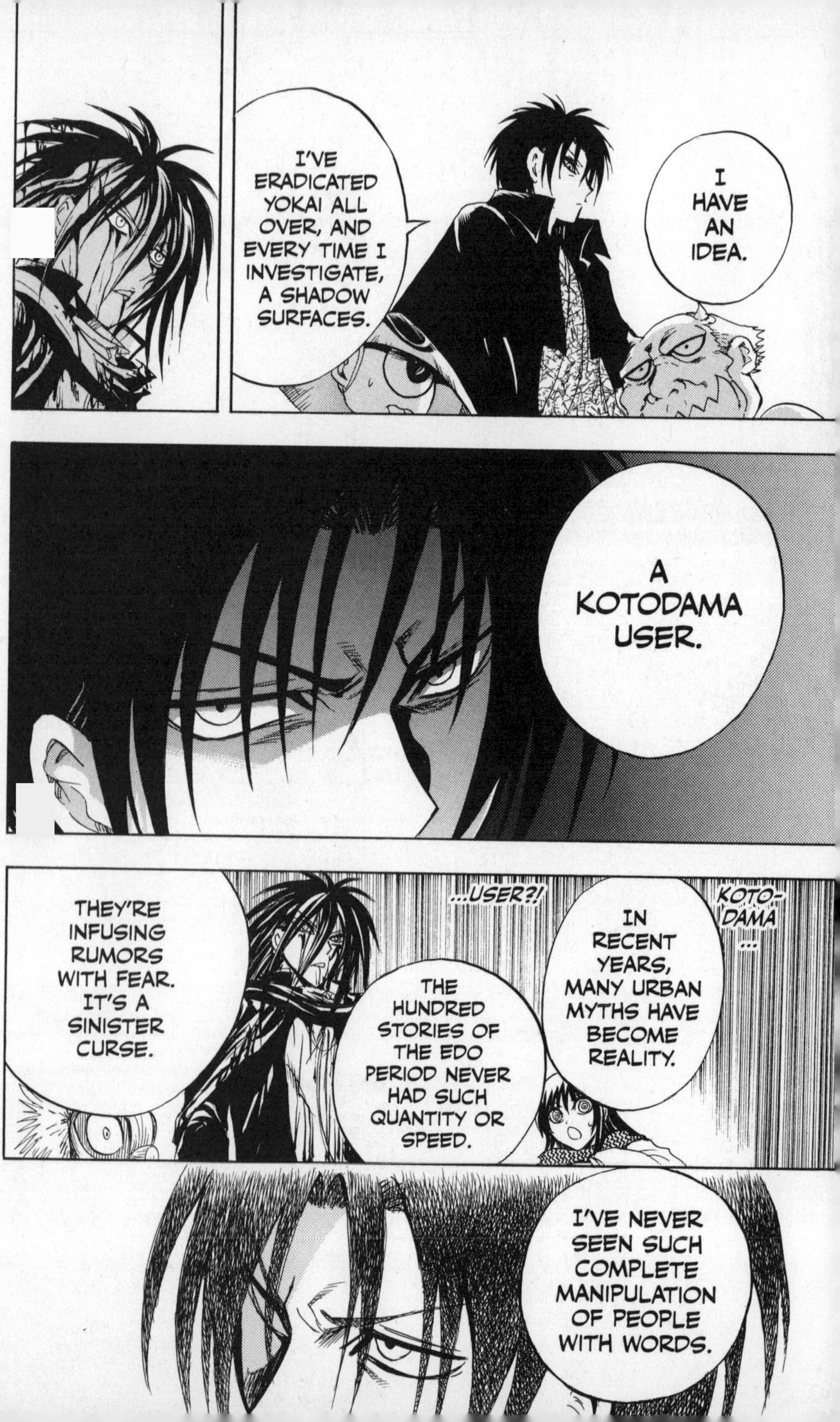
I HAVE AN IDEA.
I'VE ERADICATED YOKAI ALL OVER, AND EVERY TIME I INVESTIGATE, A SHADOW SURFACES.
A KOTODAMA USER.
KOTO-DAMA...
...USER?!
IN RECENT YEARS, MANY URBAN MYTHS HAVE BECOME REALITY.
THE HUNDRED STORIES OF THE EDO PERIOD NEVER HAD SUCH QUANTITY OR SPEED.
THEY'RE INFUSING RUMORS WITH FEAR. IT'S A SINISTER CURSE.
I'VE NEVER SEEN SUCH COMPLETE MANIPULATION OF PEOPLE WITH WORDS.

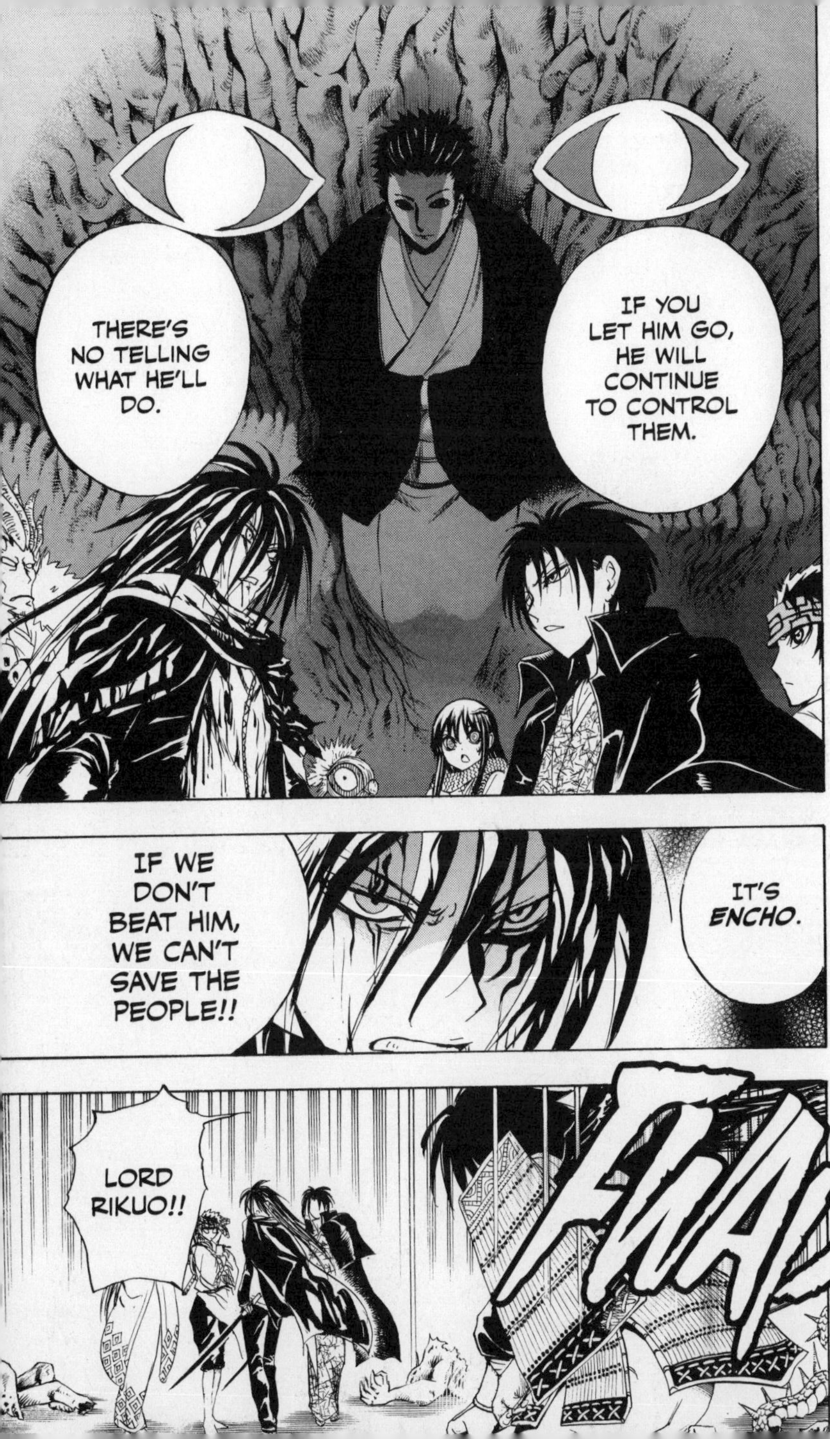
IF YOU LET HIM GO, HE WILL CONTINUE TO CONTROL THEM.
THERE'S NO TELLING WHAT HE'LL DO.
IT'S *ENCHO*.
IF WE DON'T BEAT HIM, WE CAN'T SAVE THE PEOPLE!!
FWAP
LORD RIKUO!!

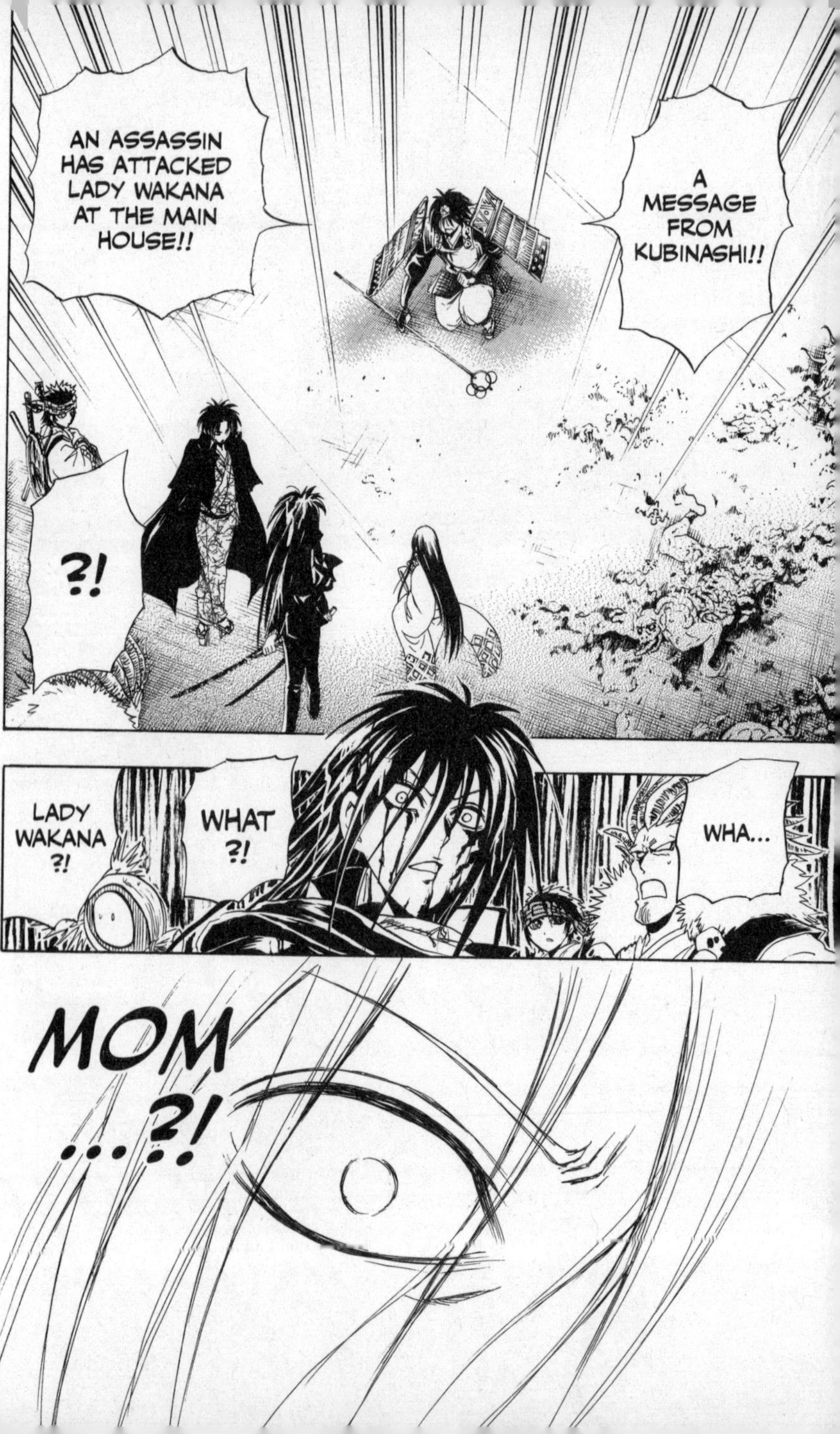
A MESSAGE FROM KUBINASHI!!
AN ASSASSIN HAS ATTACKED LADY WAKANA AT THE MAIN HOUSE!!
?!
WHA...
WHAT ?!
LADY WAKANA ?!
MOM ...?!

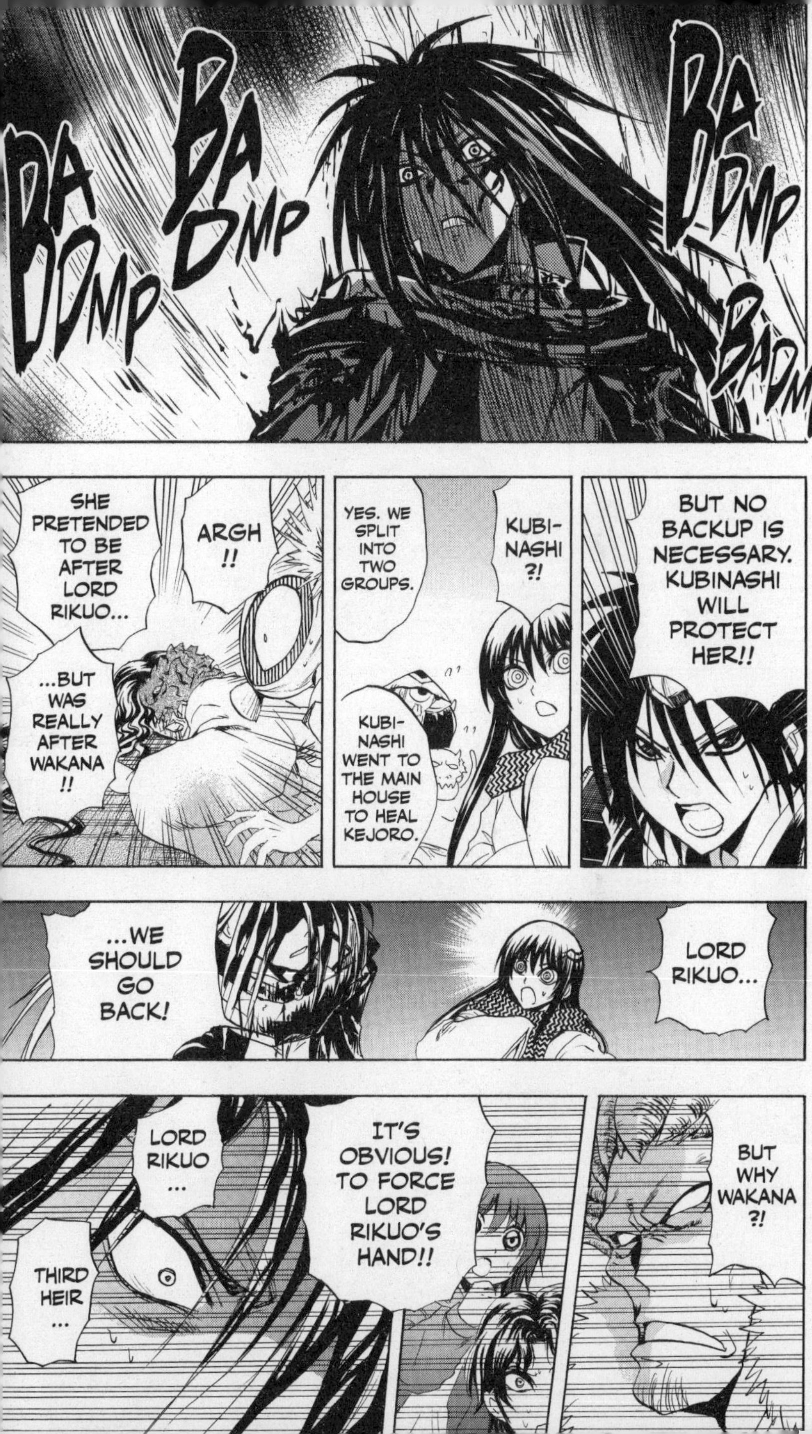
BA DMP
BADMP
BA DMP
BA DMP
BUT NO BACKUP IS NECESSARY. KUBINASHI WILL PROTECT HER!!
KUBI-NASHI ?!
YES. WE SPLIT INTO TWO GROUPS.
KUBI-NASHI WENT TO THE MAIN HOUSE TO HEAL KEJORO.
ARGH !!
SHE PRETENDED TO BE AFTER LORD RIKUO...
...BUT WAS REALLY AFTER WAKANA !!
LORD RIKUO...
...WE SHOULD GO BACK!
BUT WHY WAKANA ?!
IT'S OBVIOUS! TO FORCE LORD RIKUO'S HAND!!
LORD RIKUO ...
THIRD HEIR ...

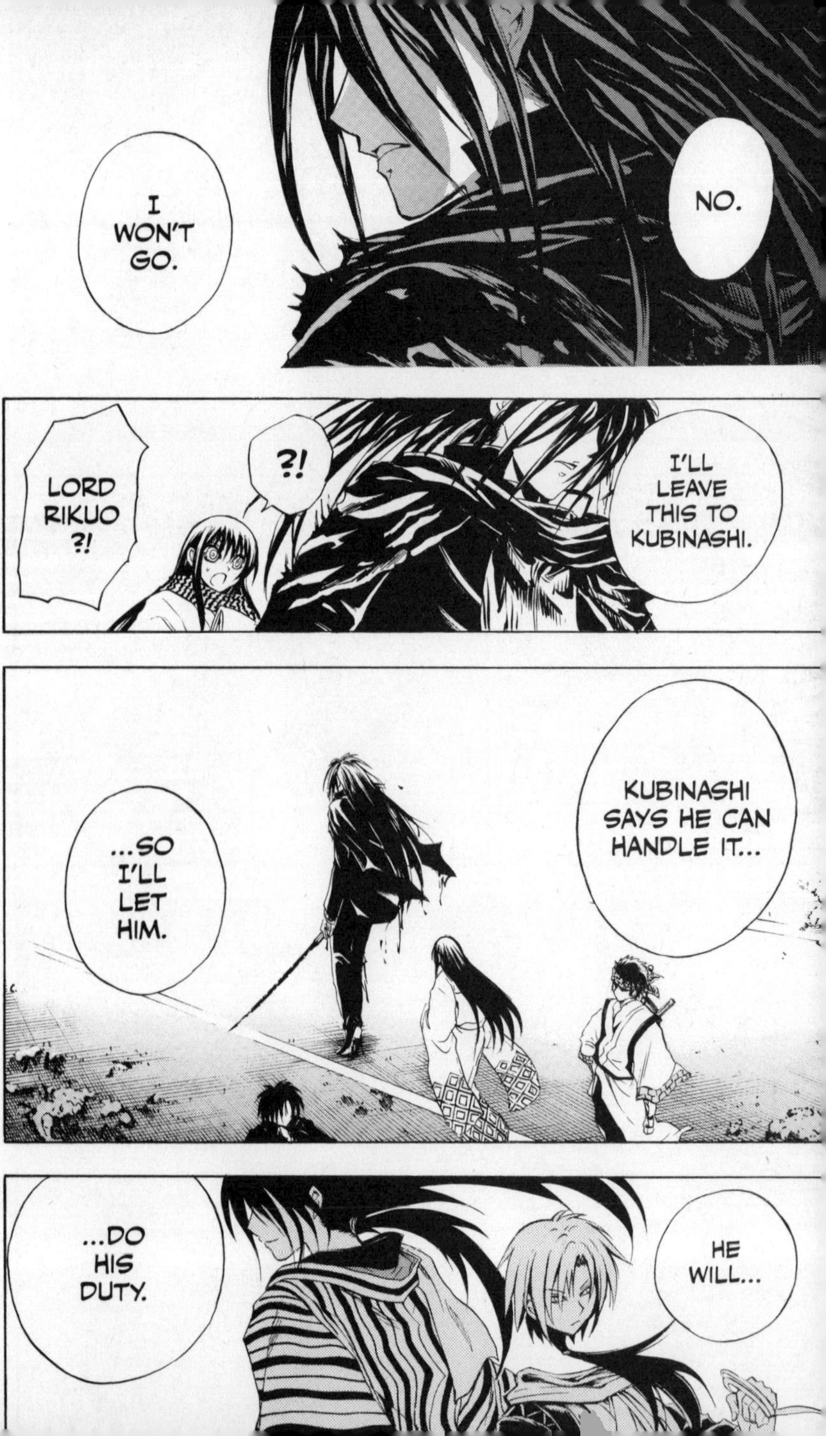
NO.
I WON'T GO.
I'LL LEAVE THIS TO KUBINASHI.
?!
LORD RIKUO ?!
KUBINASHI SAYS HE CAN HANDLE IT...
...SO I'LL LET HIM.
HE WILL...
...DO HIS DUTY.

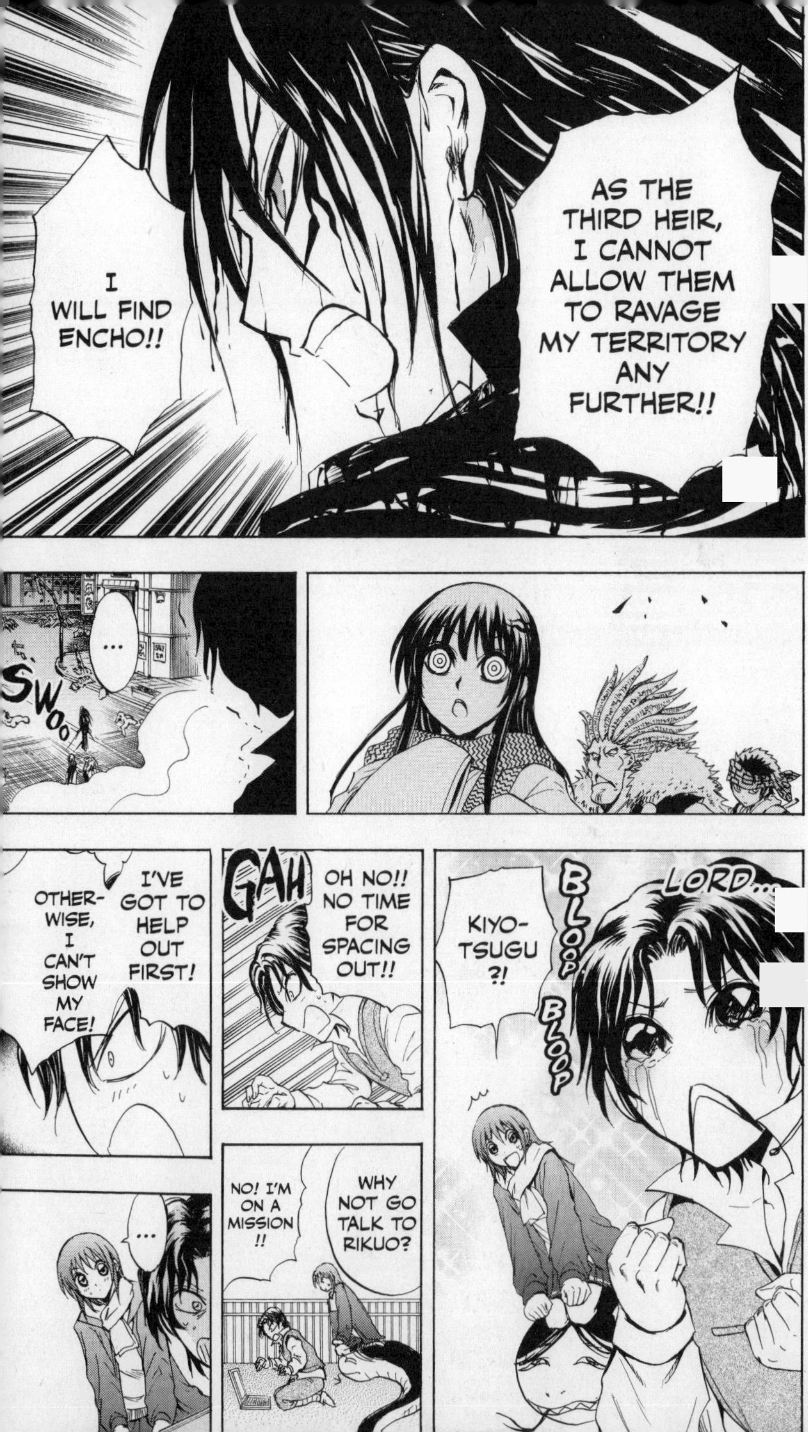
AS THE THIRD HEIR, I CANNOT ALLOW THEM TO RAVAGE MY TERRITORY ANY FURTHER!!
I WILL FIND ENCHO!!
...
SWOOO
LORD...
BLOOP BLOOP
KIYO-TSUGU?!
GAH
OH NO!! NO TIME FOR SPACING OUT!!
I'VE GOT TO HELP OUT FIRST!
OTHER-WISE, I CAN'T SHOW MY FACE!
WHY NOT GO TALK TO RIKUO?
NO! I'M ON A MISSION!!
...

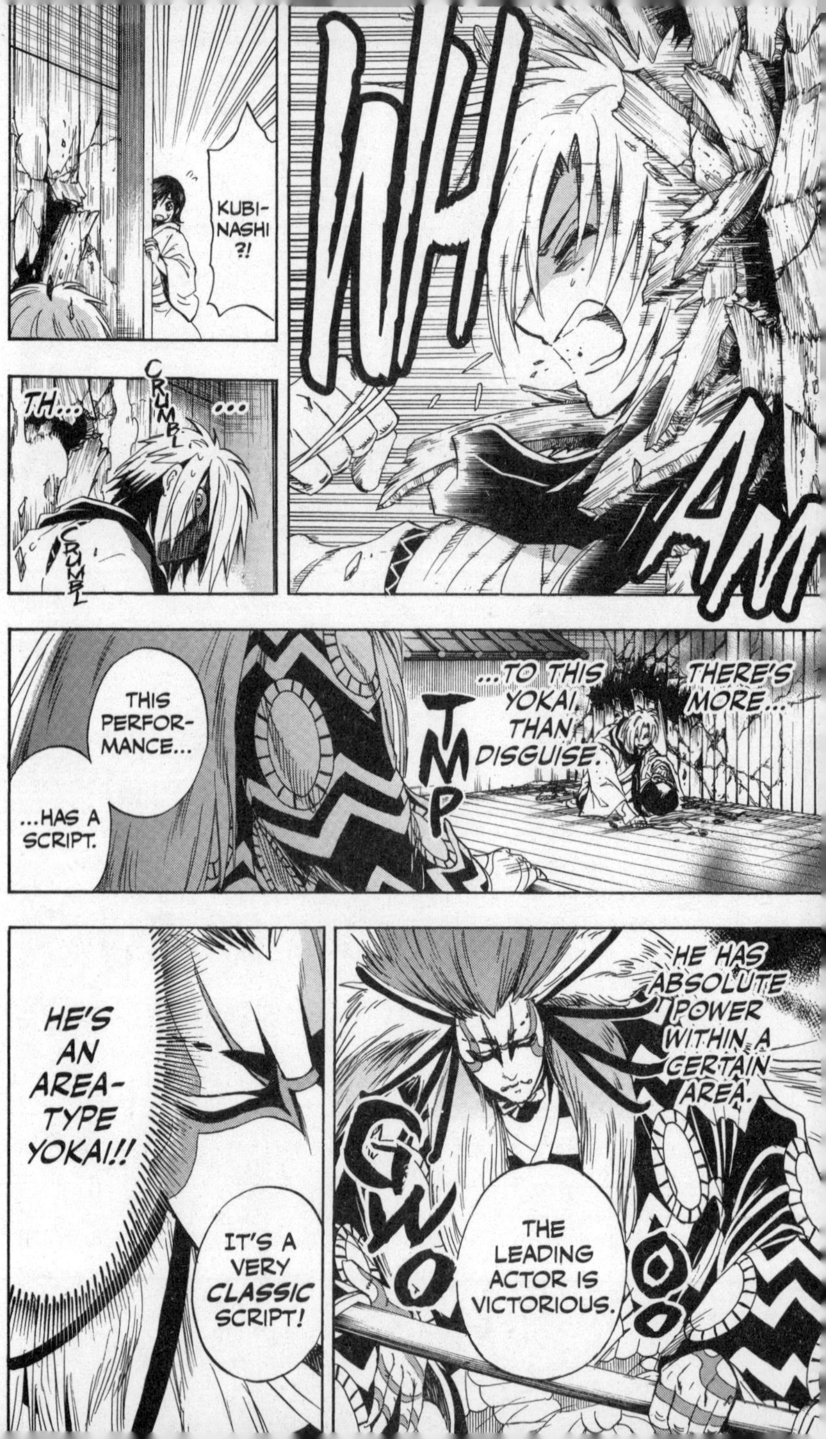
WHAM
KUBI-NASHI?!
TH...
CRUMBL
...
CRUMBL
THERE'S MORE...
...TO THIS YOKAI THAN DISGUISE.
TMP
THIS PERFORMANCE...
...HAS A SCRIPT.
HE HAS ABSOLUTE POWER WITHIN A CERTAIN AREA.
GWOO
THE LEADING ACTOR IS VICTORIOUS.
HE'S AN AREA-TYPE YOKAI!!
IT'S A VERY CLASSIC SCRIPT!

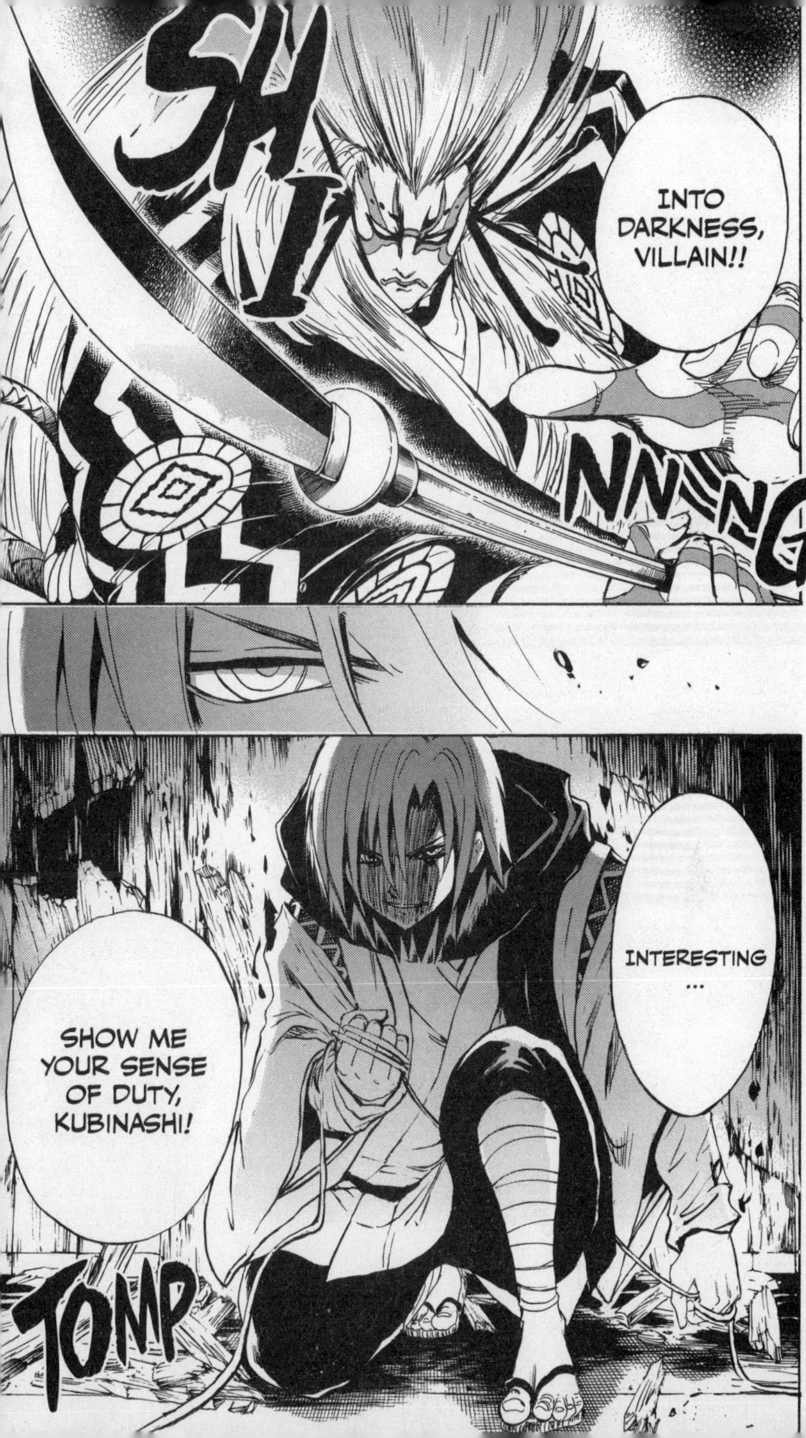
INTO DARKNESS, VILLAIN!!
SHINNNG
INTERESTING ...
SHOW ME YOUR SENSE OF DUTY, KUBINASHI!
TOMP

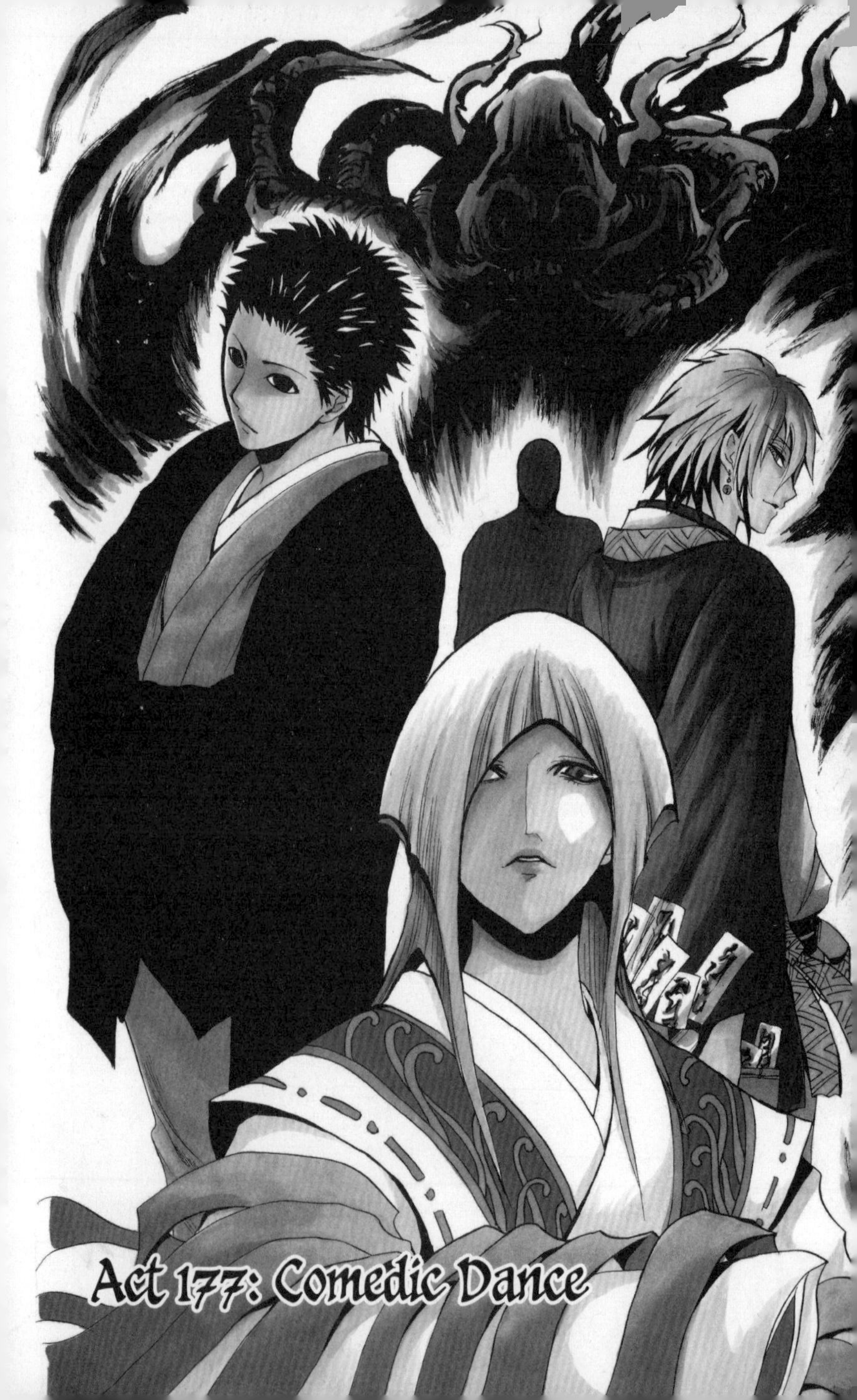
Act 177: Comedic Dance

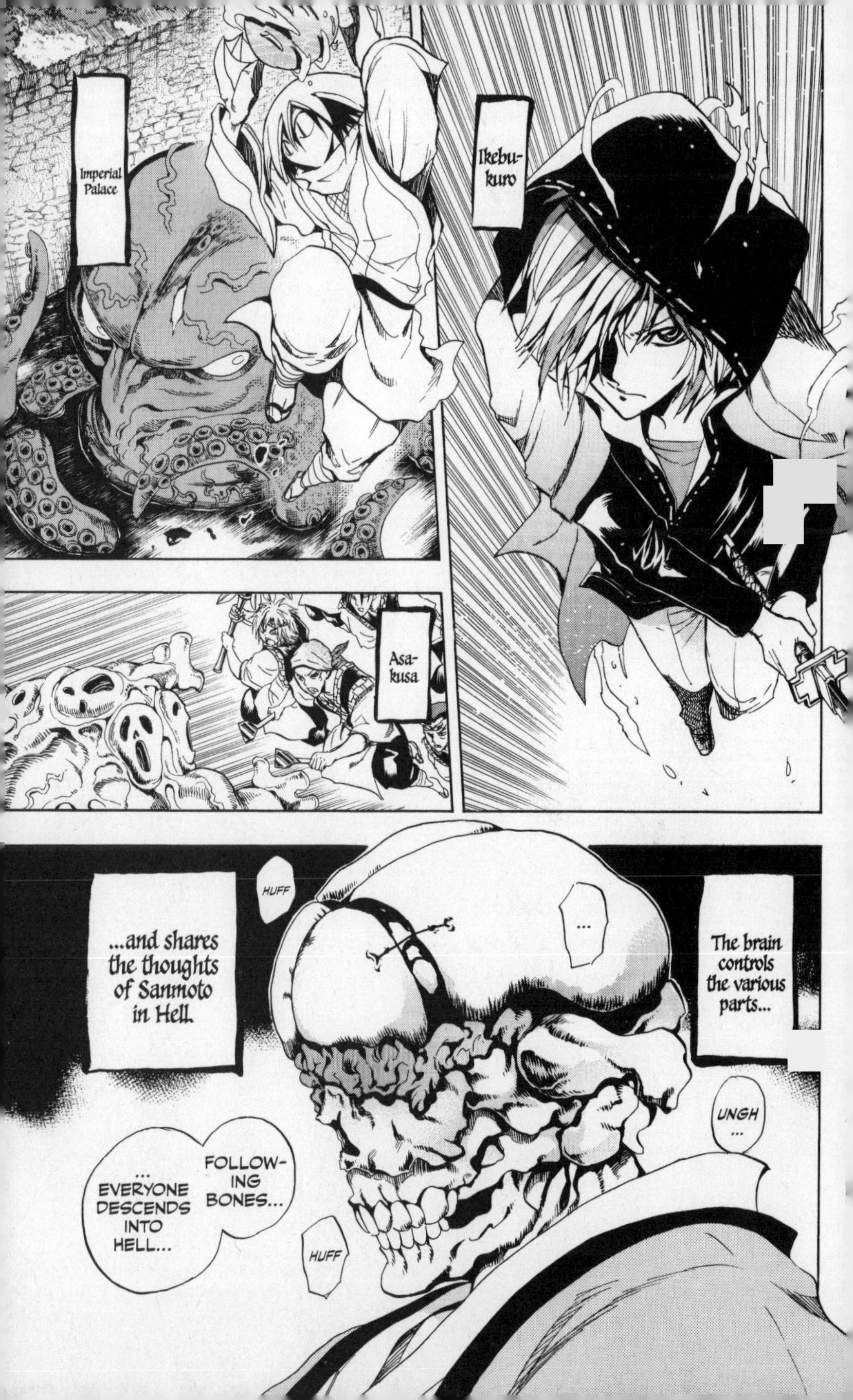
Ikebukuro
Imperial Palace
Asakusa
The brain controls the various parts...
...
HUFF
...and shares the thoughts of Sanmoto in Hell.
UNGH...
FOLLOWING BONES...
...EVERYONE DESCENDS INTO HELL...
HUFF

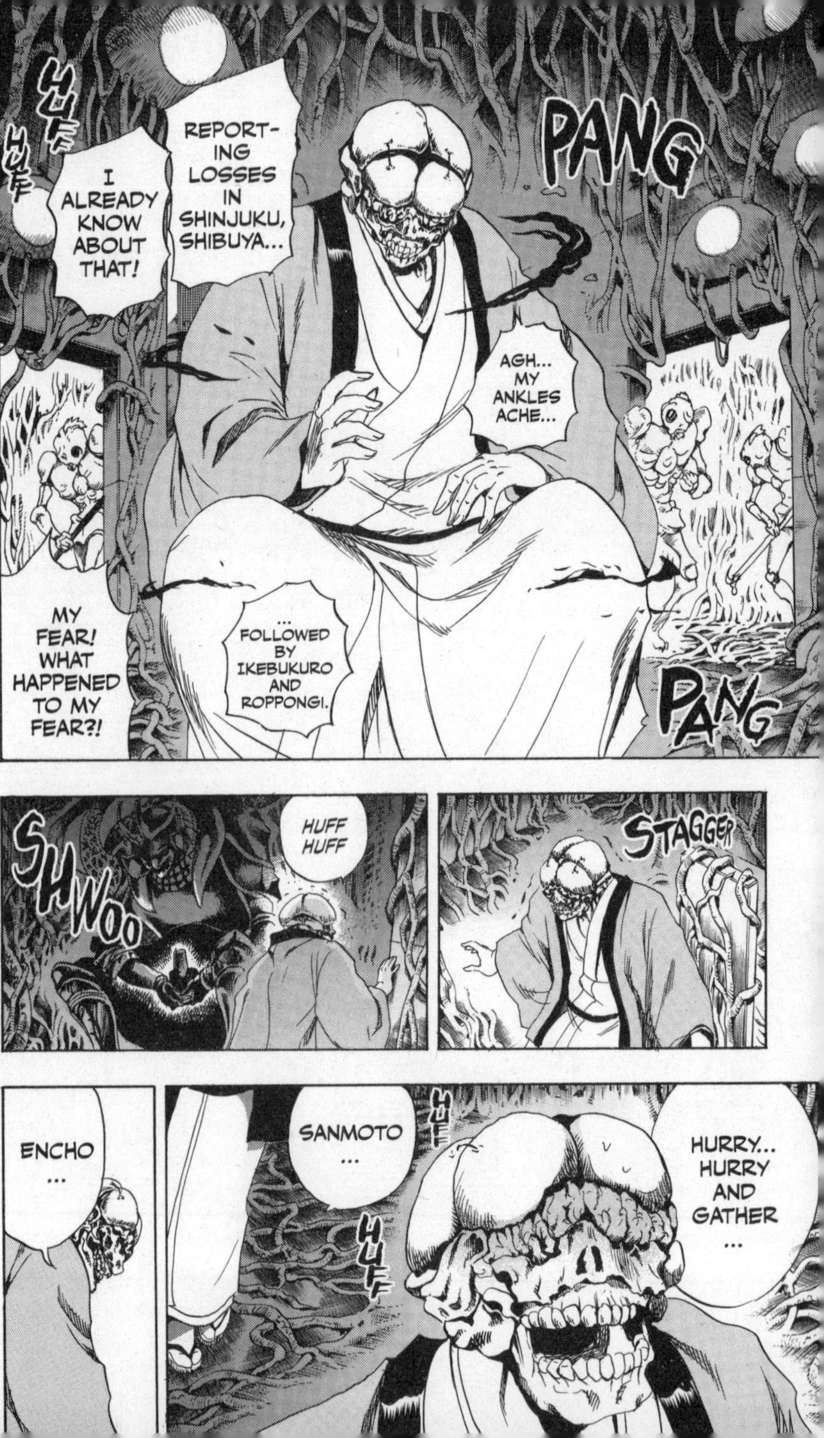
PANG
REPORTING LOSSES IN SHINJUKU, SHIBUYA...
I ALREADY KNOW ABOUT THAT!
HUFF HUFF
AGH... MY ANKLES ACHE...
... FOLLOWED BY IKEBUKURO AND ROPPONGI.
PANG
MY FEAR! WHAT HAPPENED TO MY FEAR?!
STAGGER
HUFF HUFF
SHWOO
HURRY... HURRY AND GATHER ...
HUFF
SANMOTO ...
HUFF
ENCHO ...

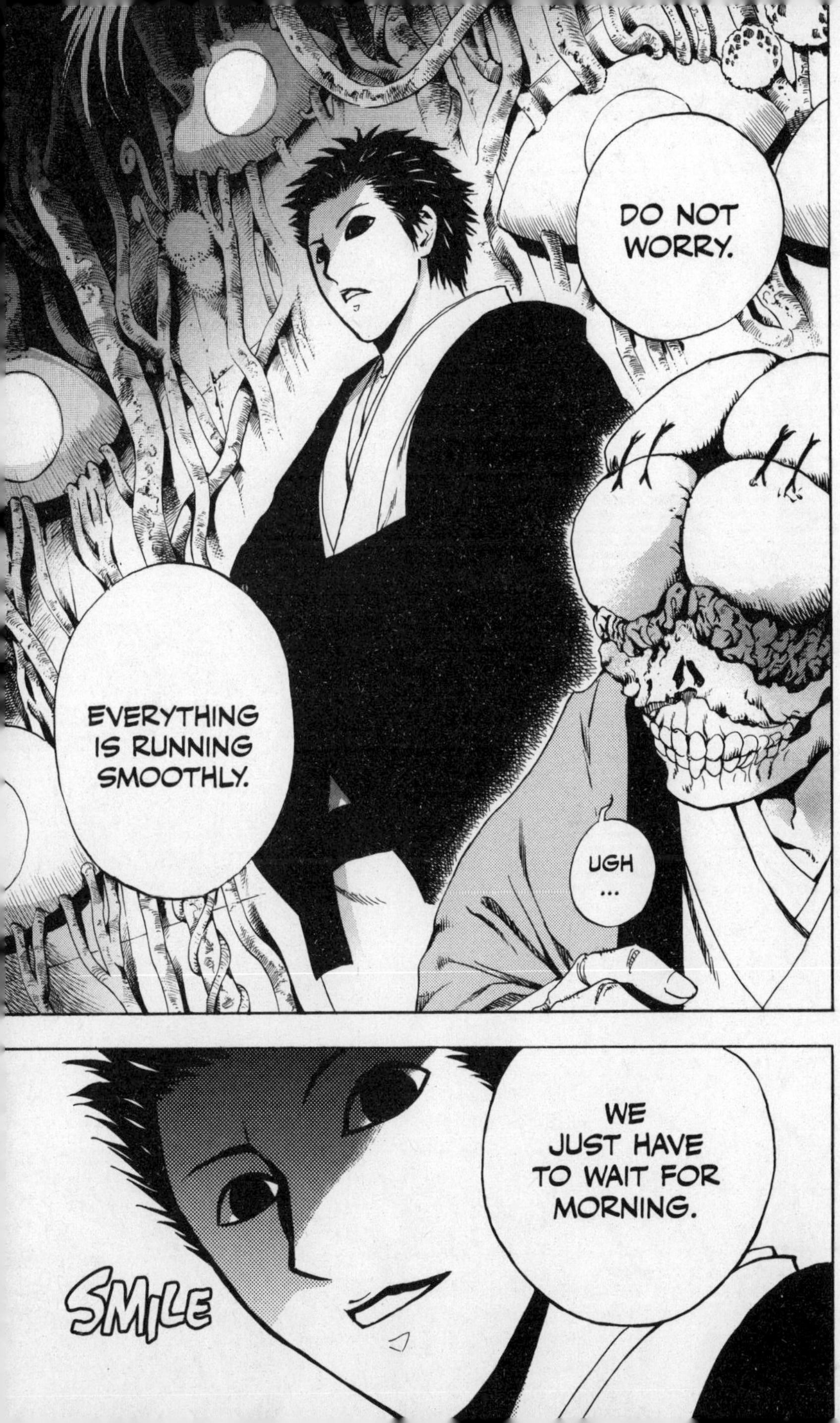
DO NOT WORRY.
EVERYTHING IS RUNNING SMOOTHLY.
UGH ...
WE JUST HAVE TO WAIT FOR MORNING.
SMILE

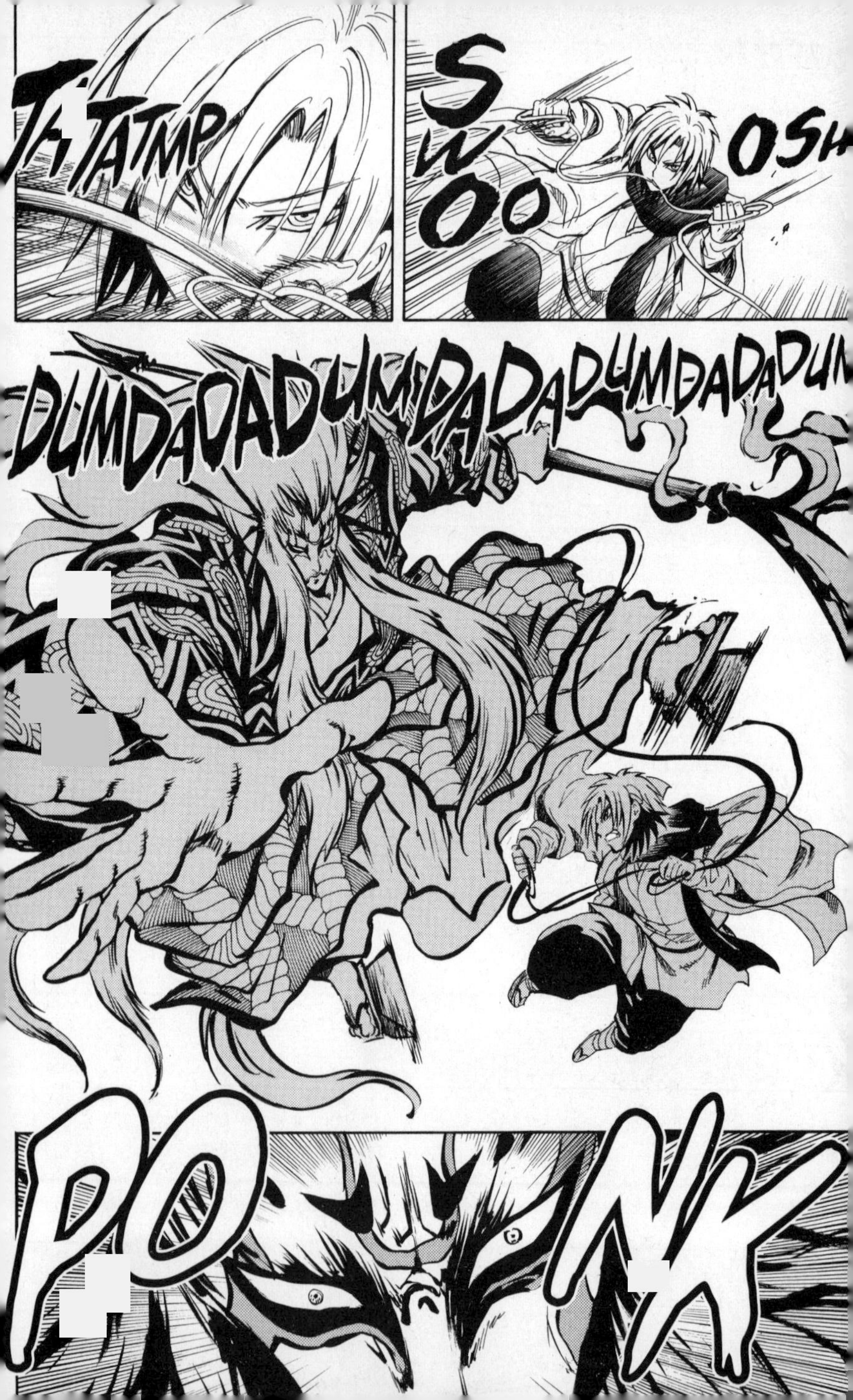
SWOO OSH
T TATMP
DUMDADADUMDADADUMDADADUM
PO NK

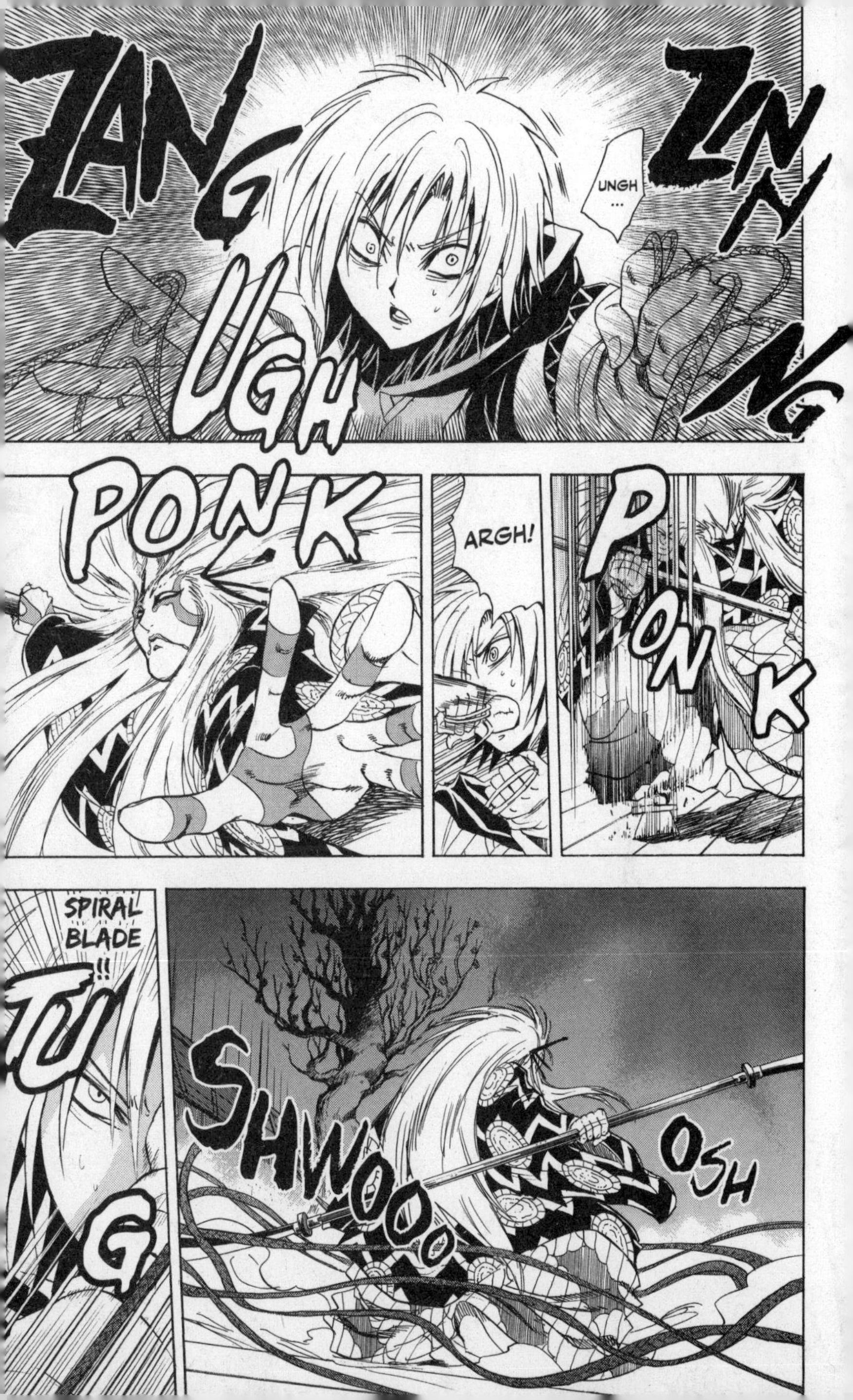
ZINNNG
UNGH ...
ZANG
UGH
PONK
ARGH!
PONK
SHWOOOOOSH
SPIRAL BLADE!!
TU
G

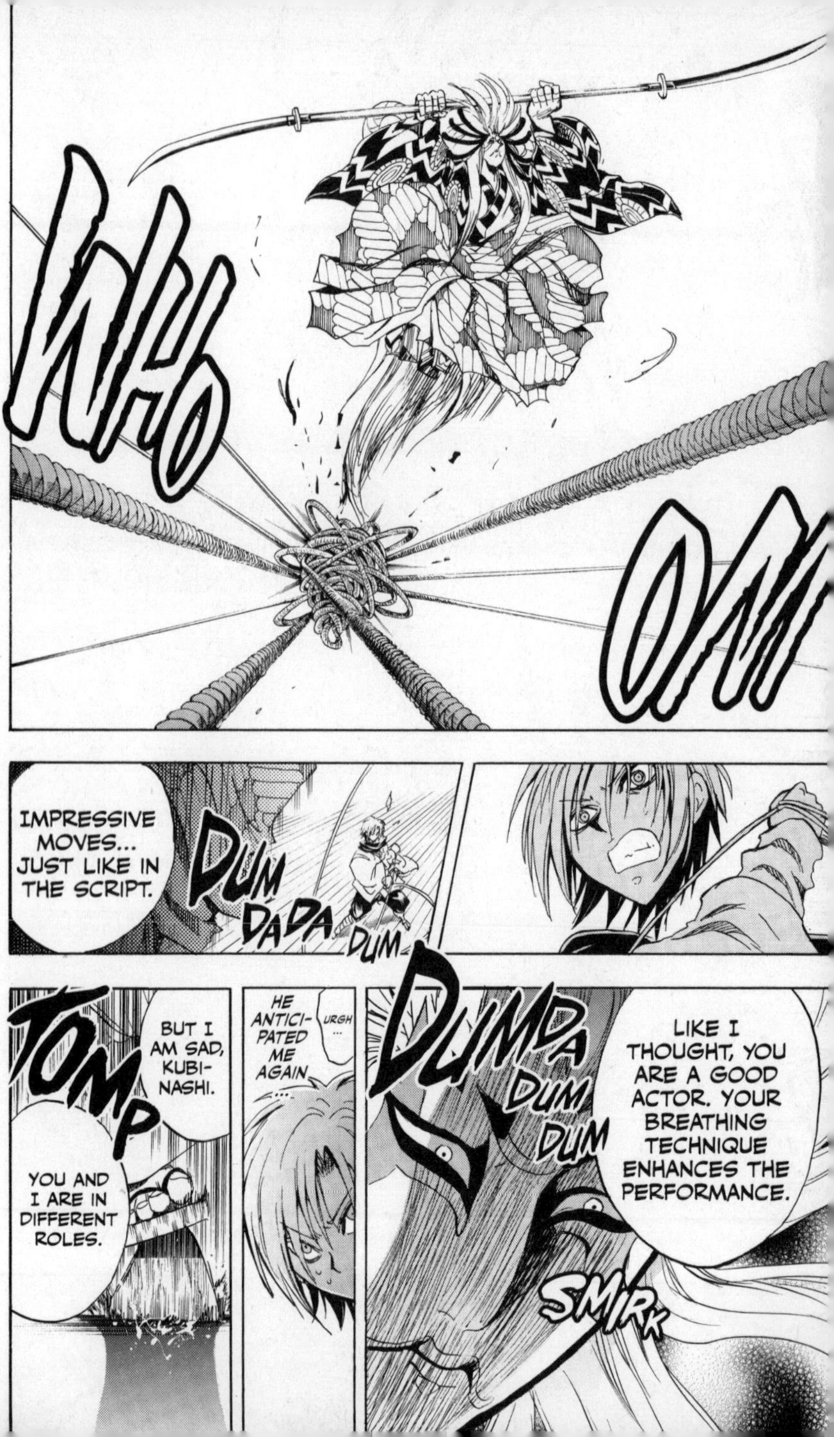
WHOOM
IMPRESSIVE MOVES... JUST LIKE IN THE SCRIPT.
DUM DADA DUM
LIKE I THOUGHT, YOU ARE A GOOD ACTOR. YOUR BREATHING TECHNIQUE ENHANCES THE PERFORMANCE.
DUMDA DUM DUM
SMIRK
URGH ...
HE ANTICI-PATED ME AGAIN....
TOMP
BUT I AM SAD, KUBI-NASHI.
YOU AND I ARE IN DIFFERENT ROLES.

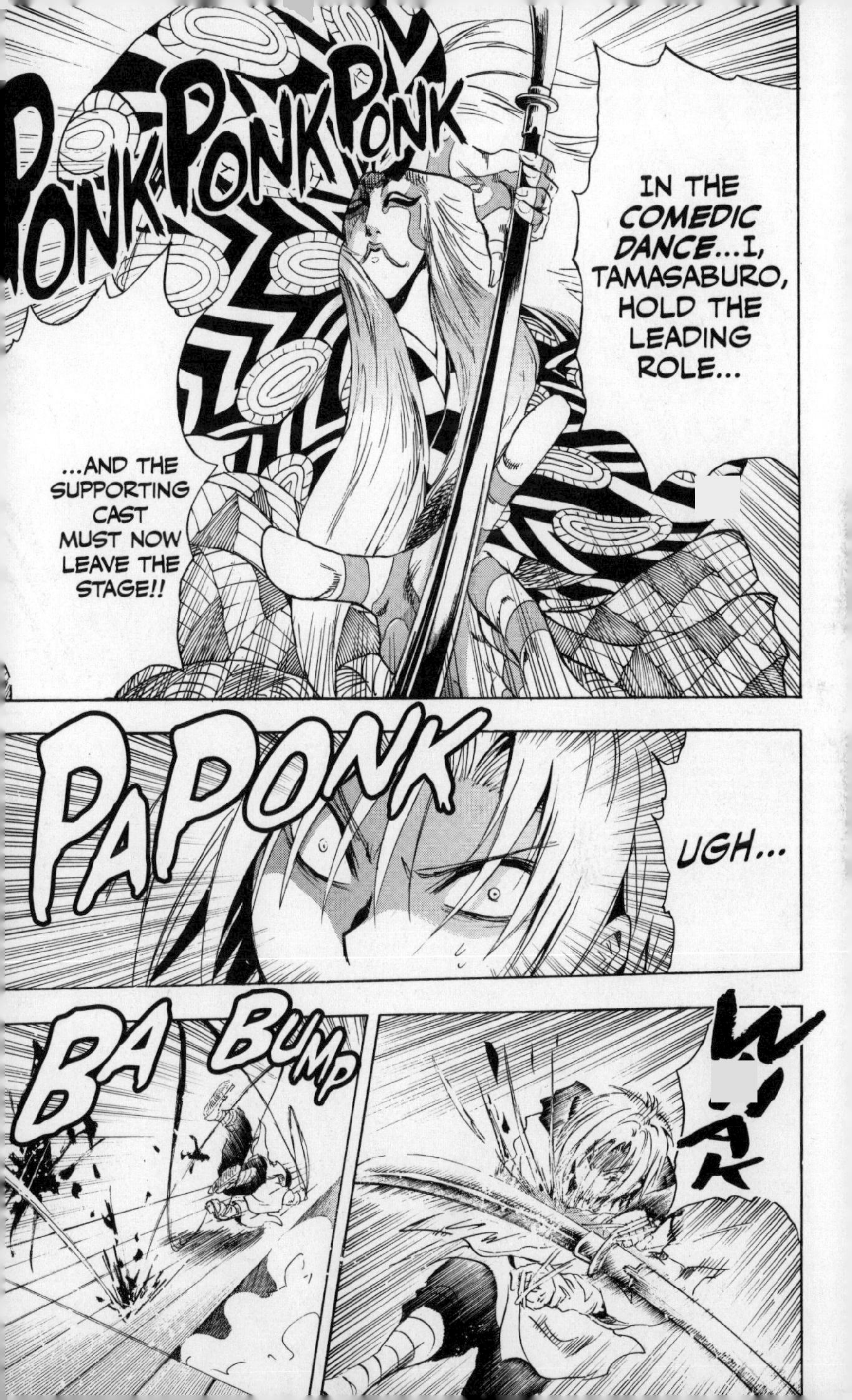
IN THE COMEDIC DANCE...I, TAMASABURO, HOLD THE LEADING ROLE...
PONK PONK PONK PONK
...AND THE SUPPORTING CAST MUST NOW LEAVE THE STAGE!!
PAPONK
UGH...
W AK
BA BUMP

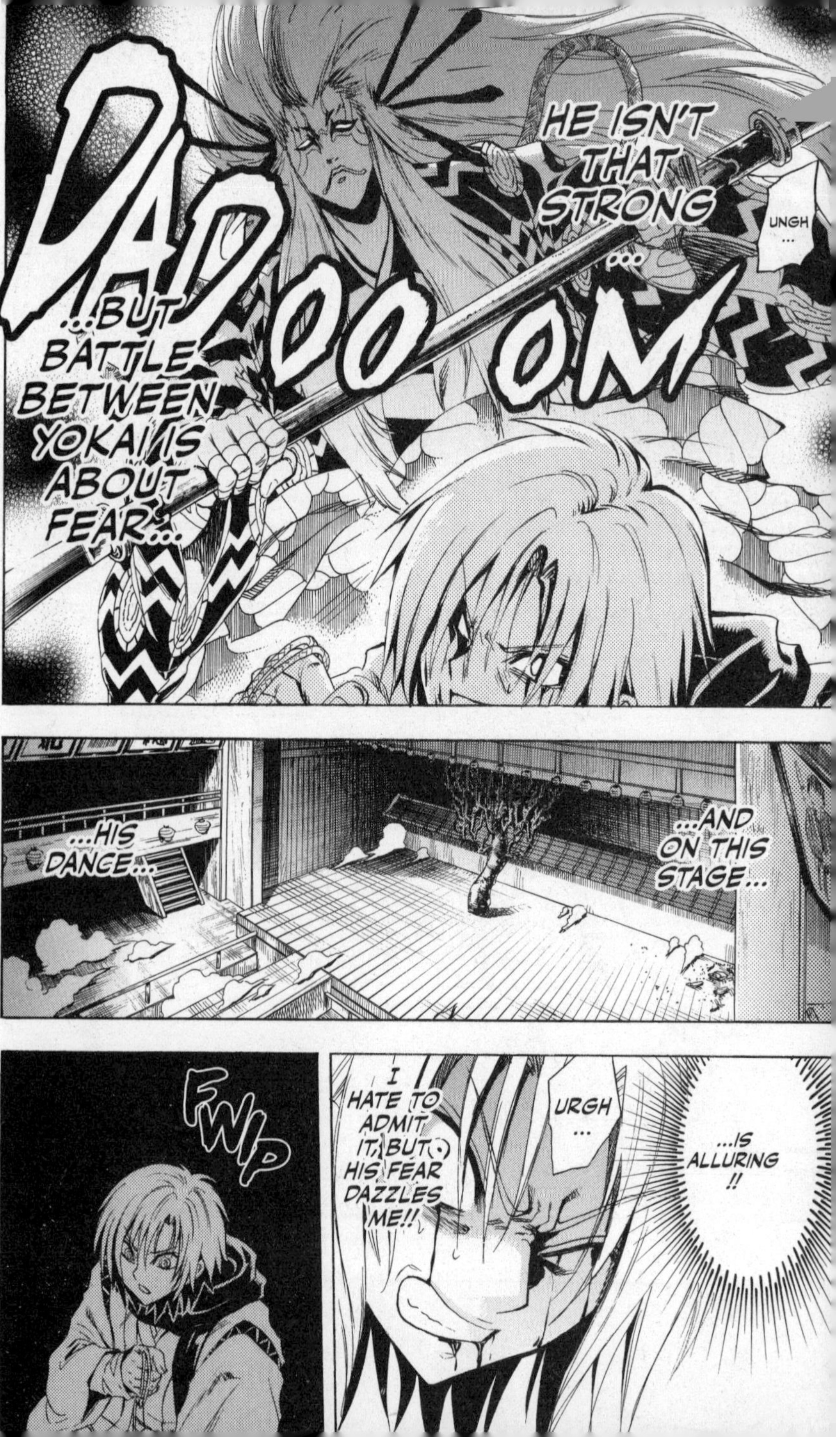
UNGH ...
HE ISN'T THAT STRONG ...
DADOOOM
...BUT BATTLE BETWEEN YOKAI IS ABOUT FEAR...
...AND ON THIS STAGE...
...HIS DANCE...
...IS ALLURING !!
URGH ...
I HATE TO ADMIT IT, BUT HIS FEAR DAZZLES ME!!
FWIP

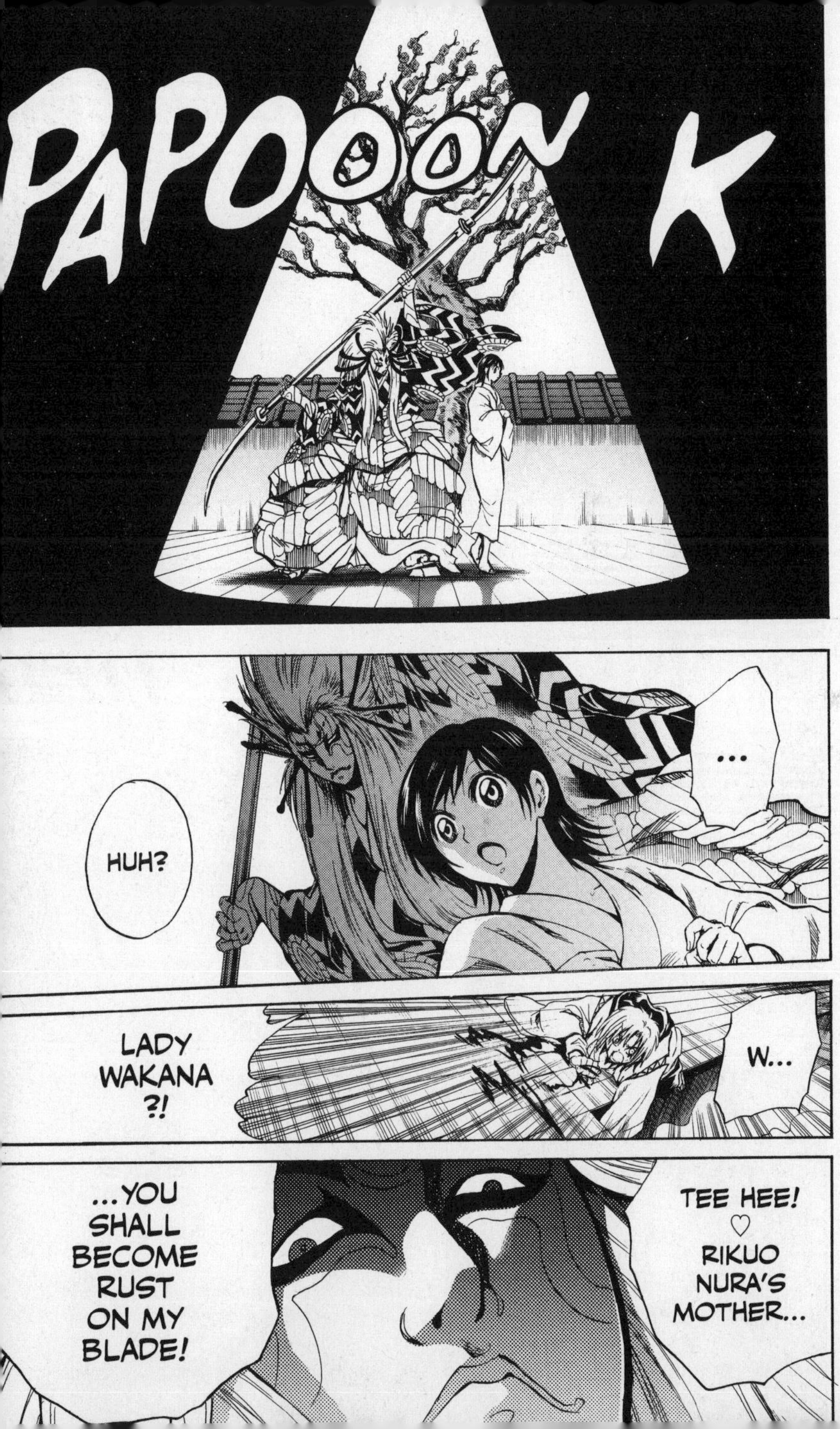
PAPOOON K
...
HUH?
W...
LADY WAKANA ?!
TEE HEE! ♡ RIKUO NURA'S MOTHER...
...YOU SHALL BECOME RUST ON MY BLADE!

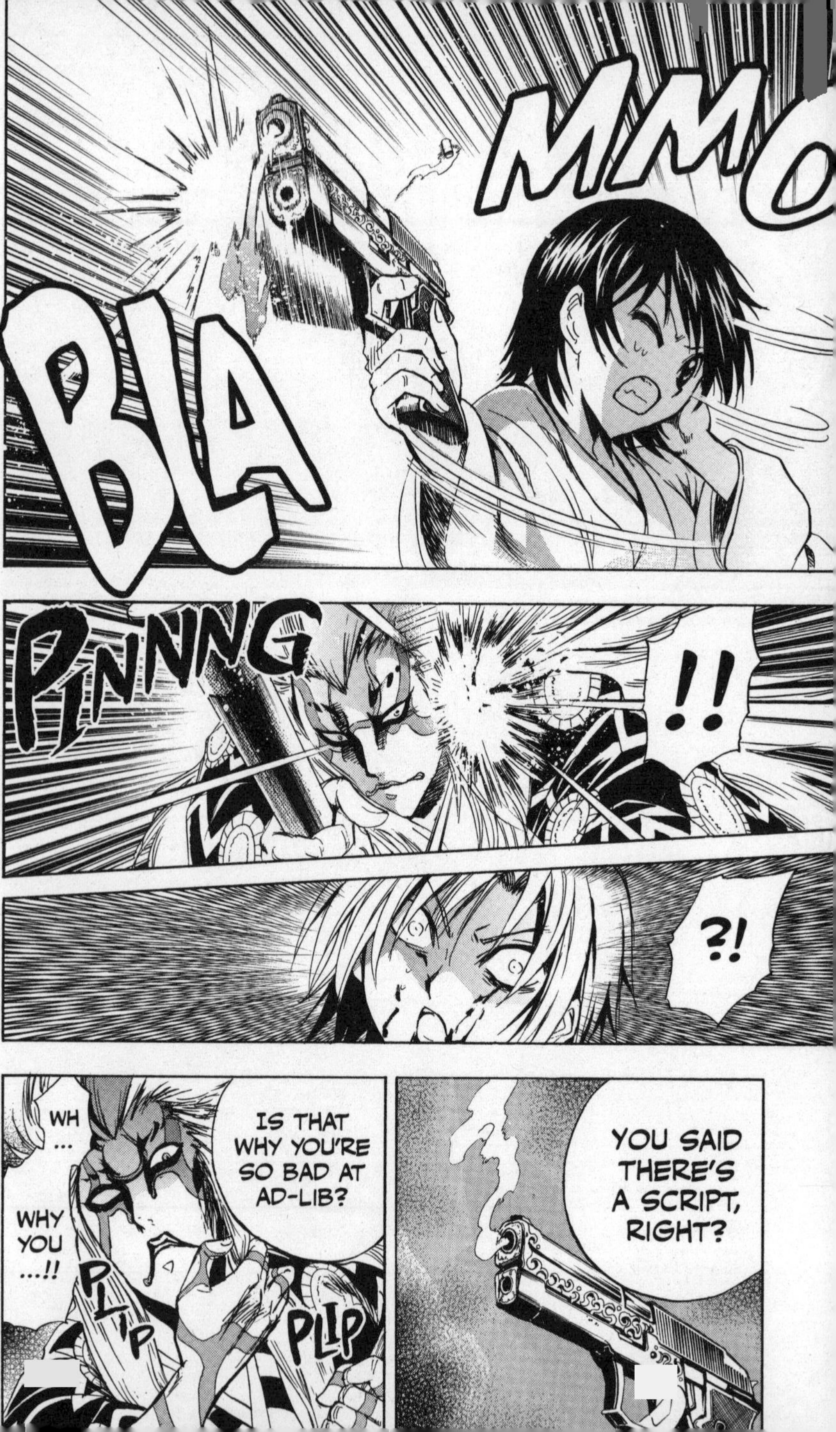
MMO
BLA
!!
PINNNG
?!
YOU SAID THERE'S A SCRIPT, RIGHT?
IS THAT WHY YOU'RE SO BAD AT AD-LIB?
WH ...
WHY YOU ...!!
PLIP
PLIP

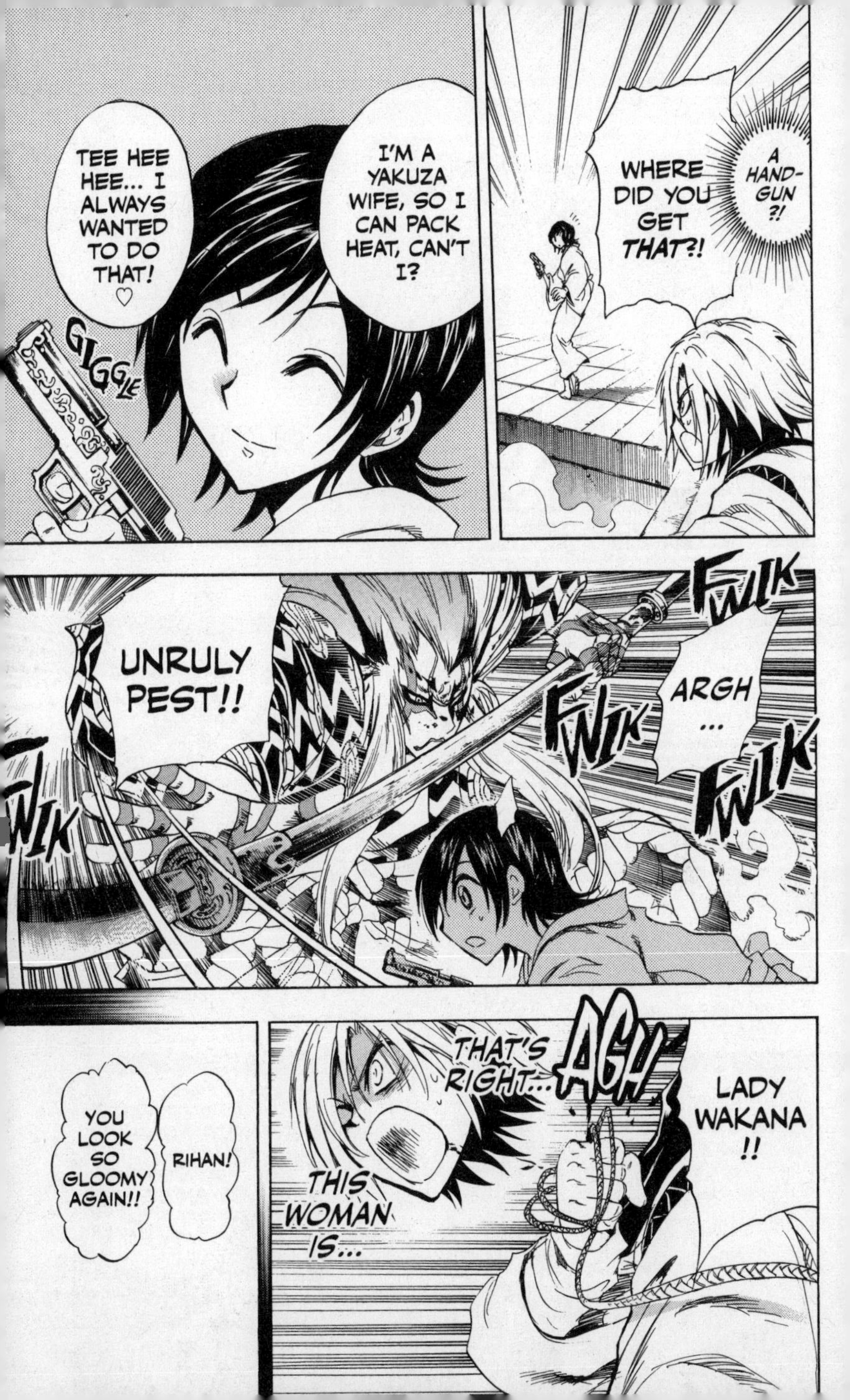
A HAND-GUN?!
WHERE DID YOU GET THAT?!
I'M A YAKUZA WIFE, SO I CAN PACK HEAT, CAN'T I?
TEE HEE HEE... I ALWAYS WANTED TO DO THAT! ♡
GIGGLE
FWIK
ARGH...
FWIK
FWIK
UNRULY PEST!!
FWIK
LADY WAKANA!!
AGH
THAT'S RIGHT...
THIS WOMAN IS...
RIHAN!
YOU LOOK SO GLOOMY AGAIN!!

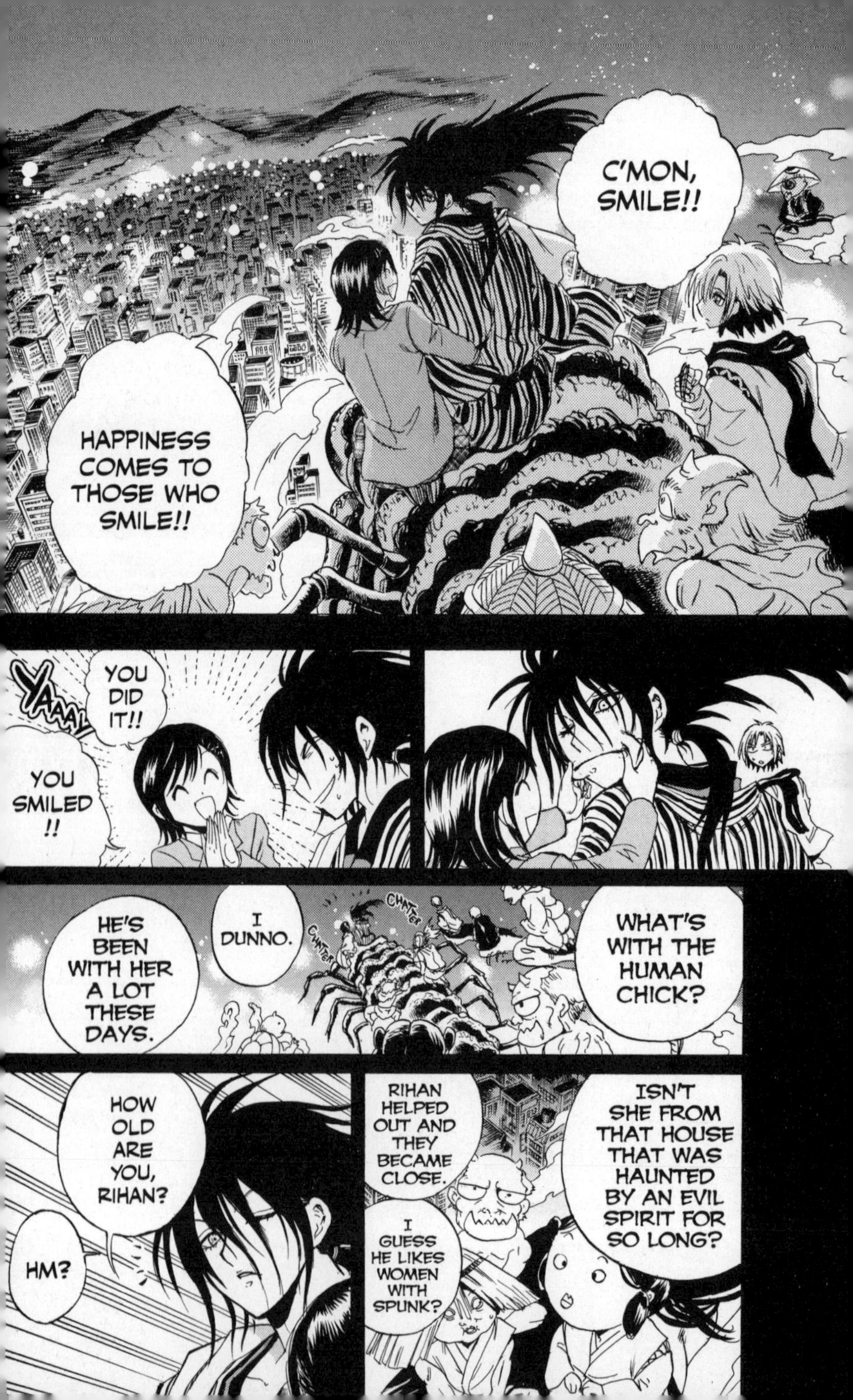
C'MON, SMILE!!
HAPPINESS COMES TO THOSE WHO SMILE!!
YAAAY
YOU DID IT!!
YOU SMILED!!
WHAT'S WITH THE HUMAN CHICK?
CHATTER
CHATTER
I DUNNO.
HE'S BEEN WITH HER A LOT THESE DAYS.
ISN'T SHE FROM THAT HOUSE THAT WAS HAUNTED BY AN EVIL SPIRIT FOR SO LONG?
RIHAN HELPED OUT AND THEY BECAME CLOSE.
I GUESS HE LIKES WOMEN WITH SPUNK?
HOW OLD ARE YOU, RIHAN?
HM?

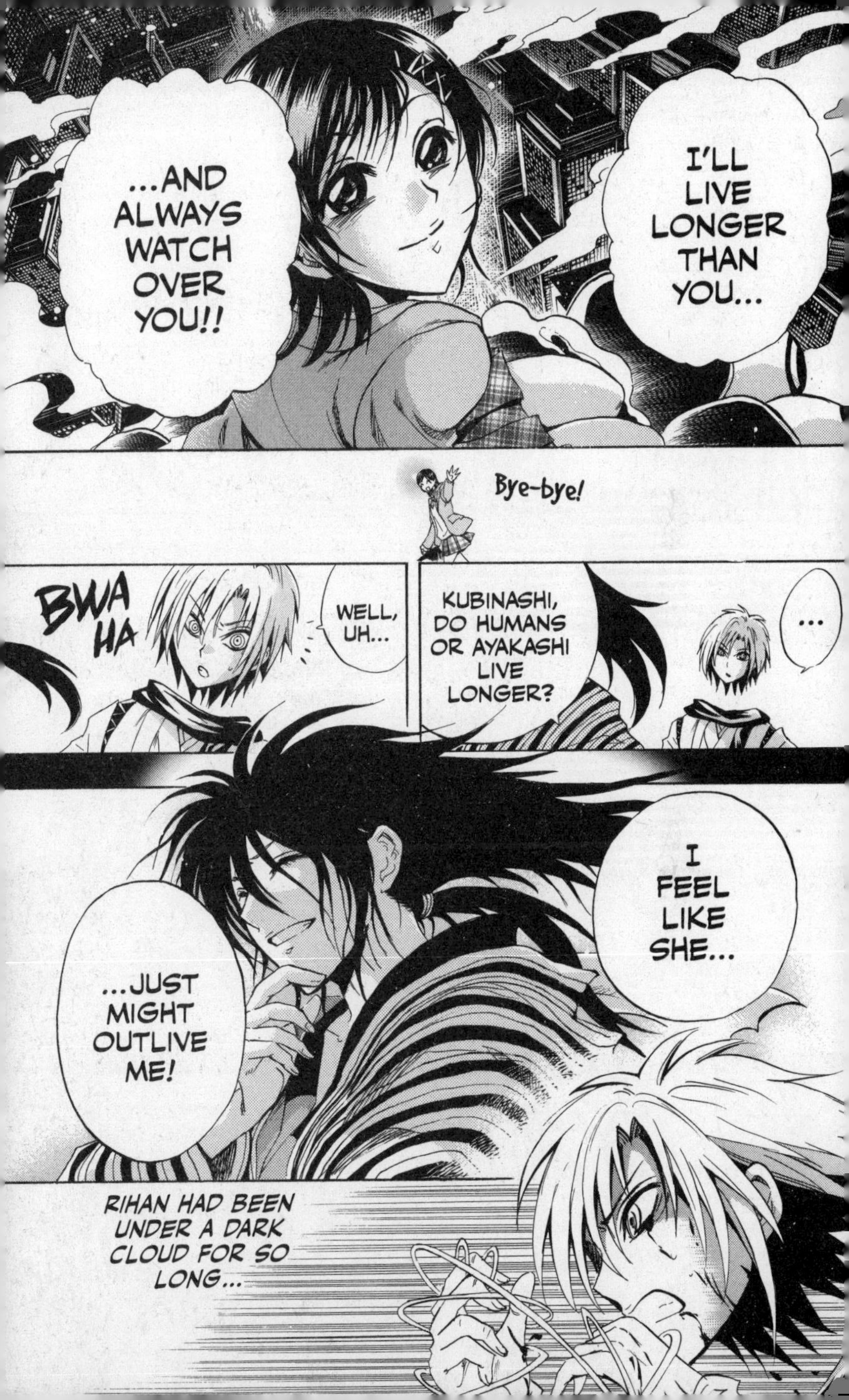
I'LL LIVE LONGER THAN YOU...
...AND ALWAYS WATCH OVER YOU!!
Bye-bye!
KUBINASHI, DO HUMANS OR AYAKASHI LIVE LONGER?
...
WELL, UH...
BWA HA
I FEEL LIKE SHE...
...JUST MIGHT OUTLIVE ME!
RIHAN HAD BEEN UNDER A DARK CLOUD FOR SO LONG...

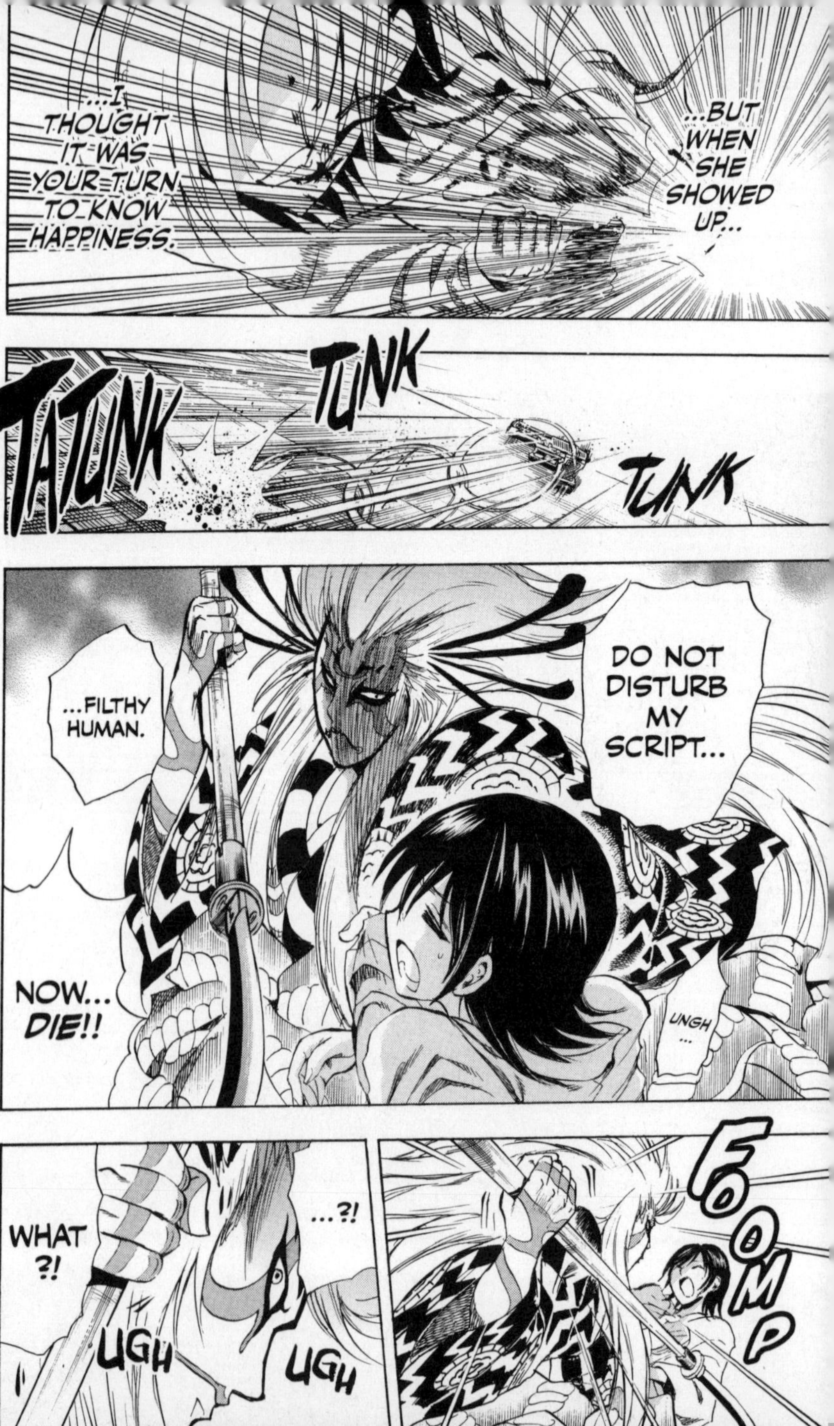
...BUT WHEN SHE SHOWED UP...
...I THOUGHT IT WAS YOUR TURN TO KNOW HAPPINESS.
TUNK
TUNK
TATUNK
DO NOT DISTURB MY SCRIPT...
UNGH ...
...FILTHY HUMAN.
NOW... *DIE!!*
FOOMP
...?!
WHAT ?!
UGH
UGH

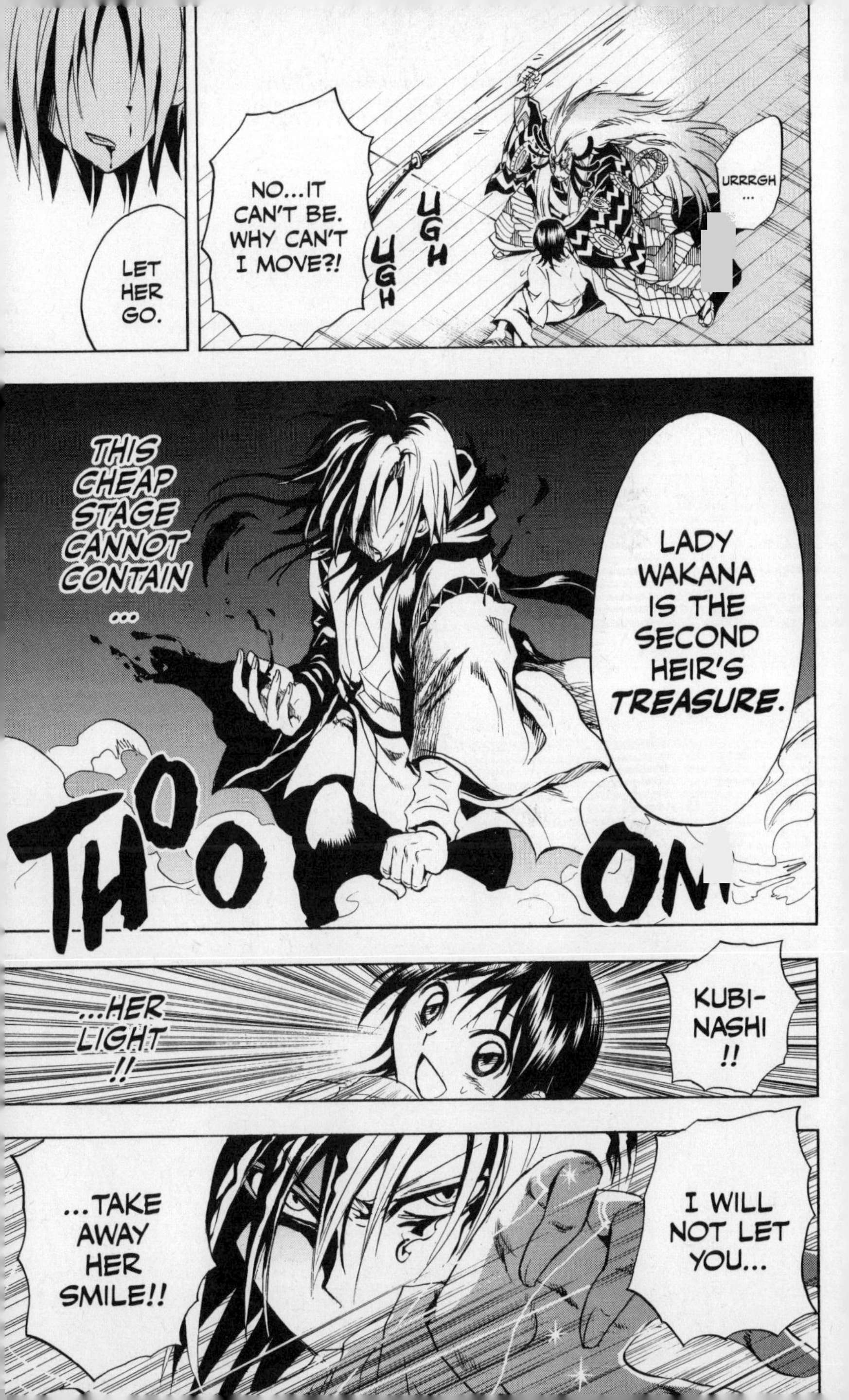
URRRGH ...
NO...IT CAN'T BE. WHY CAN'T I MOVE?!
UGH
UGH
LET HER GO.
LADY WAKANA IS THE SECOND HEIR'S TREASURE.
THIS CHEAP STAGE CANNOT CONTAIN ...
THOOOM
KUBI-NASHI !!
...HER LIGHT !!
I WILL NOT LET YOU...
...TAKE AWAY HER SMILE!!

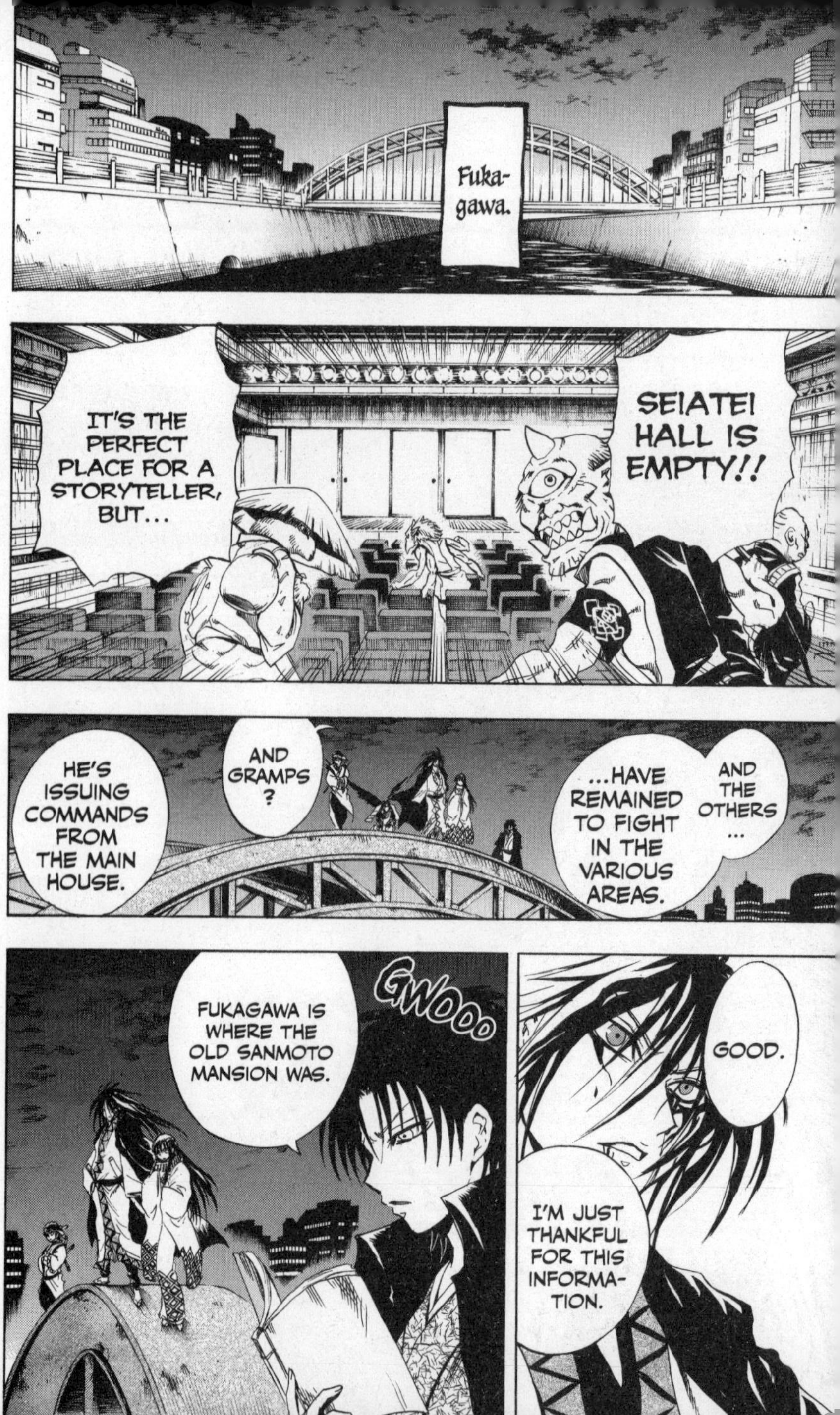
Fuka-gawa.
SEIATEI HALL IS EMPTY!!
IT'S THE PERFECT PLACE FOR A STORYTELLER, BUT...
AND THE OTHERS...
...HAVE REMAINED TO FIGHT IN THE VARIOUS AREAS.
AND GRAMPS?
HE'S ISSUING COMMANDS FROM THE MAIN HOUSE.
GOOD.
I'M JUST THANKFUL FOR THIS INFORMATION.
GWOOO
FUKAGAWA IS WHERE THE OLD SANMOTO MANSION WAS.

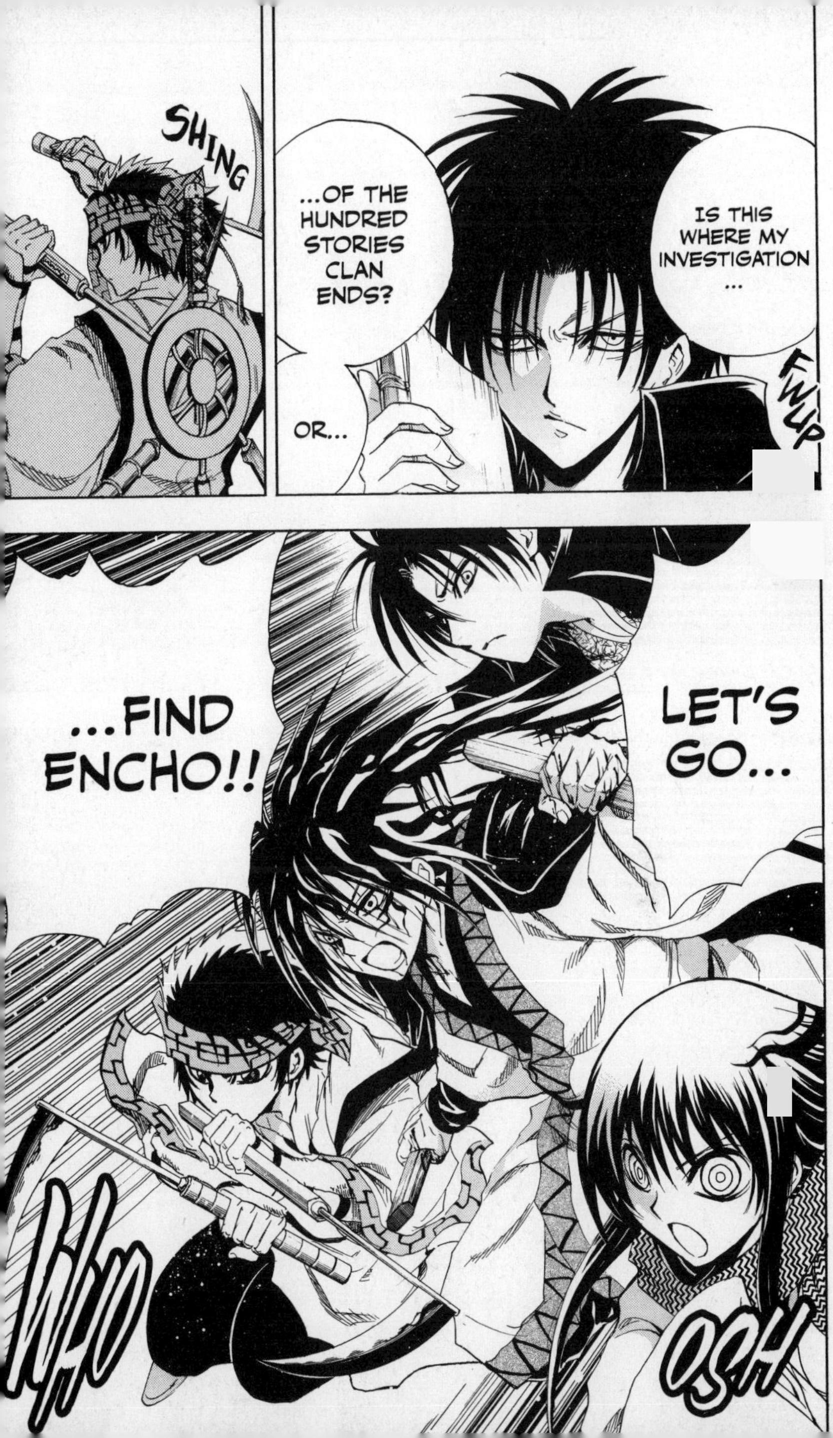
IS THIS WHERE MY INVESTIGATION ...
...OF THE HUNDRED STORIES CLAN ENDS?
OR...
FWUP
SHING
LET'S GO...
...FIND ENCHO!!
OSH

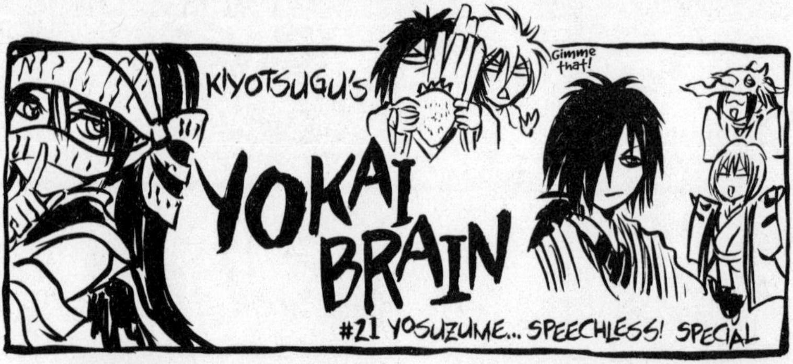
KIYOTSUGU'S
YOKAI BRAIN
Gimme that!
#21 YOSUZUME... SPEECHLESS! SPECIAL

Q: RIHAN WAS HALF-YOKAI, SO WAS HE HUMAN FOR HALF OF EACH DAY? IF HE WAS, HAVE OTOME, WAKANA AND RIKUO SEEN THAT FORM? *—YUKI-ONNA, YAMANASHI PREFECTURE*

WAKANA: RIHAN'S HUMAN FORM? I HAVEN'T SEEN IT. UNLIKE RIKUO, I DON'T THINK HE WAS HUMAN FOR HALF THE DAY.

KUROTABO: THE SECOND HEIR KEPT HIS HUMAN SIDE SUBCONSCIOUS. I DON'T KNOW WHY THAT WAS, BUT I SUPPOSE IT WAS THE RESULT OF COMING TO AN UNDERSTANDING OF HIMSELF.

NURARIHYON: HE WAS THAT WAY FROM BIRTH. HE WAS THE TYPE TO TAKE EVERYTHING POSITIVELY.

Q: THIS QUESTION IS FOR KUBINASHI. WHAT'S THE HARDEST THING THAT HAS HAPPENED TO YOU SINCE JOINING THE NURA CLAN? *—NACCHI, NIIGATA PREFECTURE*

KUBINASHI: IT WAS WHEN RIHAN—I MEAN LORD RIHAN—WORKED ME REALLY HARD. AND ALSO DEALING WITH KINO—I MEAN KEJORO!

Q: HAS YOSUZUME EVER TALKED TO THE SHIKOKU YOKAI? *—NOBU-CHAN, KANAGAWA PREFECTURE*

YOSUZUME:

RIKUO: C'MON! SAY SOMETHING!

Q: THIS IS FOR GOZUMARU! HAVE YOU EVER MISTAKEN MEZUMARU FOR A GIRL? *—MAYU YAMADA, SAITAMA PREFECTURE*

GOZUMARU: N-NOOO!! OF COURSE NOT!!

MEZUMARU: HE HAS. I'D NEVER SEEN HIM ACT THAT WAY BEFORE!

GOZUMARU: IDIOT!! WHAT'RE YOU SAYING?! I'LL KILL YOU!!!

Q: LORD RIKUO! THIS MAY SEEM SUDDEN, BUT GO OUT WITH ME! PLEASE! I LOVE LOVE LOVE LOVE LOVE LOVE LOVE YOU! *—THE TIP OF NENEKIRI-MARU, MIE PREFECTURE*

TSURARA: NOT HAPPENING!! LORD RIKUO IS VERY BUSY! HE DOESN'T HAVE TIME FOR DATING WOMEN! RIGHT, LORD RIKUO?!

Q: DOES IBARAKI-DOJI LIKE STRAWBERRIES? IF HE DOES, I'LL TAKE HIM SOME IN HELL!!!! *—GURENMARU, FUKUSHIMA PREFECTURE*

IBARAKI-DOJI: YEAH, GIMME!

Q: I HAVE A QUESTION FOR THE NIGHT RIKUO! DO YOU LIKE SWEETS? I DO! *—TACCHII, HIROSHIMA PREFECTURE*

NIGHT RIKUO: YEAH, GIMME!

Q: RYUJI, THE SECOND KANJI OF YOUR NAME MEANS "SECOND," SO IS THERE A RYUICHI WHO'S "FIRST" AND RYUZO WHO'S "THIRD"? *—HAKUA, YAMAGUCHI PREFECTURE*

RYUJI: LET ME JUST SAY THAT IN ORDER TO AVOID THE FOX'S CURSE, MANY ELDEST SONS IN THE KEIKAIN CLAN GET NAMES MEANING "SECOND" OR "NEXT." I WON'T SAY WHETHER I'M THE ELDEST OR NOT.

Q: ALL THE ONMYOJI LIVE IN KYOTO, SO WHY IS YURA THE ONLY ONE WHO SPEAKS THE KYOTO DIALECT? *—BALANCE BALL, NIIGATA PREFECTURE AND MIKANMARU, TOKYO PREFECTURE*

YURA: BECAUSE THEY'RE ALL NERDS! FOR SOME REASON, THEY INSIST ON STANDARD JAPANESE!

Q: AWASHIMA CHANGES FROM BOY TO GIRL DEPENDING ON WHETHER IT'S NIGHT OR DAY, BUT WHICH DOES SHE/ HE PREFER IN LOVE? *—YUKI-USAGI, YAMANASHI PREFECTURE*

AWASHIMA: WOMEN! BUT, UH...WHEN IT COMES TO MEN, RIKUO WOULDN'T BE SO BAD! ♪

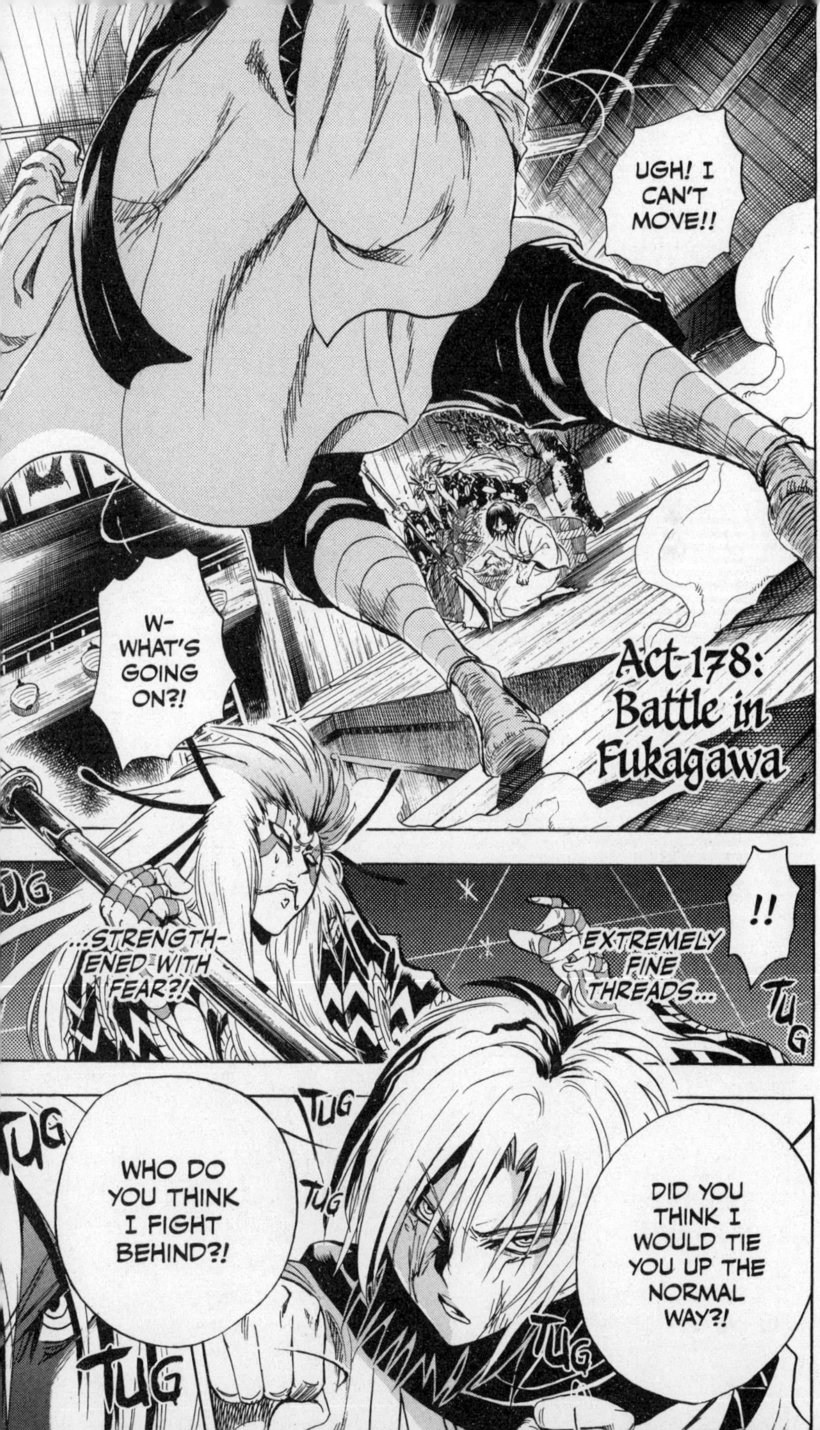
UGH! I CAN'T MOVE!!
W-WHAT'S GOING ON?!
Act 178: Battle in Fukagawa
!!
EXTREMELY FINE THREADS...
TUG
TUG
...STRENGTH-ENED WITH FEAR?!
DID YOU THINK I WOULD TIE YOU UP THE NORMAL WAY?!
TUG
TUG
TUG
WHO DO YOU THINK I FIGHT BEHIND?!
TUG
TUG

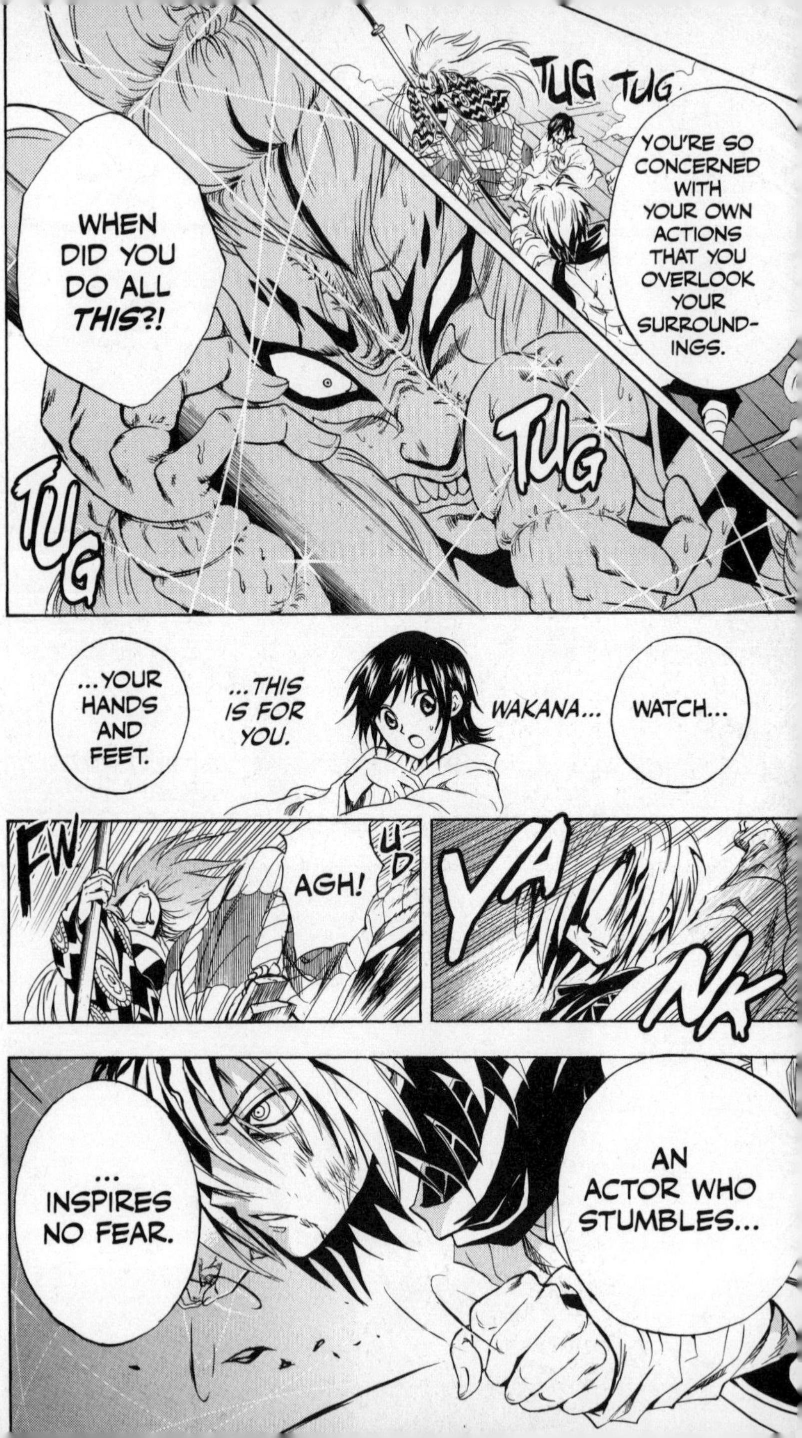
TUG TUG
YOU'RE SO CONCERNED WITH YOUR OWN ACTIONS THAT YOU OVERLOOK YOUR SURROUND-INGS.
WHEN DID YOU DO ALL *THIS*?!
TUG
TUG
WATCH...
WAKANA...
...THIS IS FOR YOU.
...YOUR HANDS AND FEET.
YANK
FW
UD
AGH!
AN ACTOR WHO STUMBLES...
... INSPIRES NO FEAR.

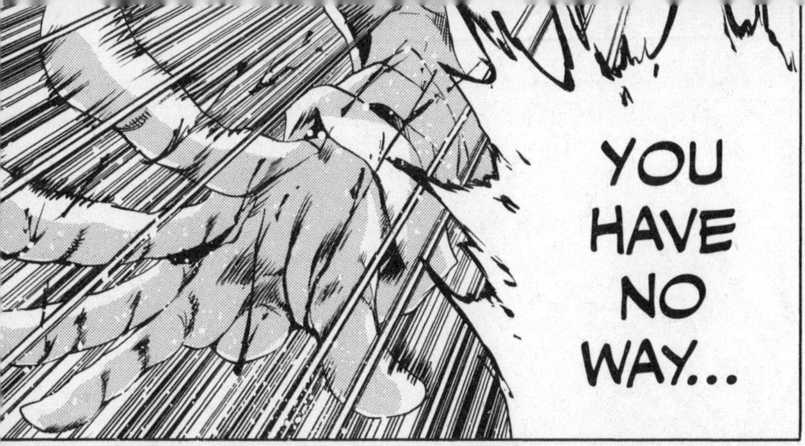
YOU HAVE NO WAY...
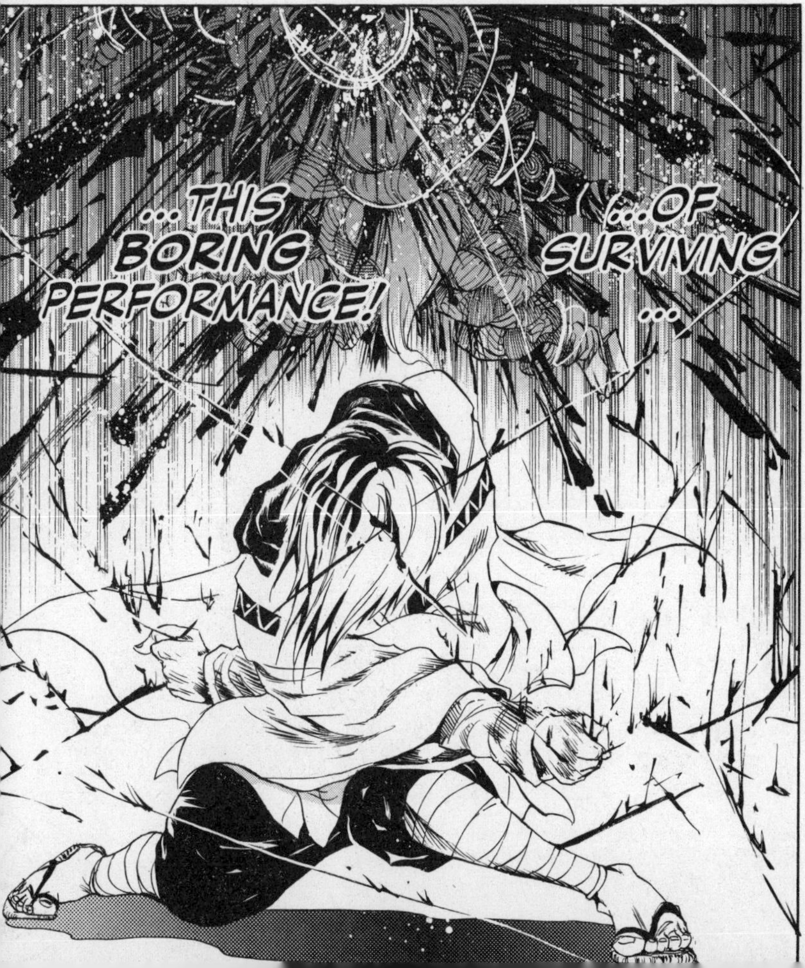
...OF SURVIVING ...
...THIS BORING PERFORMANCE!

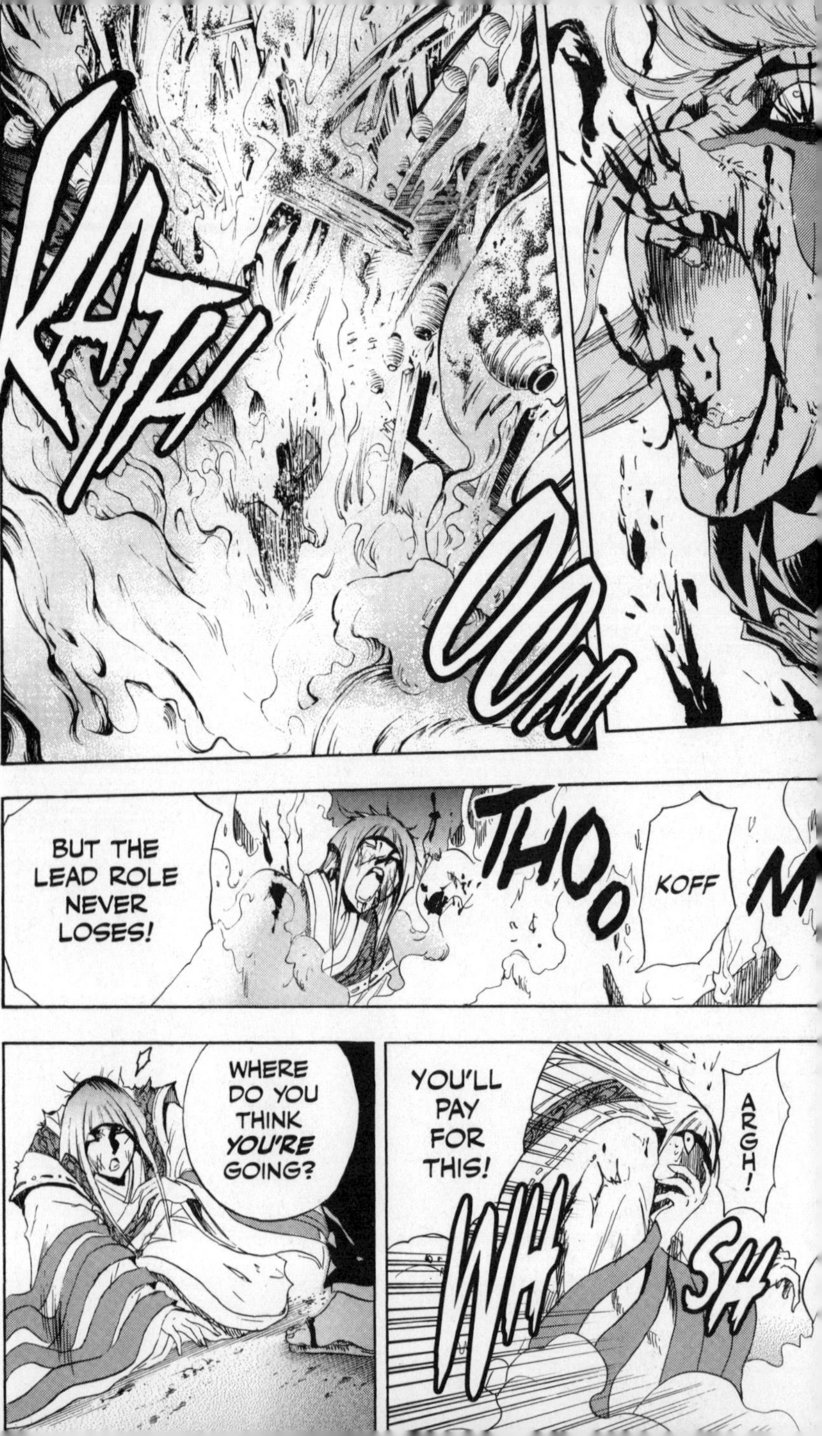
KOFF
BUT THE LEAD ROLE NEVER LOSES!
ARGH!
YOU'LL PAY FOR THIS!
WHSH
WHERE DO YOU THINK *YOU'RE* GOING?

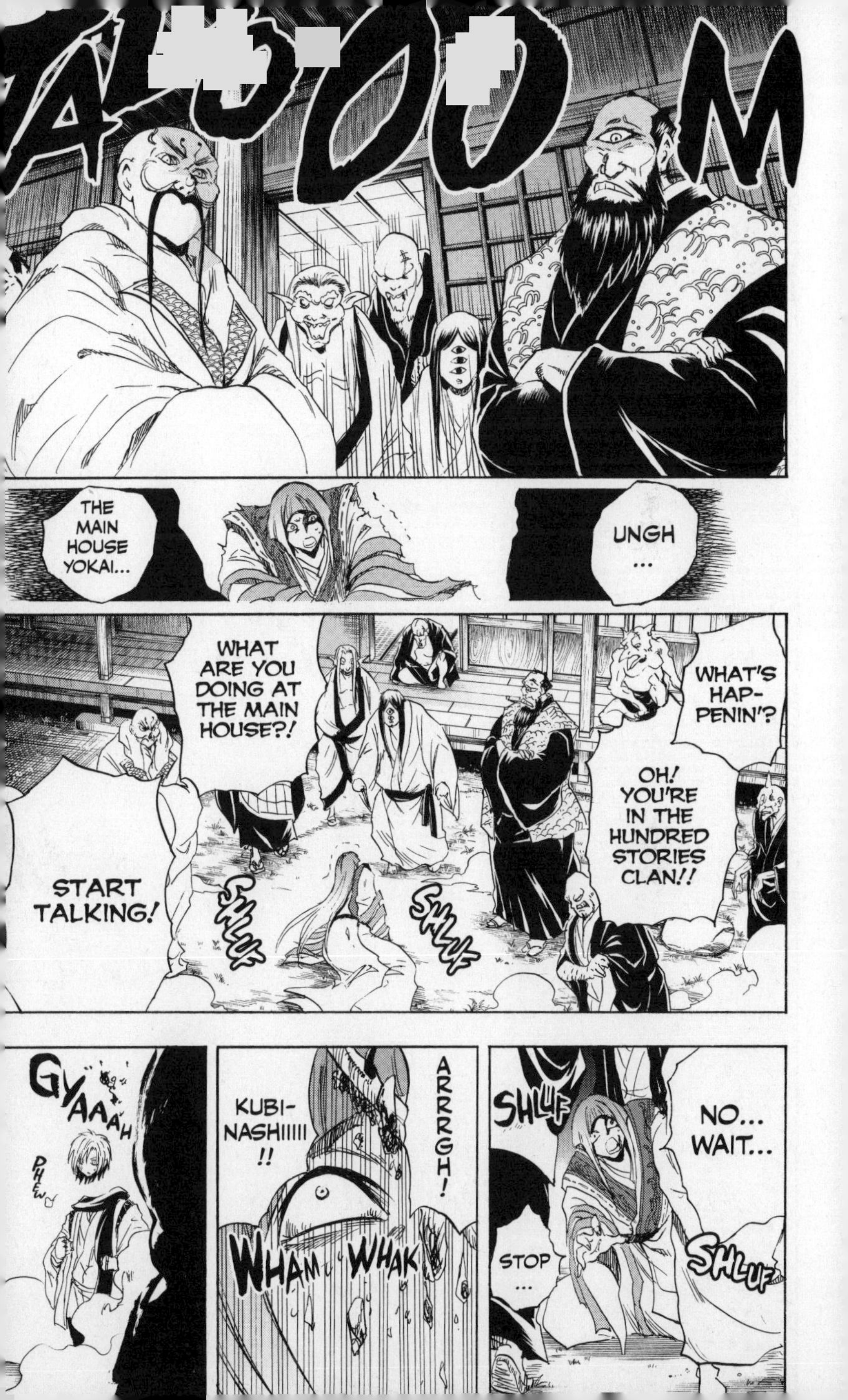
UNGH ...
THE MAIN HOUSE YOKAI...
WHAT'S HAP-PENIN'?
OH! YOU'RE IN THE HUNDRED STORIES CLAN!!
WHAT ARE YOU DOING AT THE MAIN HOUSE?!
SHLUF
SHLUF
START TALKING!
NO... WAIT...
SHLUF
SHLUF
STOP ...
ARRRGH!
KUBI-NASHIIIII !!
WHAM
WHAK
GYAAAH
PHEW

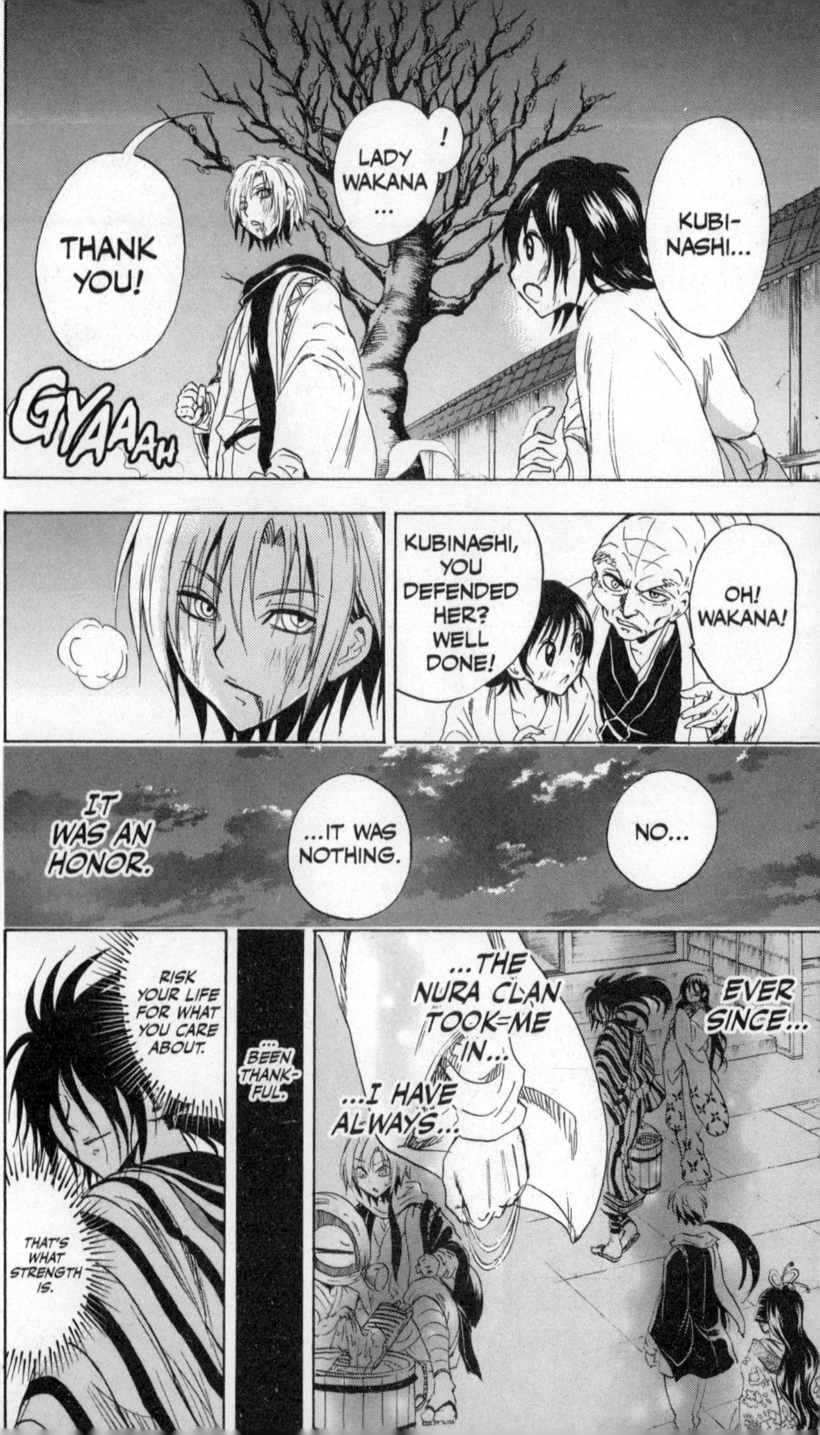
KUBI-NASHI...
!
LADY WAKANA ...
THANK YOU!
GYAAAAH
OH! WAKANA!
KUBINASHI, YOU DEFENDED HER? WELL DONE!
NO...
...IT WAS NOTHING.
IT WAS AN HONOR.
EVER SINCE...
...THE NURA CLAN TOOK ME IN...
...I HAVE ALWAYS...
...BEEN THANKFUL.
RISK YOUR LIFE FOR WHAT YOU CARE ABOUT.
THAT'S WHAT STRENGTH IS.

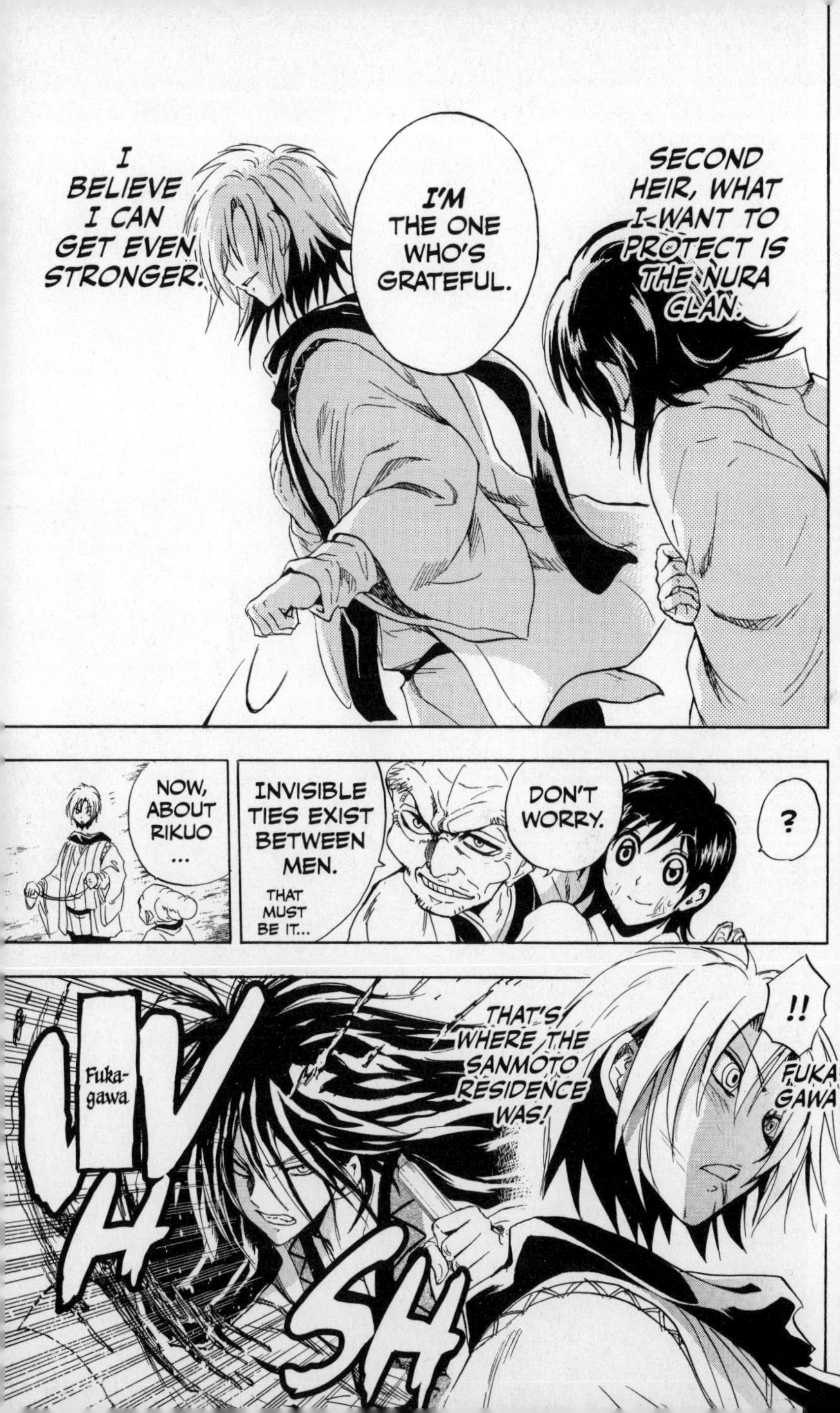
SECOND HEIR, WHAT I WANT TO PROTECT IS THE NURA CLAN.
I'M THE ONE WHO'S GRATEFUL.
I BELIEVE I CAN GET EVEN STRONGER.
?
DON'T WORRY.
INVISIBLE TIES EXIST BETWEEN MEN.
THAT MUST BE IT...
NOW, ABOUT RIKUO ...
!!
FUKA-GAWA?!
THAT'S WHERE THE SANMOTO RESIDENCE WAS!
Fuka-gawa

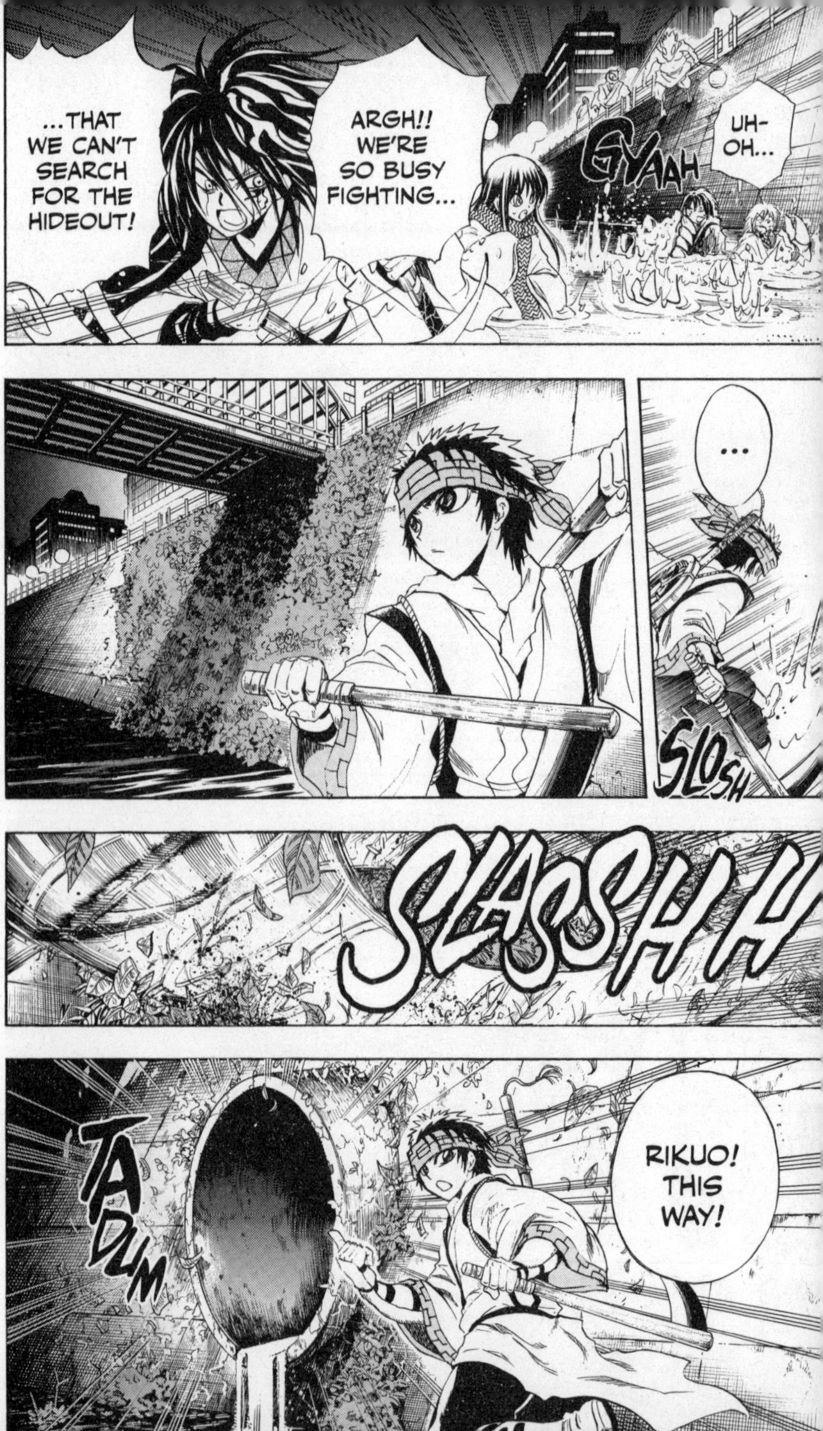
UH-OH...
GYAAH
ARGH!! WE'RE SO BUSY FIGHTING...
...THAT WE CAN'T SEARCH FOR THE HIDEOUT!
...
SLOSH
SLASSHH
RIKUO! THIS WAY!
TADUM

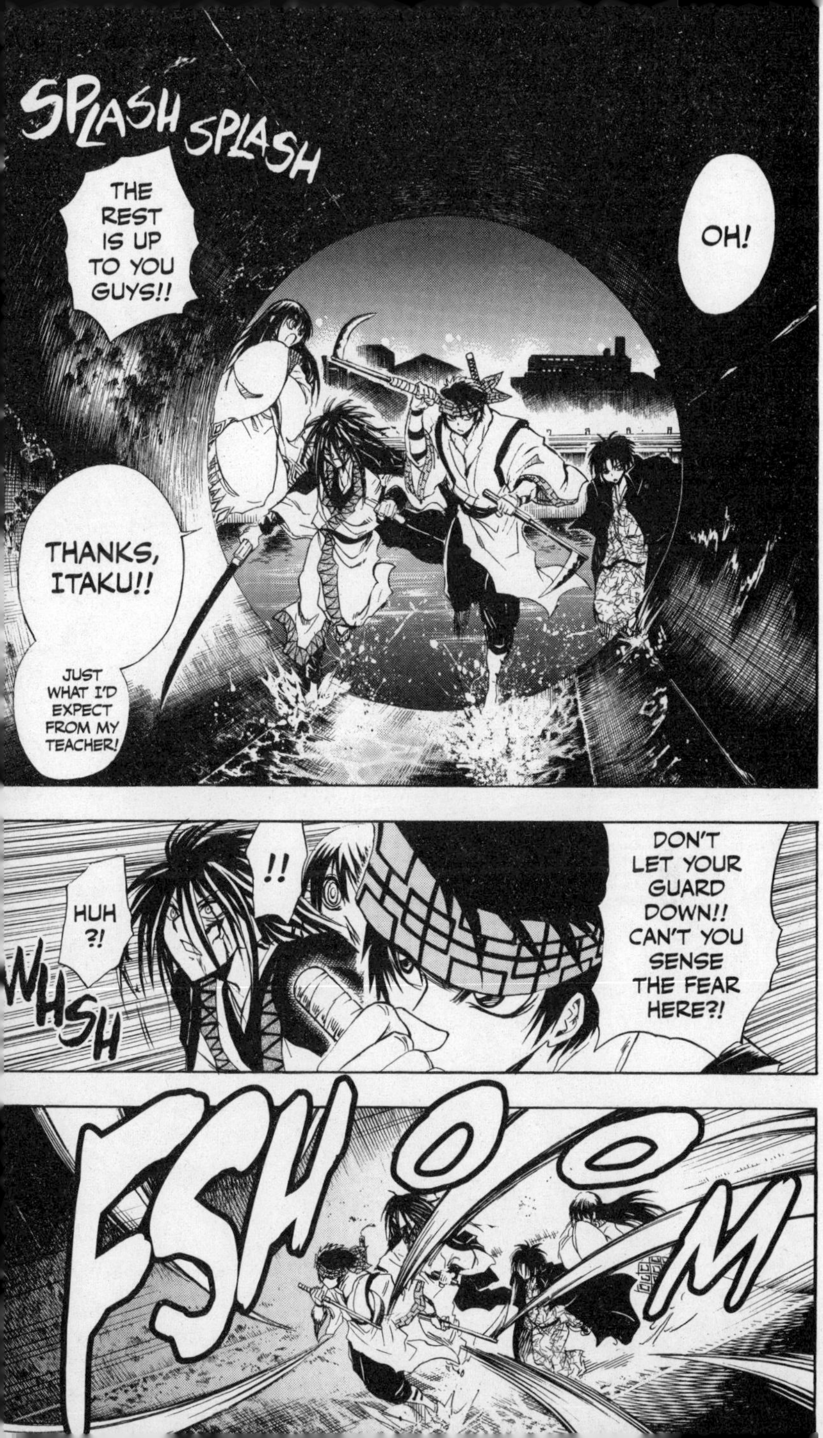
SPLASH SPLASH
THE REST IS UP TO YOU GUYS!!
OH!
THANKS, ITAKU!!
JUST WHAT I'D EXPECT FROM MY TEACHER!
DON'T LET YOUR GUARD DOWN!! CAN'T YOU SENSE THE FEAR HERE?!
!!
HUH ?!
WHSH
FSHOOOM

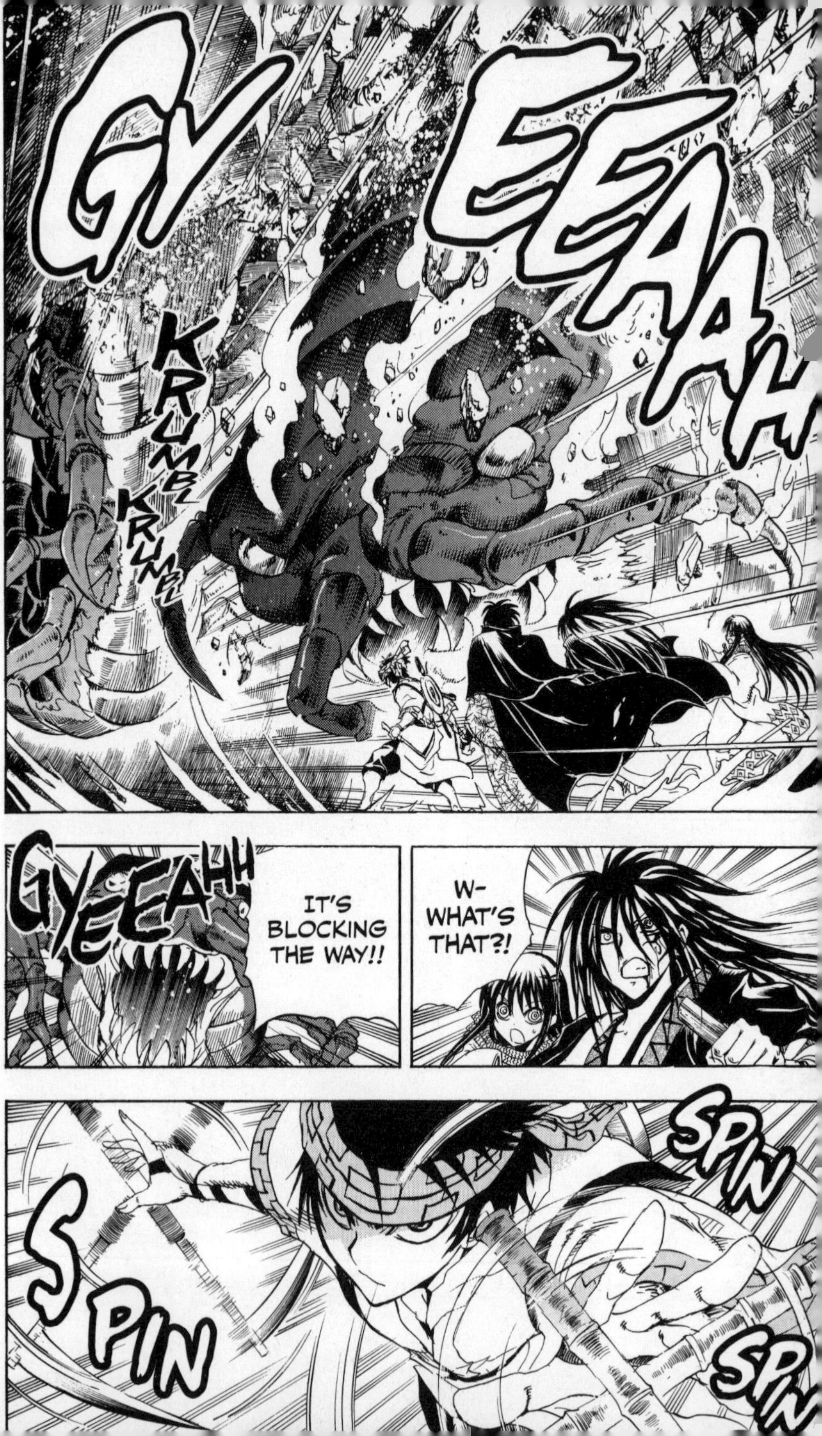
GYEEAAH
KRUMBL
KRUMBL
W- WHAT'S THAT?!
IT'S BLOCKING THE WAY!!
GYEEAH!!
SPIN
SPIN
SPIN
SPIN

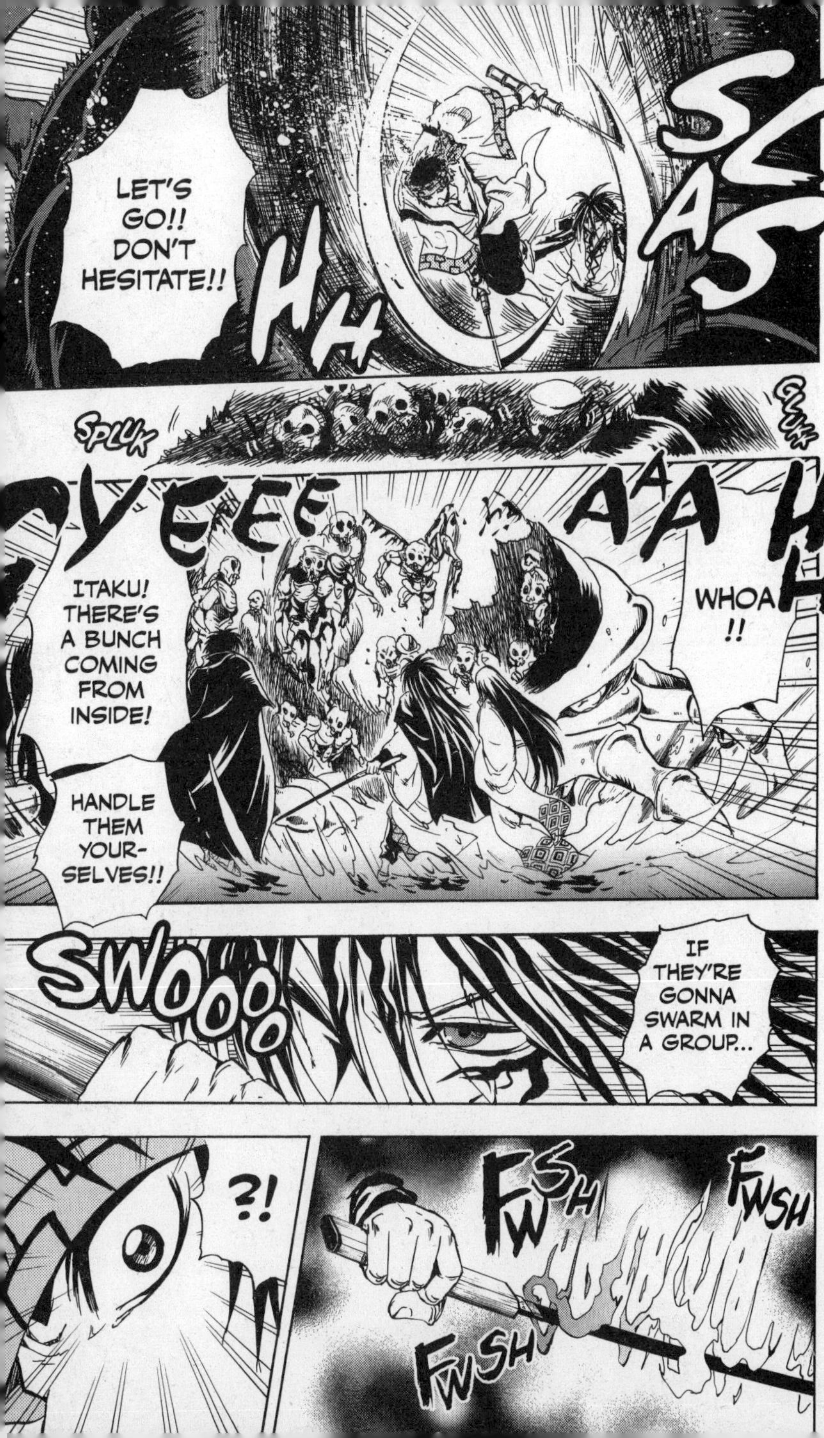

SLASHH
LET'S GO!! DON'T HESITATE!!
GLUK
SPLUK
YEEEAAAHH
WHOA!!
ITAKU! THERE'S A BUNCH COMING FROM INSIDE!
HANDLE THEM YOURSELVES!!
IF THEY'RE GONNA SWARM IN A GROUP...
SWOOOO
FWSH
FWSH
FWSH
?!

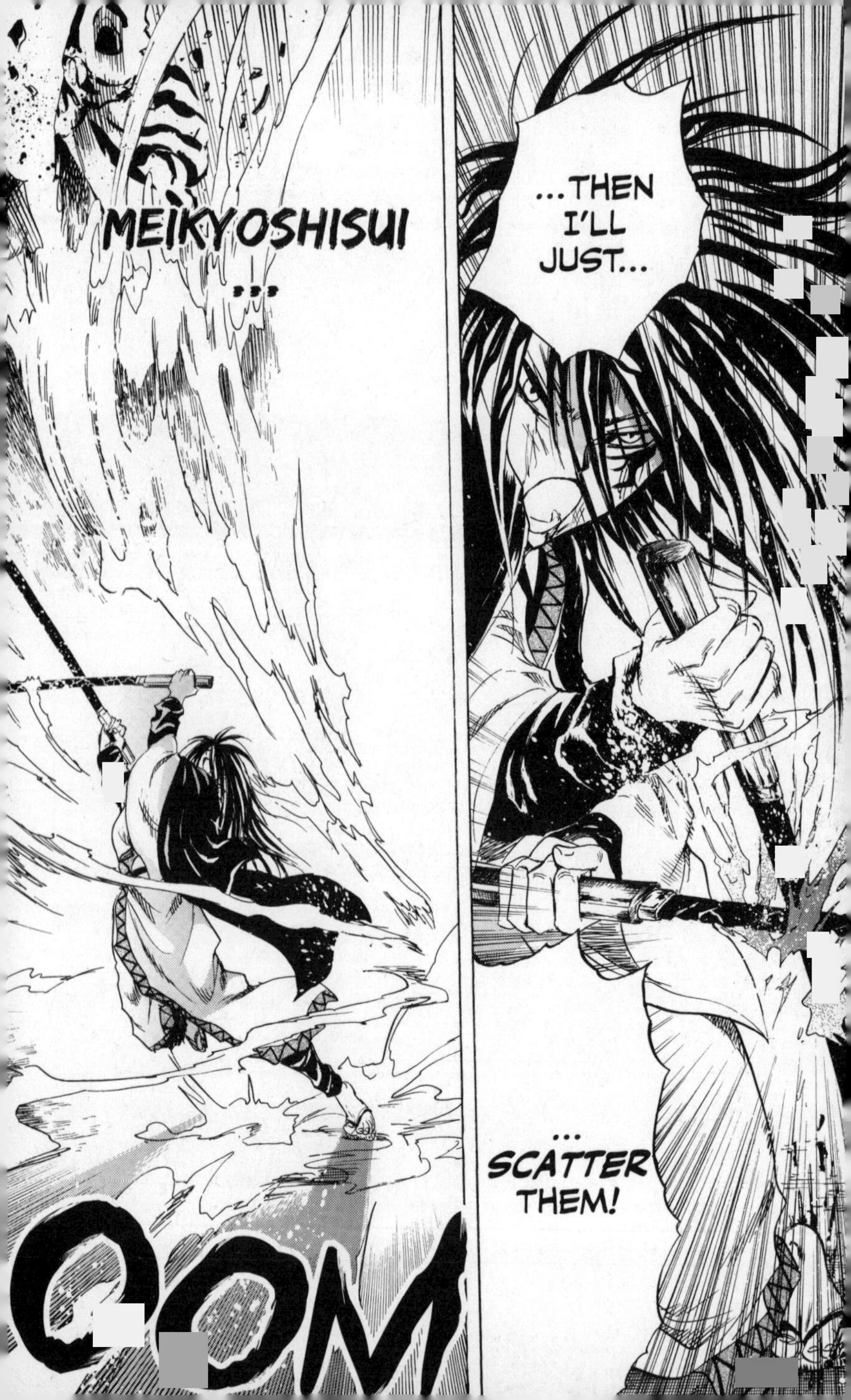
...THEN I'LL JUST...
...SCATTER THEM!
MEIKYOSHISUI...
OOM

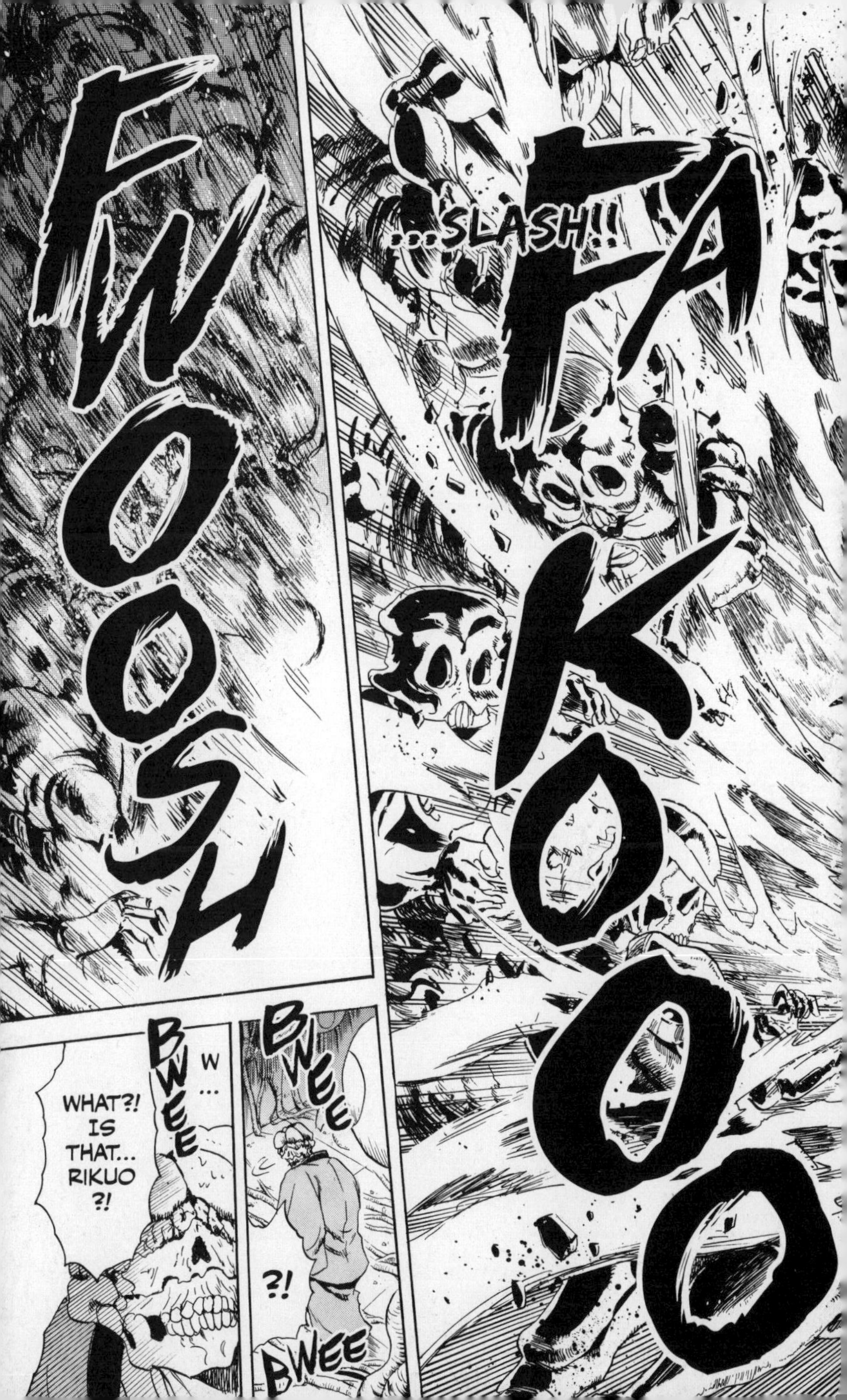
...SLASH!!
TAKOOO
FWOOOSH
BWEE
BWEE
?!
BWEE
W...
BWEE
WHAT?! IS THAT... RIKUO ?!

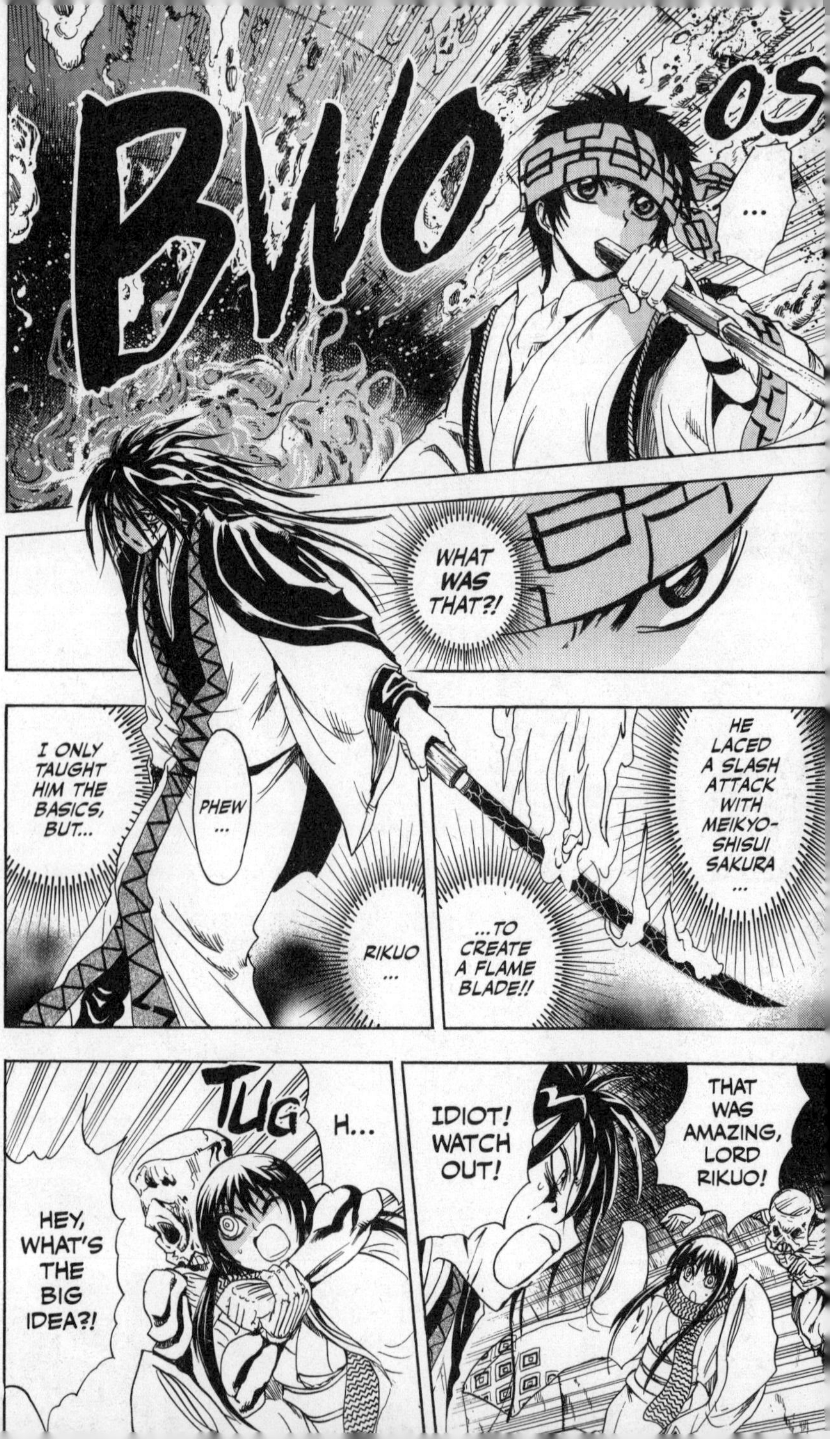
BWOOSH
...
WHAT WAS THAT?!
HE LACED A SLASH ATTACK WITH MEIKYO-SHISUI SAKURA ...
...TO CREATE A FLAME BLADE!!
I ONLY TAUGHT HIM THE BASICS, BUT...
PHEW ...
RIKUO ...
THAT WAS AMAZING, LORD RIKUO!
IDIOT! WATCH OUT!
TUG
H...
HEY, WHAT'S THE BIG IDEA?!

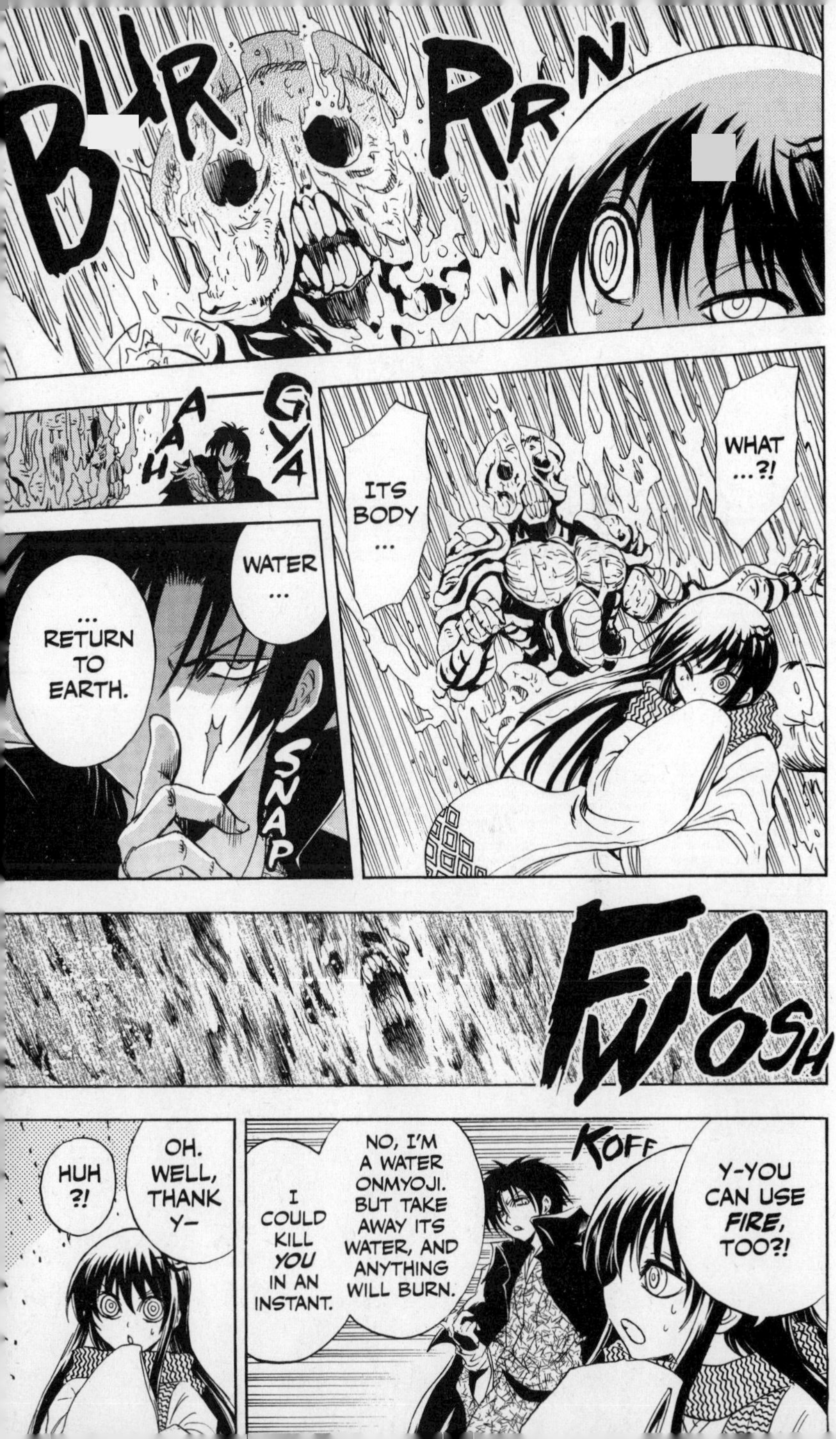
BURRRN
WHAT ...?!
ITS BODY ...
GYAAAH
WATER ...
... RETURN TO EARTH.
SNAP
FWOOSH
Y-YOU CAN USE *FIRE*, TOO?!
KOFF
NO, I'M A WATER ONMYOJI. BUT TAKE AWAY ITS WATER, AND ANYTHING WILL BURN.
I COULD KILL *YOU* IN AN INSTANT.
OH. WELL, THANK Y—
HUH ?!

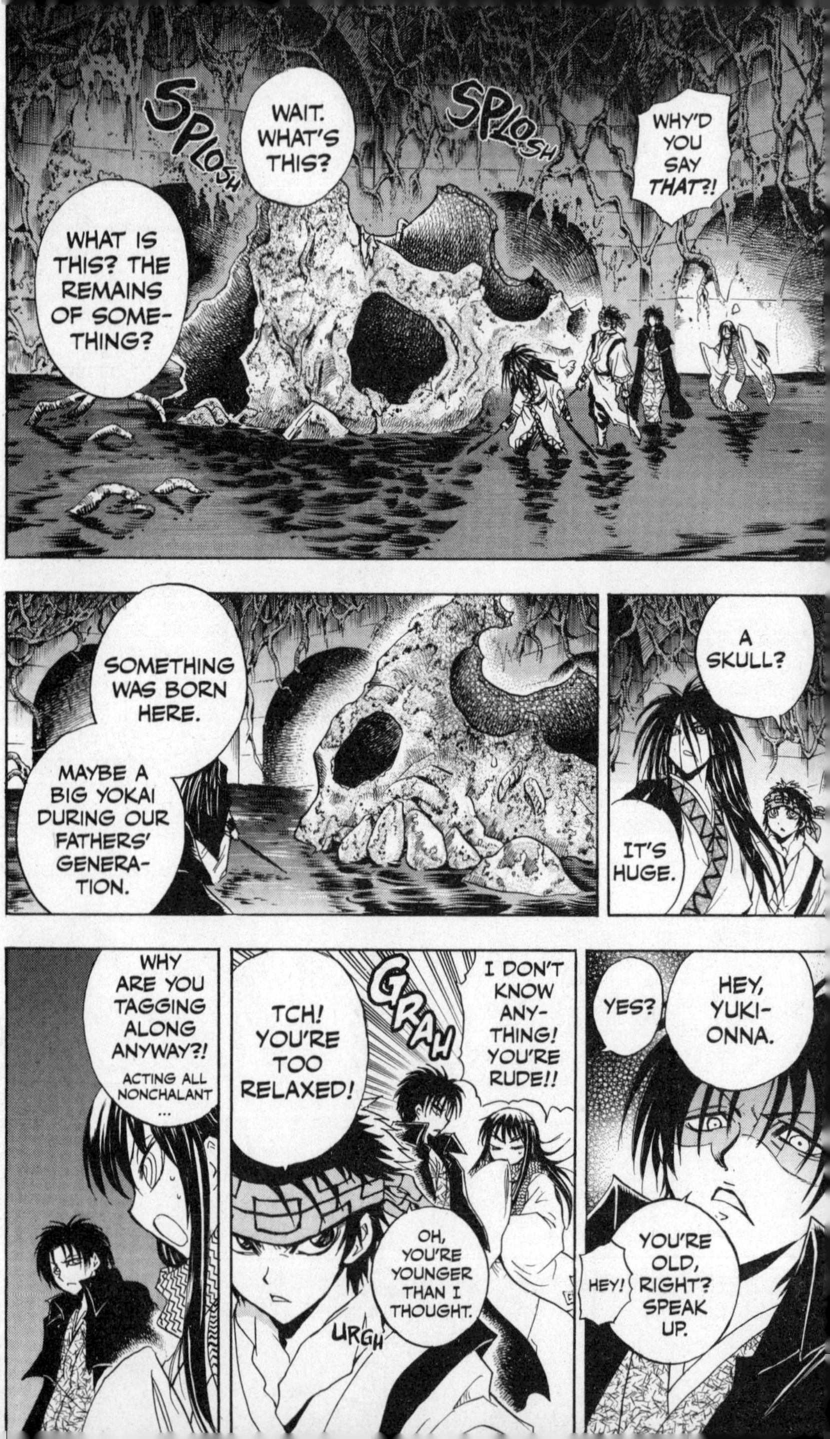
WHY'D YOU SAY *THAT*?!
SPLOSH
WAIT. WHAT'S THIS?
SPLOSH
WHAT IS THIS? THE REMAINS OF SOME-THING?
A SKULL?
IT'S HUGE.
SOMETHING WAS BORN HERE.
MAYBE A BIG YOKAI DURING OUR FATHERS' GENERA-TION.
HEY, YUKI-ONNA.
YES?
YOU'RE OLD, RIGHT? SPEAK UP.
HEY!
I DON'T KNOW ANY-THING! YOU'RE RUDE!!
GRAH
TCH! YOU'RE TOO RELAXED!
OH, YOU'RE YOUNGER THAN I THOUGHT.
URGH
WHY ARE YOU TAGGING ALONG ANYWAY?!
ACTING ALL NONCHALANT ...

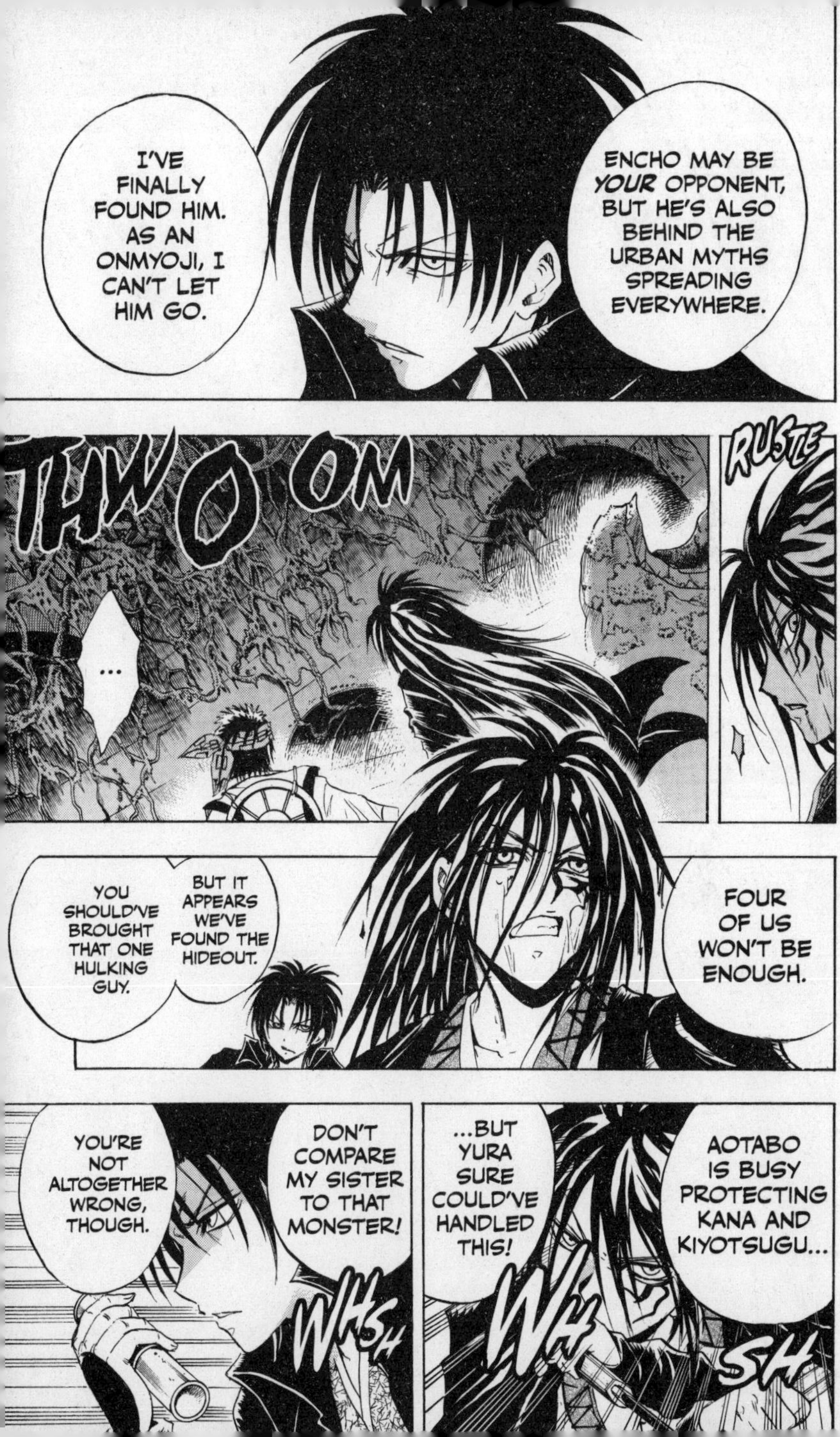
ENCHO MAY BE *YOUR* OPPONENT, BUT HE'S ALSO BEHIND THE URBAN MYTHS SPREADING EVERYWHERE.
I'VE FINALLY FOUND HIM. AS AN ONMYOJI, I CAN'T LET HIM GO.
RUSTLE
THWOOM
...
FOUR OF US WON'T BE ENOUGH.
BUT IT APPEARS WE'VE FOUND THE HIDEOUT.
YOU SHOULD'VE BROUGHT THAT ONE HULKING GUY.
AOTABO IS BUSY PROTECTING KANA AND KIYOTSUGU...
...BUT YURA SURE COULD'VE HANDLED THIS!
WHA
SH
DON'T COMPARE MY SISTER TO THAT MONSTER!
YOU'RE NOT ALTOGETHER WRONG, THOUGH.
WHSH

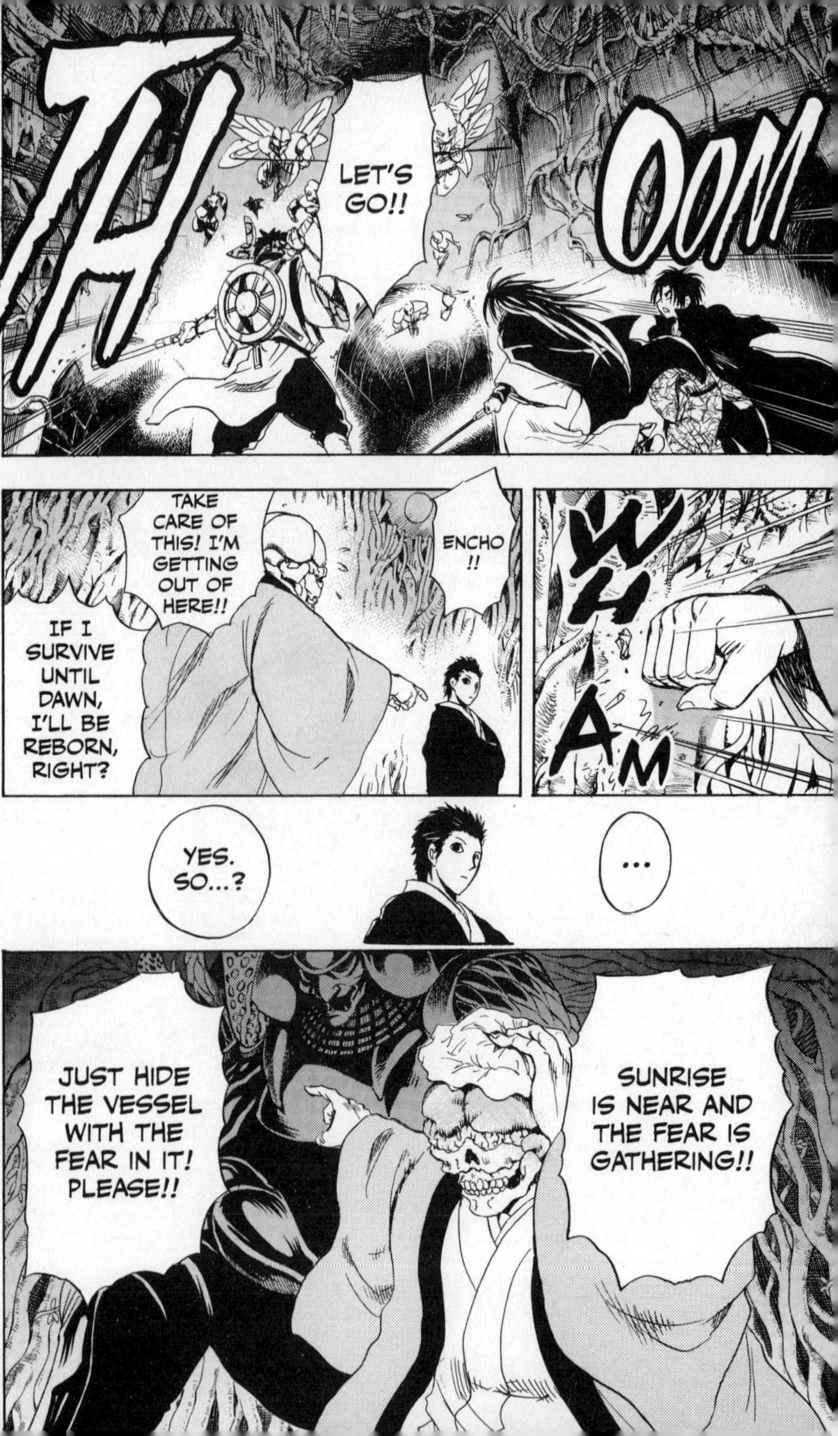
OOM
LET'S GO!!
WHAM
ENCHO!!
TAKE CARE OF THIS! I'M GETTING OUT OF HERE!!
IF I SURVIVE UNTIL DAWN, I'LL BE REBORN, RIGHT?
...
YES. SO...?
SUNRISE IS NEAR AND THE FEAR IS GATHERING!!
JUST HIDE THE VESSEL WITH THE FEAR IN IT! PLEASE!!

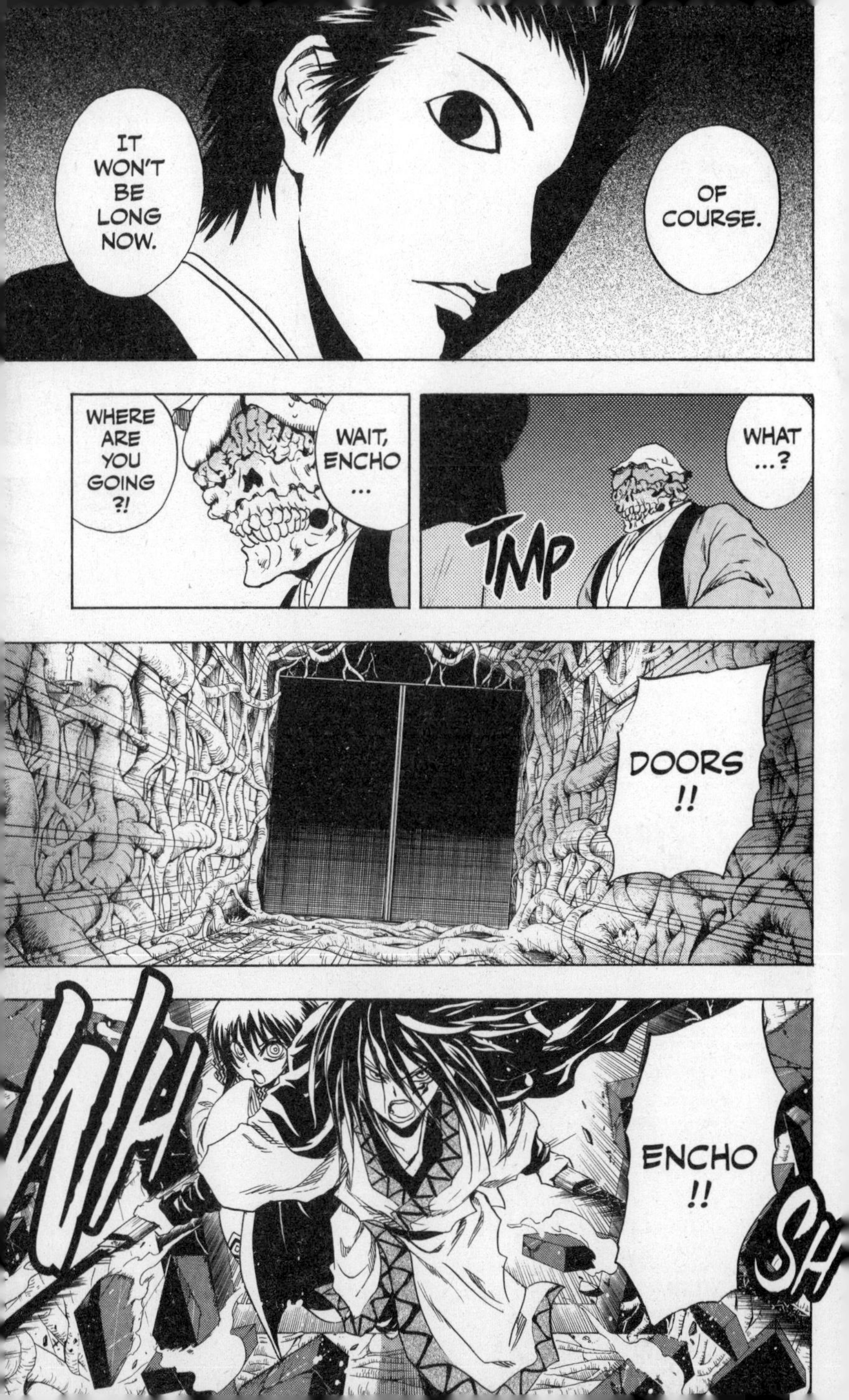
OF COURSE.
IT WON'T BE LONG NOW.
WHAT ...?
TMP
WAIT, ENCHO ...
WHERE ARE YOU GOING ?!
DOORS !!
ENCHO !!
WH
SH

A Spring Storm of Image Changes, Part 2

For Part 1, check out the inside cover!

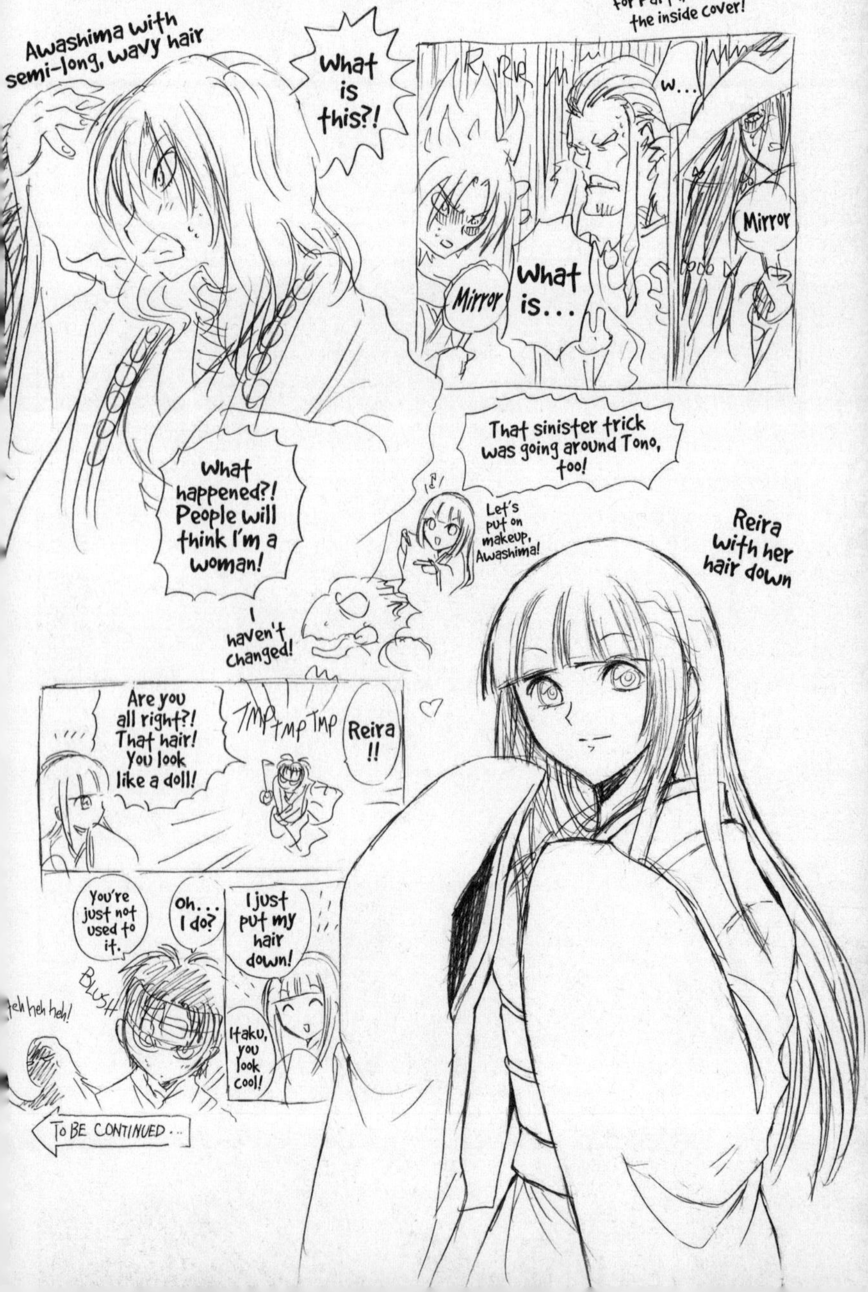

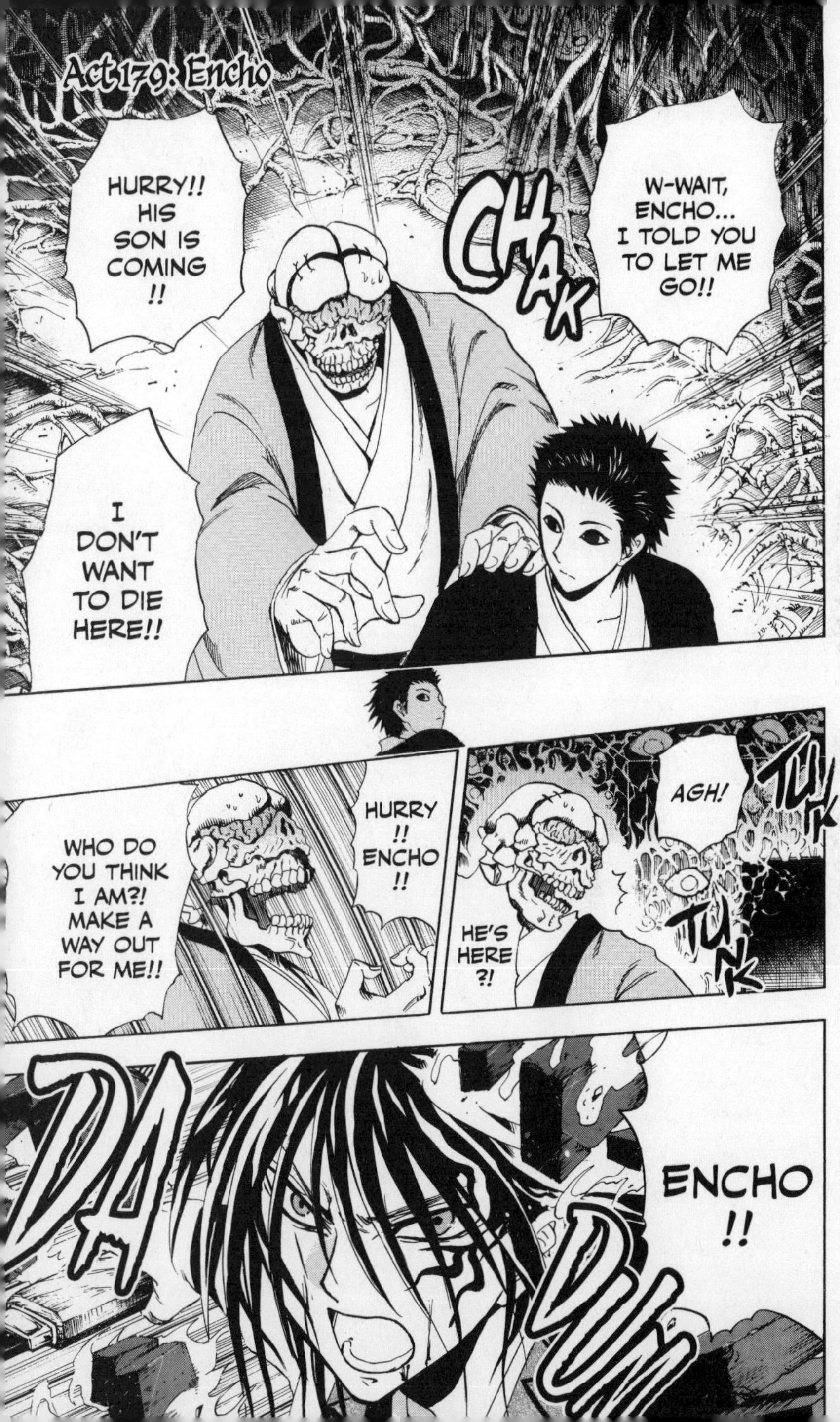
Act 179: Encho
W-WAIT, ENCHO... I TOLD YOU TO LET ME GO!!
CHAK
HURRY!! HIS SON IS COMING!!
I DON'T WANT TO DIE HERE!!
AGH!
TUNK
TUNK
HURRY!! ENCHO!!
HE'S HERE?!
WHO DO YOU THINK I AM?! MAKE A WAY OUT FOR ME!!
ENCHO!!
DA
DUUN

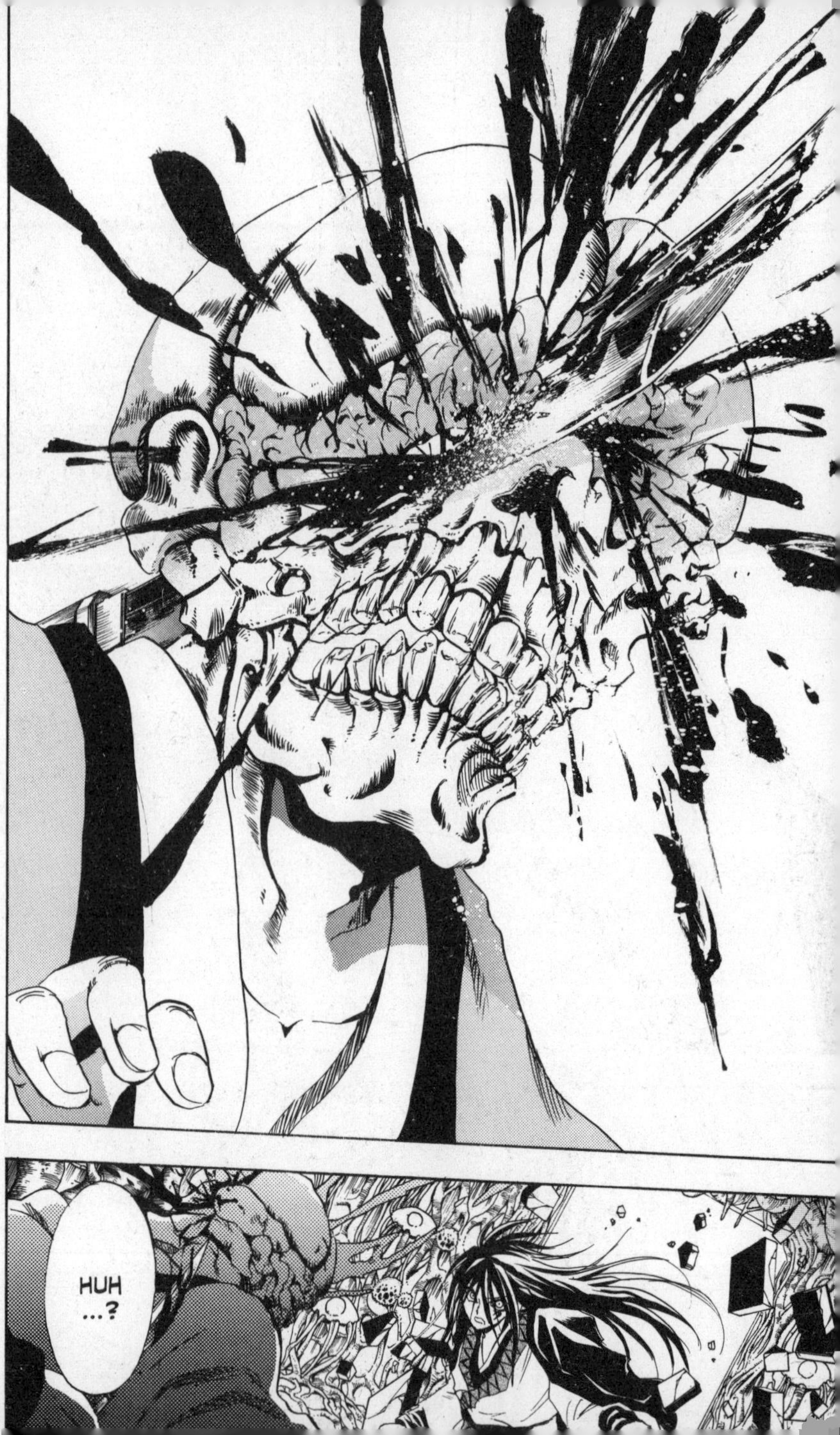
HUH ...?

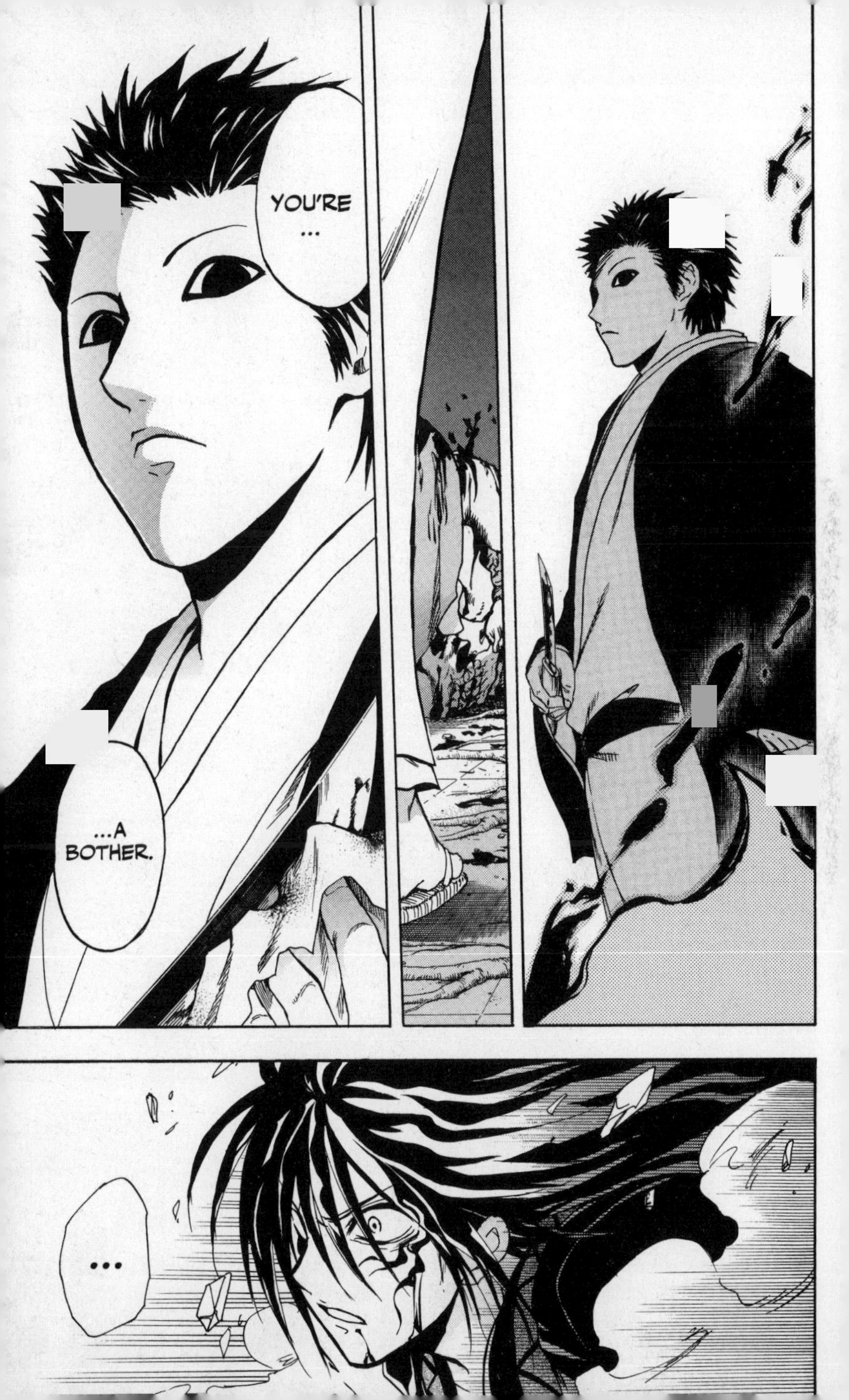
YOU'RE ...
...A BOTHER.
...

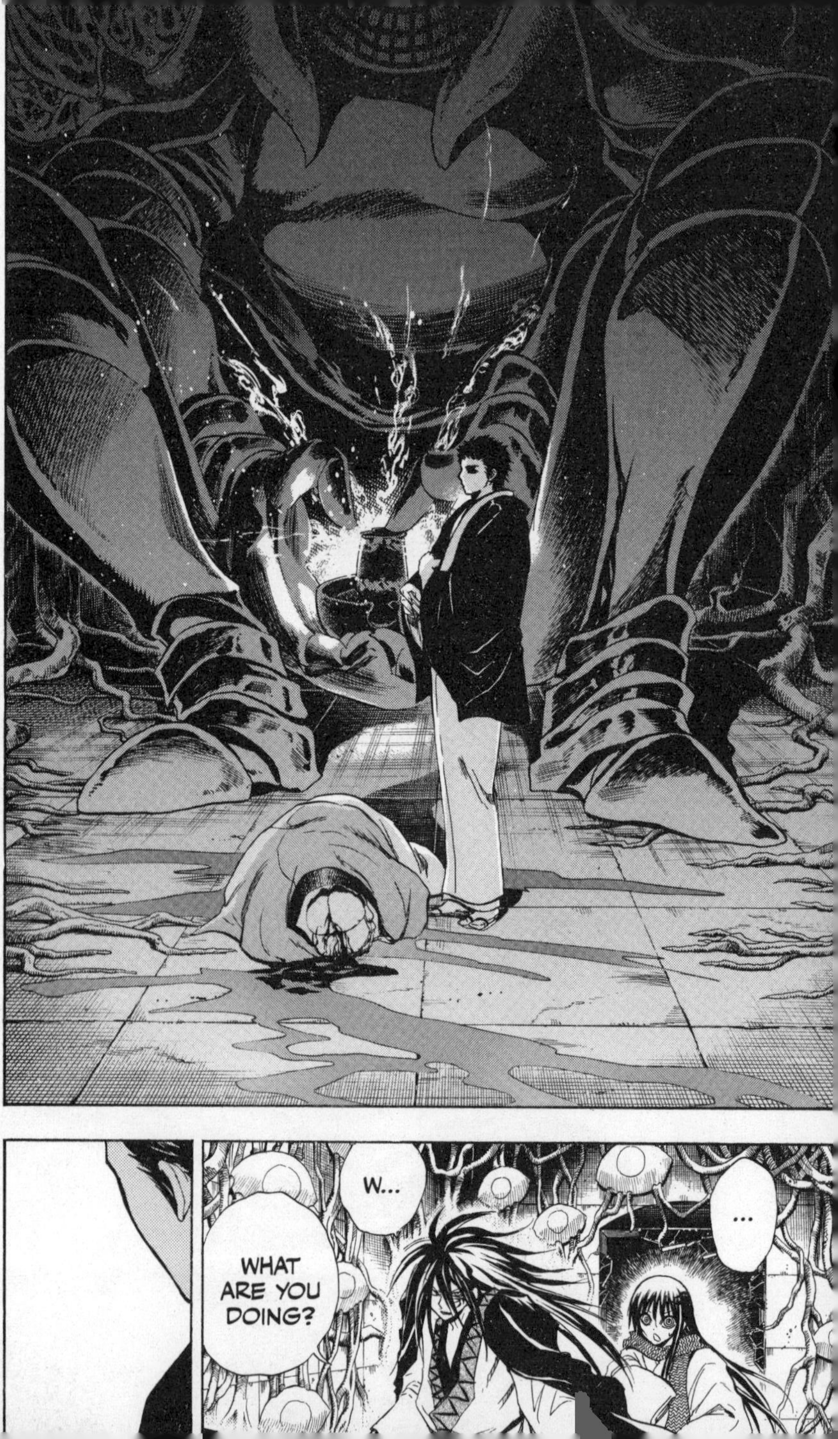
...
W...
WHAT ARE YOU DOING?

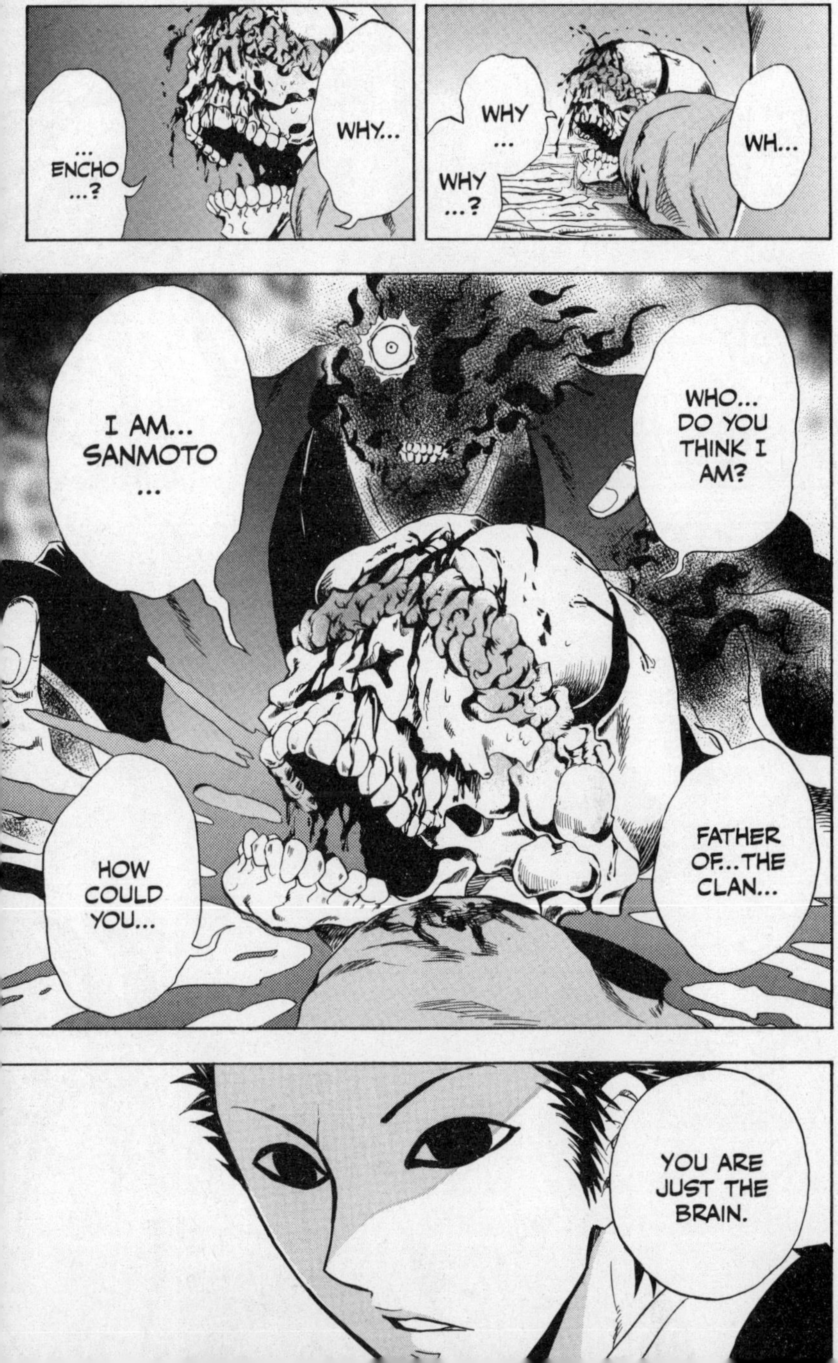
WH...
WHY ...
WHY ...?
WHY...
... ENCHO ...?
WHO... DO YOU THINK I AM?
I AM... SANMOTO ...
FATHER OF...THE CLAN...
HOW COULD YOU...
YOU ARE JUST THE BRAIN.

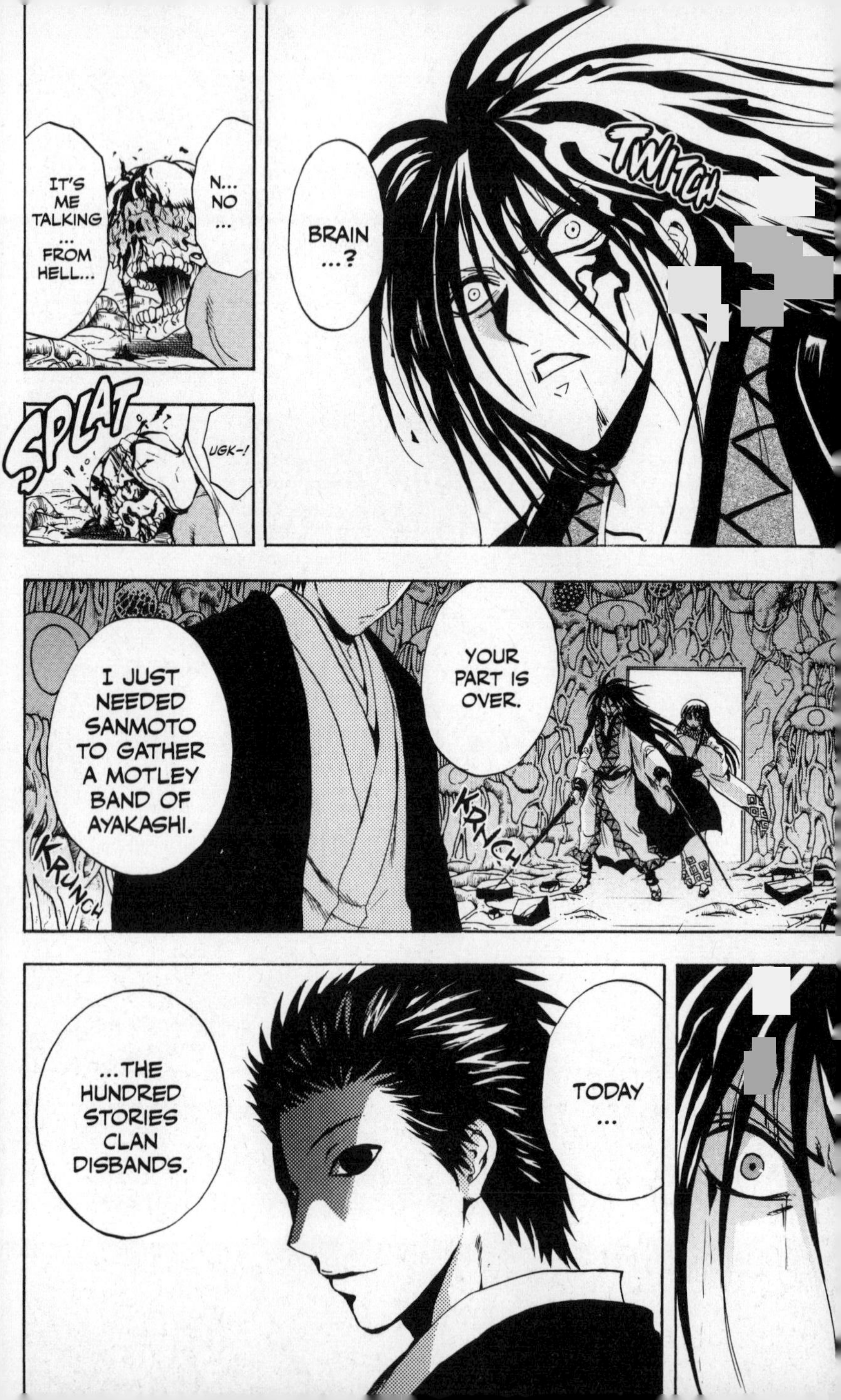
TWITCH
BRAIN ...?
N... NO ...
IT'S ME TALKING ... FROM HELL...
UGK-!
SPLAT
YOUR PART IS OVER.
KRNCH
I JUST NEEDED SANMOTO TO GATHER A MOTLEY BAND OF AYAKASHI.
KRUNCH
TODAY ...
...THE HUNDRED STORIES CLAN DISBANDS.

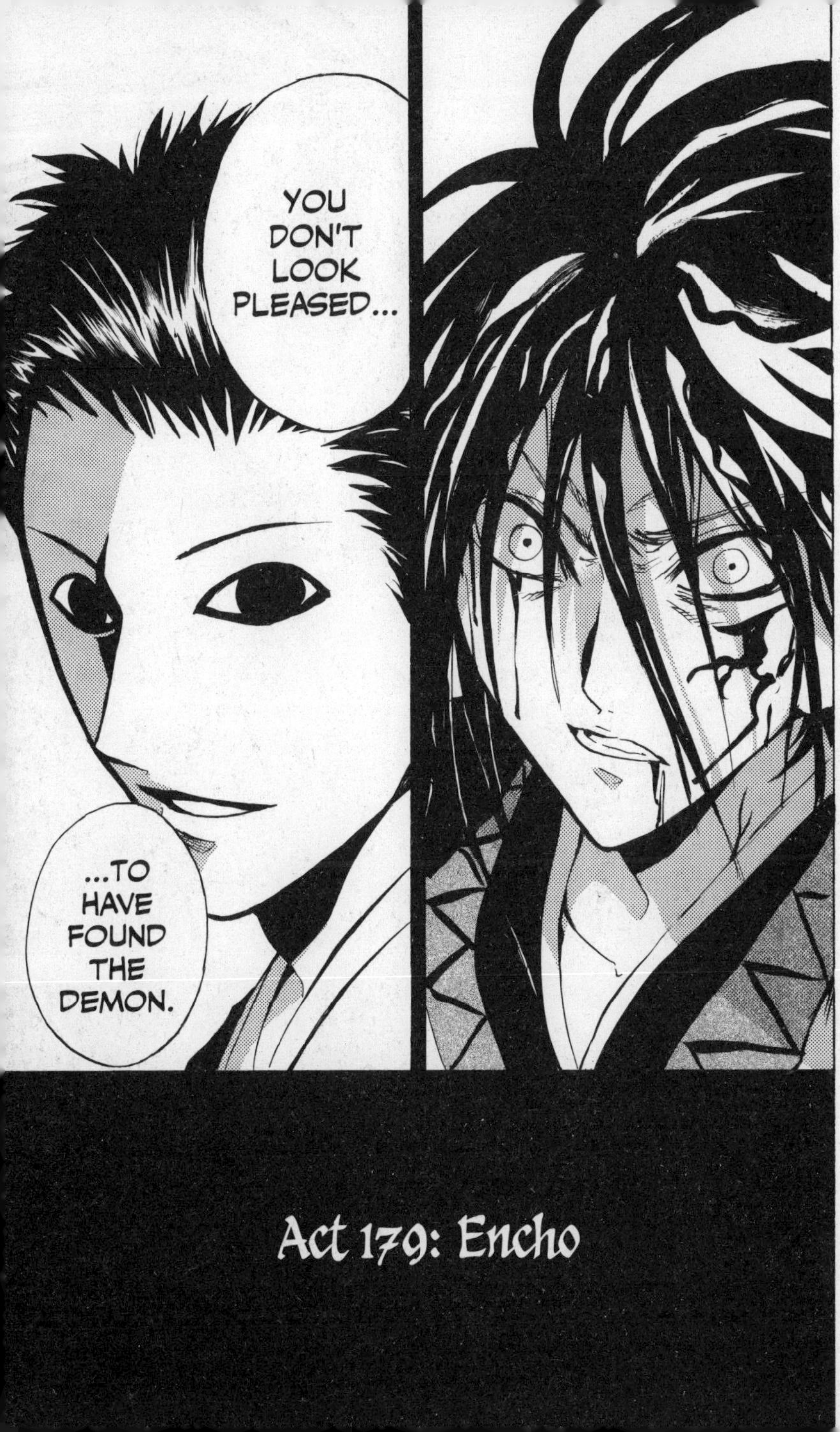
YOU DON'T LOOK PLEASED...
...TO HAVE FOUND THE DEMON.

Act 179: Encho

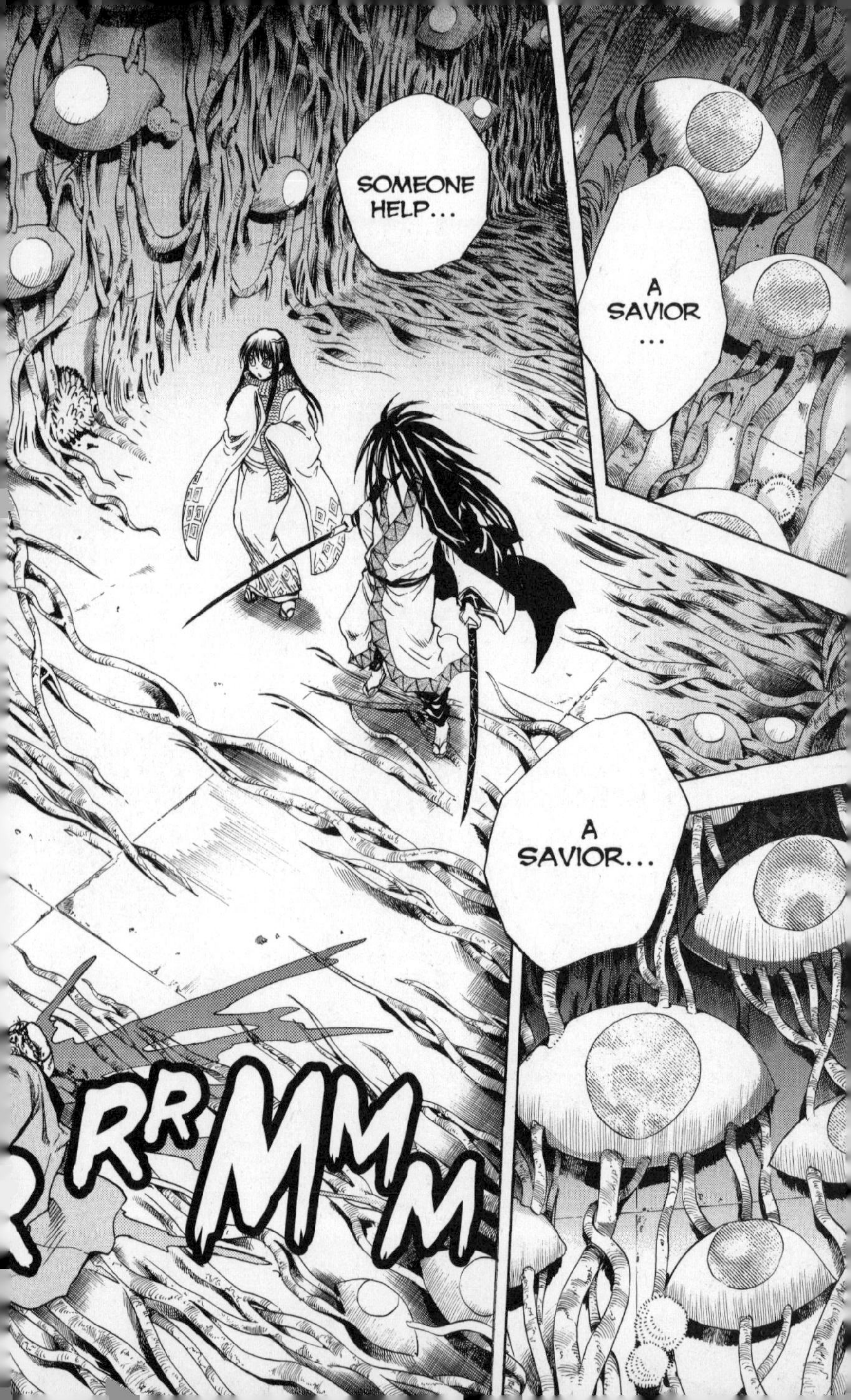
A SAVIOR …
A SAVIOR...
SOMEONE HELP...
RRMMMM

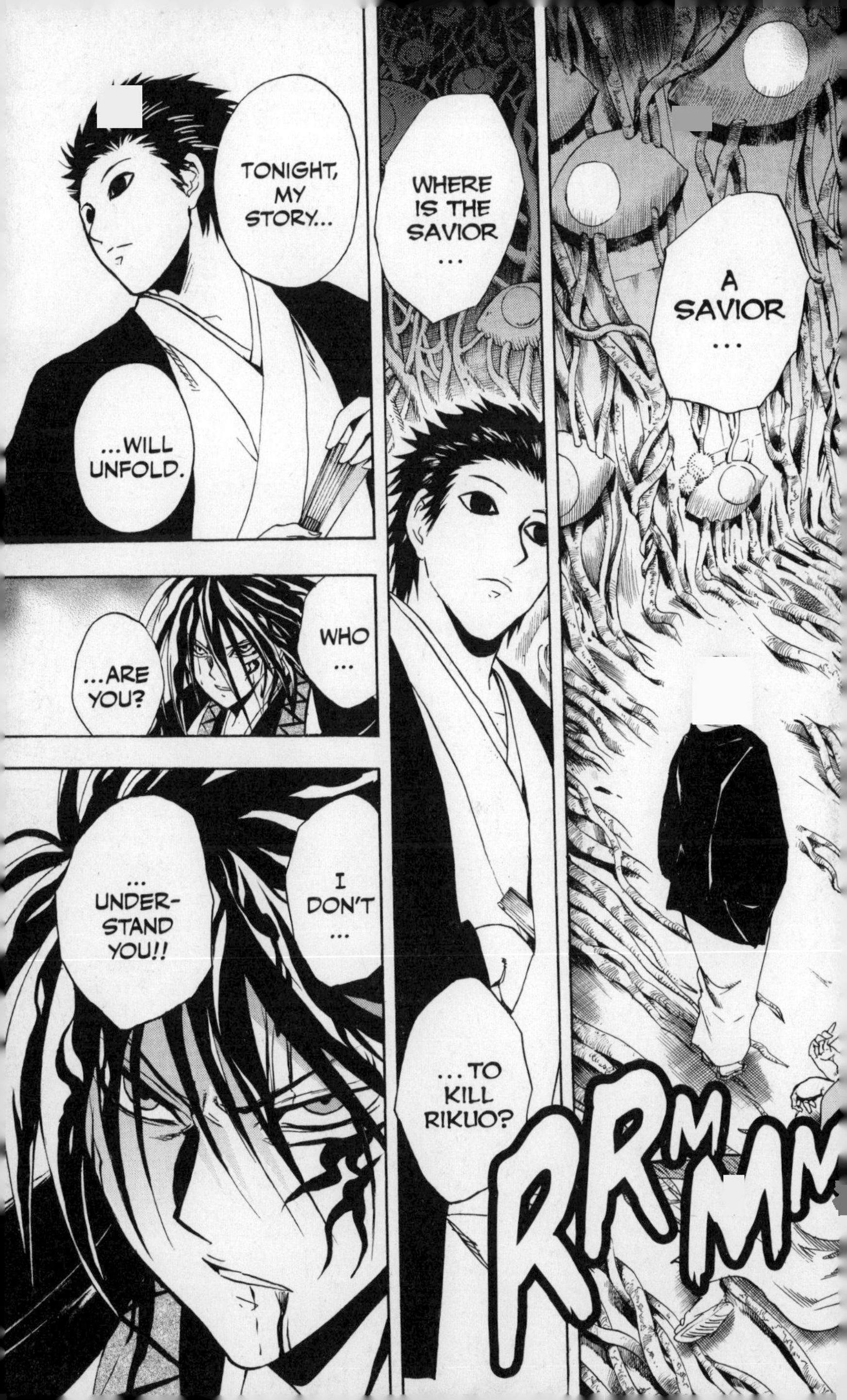
A SAVIOR ...
RRMMM
WHERE IS THE SAVIOR ...
...TO KILL RIKUO?
TONIGHT, MY STORY...
...WILL UNFOLD.
WHO ...
...ARE YOU?
I DON'T ...
... UNDER-STAND YOU!!

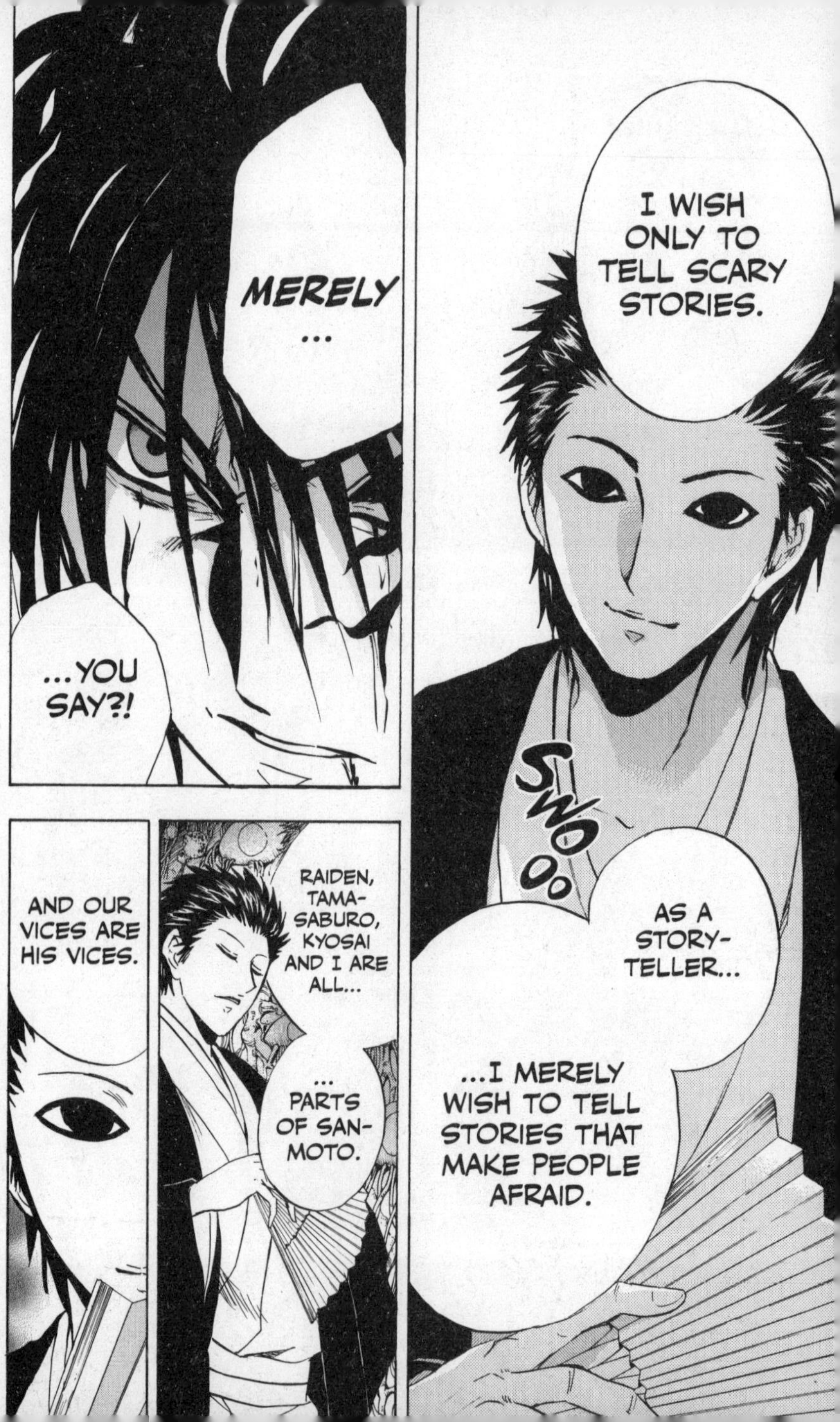
I WISH ONLY TO TELL SCARY STORIES.
SWOOO
AS A STORY-TELLER...
...I MERELY WISH TO TELL STORIES THAT MAKE PEOPLE AFRAID.
MERELY ...
...YOU SAY?!
RAIDEN, TAMA-SABURO, KYOSAI AND I ARE ALL...
... PARTS OF SAN-MOTO.
AND OUR VICES ARE HIS VICES.

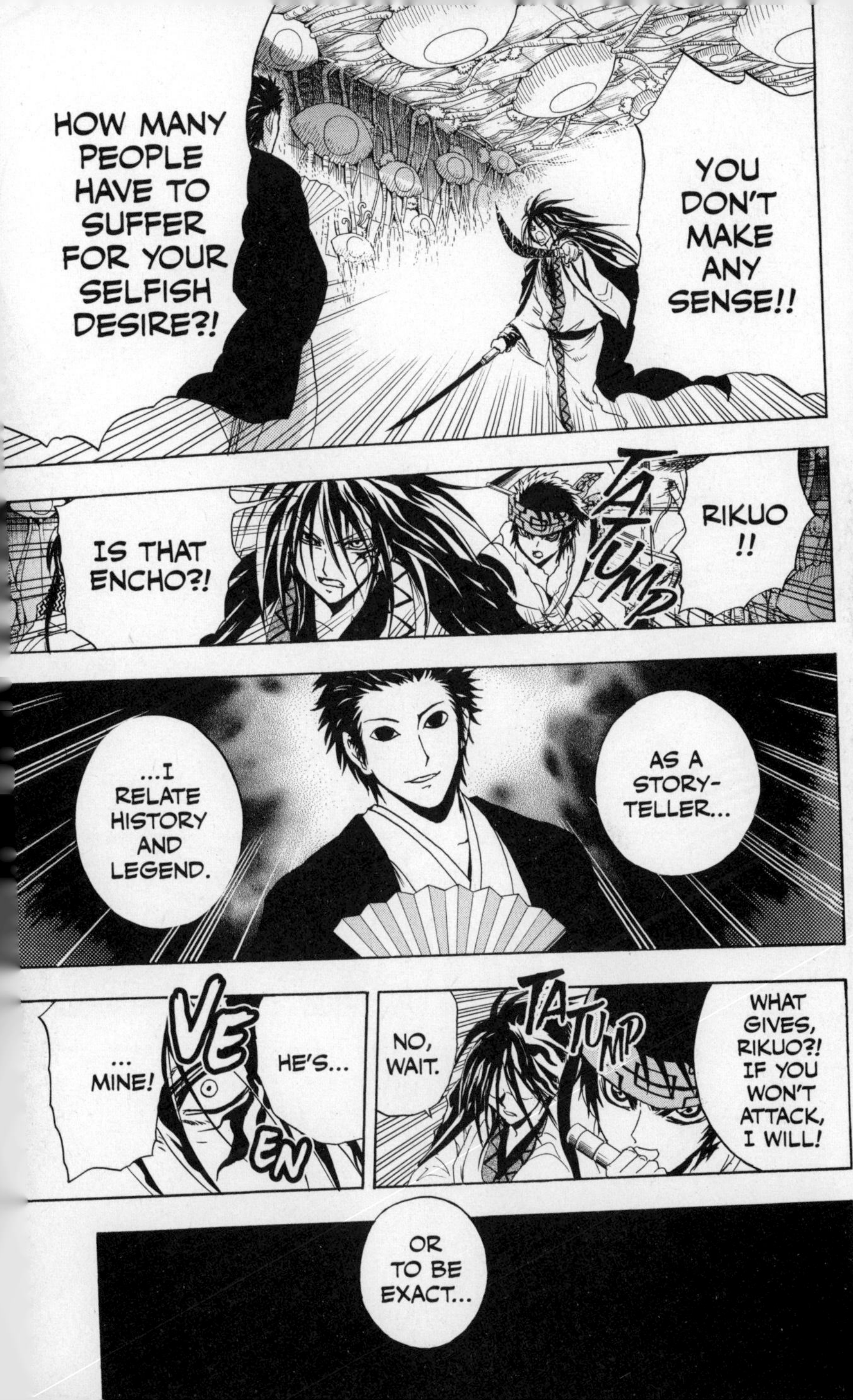
YOU DON'T MAKE ANY SENSE!!
HOW MANY PEOPLE HAVE TO SUFFER FOR YOUR SELFISH DESIRE?!
RIKUO !!
TATUMP
IS THAT ENCHO?!
AS A STORY-TELLER...
...I RELATE HISTORY AND LEGEND.
WHAT GIVES, RIKUO?! IF YOU WON'T ATTACK, I WILL!
TATUMP
NO, WAIT.
HE'S...
VEEN
... MINE!
OR TO BE EXACT...

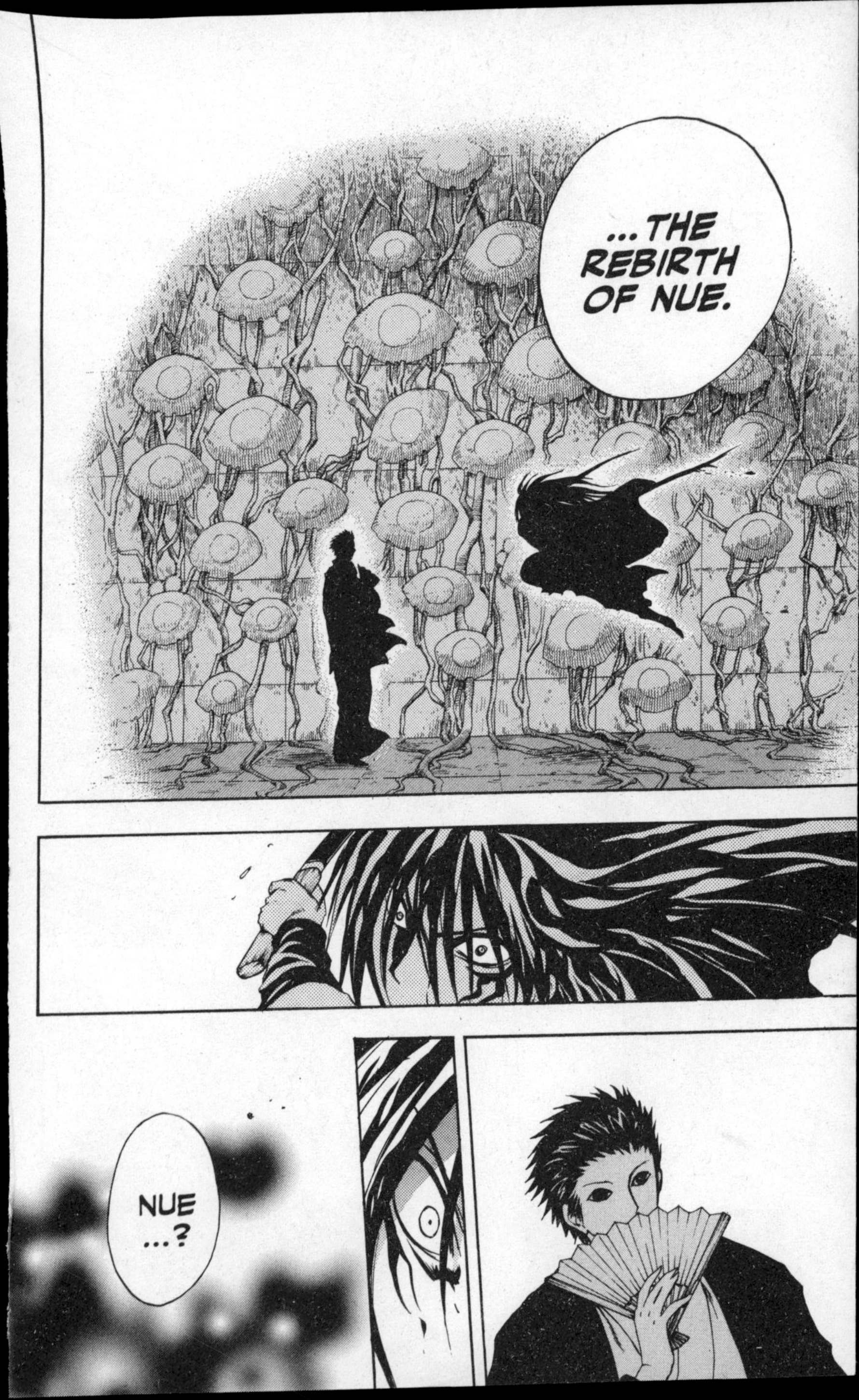
...THE REBIRTH OF NUE.
NUE ...?

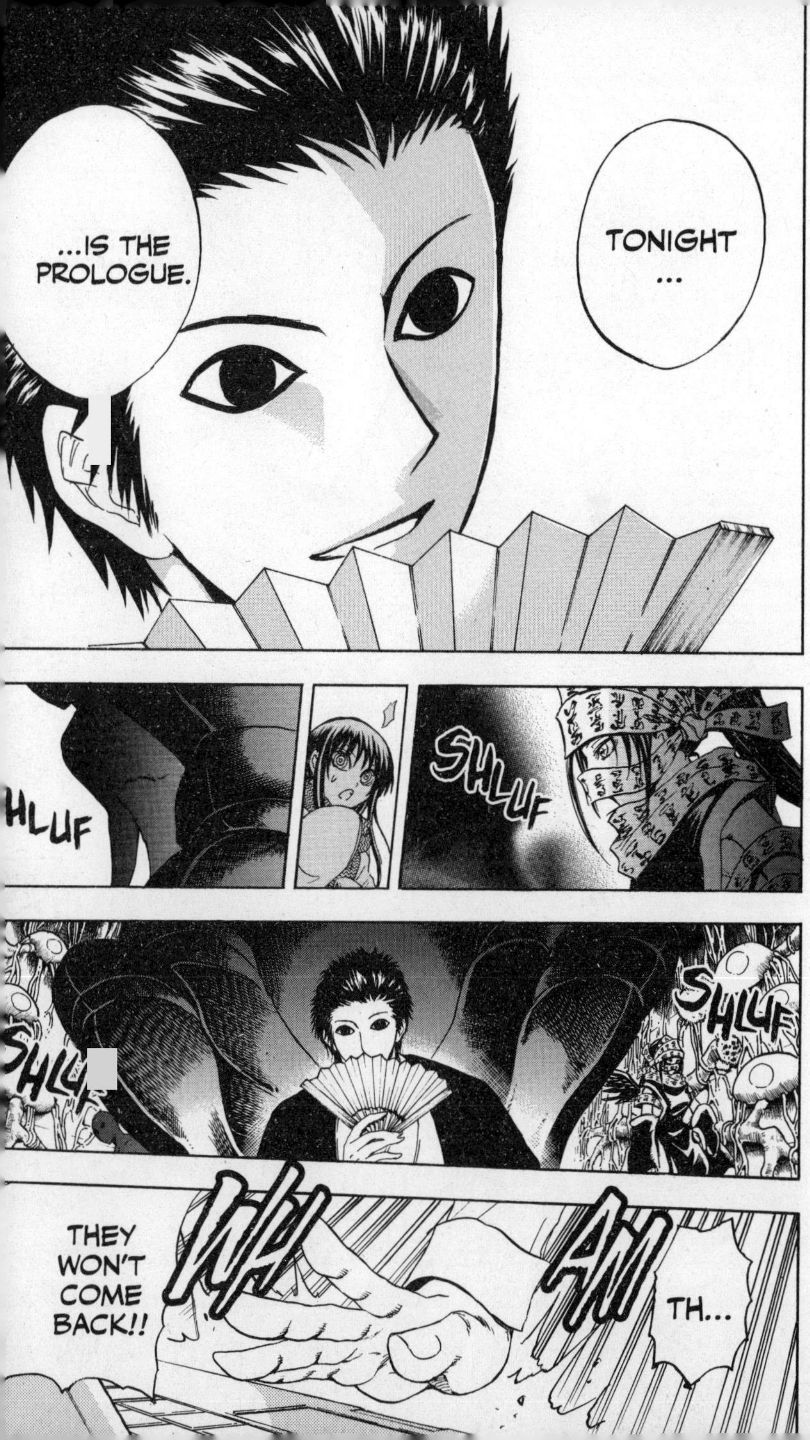
TONIGHT ...
...IS THE PROLOGUE.
SHLUF
HLUF
SHLUF
SHLU
TH...
THEY WON'T COME BACK!!

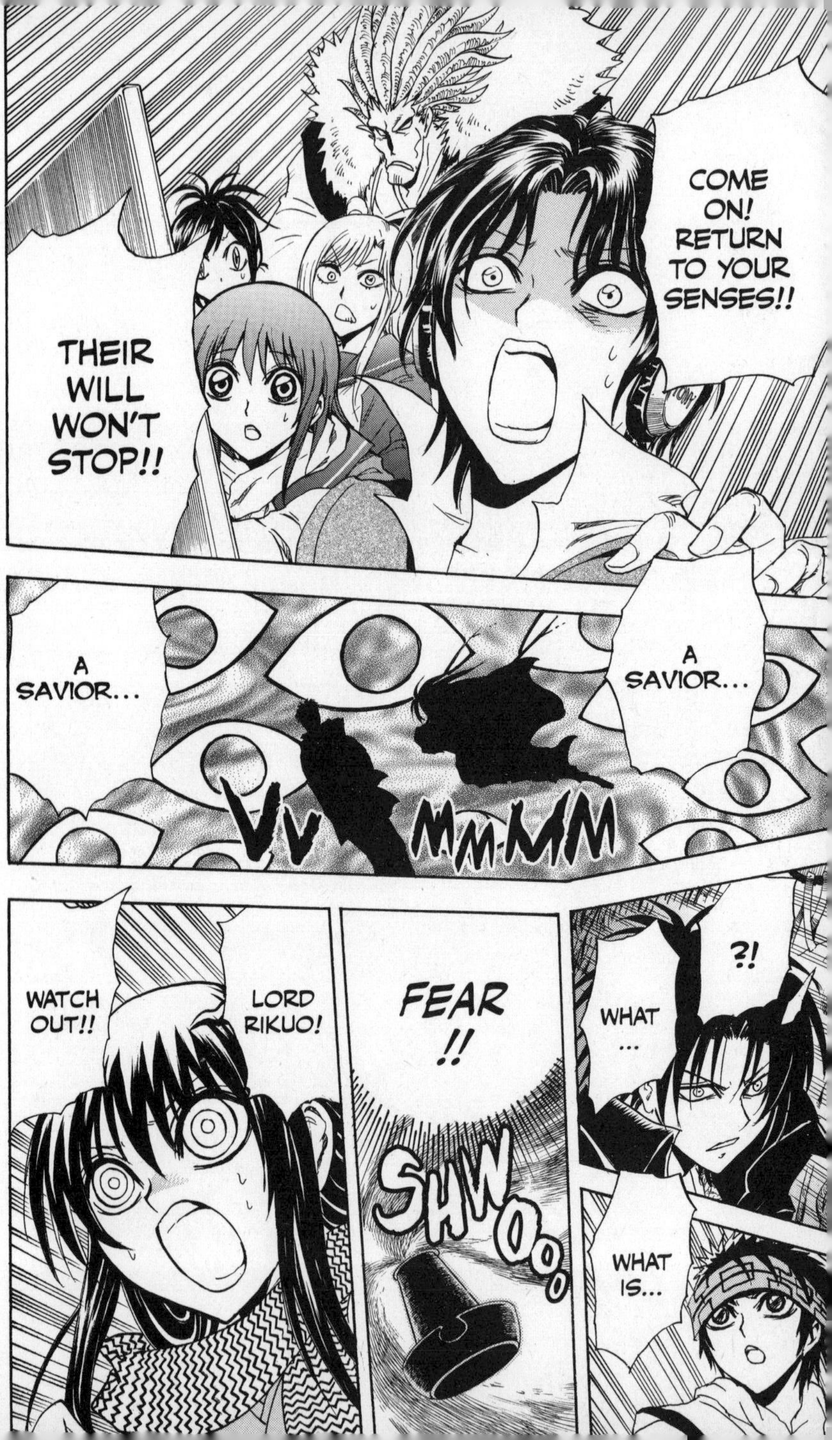
COME ON! RETURN TO YOUR SENSES!!
THEIR WILL WON'T STOP!!
A SAVIOR...
A SAVIOR...
VV MMMMM
?!
WHAT ...
WHAT IS...
FEAR !!
SHWOOO
LORD RIKUO!
WATCH OUT!!

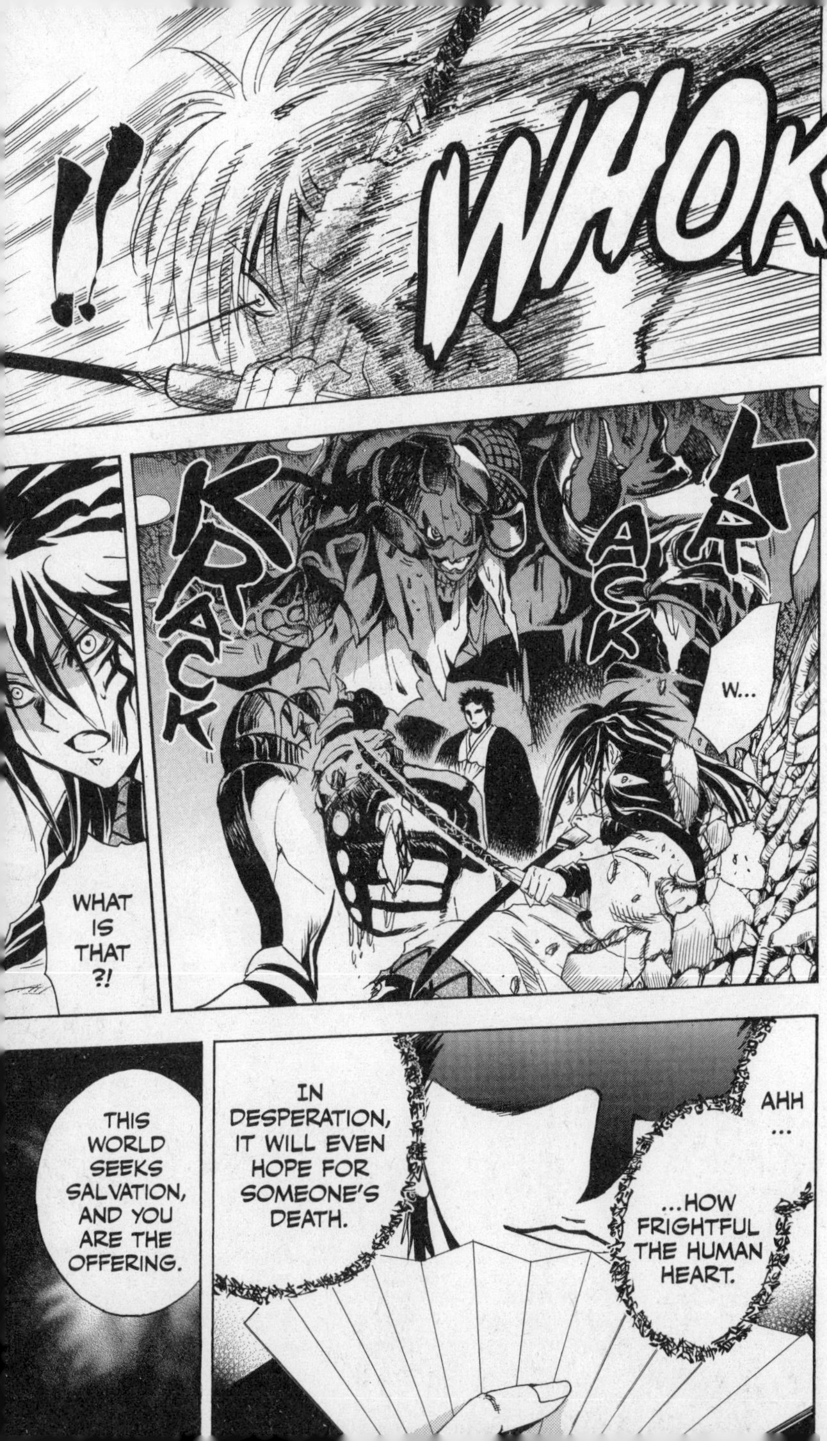
WHOK
!!
KRACK
KRACK
W...
WHAT IS THAT?!
AHH...
...HOW FRIGHTFUL THE HUMAN HEART.
IN DESPERATION, IT WILL EVEN HOPE FOR SOMEONE'S DEATH.
THIS WORLD SEEKS SALVATION, AND YOU ARE THE OFFERING.

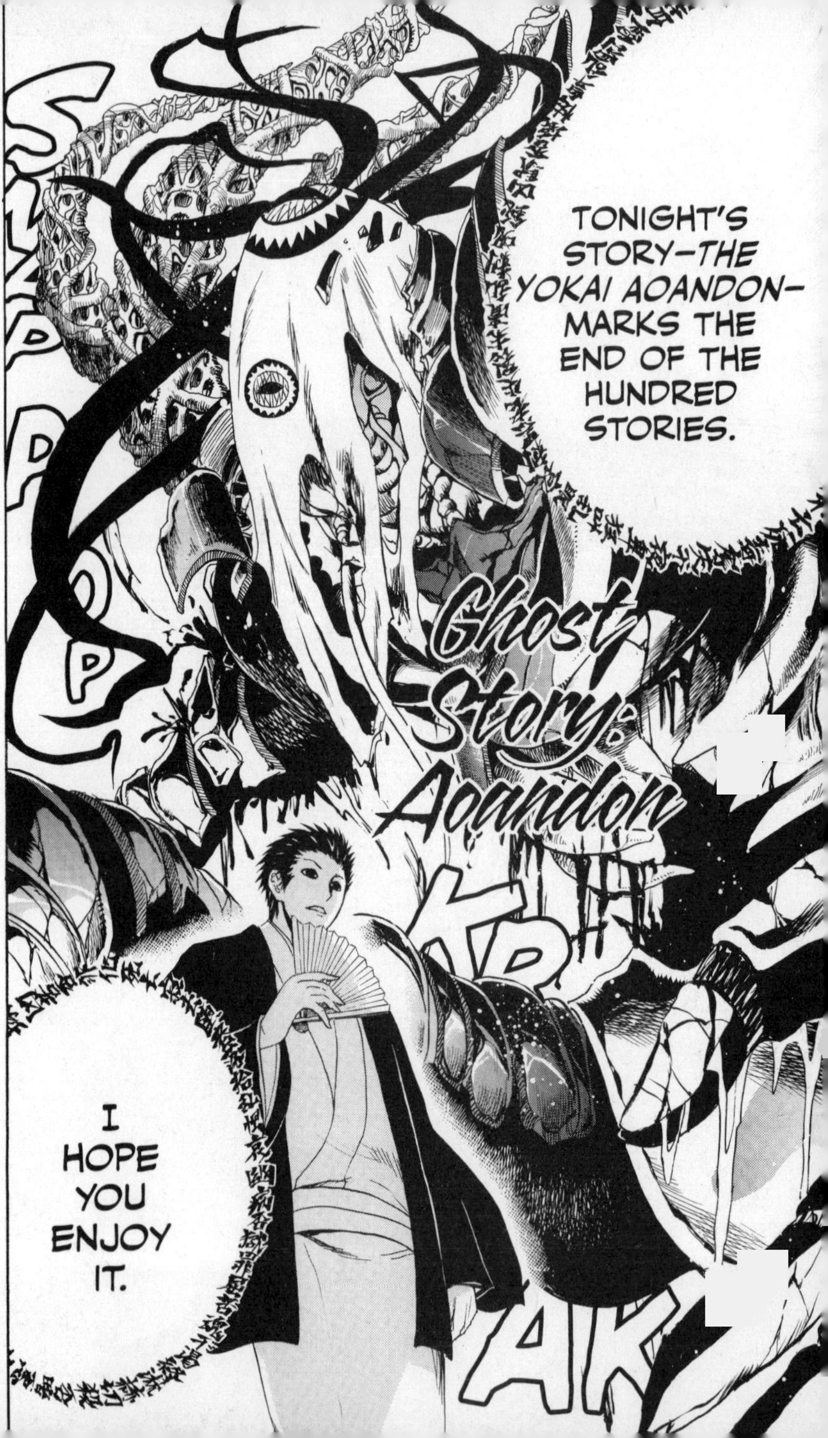
TONIGHT'S STORY—THE YOKAI AOANDON—MARKS THE END OF THE HUNDRED STORIES.
Ghost Story: Aoandon
I HOPE YOU ENJOY IT.

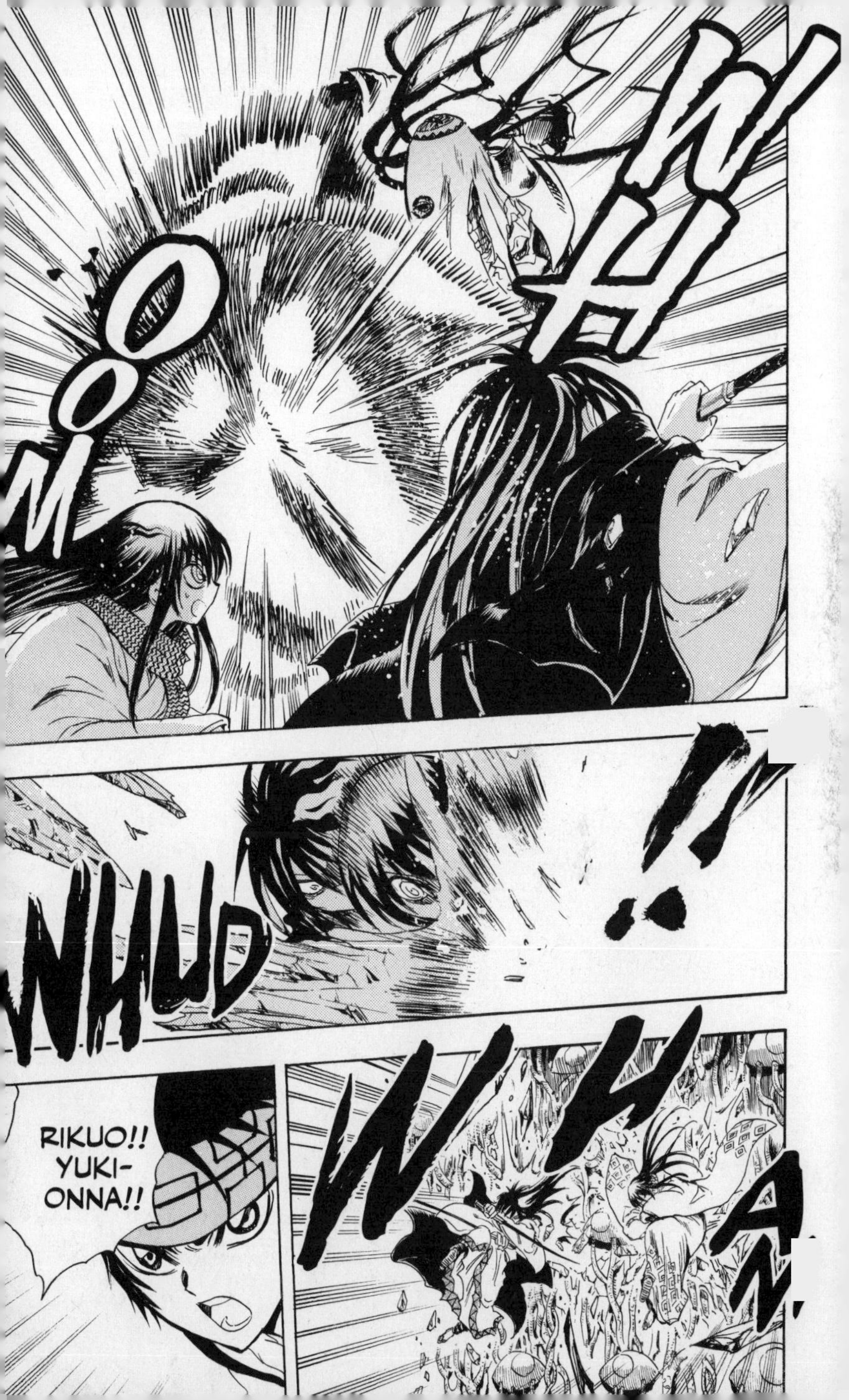
WHAM
WHOOM
!!
WHUD
RIKUO!! YUKI-ONNA!!
WHAM

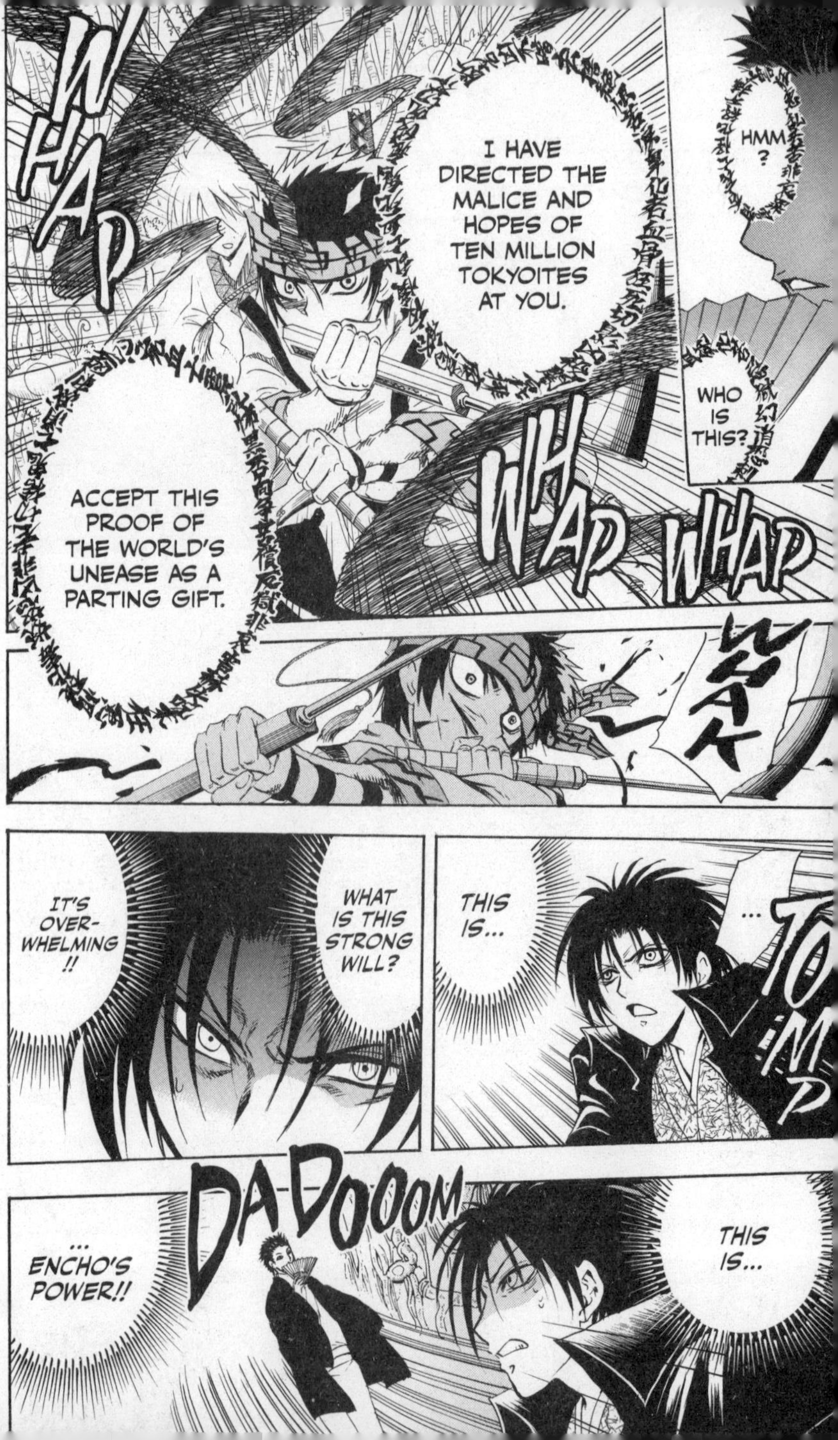
HMM?
WHO IS THIS?
I HAVE DIRECTED THE MALICE AND HOPES OF TEN MILLION TOKYOITES AT YOU.
WHAP
ACCEPT THIS PROOF OF THE WORLD'S UNEASE AS A PARTING GIFT.
WHAP WHAP
WAK
THIS IS...
...
TOMP
WHAT IS THIS STRONG WILL?
IT'S OVER-WHELMING!!
THIS IS...
DA-DOOOM
...ENCHO'S POWER!!

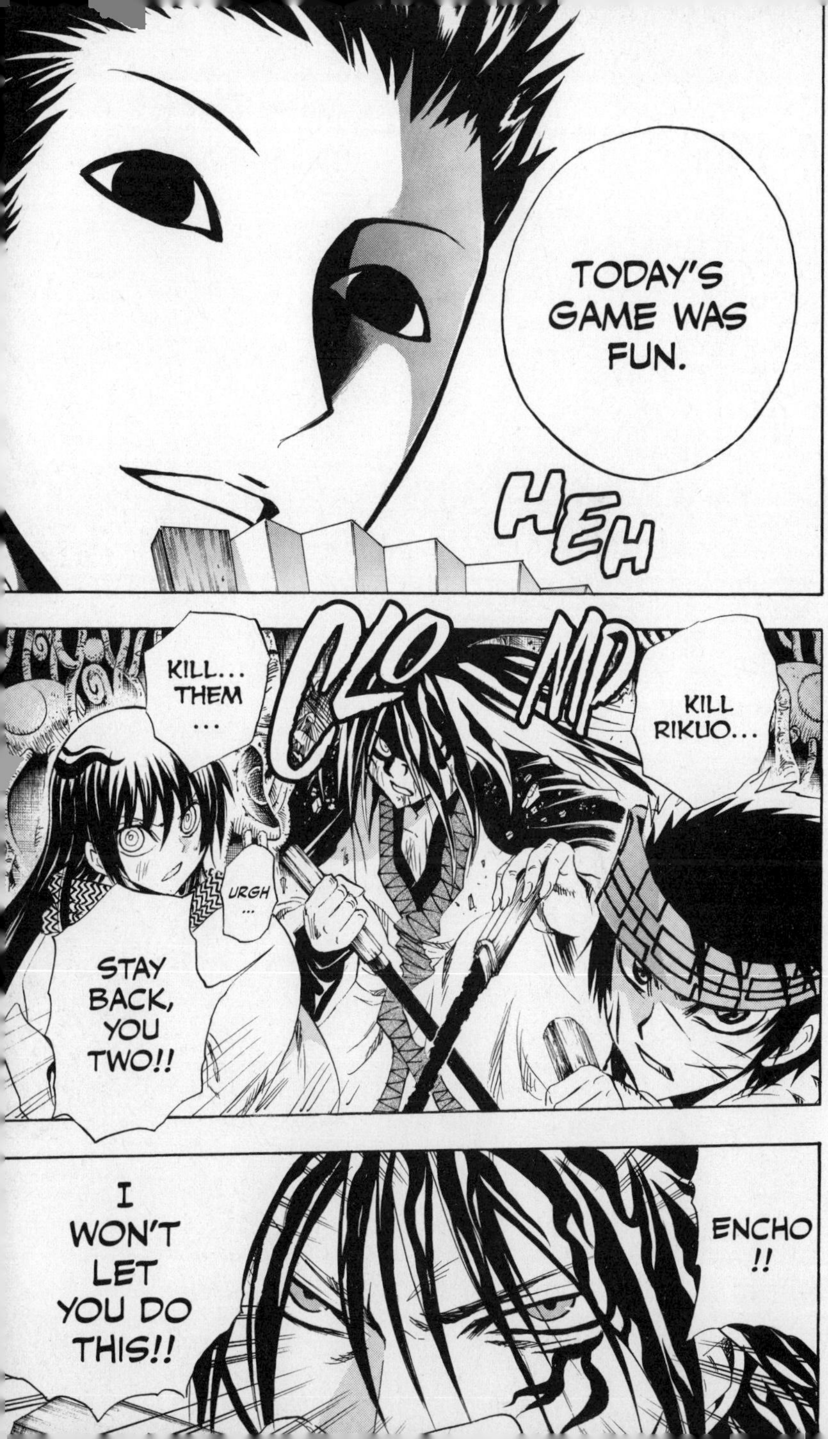
TODAY'S GAME WAS FUN.
HEH
KILL RIKUO...
CLOMP
KILL... THEM ...
URGH ...
STAY BACK, YOU TWO!!
ENCHO !!
I WON'T LET YOU DO THIS!!

A Spring Storm of Image Changes, Part 3
~Yura Keikain with Long Hair~

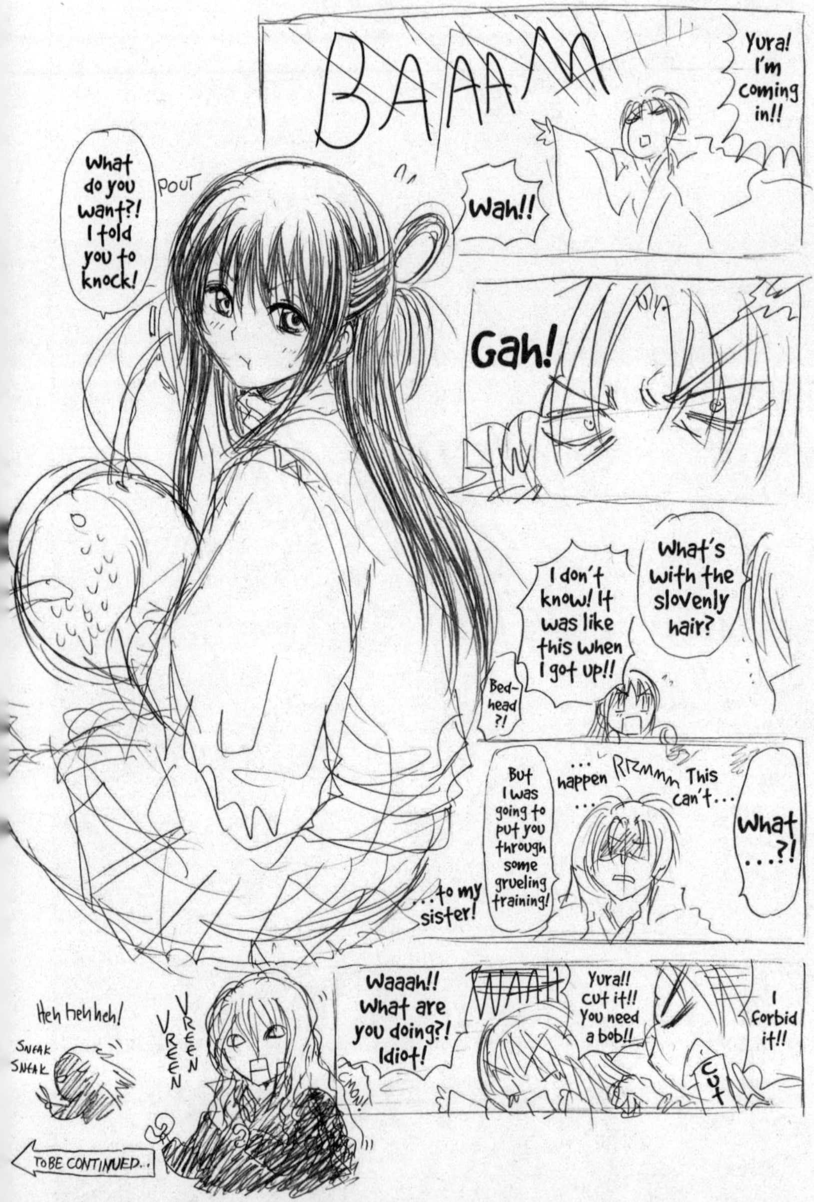
BAAAM
Yura! I'm coming in!!
Wah!!
Gah!
What's with the slovenly hair?
I don't know! It was like this when I got up!!
Bed-head?!
What...?!
This can't...
RRZMMM
...happen
But I was going to put you through some grueling training!
...to my sister!
What do you want?! I told you to knock!
POUT
I forbid it!!
Yura!! Cut it!! You need a bob!!
WAAH
CUT
Waaah!! What are you doing?! Idiot!
C'MON!
VREEN VREEN
Heh heh heh!
SNEAK SNEAK
TO BE CONTINUED...

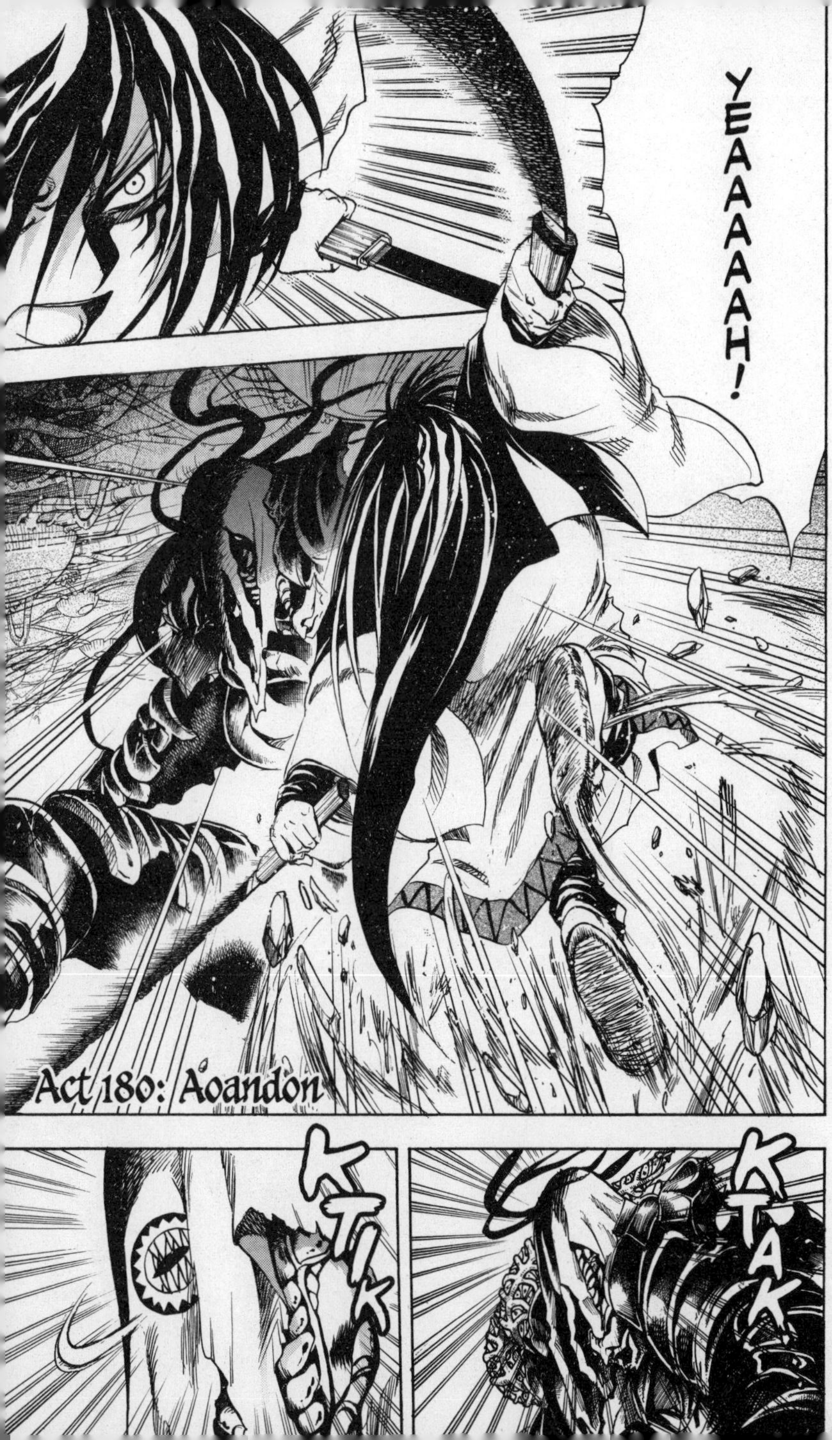
YEAAAAAH!
Act 180: Aoandon
KTAK
KTIK

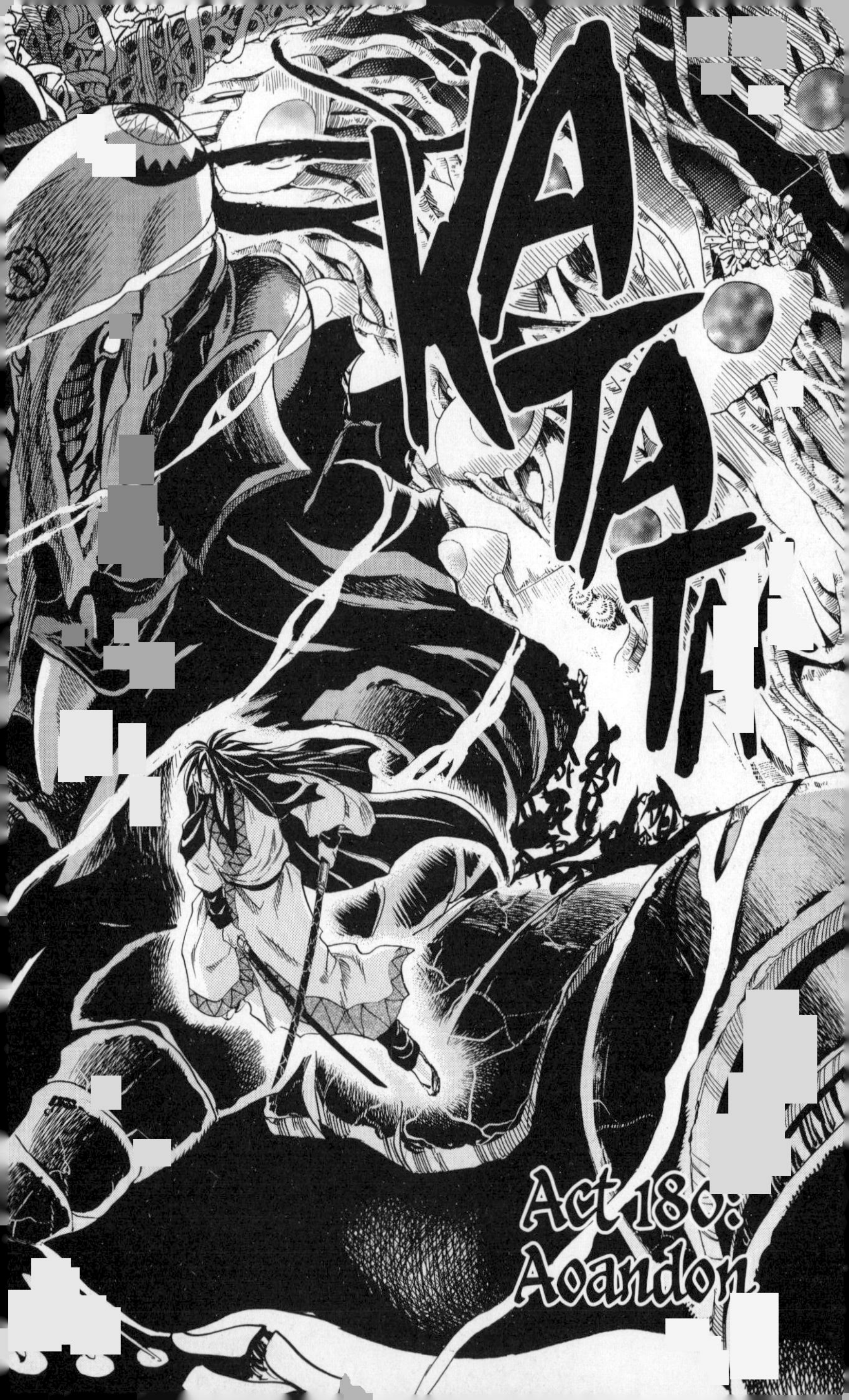
KATATA
Act 180:
Aoandon

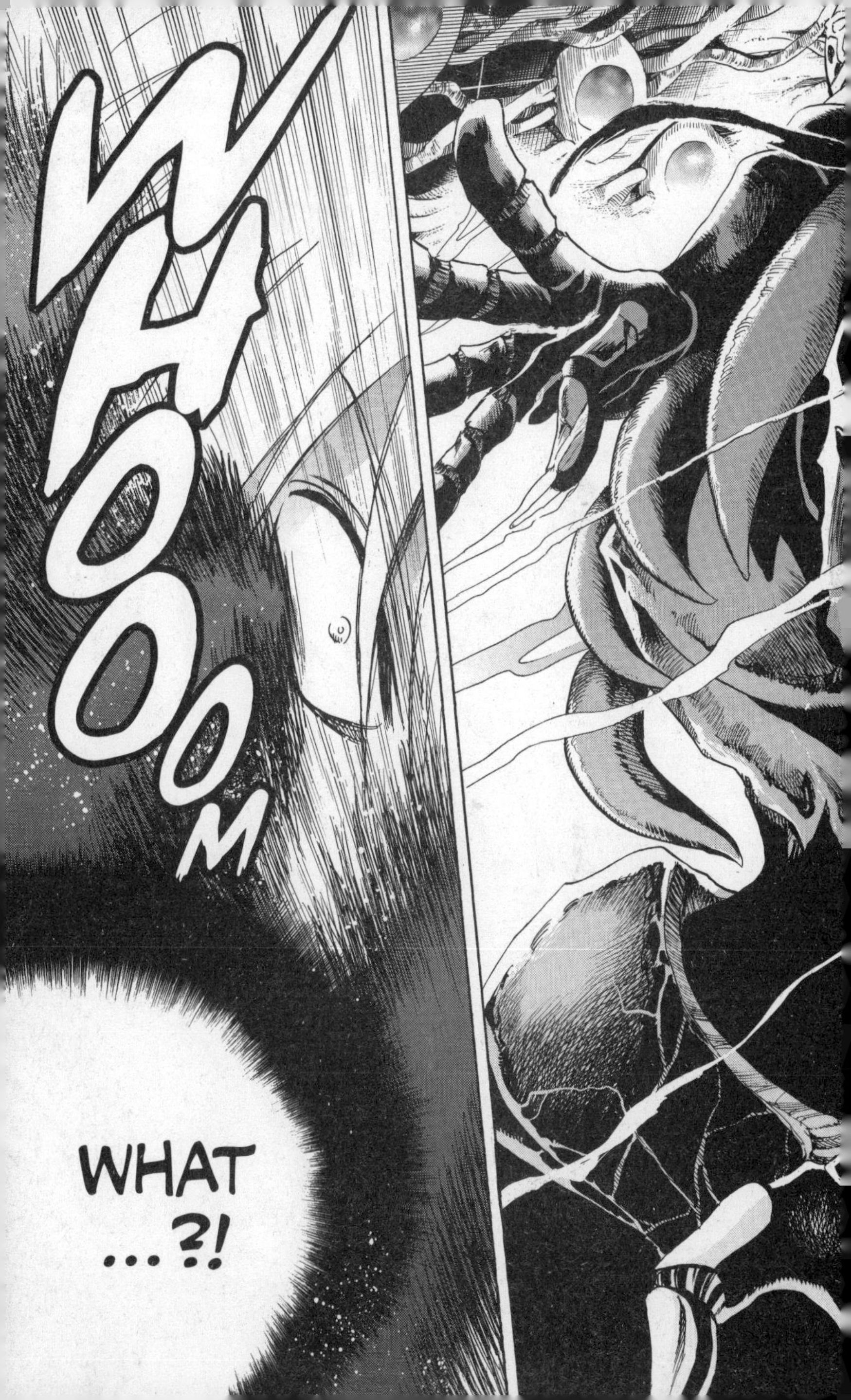
WHOOOOM
WHAT ...?!

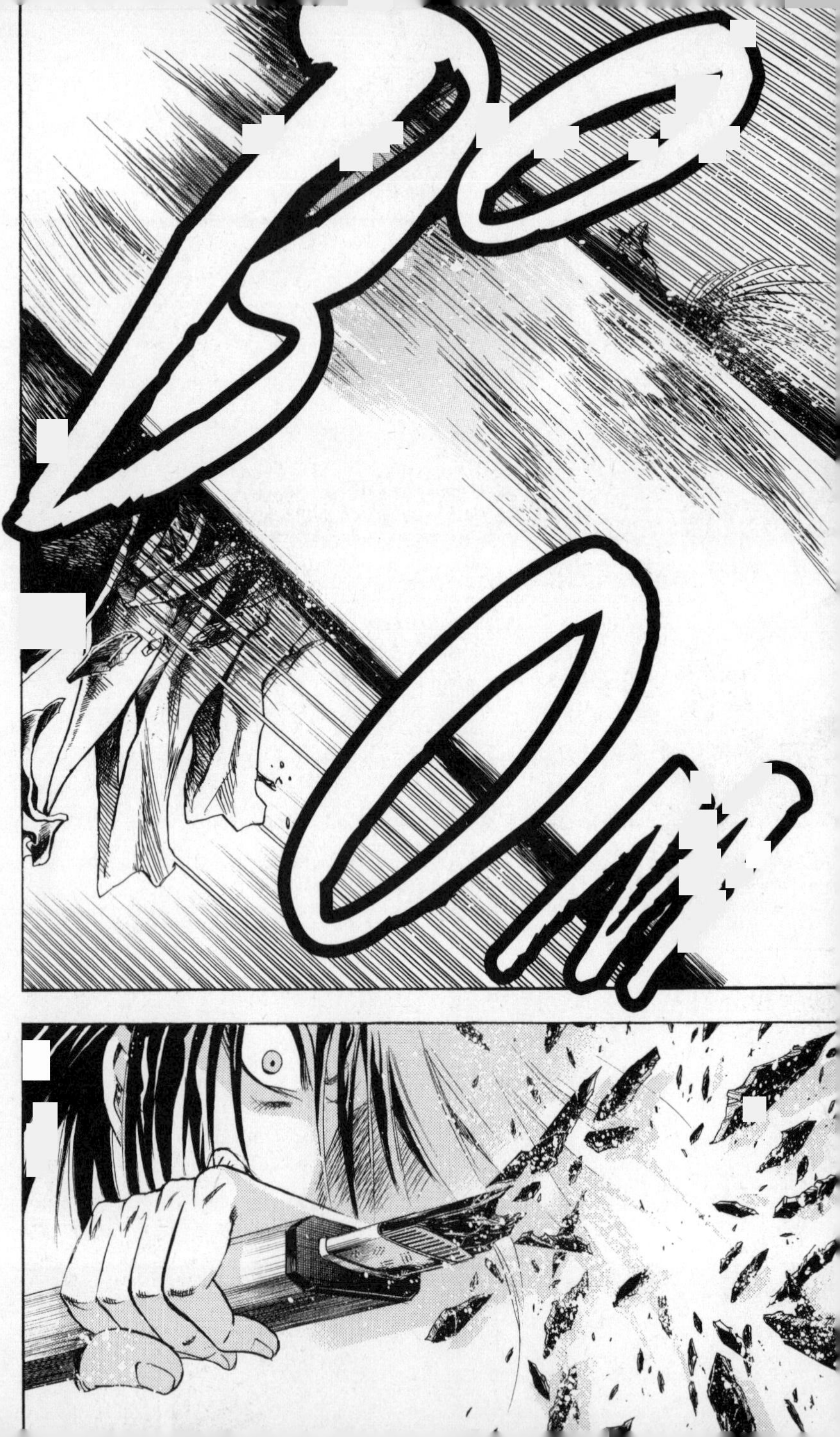

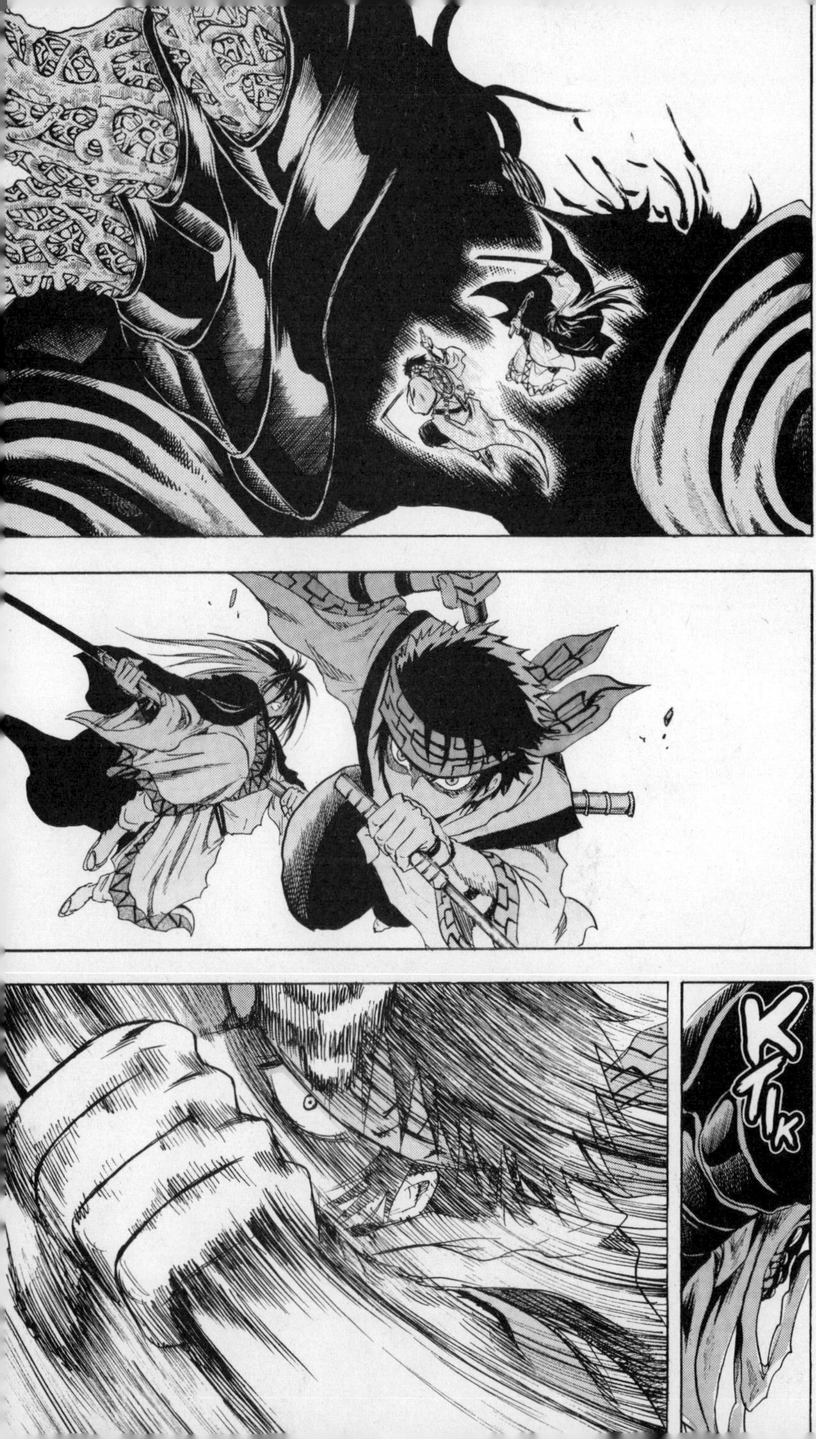
KTIK

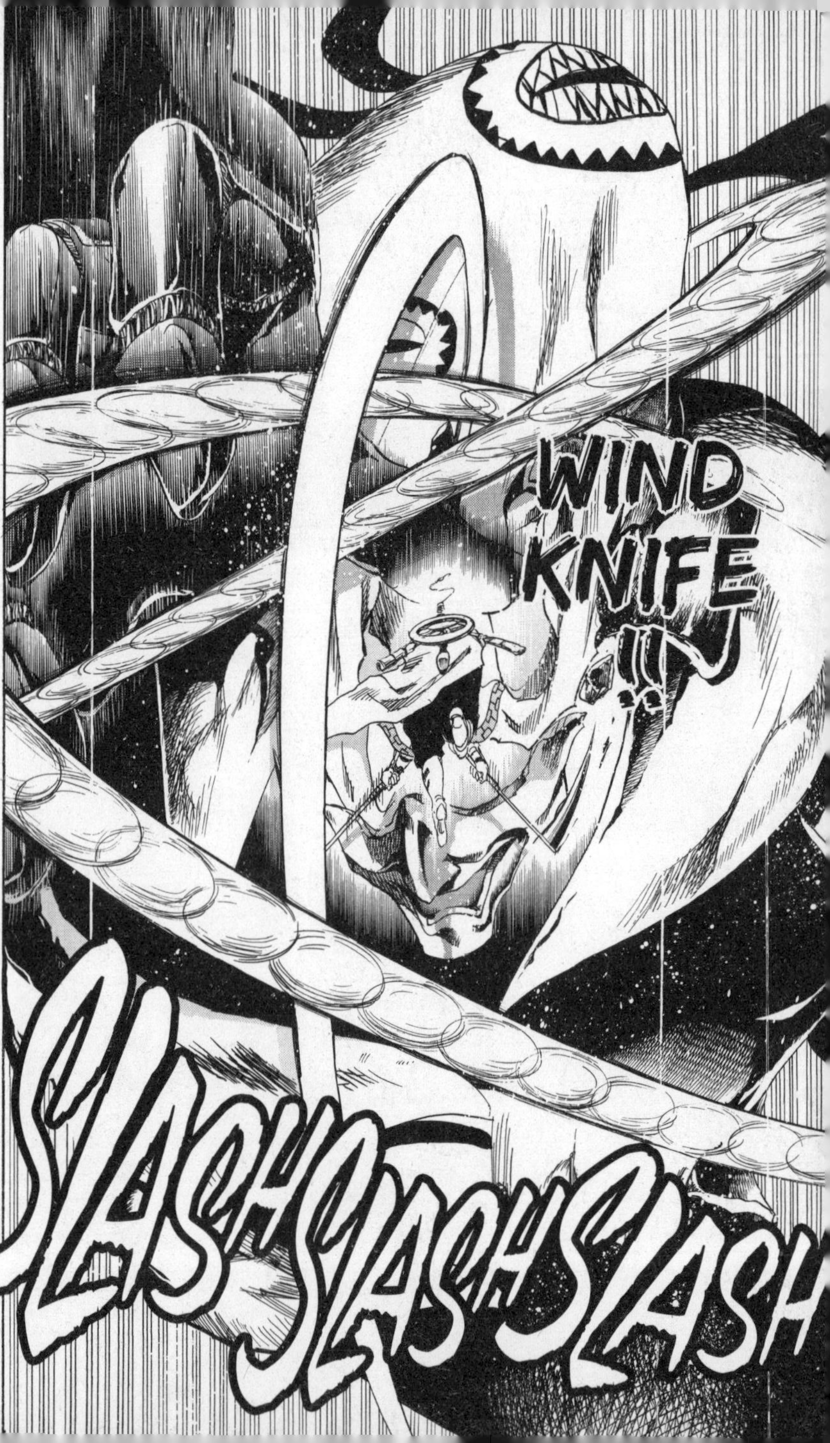
WIND KNIFE!!
SLASH SLASH SLASH

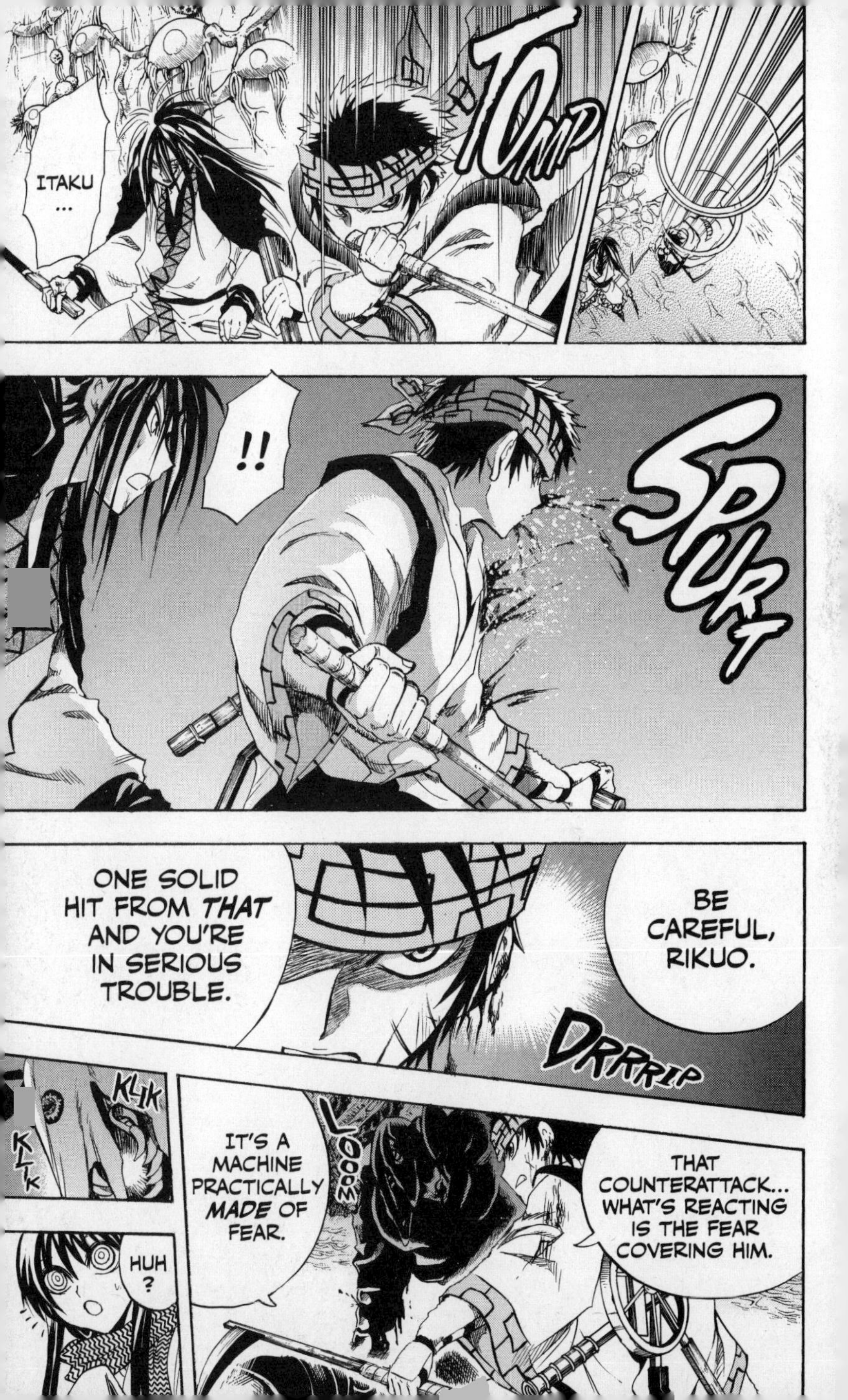
TOMP
ITAKU ...
SPURT
!!
BE CAREFUL, RIKUO.
ONE SOLID HIT FROM *THAT* AND YOU'RE IN SERIOUS TROUBLE.
DRRRRIP
THAT COUNTERATTACK... WHAT'S REACTING IS THE FEAR COVERING HIM.
LOOOOM
IT'S A MACHINE PRACTICALLY *MADE* OF FEAR.
KLIK
KLIK
HUH ?

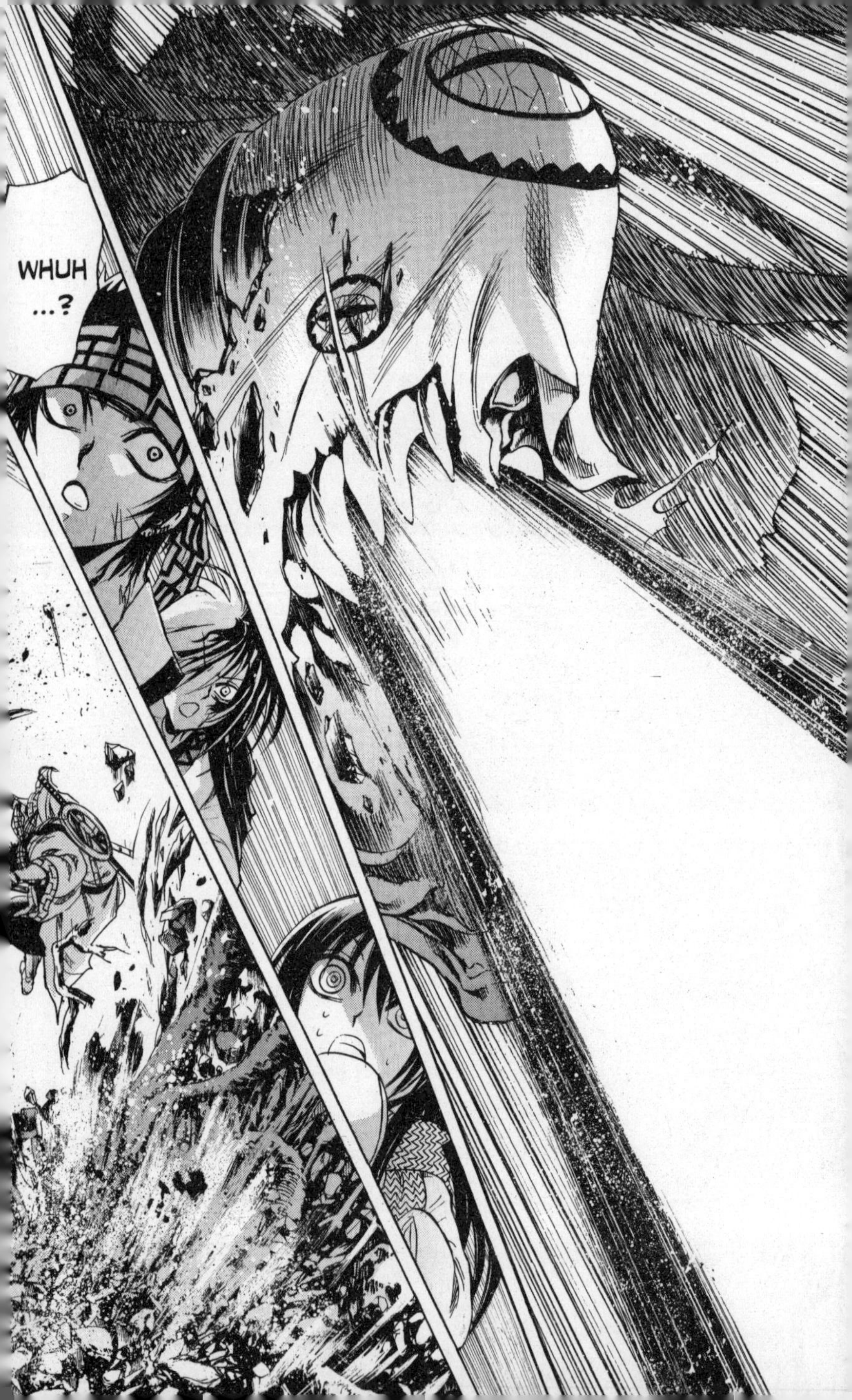
WHUH ...?

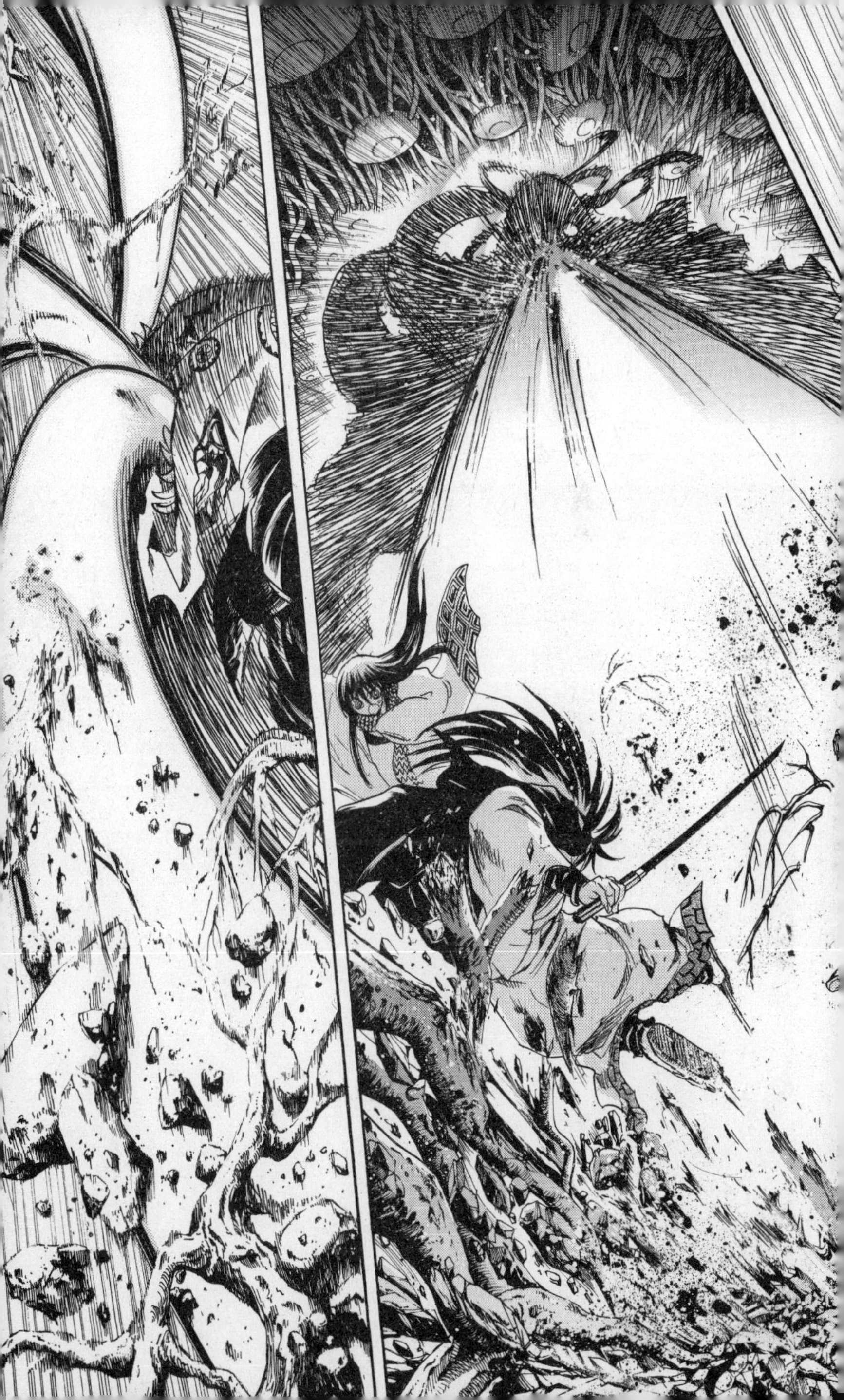

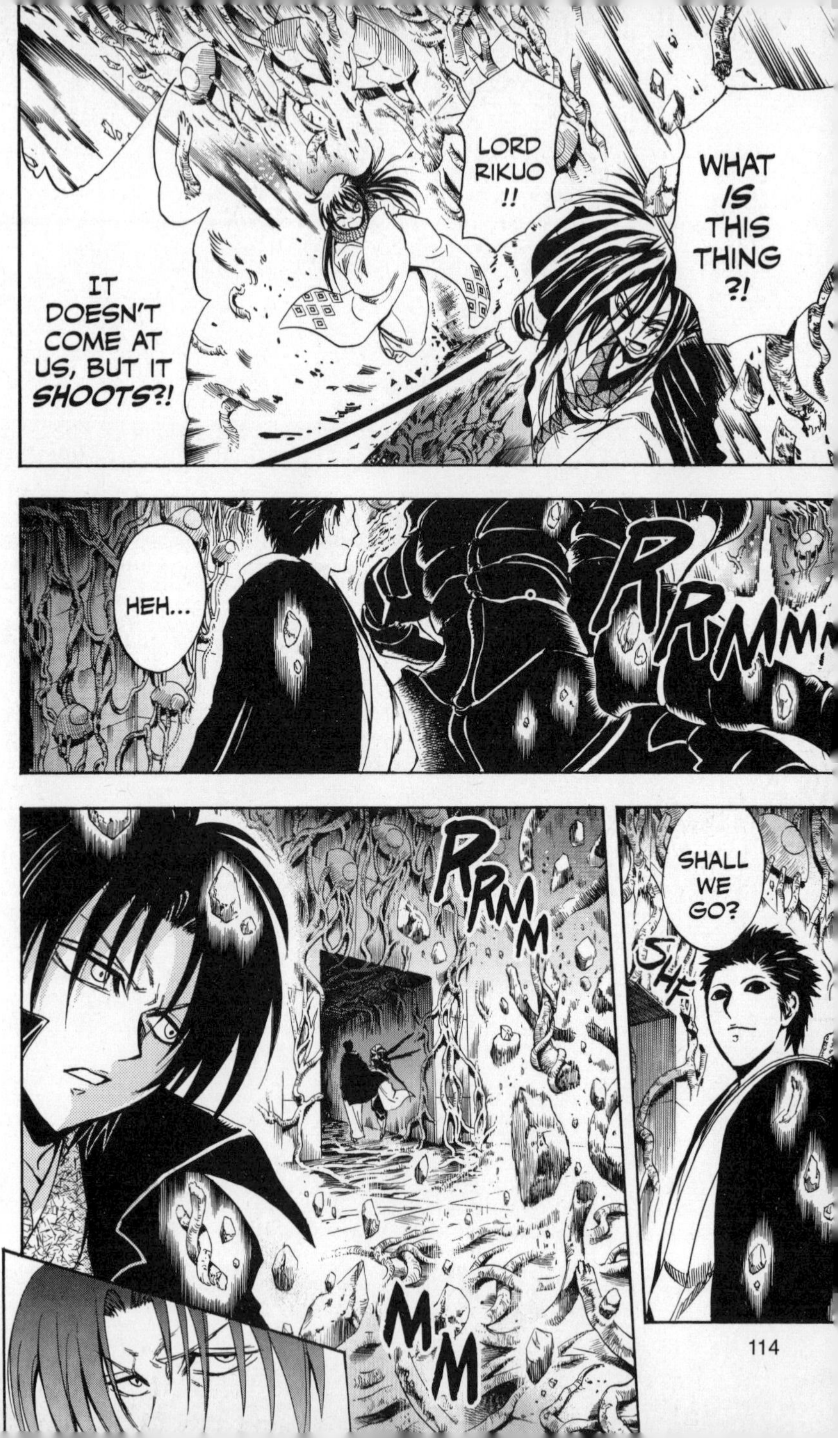
WHAT IS THIS THING?!
LORD RIKUO!!
IT DOESN'T COME AT US, BUT IT SHOOTS?!
RRMMM
HEH...
SHALL WE GO?
SHF
RRMM
MM

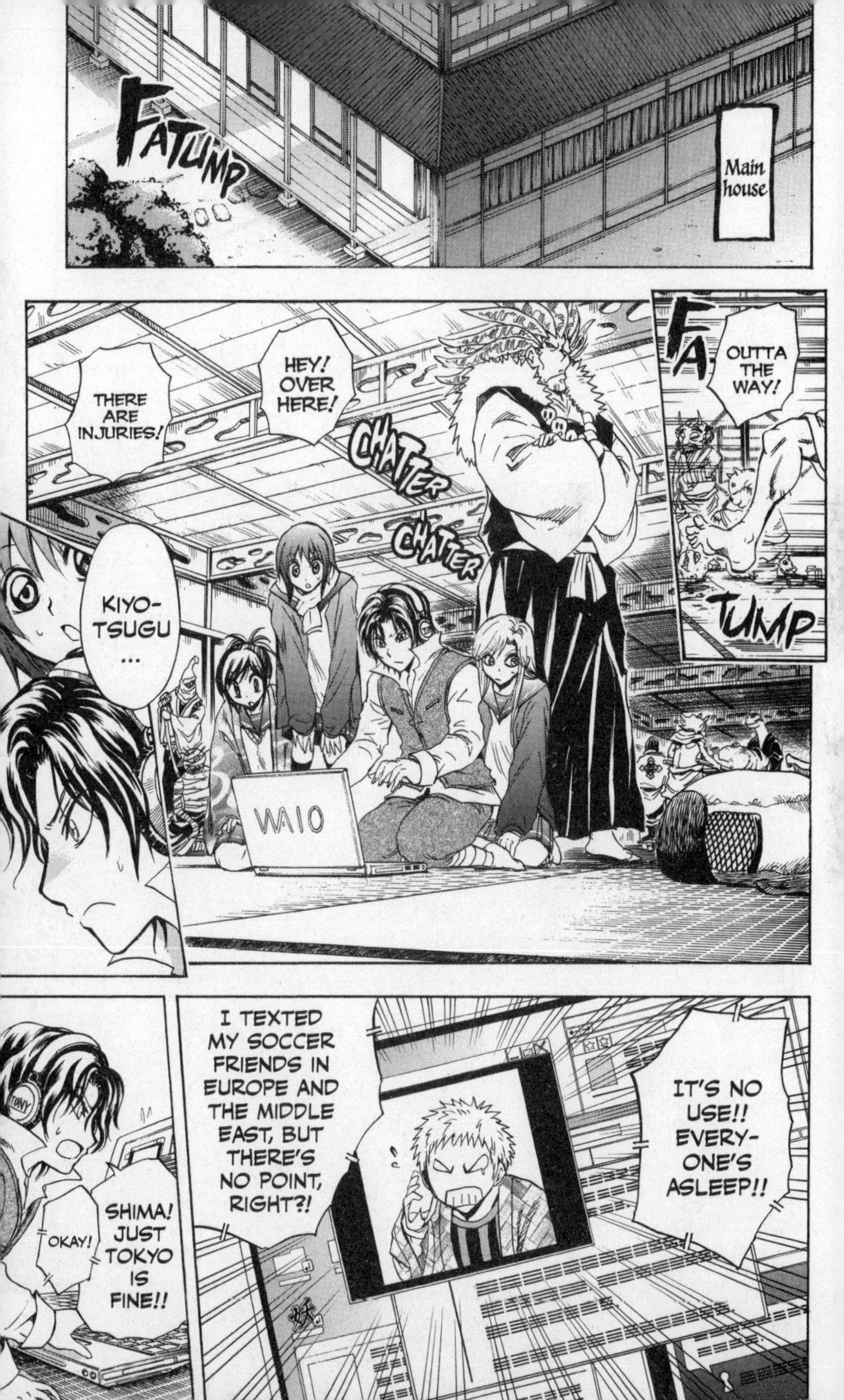
FATUMP
Main house
FA
OUTTA THE WAY!
TUMP
HEY! OVER HERE!
CHATTER
CHATTER
THERE ARE INJURIES!
KIYO-TSUGU...
IT'S NO USE!! EVERY-ONE'S ASLEEP!!
I TEXTED MY SOCCER FRIENDS IN EUROPE AND THE MIDDLE EAST, BUT THERE'S NO POINT, RIGHT?!
SHIMA! JUST TOKYO IS FINE!!
OKAY!
WAIO
TONY

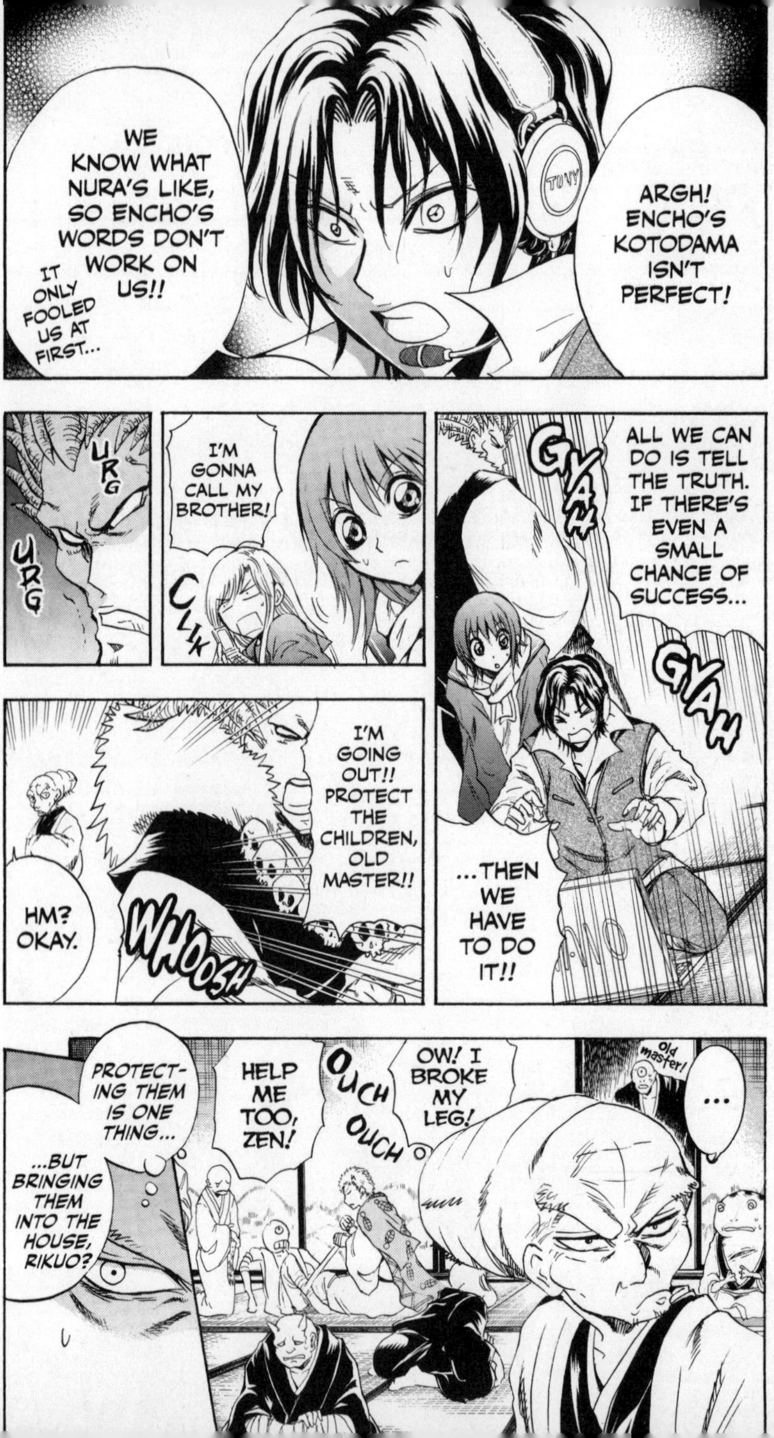
ARGH! ENCHO'S KOTODAMA ISN'T PERFECT!
WE KNOW WHAT NURA'S LIKE, SO ENCHO'S WORDS DON'T WORK ON US!!
IT ONLY FOOLED US AT FIRST...
ALL WE CAN DO IS TELL THE TRUTH. IF THERE'S EVEN A SMALL CHANCE OF SUCCESS...
GYAH
GYAH
...THEN WE HAVE TO DO IT!!
I'M GONNA CALL MY BROTHER!
CLIK
URG
URG
I'M GOING OUT!! PROTECT THE CHILDREN, OLD MASTER!!
WHOOSH
HM? OKAY.
old master!
...
OW! I BROKE MY LEG!
OUCH
OUCH
OUCH
HELP ME TOO, ZEN!
PROTECTING THEM IS ONE THING...
...BUT BRINGING THEM INTO THE HOUSE, RIKUO?

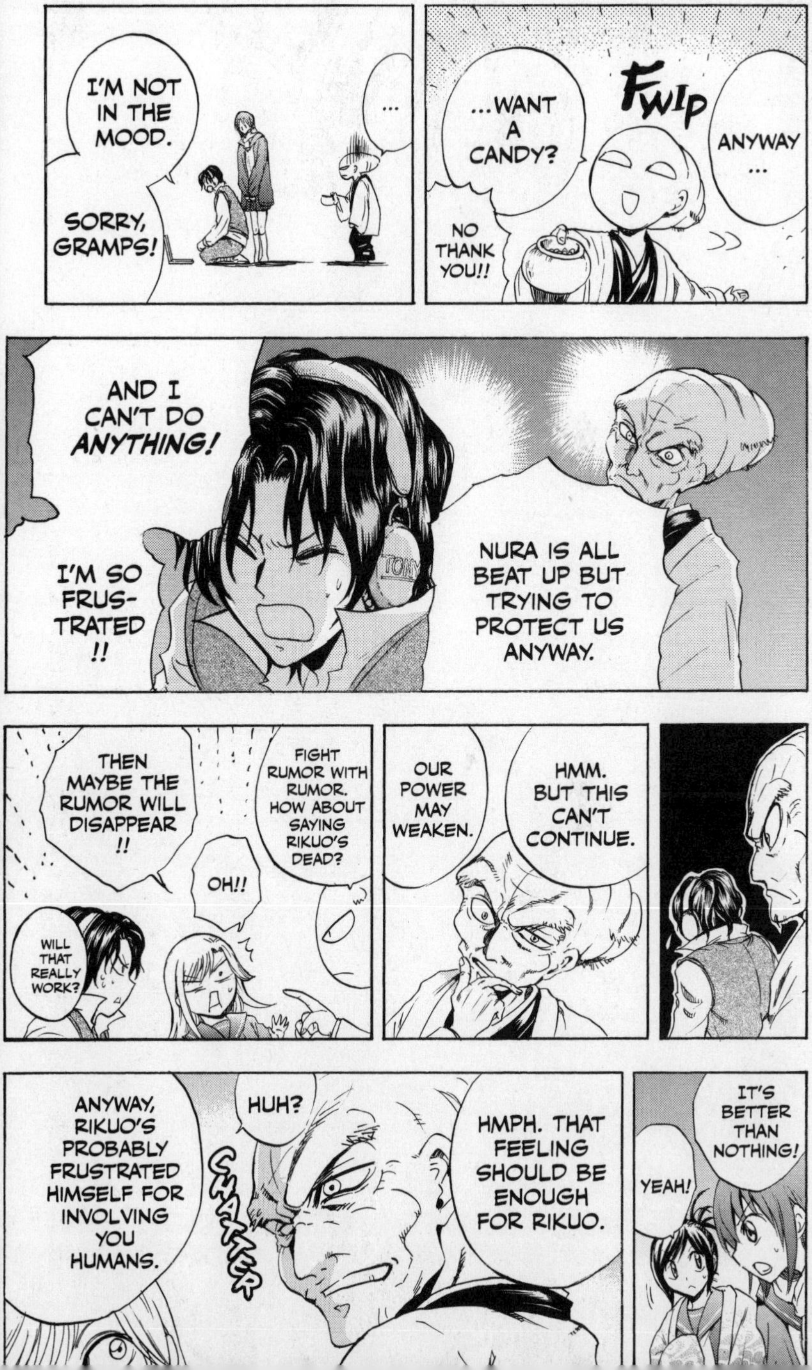
ANYWAY ...
FWIP
...WANT A CANDY?
NO THANK YOU!!
...
I'M NOT IN THE MOOD.
SORRY, GRAMPS!
NURA IS ALL BEAT UP BUT TRYING TO PROTECT US ANYWAY.
AND I CAN'T DO ANYTHING!
I'M SO FRUS-TRATED!!
HMM. BUT THIS CAN'T CONTINUE.
OUR POWER MAY WEAKEN.
FIGHT RUMOR WITH RUMOR. HOW ABOUT SAYING RIKUO'S DEAD?
THEN MAYBE THE RUMOR WILL DISAPPEAR!!
OH!!
WILL THAT REALLY WORK?
IT'S BETTER THAN NOTHING!
YEAH!
ANYWAY, RIKUO'S PROBABLY FRUSTRATED HIMSELF FOR INVOLVING YOU HUMANS.
HUH?
HMPH. THAT FEELING SHOULD BE ENOUGH FOR RIKUO.
CHATTER

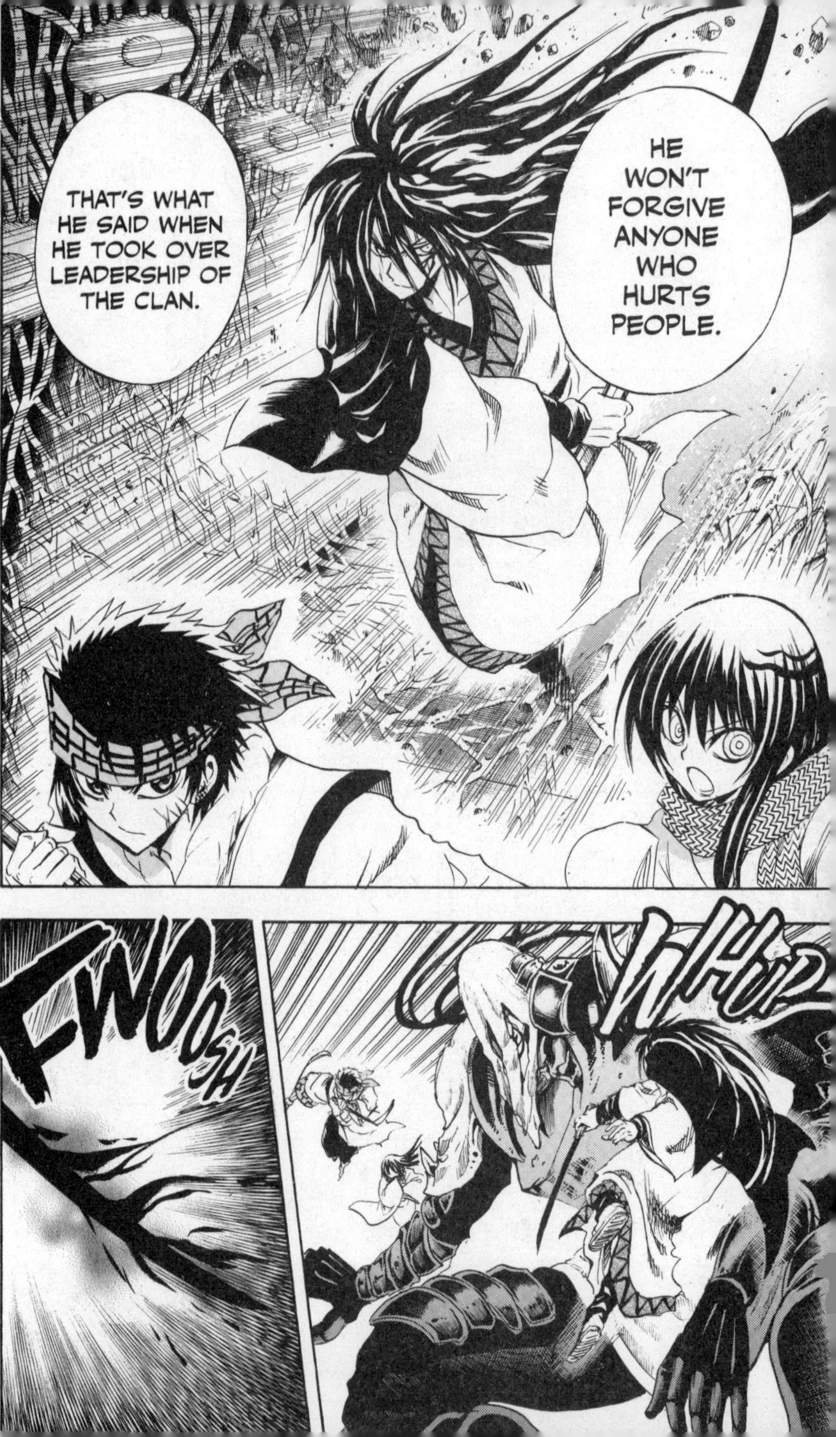
HE WON'T FORGIVE ANYONE WHO HURTS PEOPLE.
THAT'S WHAT HE SAID WHEN HE TOOK OVER LEADERSHIP OF THE CLAN.
FWOOSH

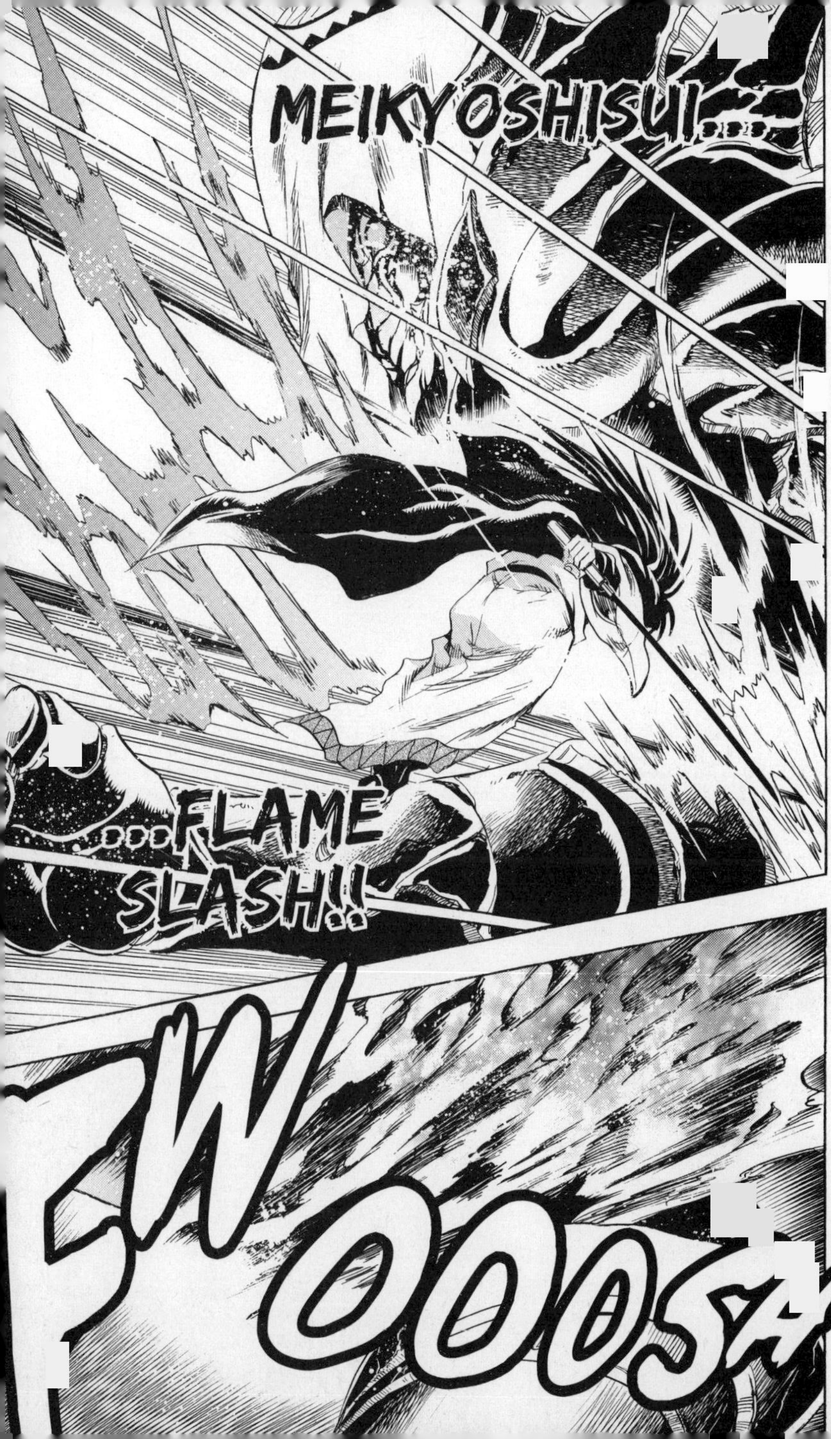
MEIKYOSHISUI...
...FLAME SLASH!!
WOOOSH

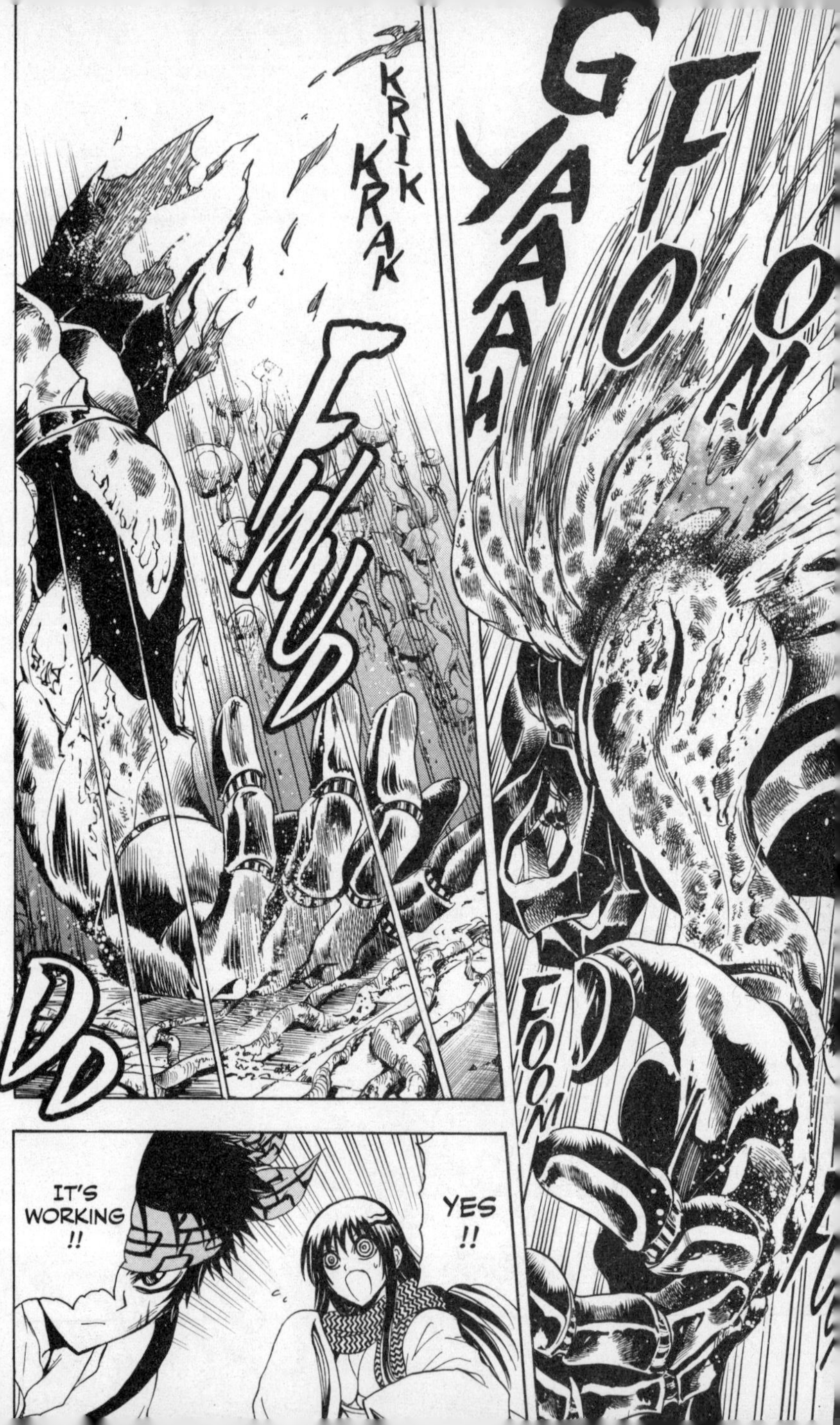
YAAAH
FOOM
KRIK KRAK
YES !!
IT'S WORKING !!

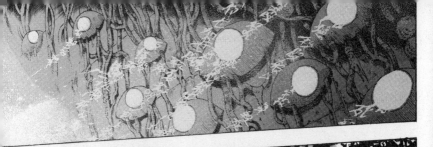

?!

RRRMMMMMM

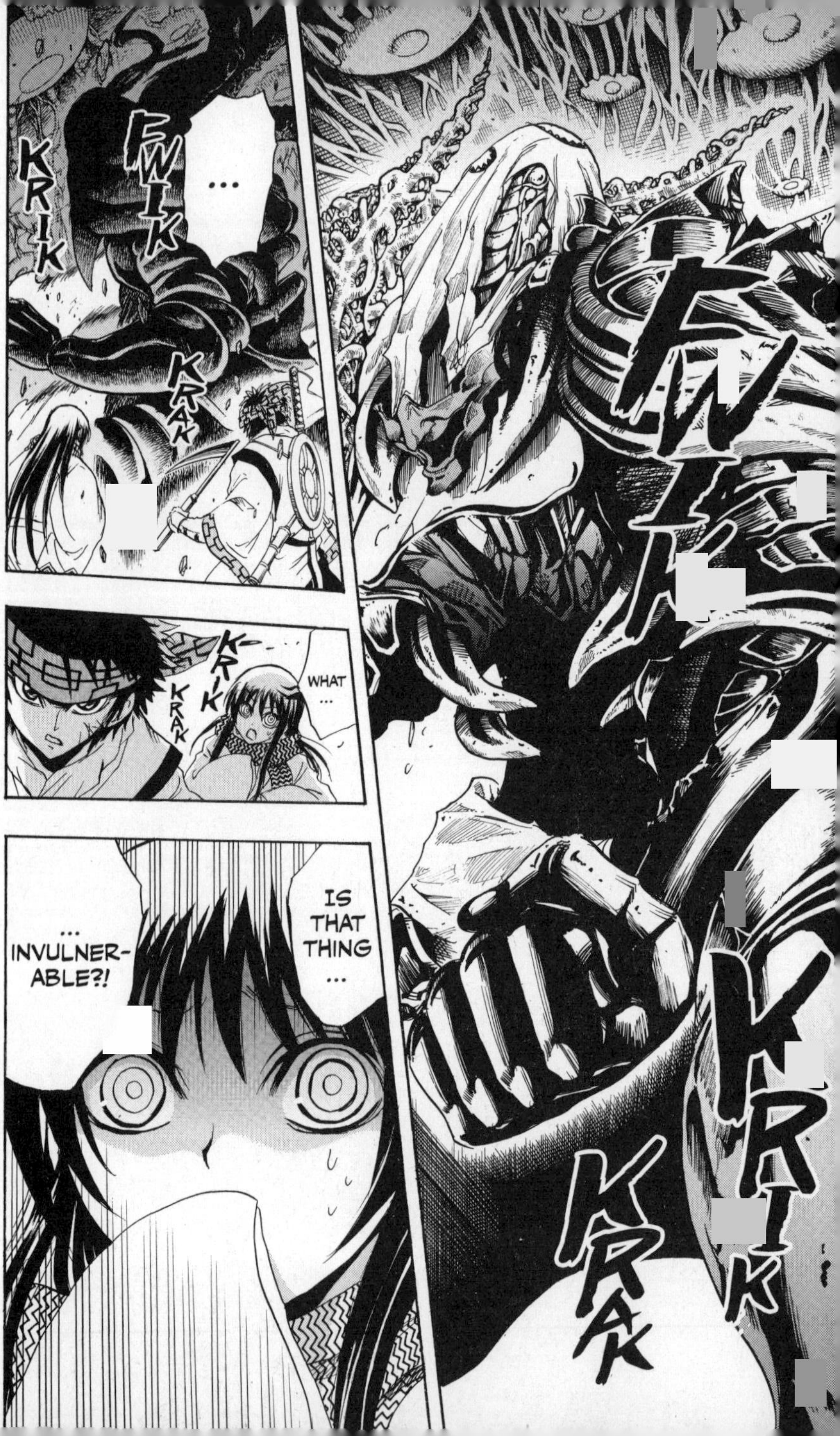
KRIK
KRAK
FWIK
...
KRIK
KRAK
K-RIK
KRAK
WHAT ...
IS THAT THING ...
... INVULNER-ABLE?!

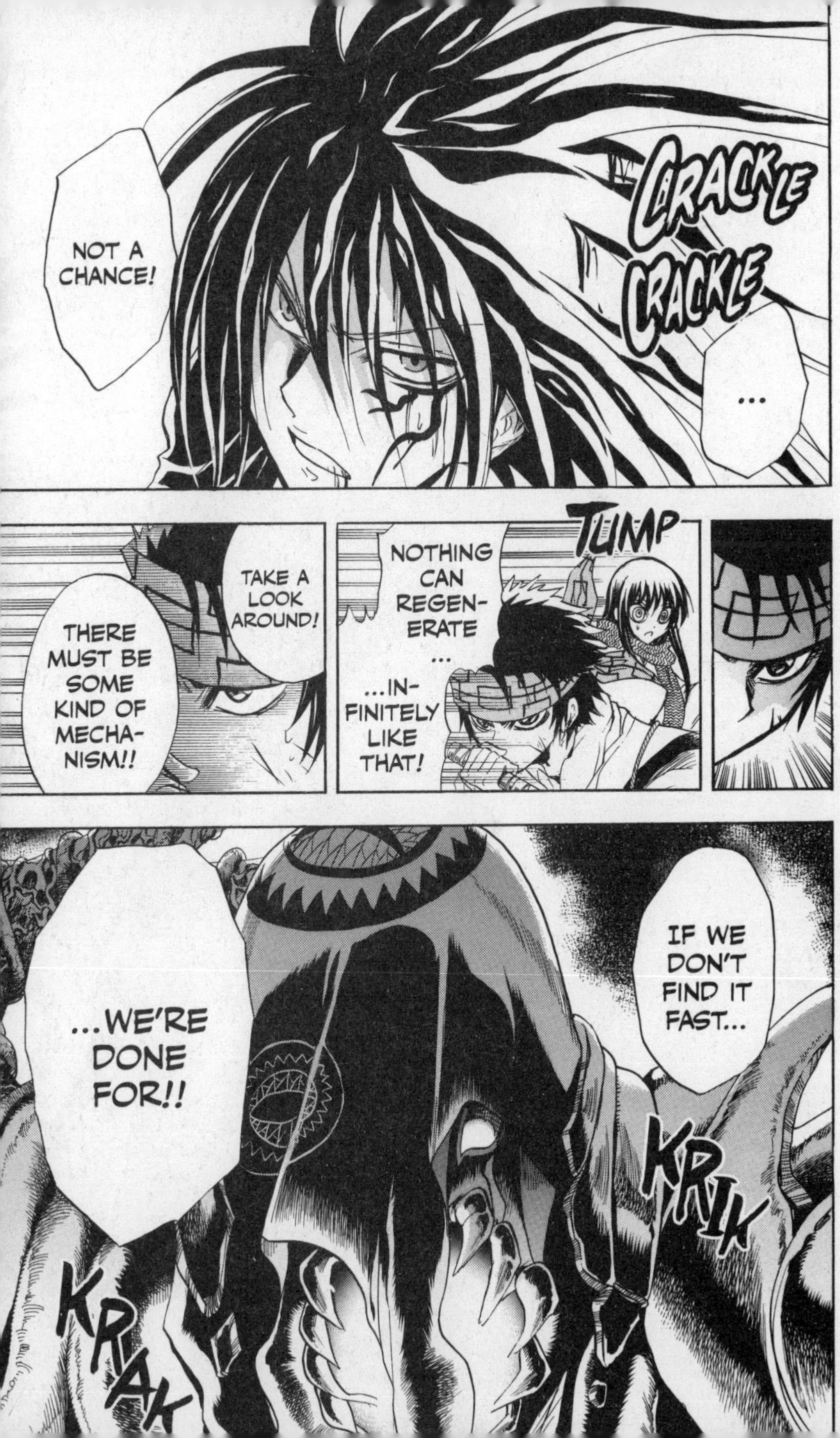
CRACKLE
CRACKLE
...
NOT A CHANCE!
TUMP
NOTHING CAN REGENERATE...
...INFINITELY LIKE THAT!
TAKE A LOOK AROUND!
THERE MUST BE SOME KIND OF MECHANISM!!
IF WE DON'T FIND IT FAST...
...WE'RE DONE FOR!!
KRIK
KRAK

Act 181: A Way Out

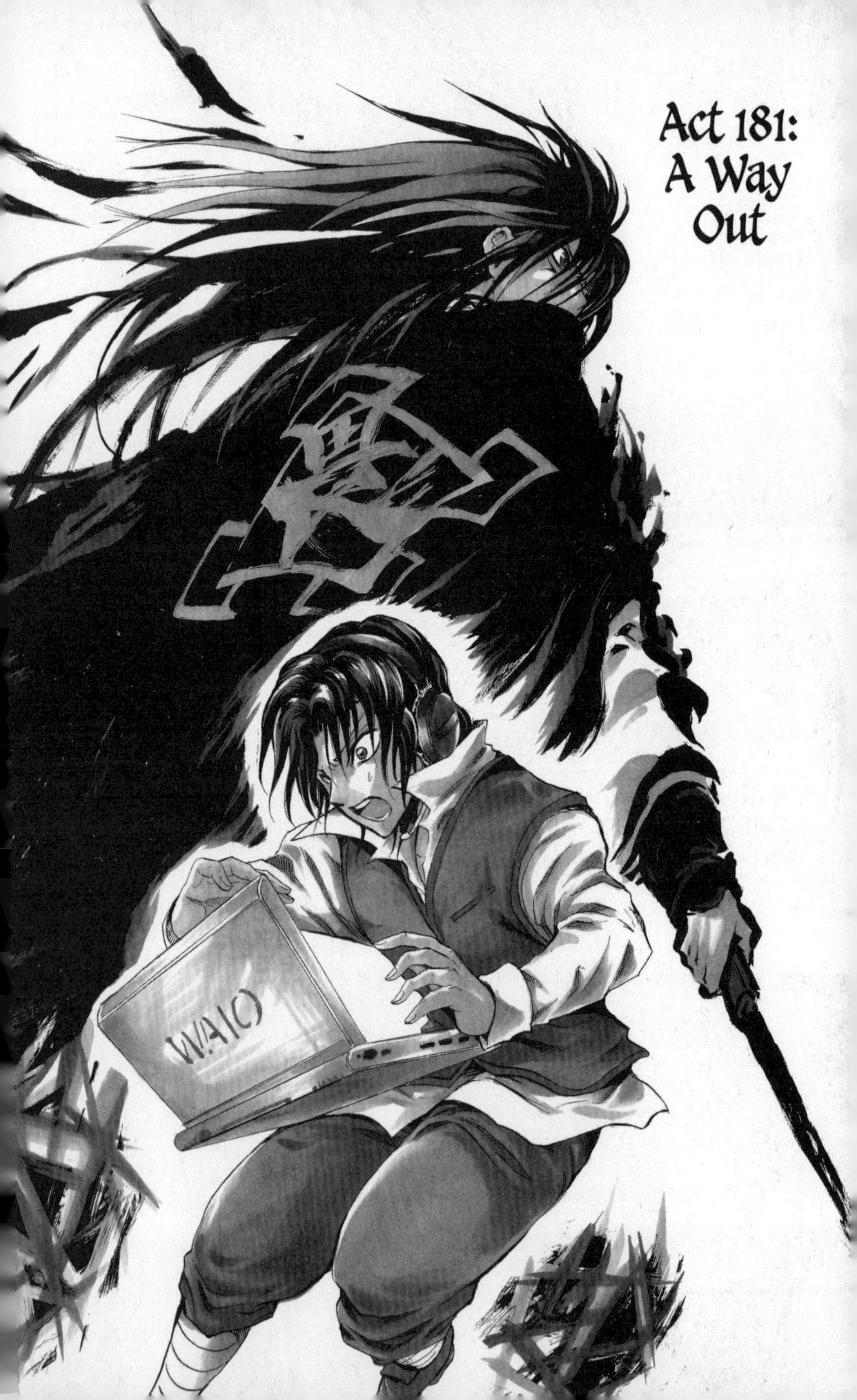

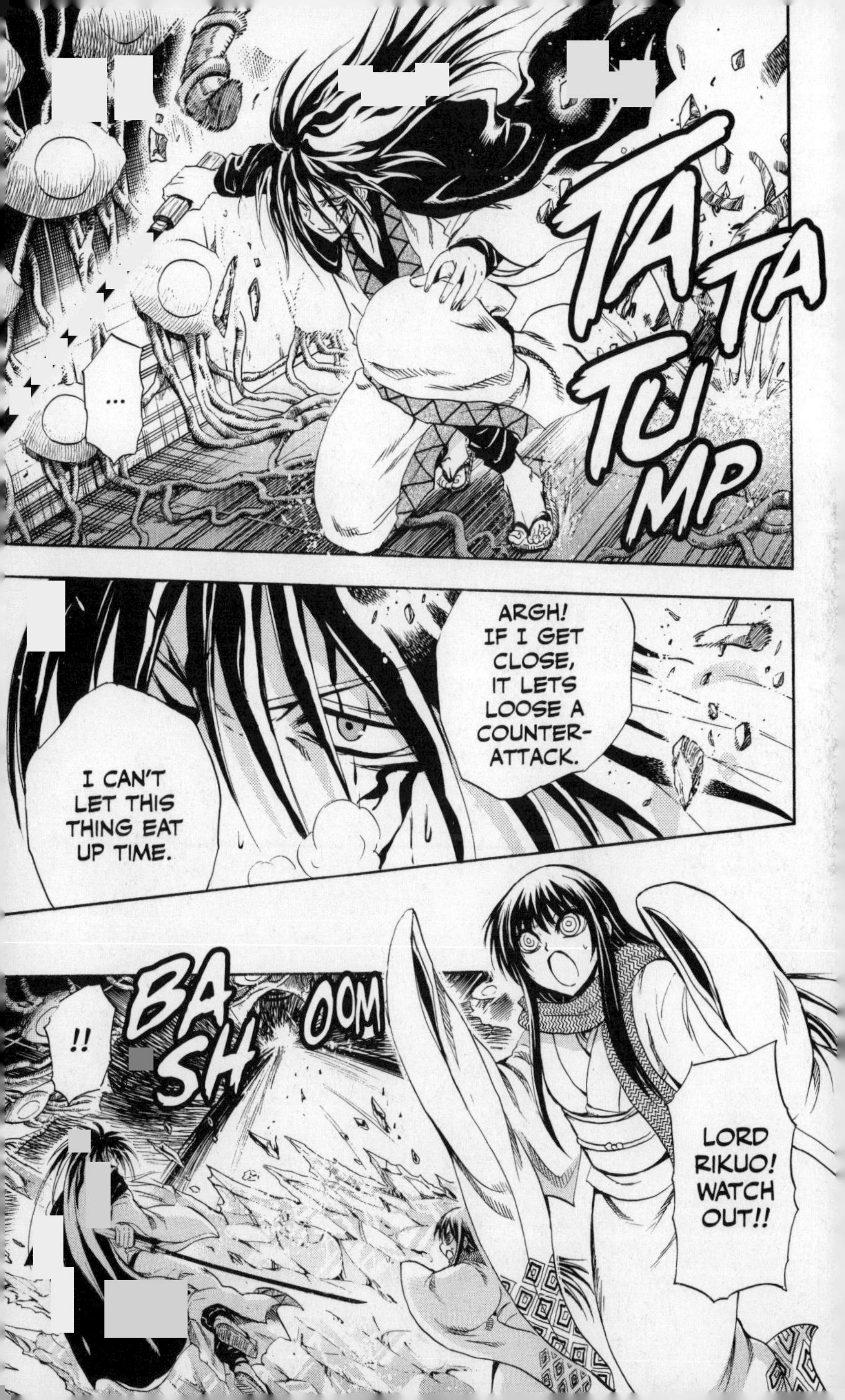
TATATUMP
...
ARGH! IF I GET CLOSE, IT LETS LOOSE A COUNTER-ATTACK.
I CAN'T LET THIS THING EAT UP TIME.
LORD RIKUO! WATCH OUT!!
BASHOOM
!!

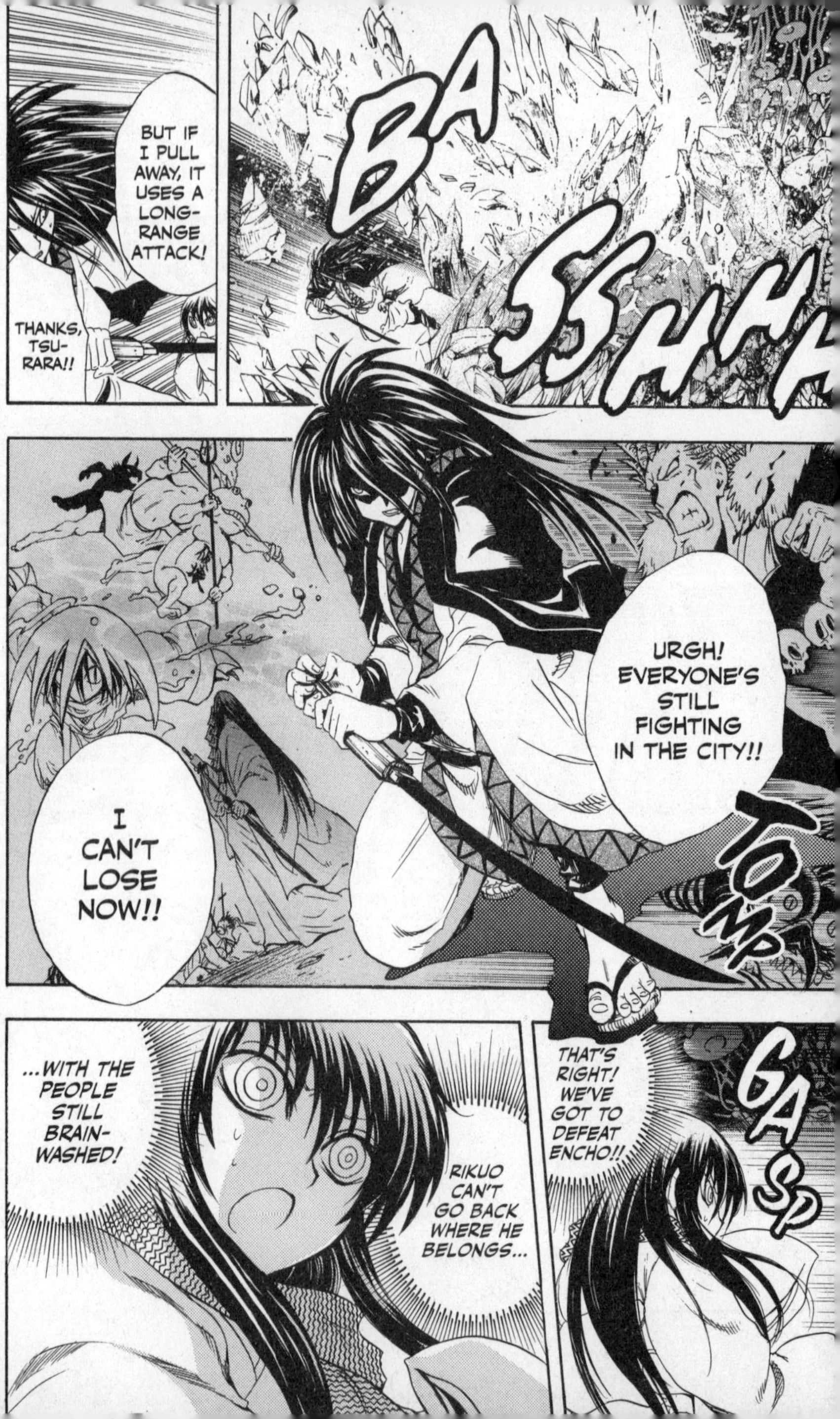
BA
SSHHH
BUT IF I PULL AWAY, IT USES A LONG-RANGE ATTACK!
THANKS, TSURARA!!
URGH! EVERYONE'S STILL FIGHTING IN THE CITY!!
TOMP
I CAN'T LOSE NOW!!
GASP
THAT'S RIGHT! WE'VE GOT TO DEFEAT ENCHO!!
RIKUO CAN'T GO BACK WHERE HE BELONGS...
...WITH THE PEOPLE STILL BRAIN-WASHED!

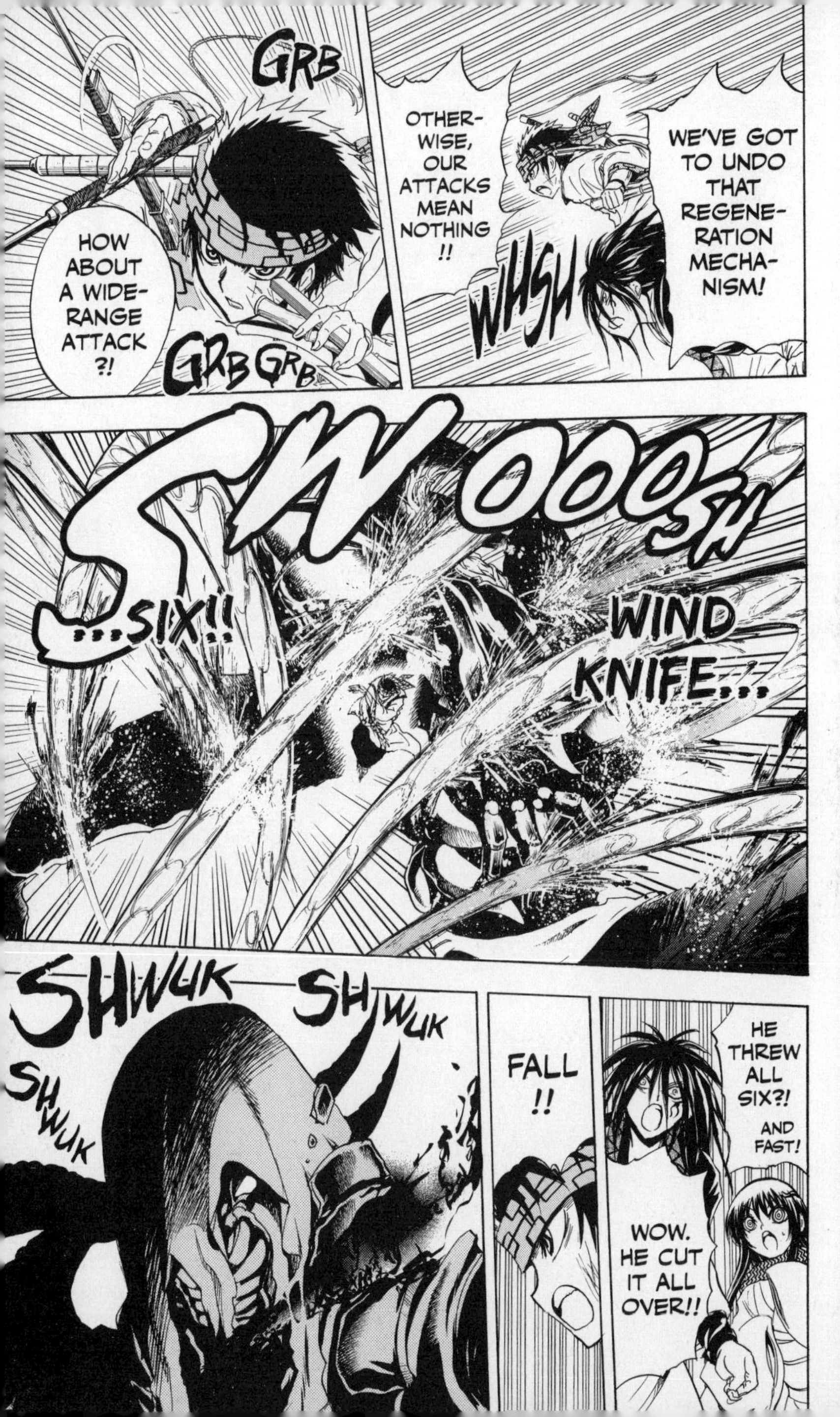
WE'VE GOT TO UNDO THAT REGENERATION MECHANISM!
OTHERWISE, OUR ATTACKS MEAN NOTHING!!
WHSH
GRB
HOW ABOUT A WIDE-RANGE ATTACK?!
GRB GRB
SWOOOSH
WIND KNIFE...
...SIX!!
HE THREW ALL SIX?!
AND FAST!
FALL!!
WOW. HE CUT IT ALL OVER!!
SHWUK
SHWUK
SHWUK

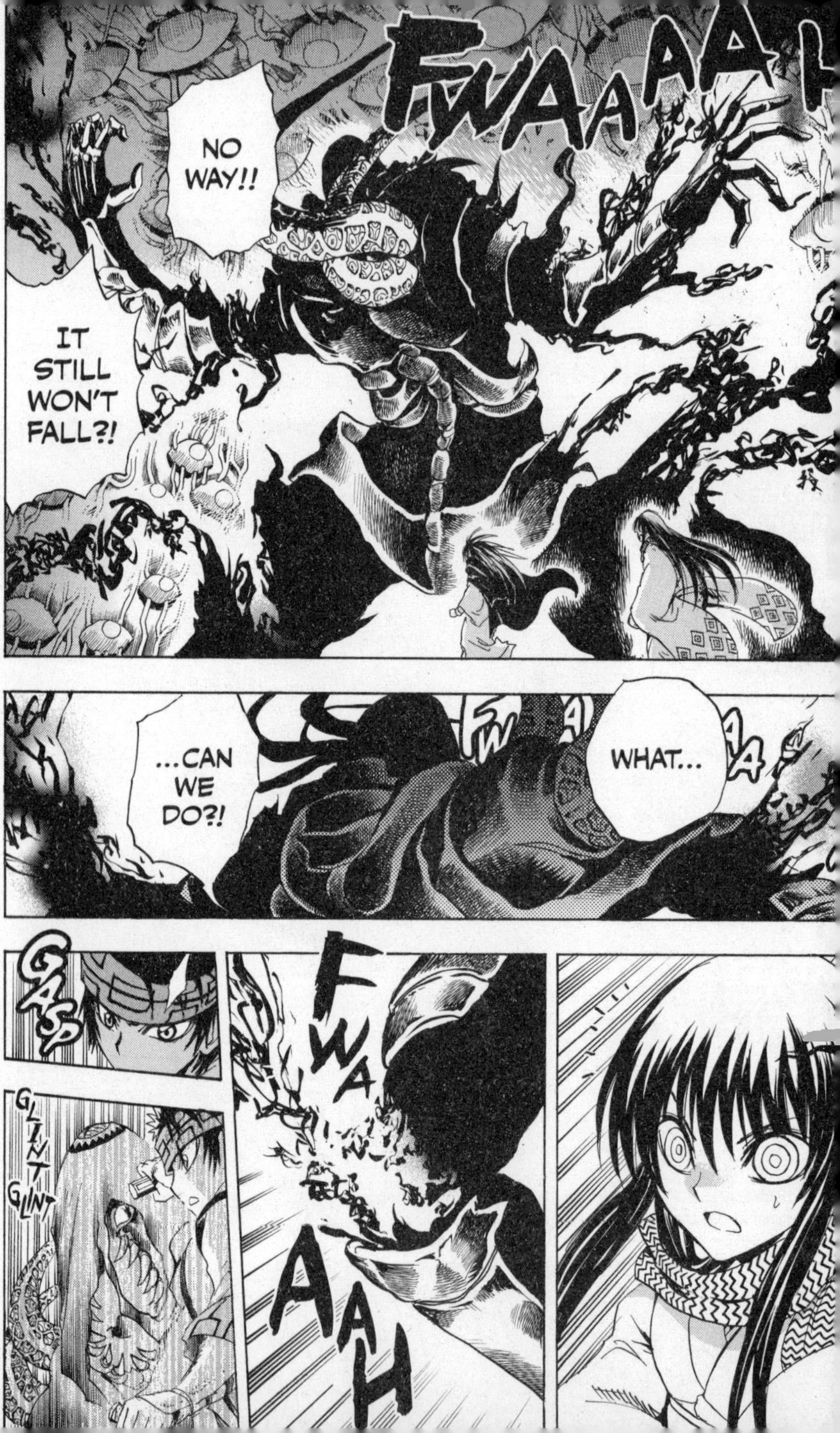
FWAAAAH
NO WAY!!
IT STILL WON'T FALL?!
WHAT...
FWAAAA
...CAN WE DO?!
FWAAAH
GASP
GLINT GLINT

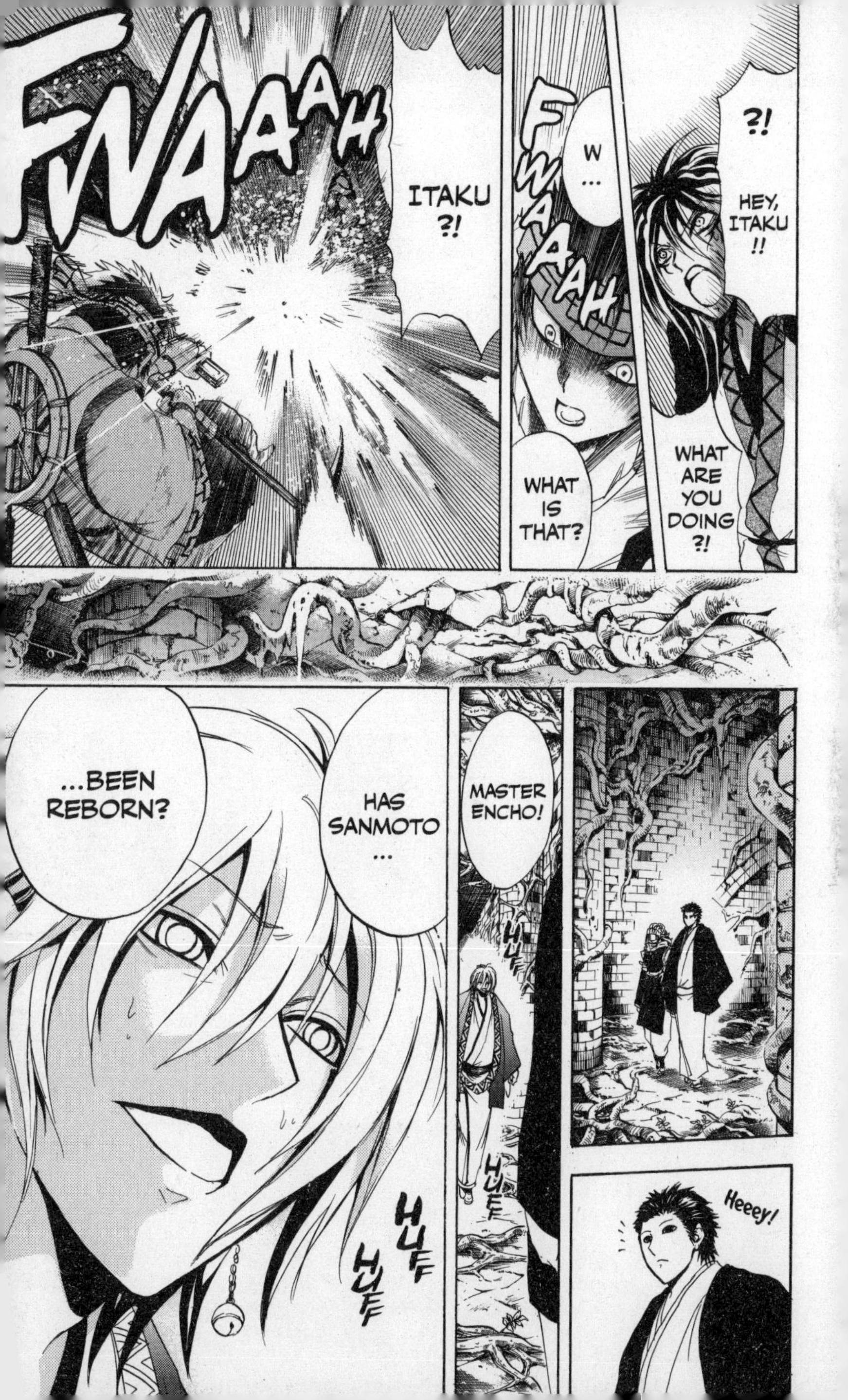
?!
HEY, ITAKU !!
WHAT ARE YOU DOING ?!
FWAAAAH
W ...
WHAT IS THAT?
FWAAAH
ITAKU ?!
Heeey!
MASTER ENCHO!
HUFF
HUFF
HAS SANMOTO ...
...BEEN REBORN?
HUFF
HUFF

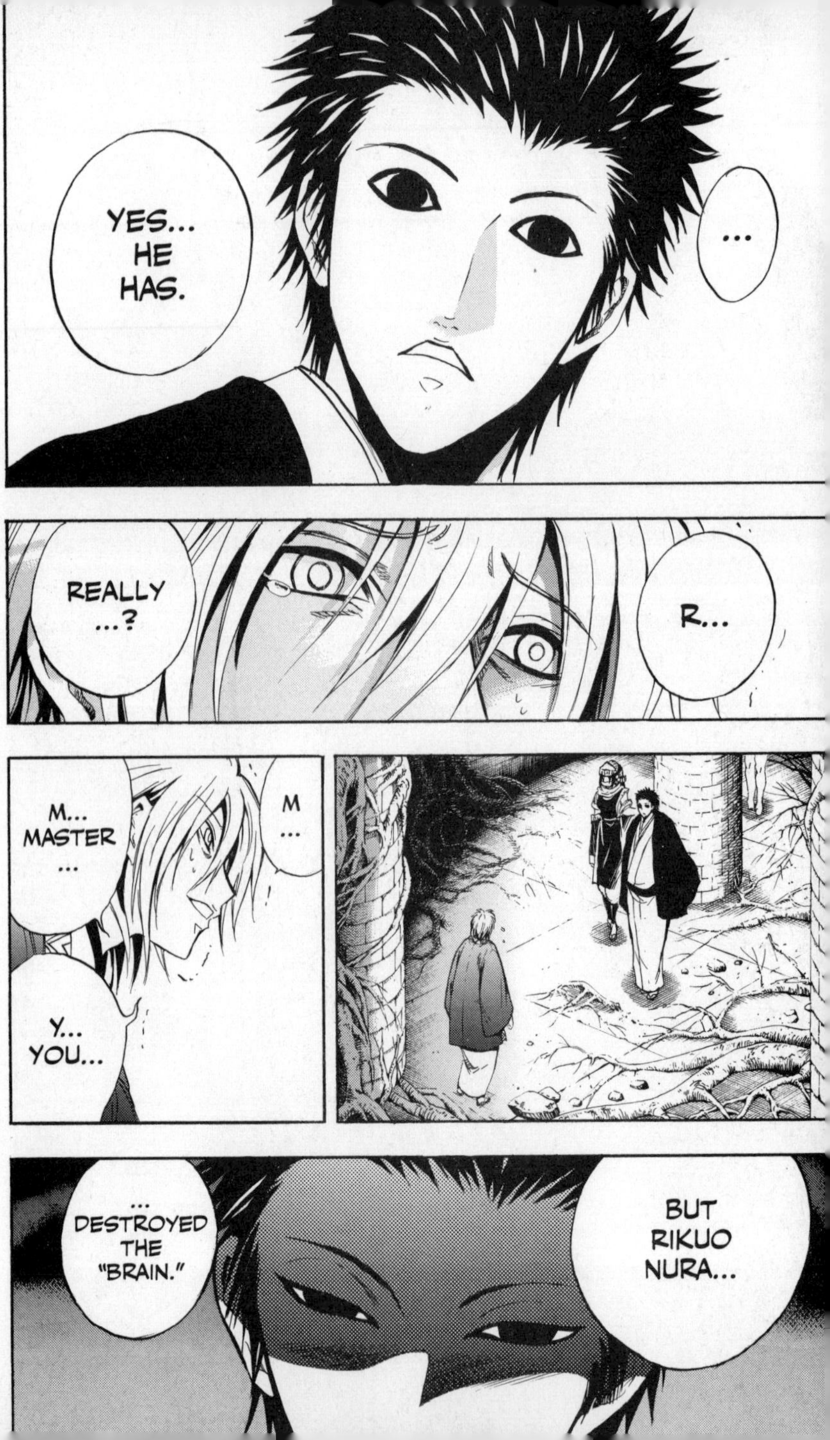
...
YES... HE HAS.
R...
REALLY ...?
M ...
M... MASTER ...
Y... YOU...
BUT RIKUO NURA...
... DESTROYED THE "BRAIN."

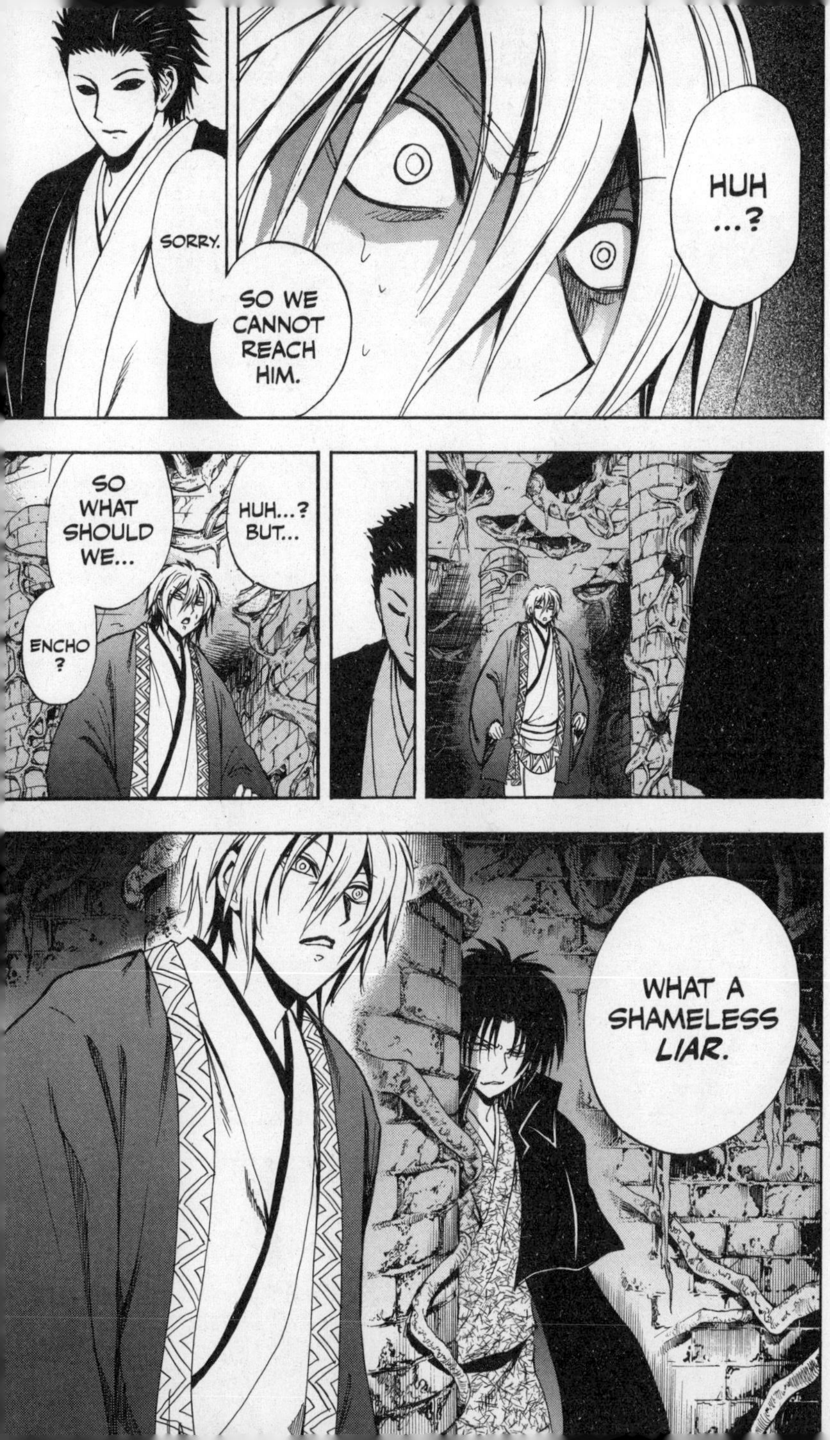
HUH ...?
SO WE CANNOT REACH HIM.
SORRY.
HUH...? BUT...
SO WHAT SHOULD WE...
ENCHO ?
WHAT A SHAMELESS *LIAR*.

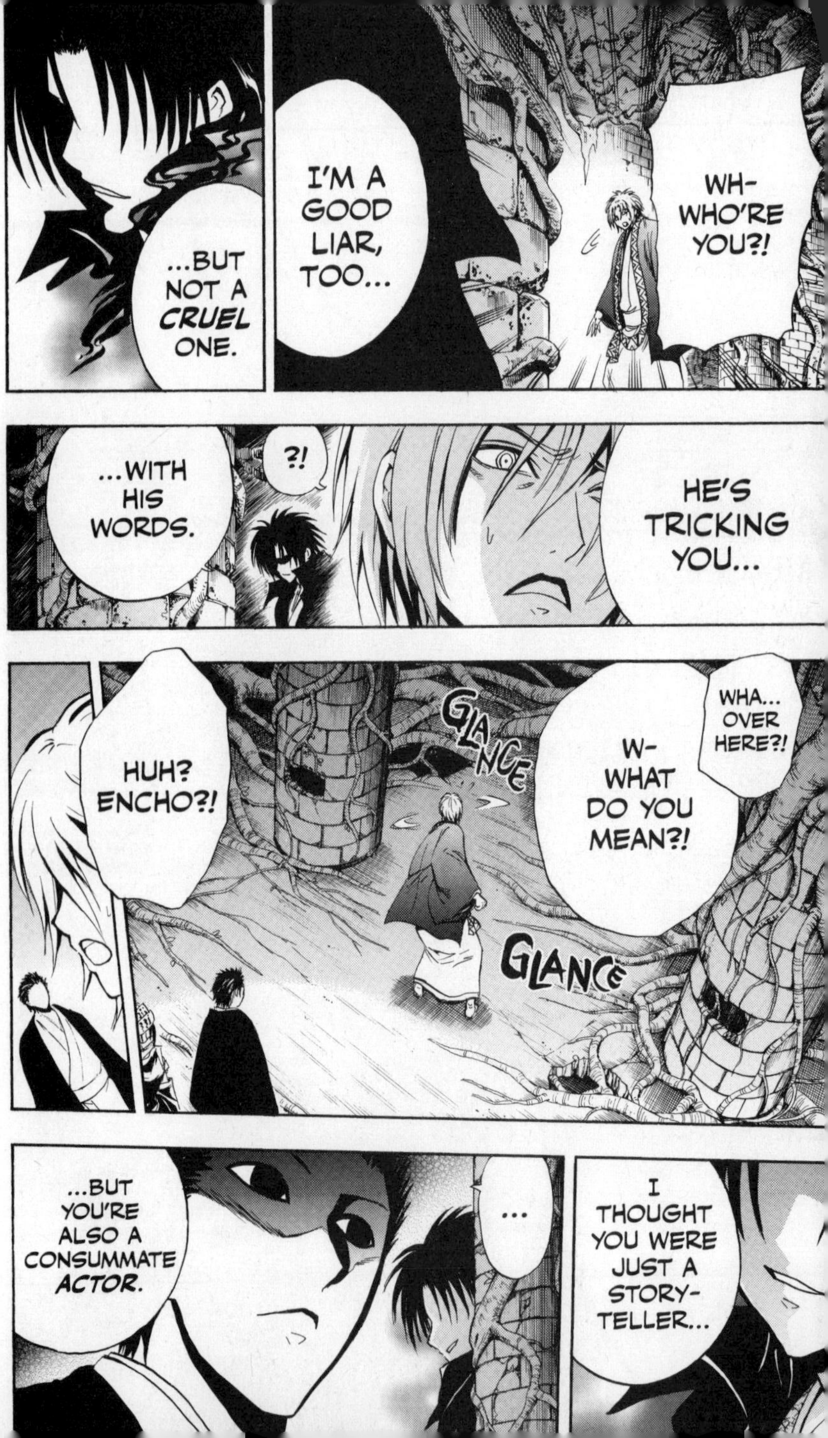
WH- WHO'RE YOU?!
I'M A GOOD LIAR, TOO...
...BUT NOT A *CRUEL* ONE.
HE'S TRICKING YOU...
?!
...WITH HIS WORDS.
WHA... OVER HERE?!
W- WHAT DO YOU MEAN?!
GLANCE
GLANCE
HUH? ENCHO?!
I THOUGHT YOU WERE JUST A STORY-TELLER...
...
...BUT YOU'RE ALSO A CONSUMMATE *ACTOR*.

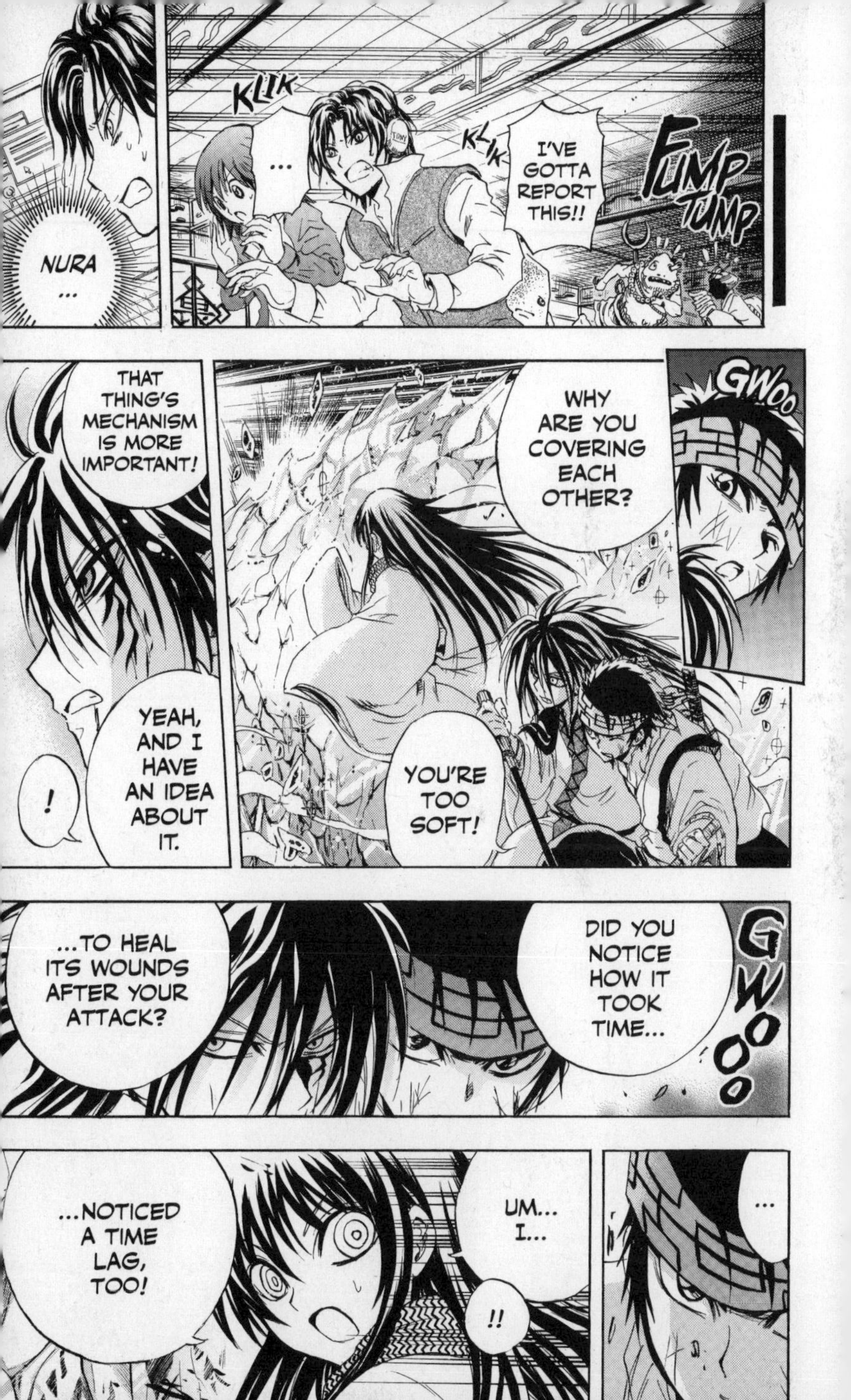

FUMP TUMP
KLIK KLIK
I'VE GOTTA REPORT THIS!!
...
NURA ...
GWOO
WHY ARE YOU COVERING EACH OTHER?
YOU'RE TOO SOFT!
THAT THING'S MECHANISM IS MORE IMPORTANT!
YEAH, AND I HAVE AN IDEA ABOUT IT.
!
GWOOOO
DID YOU NOTICE HOW IT TOOK TIME...
...TO HEAL ITS WOUNDS AFTER YOUR ATTACK?
...
UM... I...
!!
...NOTICED A TIME LAG, TOO!

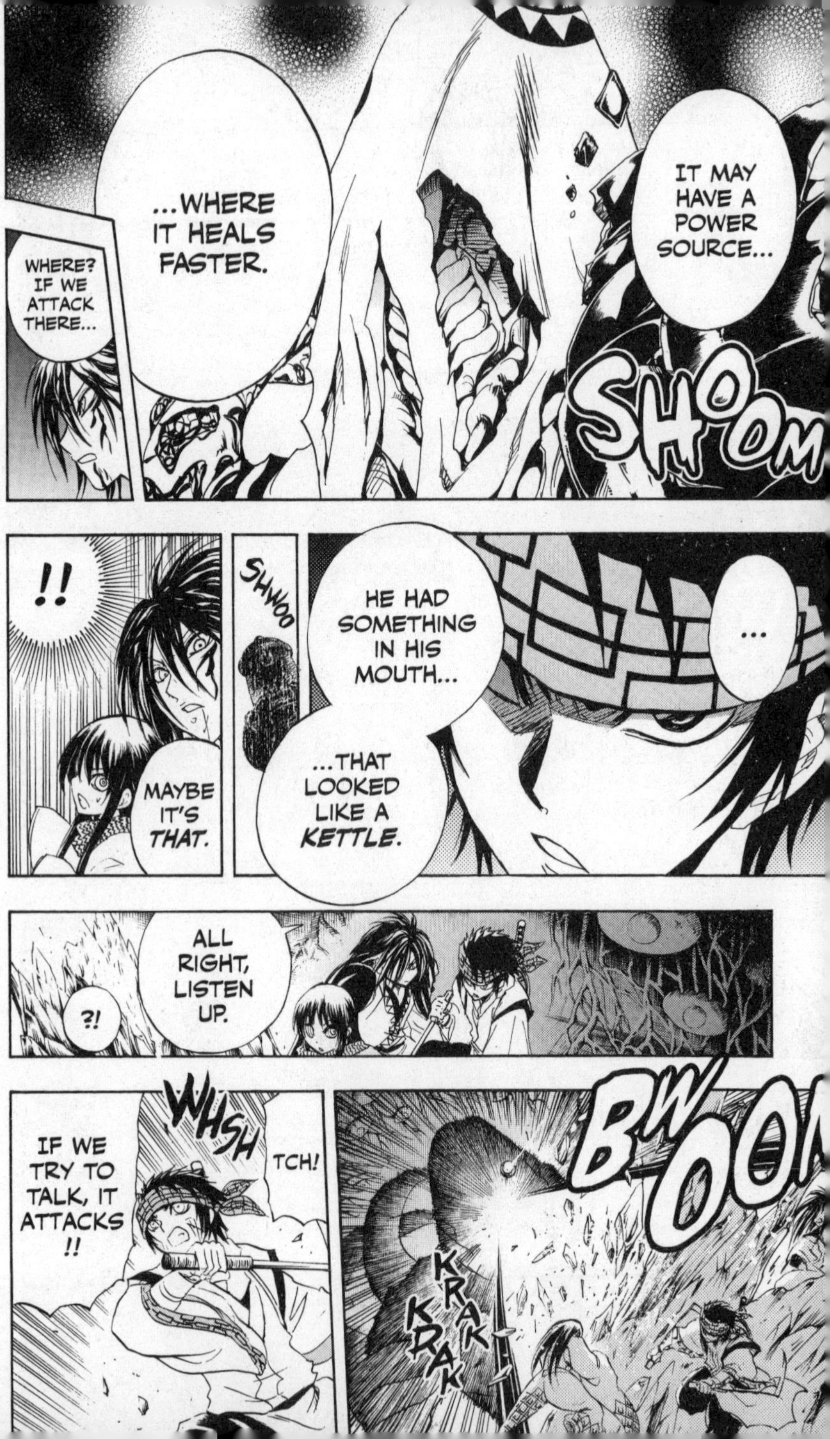
IT MAY HAVE A POWER SOURCE...
SHOOM
...WHERE IT HEALS FASTER.
WHERE? IF WE ATTACK THERE...
...
HE HAD SOMETHING IN HIS MOUTH...
...THAT LOOKED LIKE A *KETTLE*.
SHWOO
!!
MAYBE IT'S *THAT*.
ALL RIGHT, LISTEN UP.
?!
BWOOM
KRAK
KDAK
WHSH
TCH!
IF WE TRY TO TALK, IT ATTACKS!!

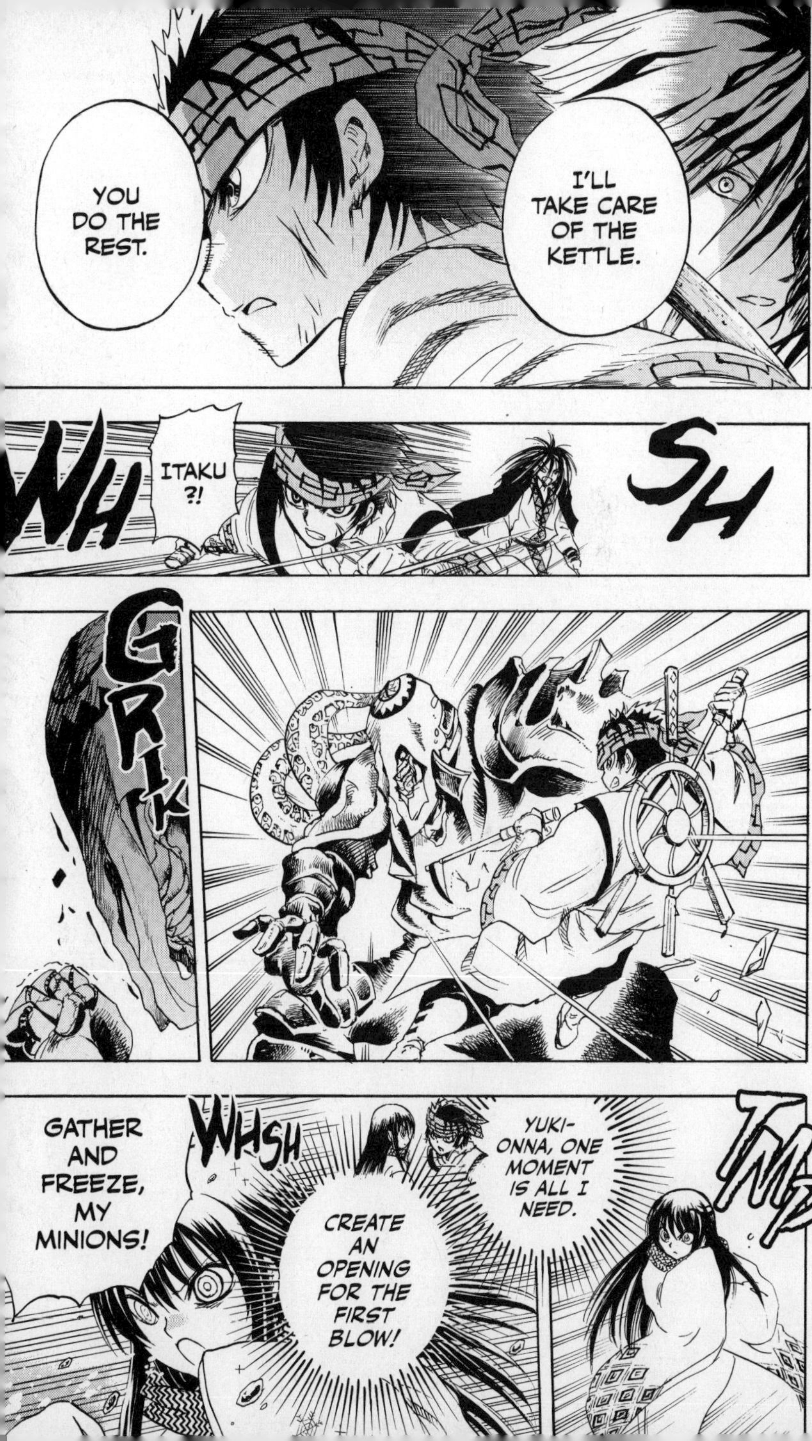
I'LL TAKE CARE OF THE KETTLE.
YOU DO THE REST.
SH
ITAKU ?!
WH
GRIK
TMP
YUKI-ONNA, ONE MOMENT IS ALL I NEED.
CREATE AN OPENING FOR THE FIRST BLOW!
WHSH
GATHER AND FREEZE, MY MINIONS!

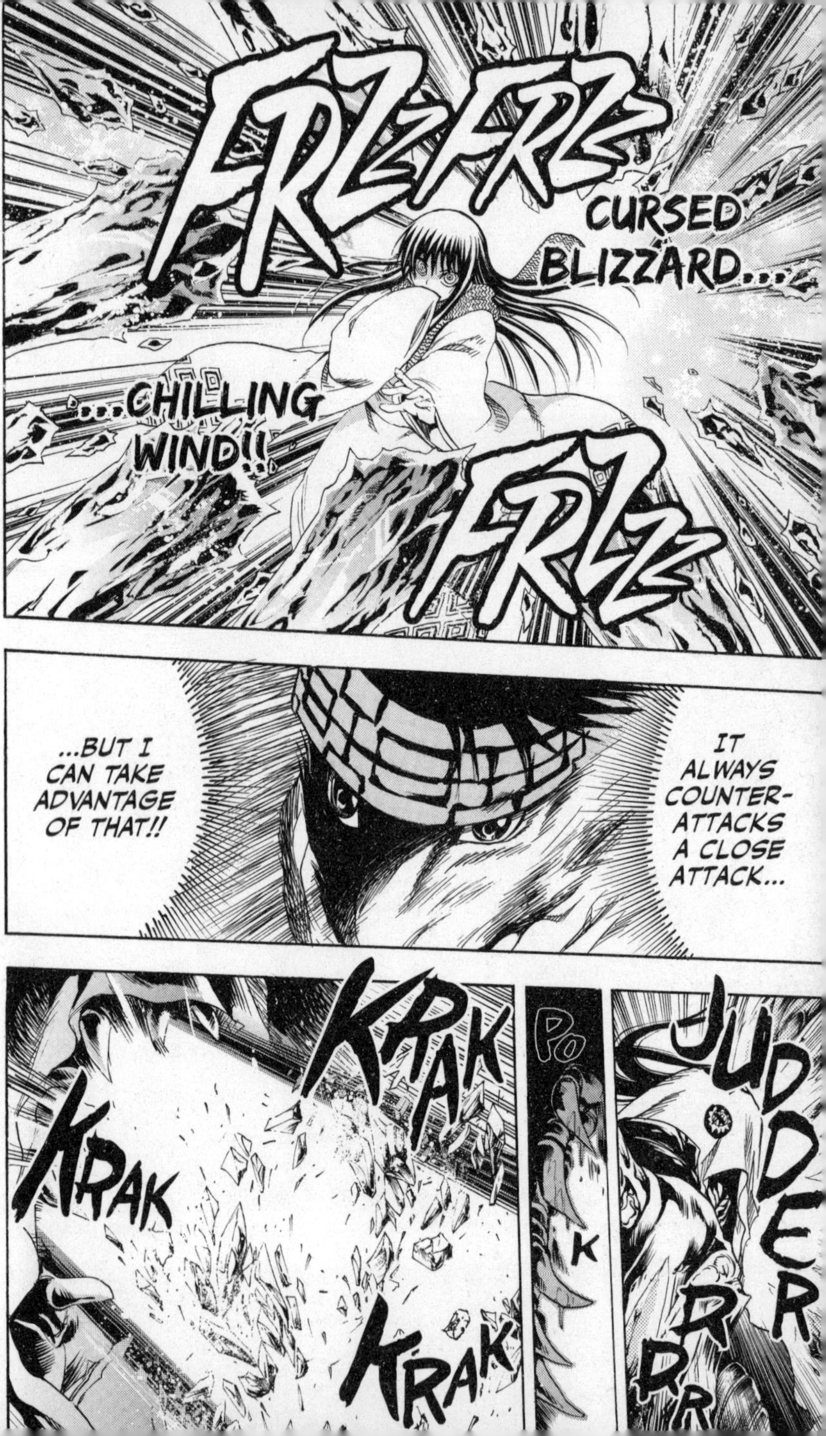
FRZFRZ
CURSED BLIZZARD...
...CHILLING WIND!!
FRZZ
IT ALWAYS COUNTER-ATTACKS A CLOSE ATTACK...
...BUT I CAN TAKE ADVANTAGE OF THAT!!
JUDDERRRR
PO
K
KRAK
KRAK
KRAK

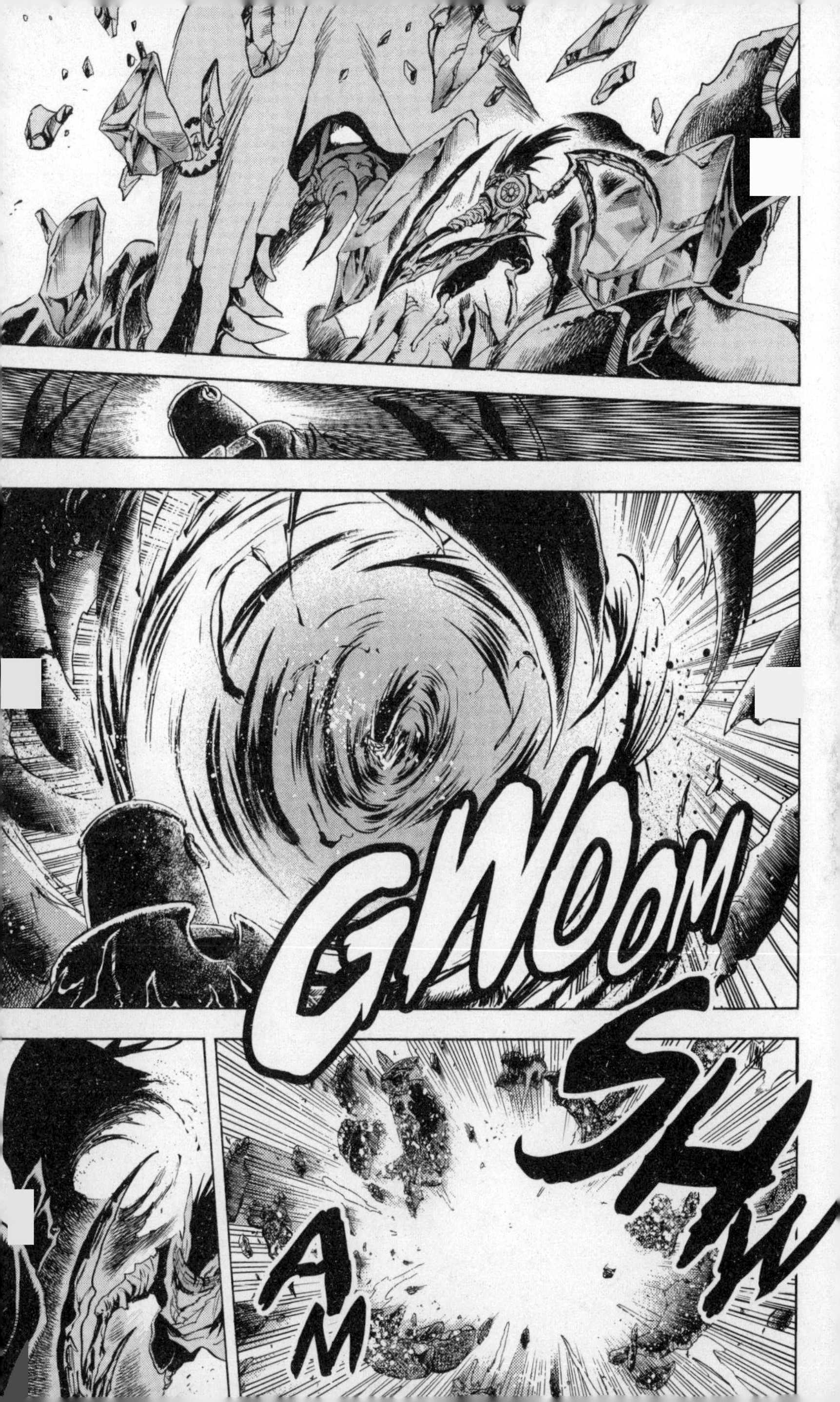
GWOOM
SHWAM

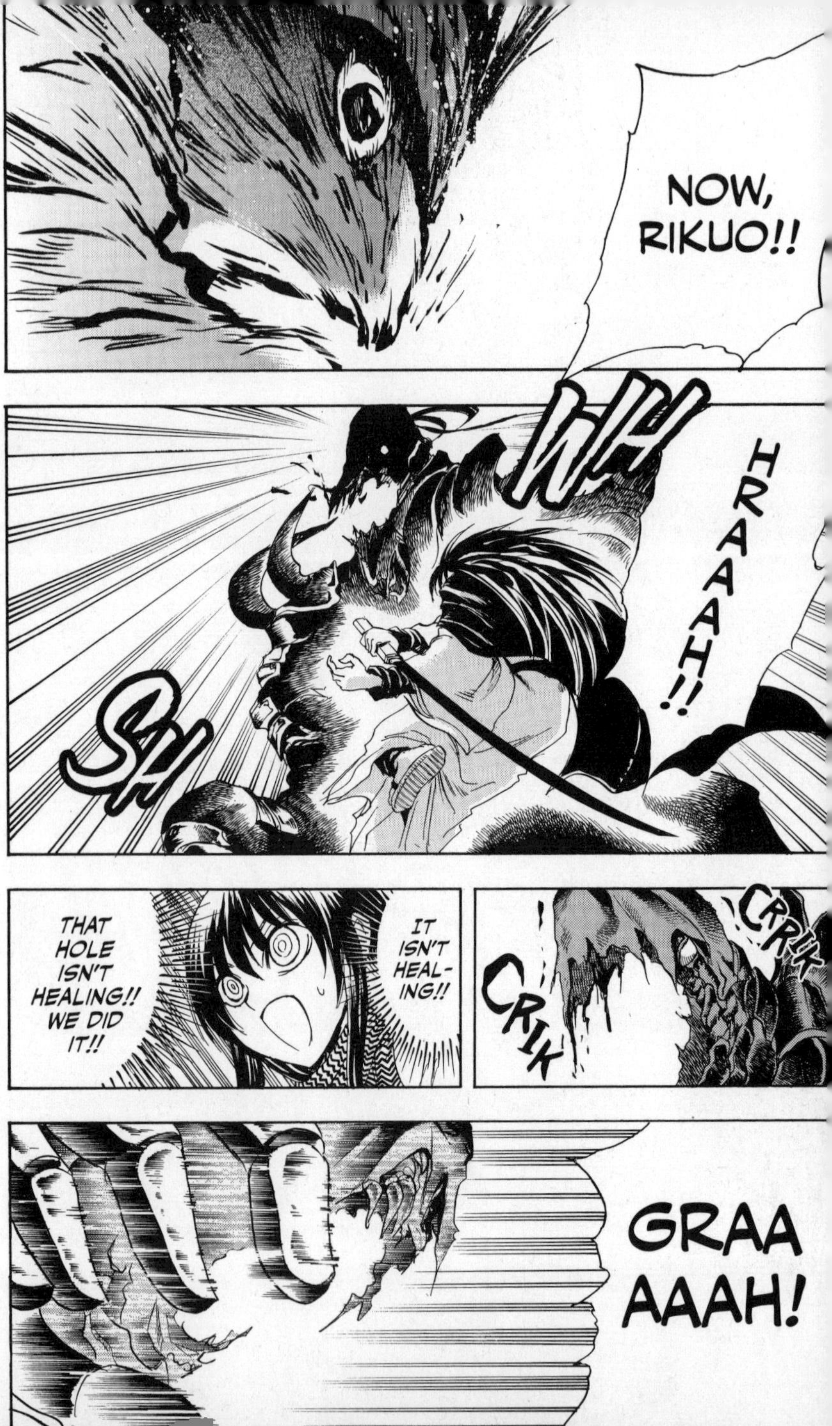
NOW, RIKUO!!
HRAAAAH!!
WH
SH
CRIK
CRIK
IT ISN'T HEAL-ING!!
THAT HOLE ISN'T HEALING!! WE DID IT!!
GRAA AAAH!

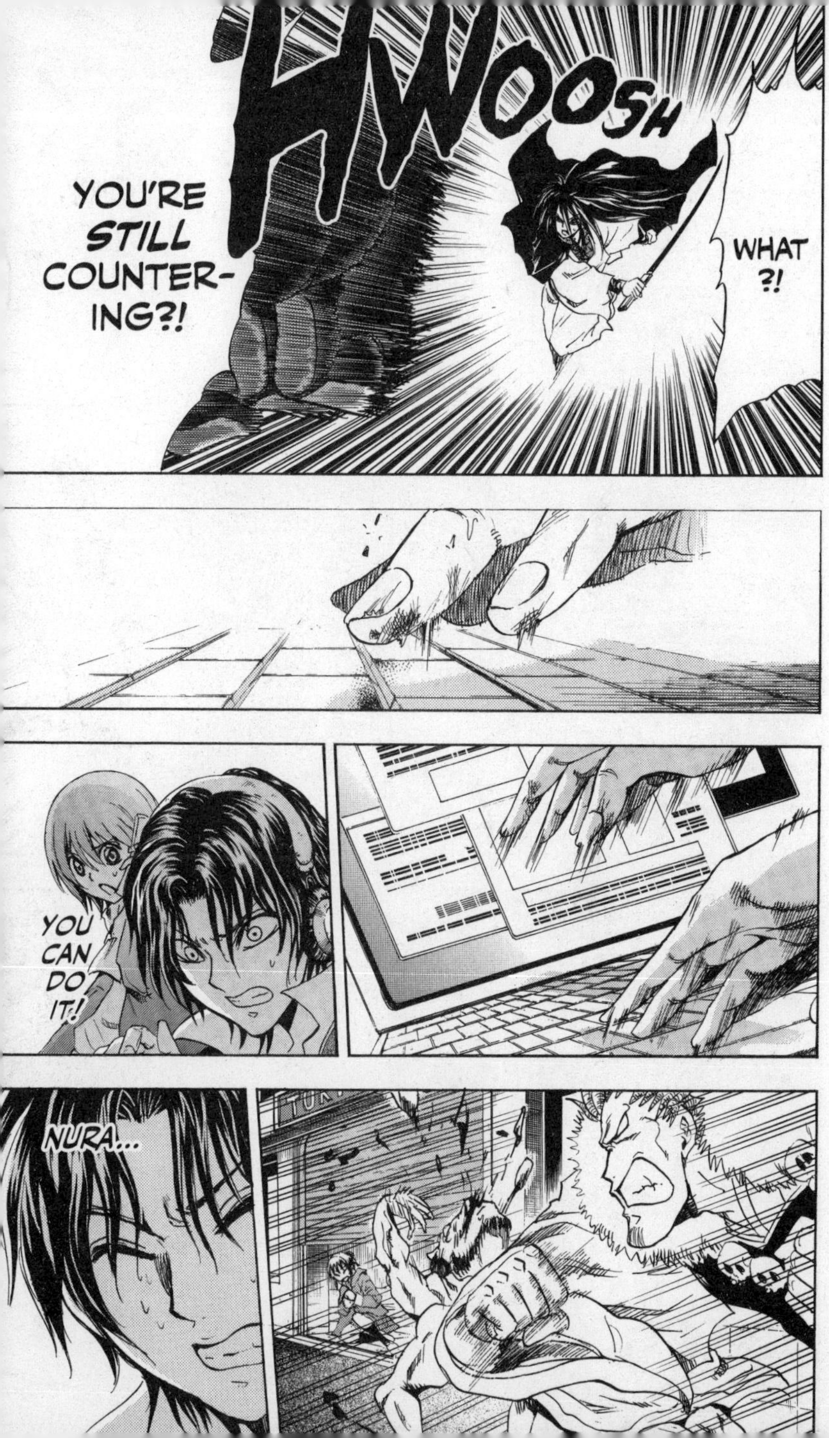
HWOOSH
WHAT?!
YOU'RE STILL COUNTER-ING?!
YOU CAN DO IT!
NURA...

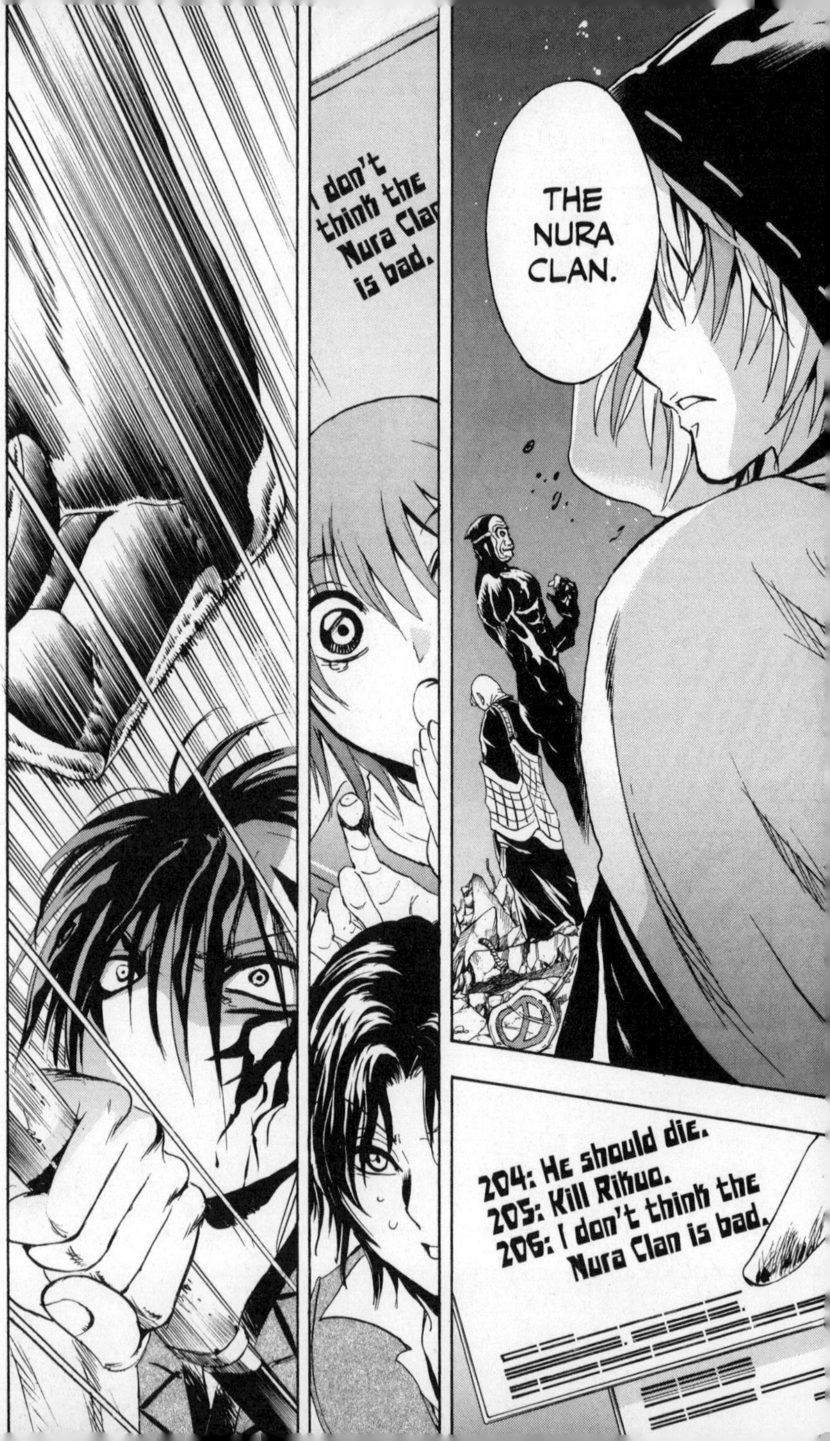
THE NURA CLAN.
204: He should die.
205: Kill Rikuo.
206: I don't think the Nura Clan is bad.
I don't think the Nura Cla is bad.

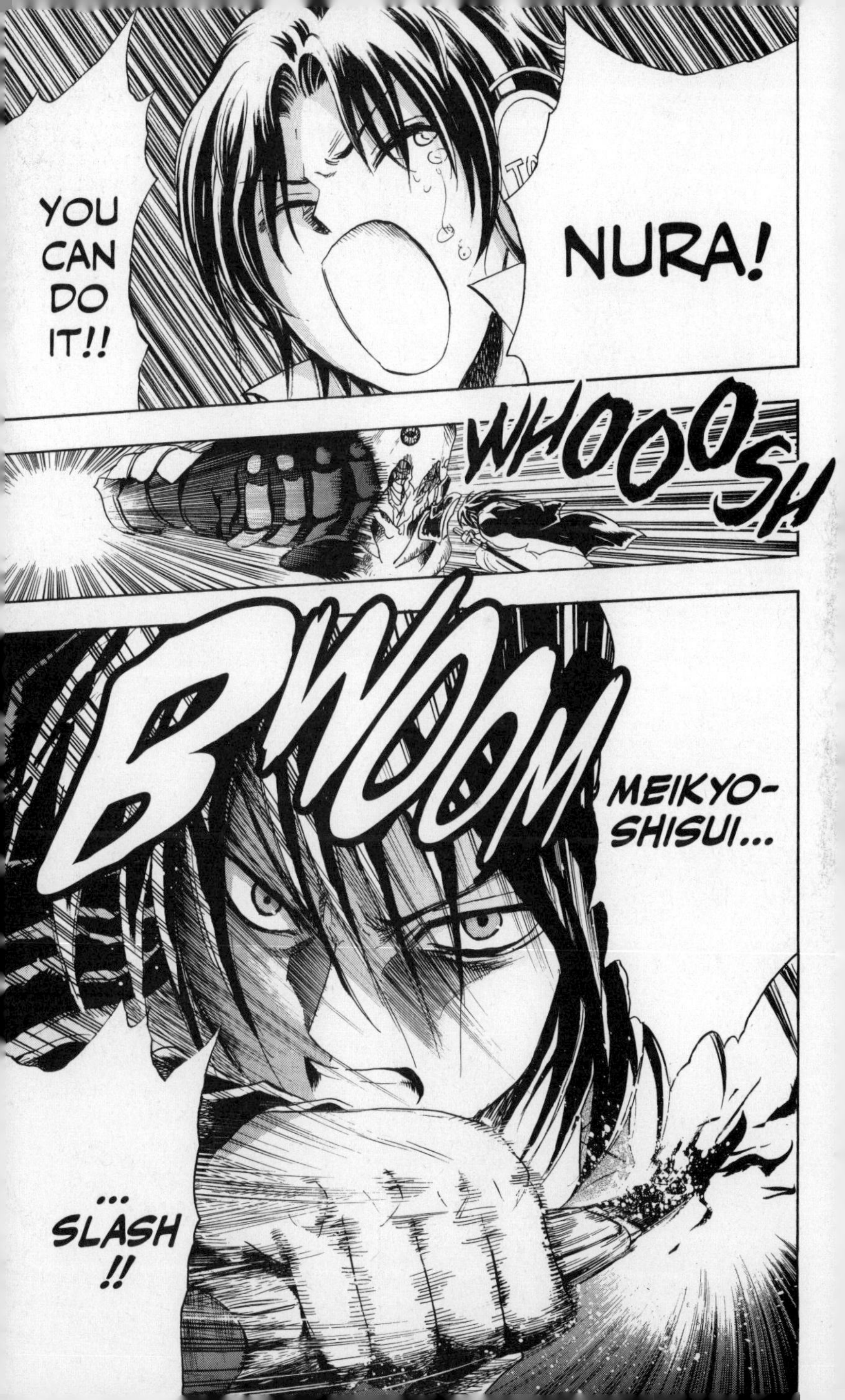
NURA!
YOU CAN DO IT!!
WHOOOOSH
BWOOM
MEIKYO-SHISUI...
...SLASH!!

A Spring Storm of Image Changes, Part 4

~At School~

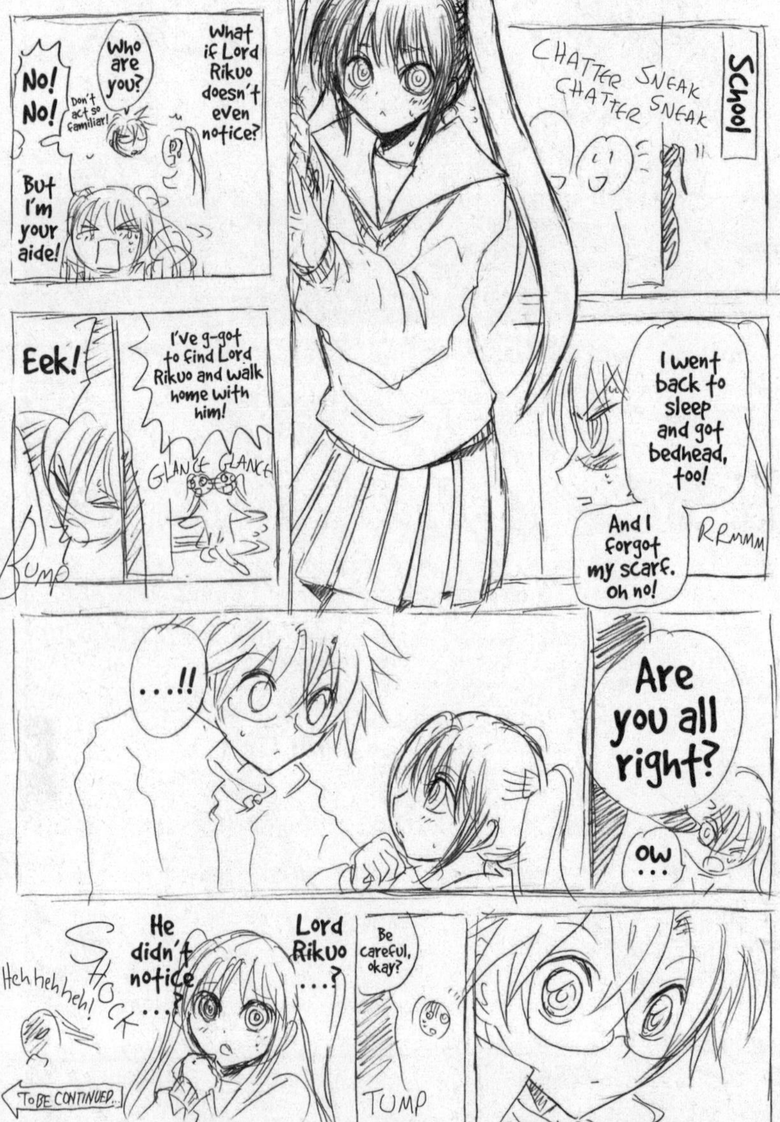
School
CHATTER CHATTER
SNEAK SNEAK
I went back to sleep and got bedhead, too!
And I forgot my scarf. Oh no!
RRMMM
What if Lord Rikuo doesn't even notice?
Who are you?
Don't act so familiar!
No! No!
But I'm your aide!
I've g-got to find Lord Rikuo and walk home with him!
GLANCE GLANCE
Eek!
BUMP
Are you all right?
Ow...
....!!
Be careful, okay?
TUMP
Lord Rikuo...?
He didn't notice...?
SHOCK
Heh heh heh!
TO BE CONTINUED...

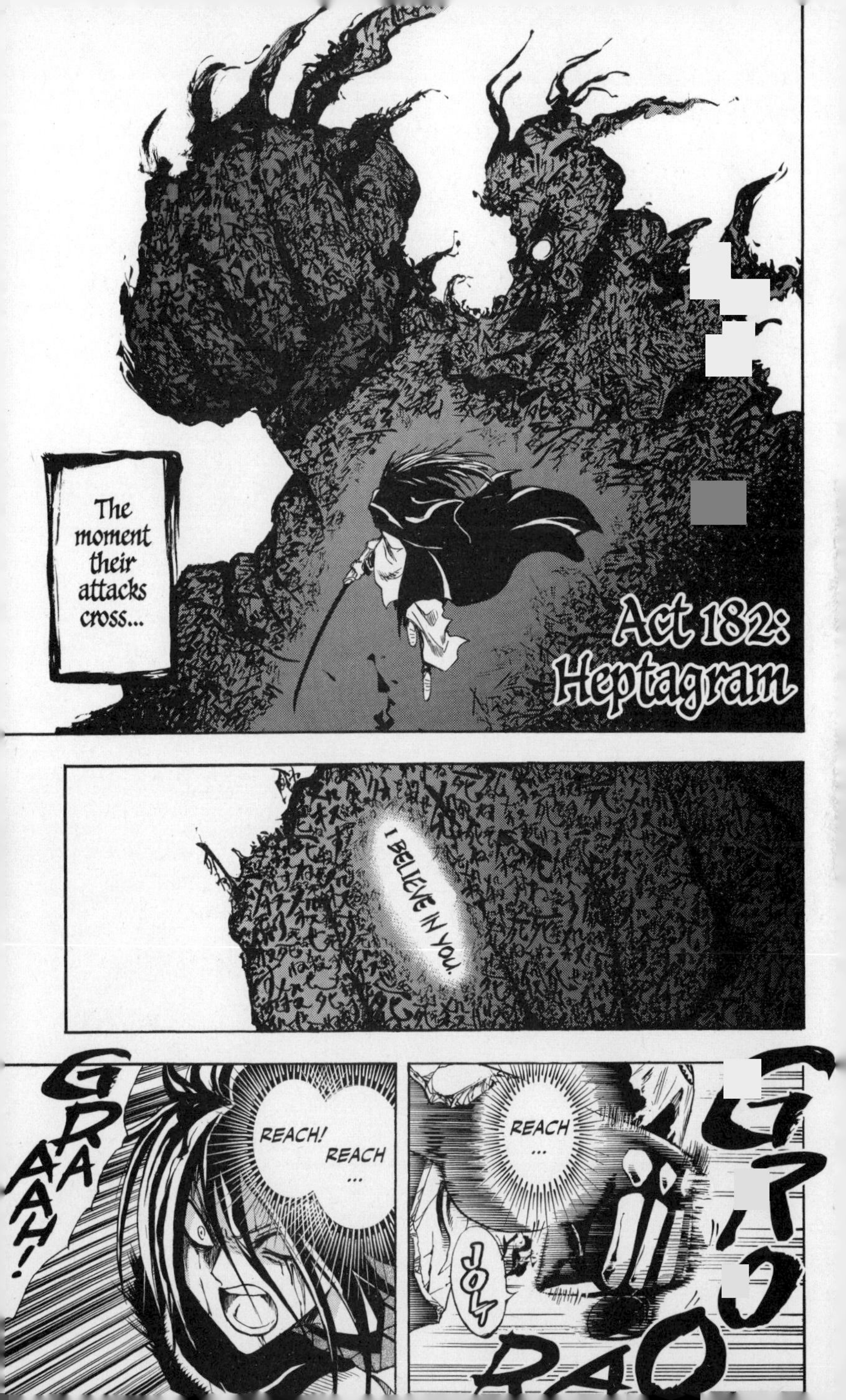
The moment their attacks cross...
Act 182: Heptagram
I BELIEVE IN YOU.
REACH ...
JOLT
RAO
REACH! REACH ...
GRAAAH!

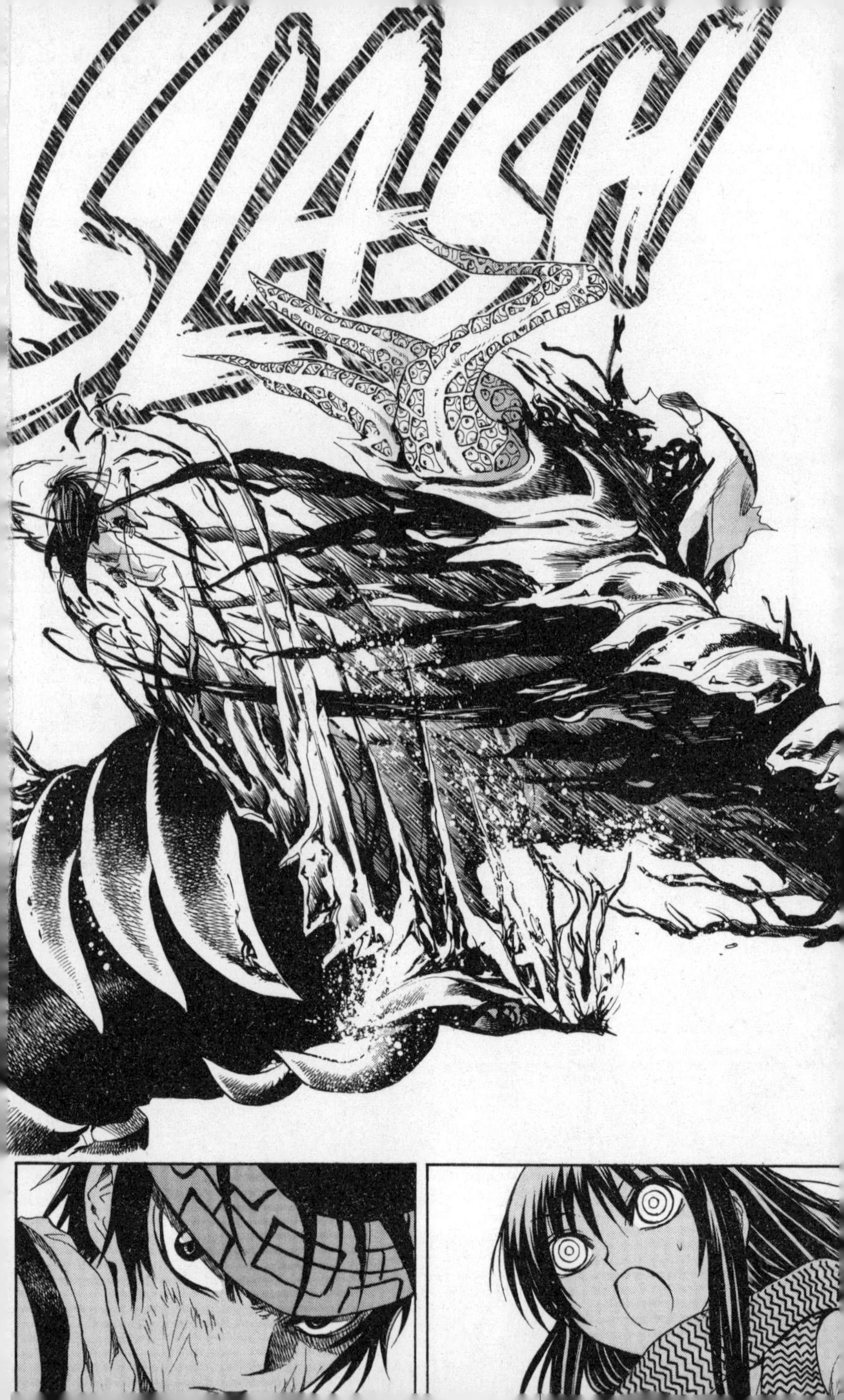
SLASH

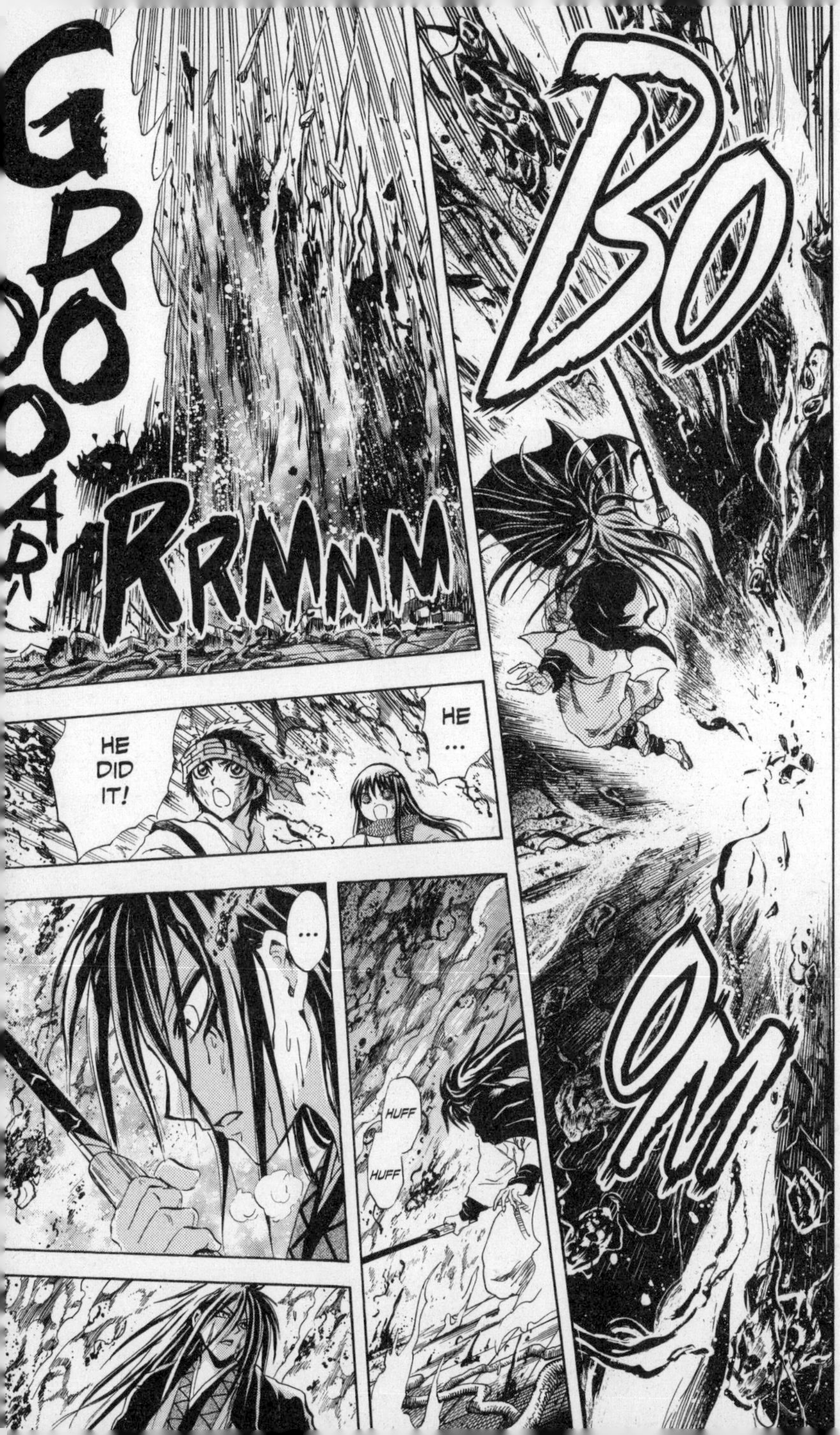
BO
OM
GROOAR
RRMMM
HE ...
HE DID IT!
HUFF HUFF
...

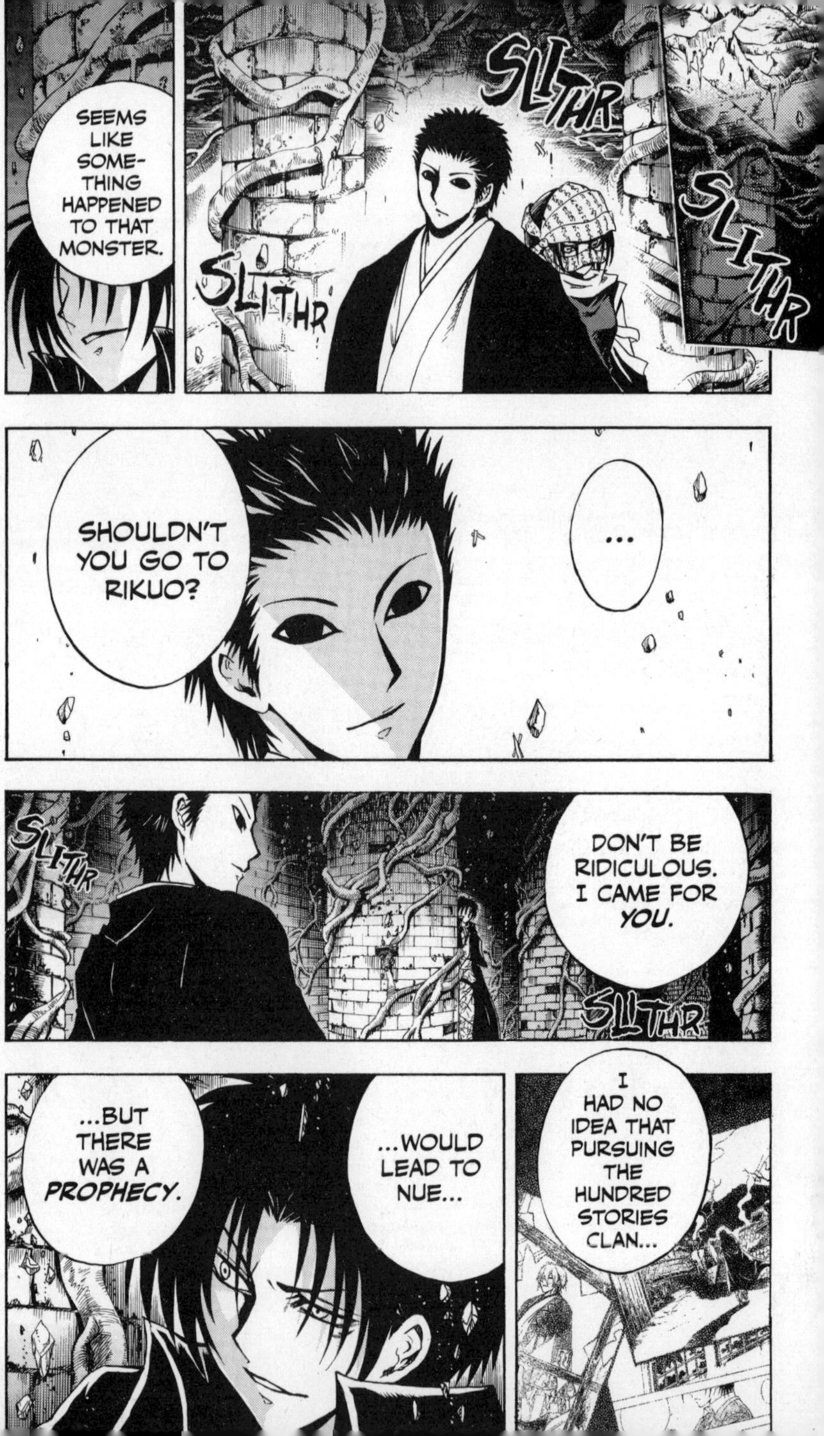
SLITHR
SLITHR
SLITHR
SEEMS LIKE SOMETHING HAPPENED TO THAT MONSTER.
...
SHOULDN'T YOU GO TO RIKUO?
DON'T BE RIDICULOUS. I CAME FOR *YOU*.
SLITHR
SLITHR
I HAD NO IDEA THAT PURSUING THE HUNDRED STORIES CLAN...
...WOULD LEAD TO NUE...
...BUT THERE WAS A *PROPHECY*.

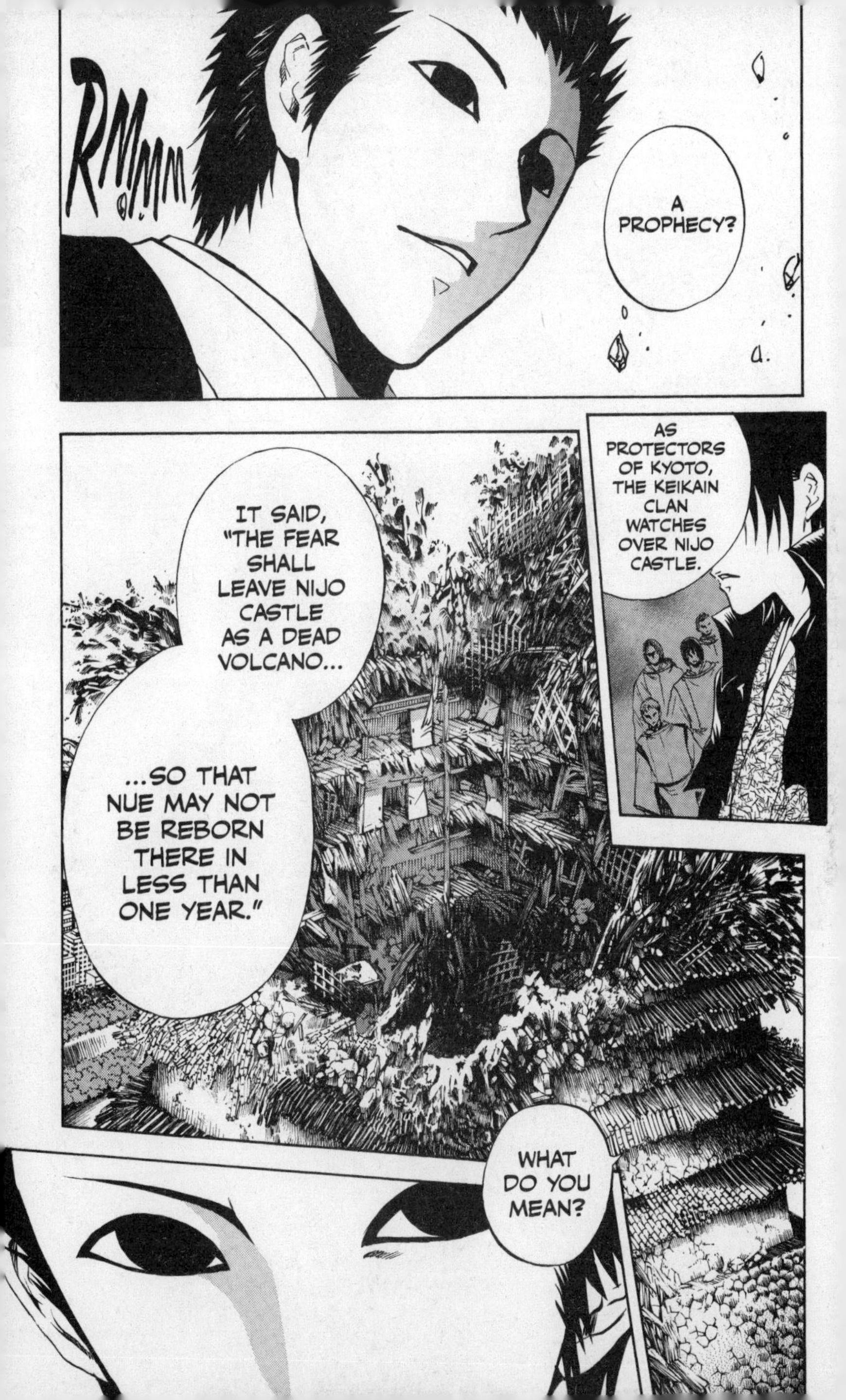
A PROPHECY?
RMMM
AS PROTECTORS OF KYOTO, THE KEIKAIN CLAN WATCHES OVER NIJO CASTLE.
IT SAID, "THE FEAR SHALL LEAVE NIJO CASTLE AS A DEAD VOLCANO...
...SO THAT NUE MAY NOT BE REBORN THERE IN LESS THAN ONE YEAR."
WHAT DO YOU MEAN?

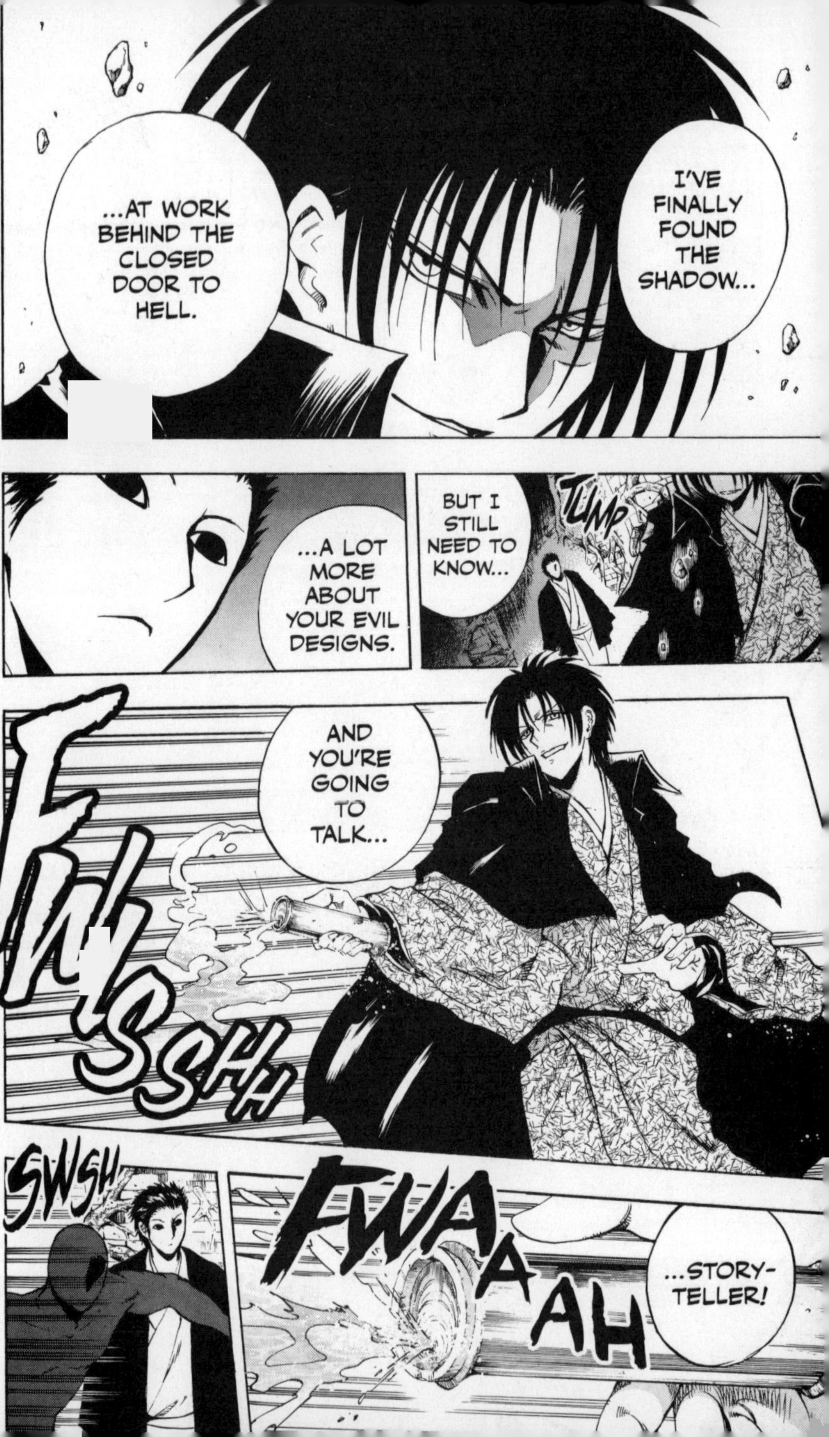
I'VE FINALLY FOUND THE SHADOW...
...AT WORK BEHIND THE CLOSED DOOR TO HELL.
TUMP
BUT I STILL NEED TO KNOW...
...A LOT MORE ABOUT YOUR EVIL DESIGNS.
AND YOU'RE GOING TO TALK...
FWISSHH
FWAAAH
...STORY-TELLER!
SWSH

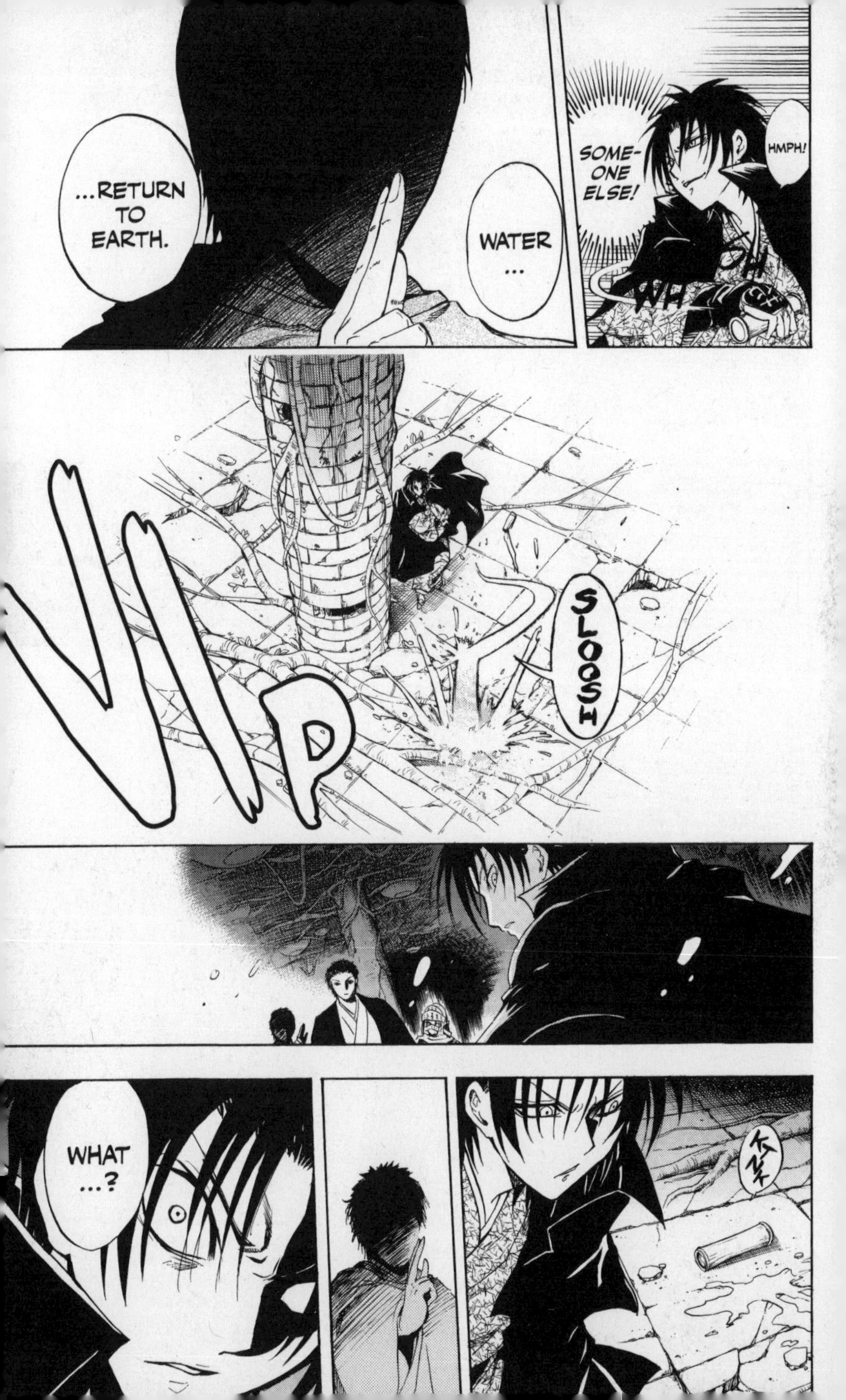
HMPH!
SOME-ONE ELSE!
WHSH
WATER ...
...RETURN TO EARTH.
SLOOSH
VIP
KTINK
WHAT ...?

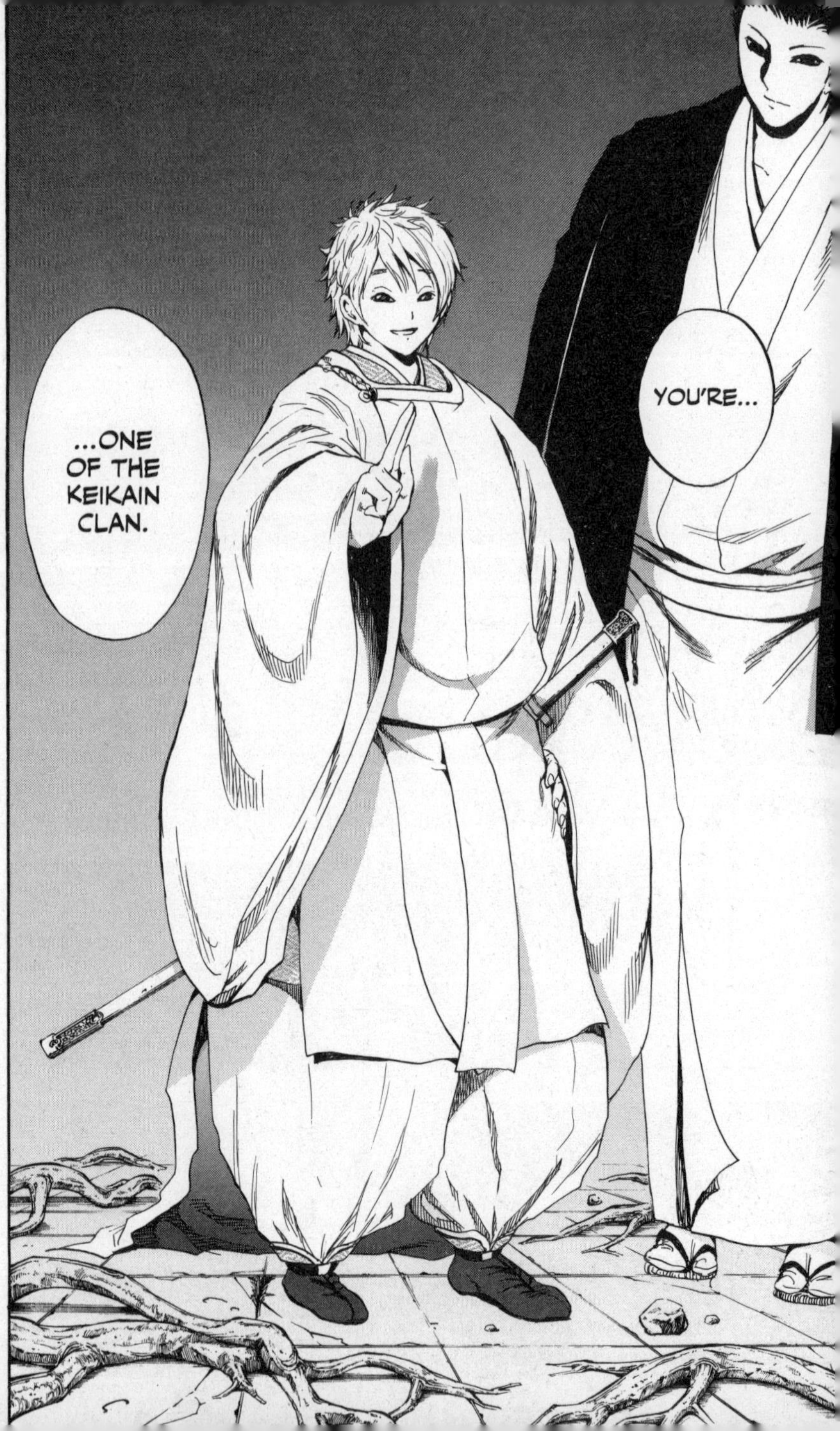
YOU'RE...
...ONE OF THE KEIKAIN CLAN.

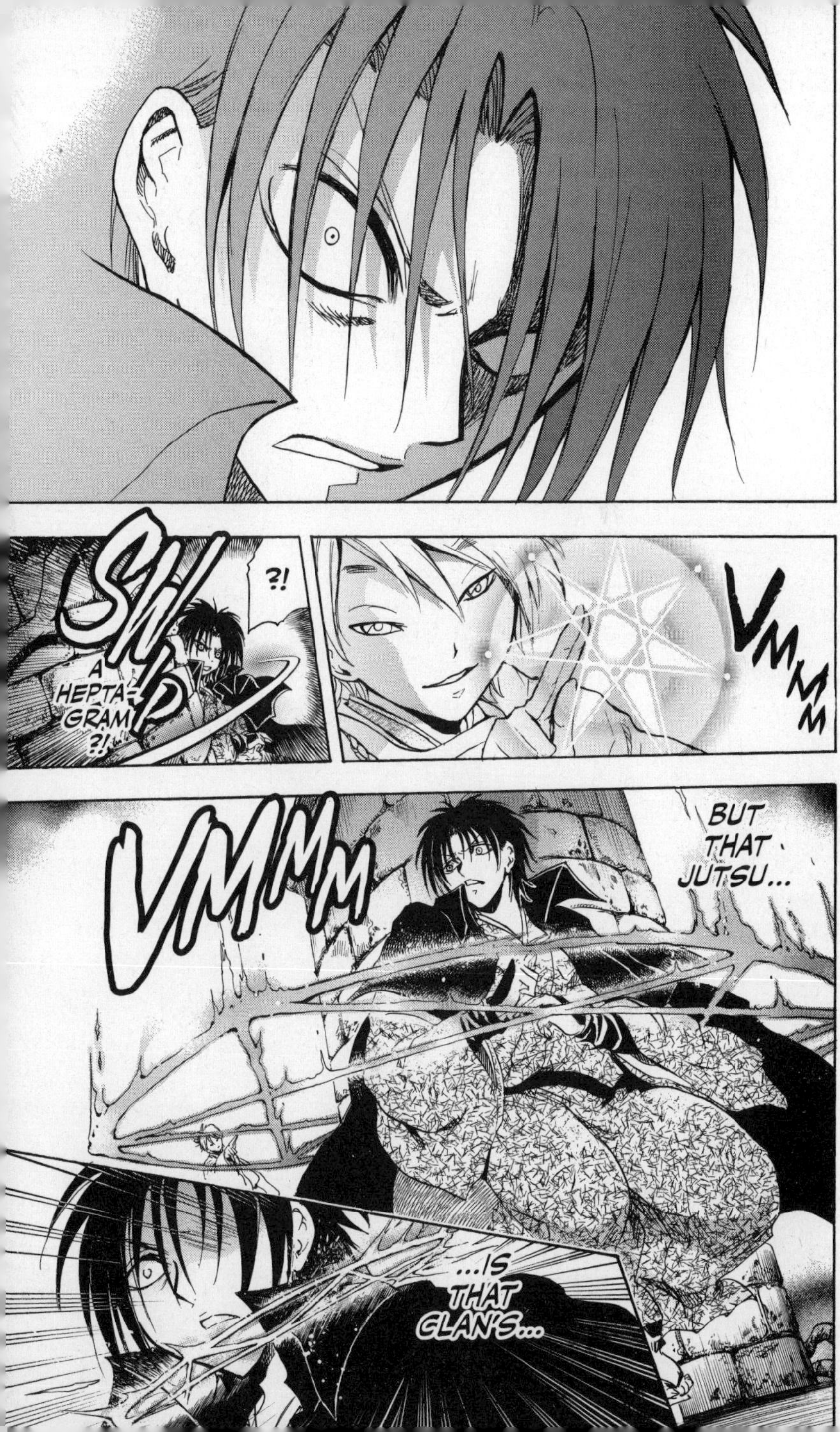
VMMM
?!
SHP
A HEPTA-GRAM ?!
VMMM
BUT THAT JUTSU...
...IS THAT CLAN'S...

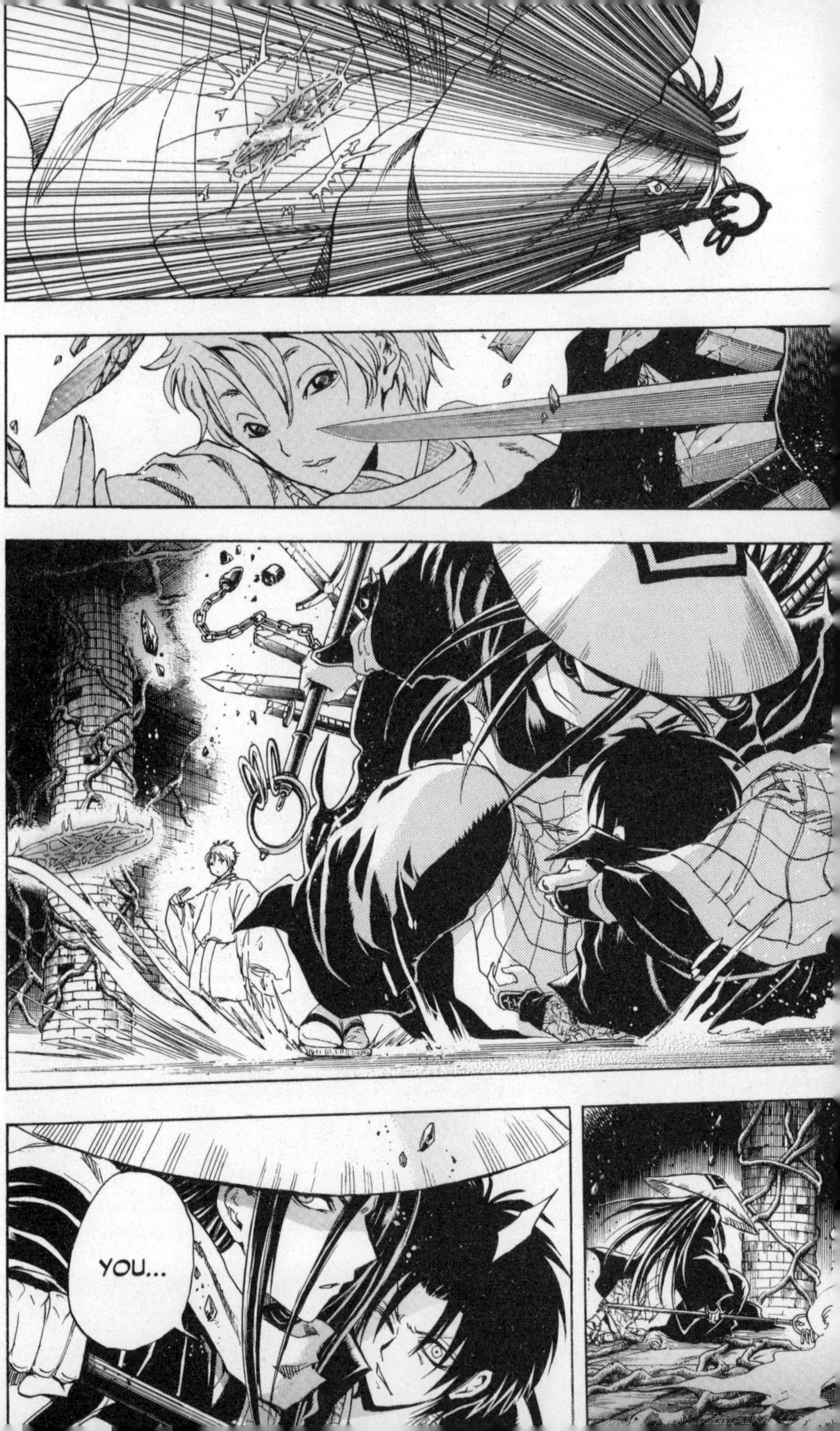
YOU...

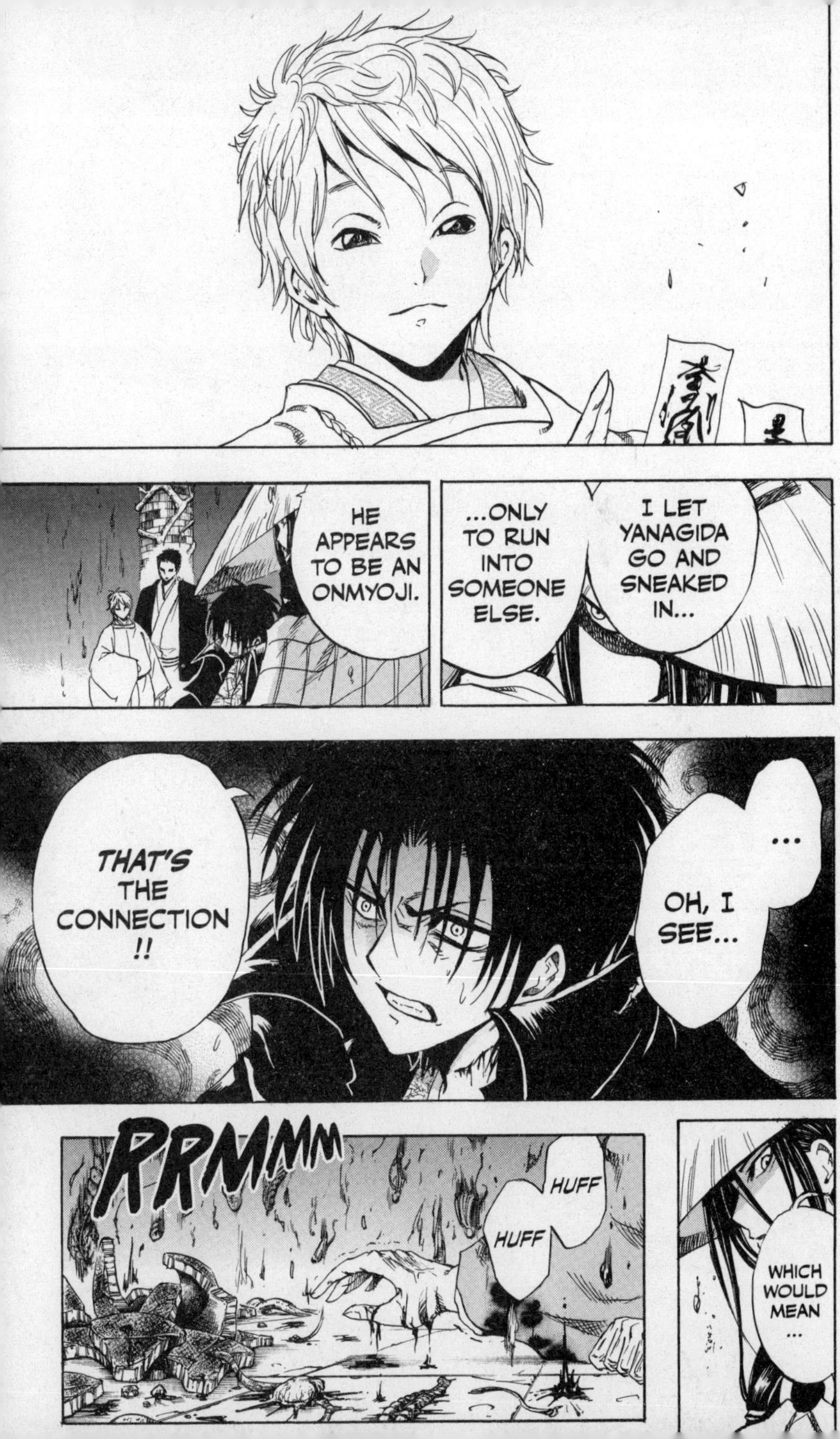
I LET YANAGIDA GO AND SNEAKED IN...
...ONLY TO RUN INTO SOMEONE ELSE.
HE APPEARS TO BE AN ONMYOJI.
...
OH, I SEE...
THAT'S THE CONNECTION !!
WHICH WOULD MEAN ...
RRMMM
HUFF
HUFF

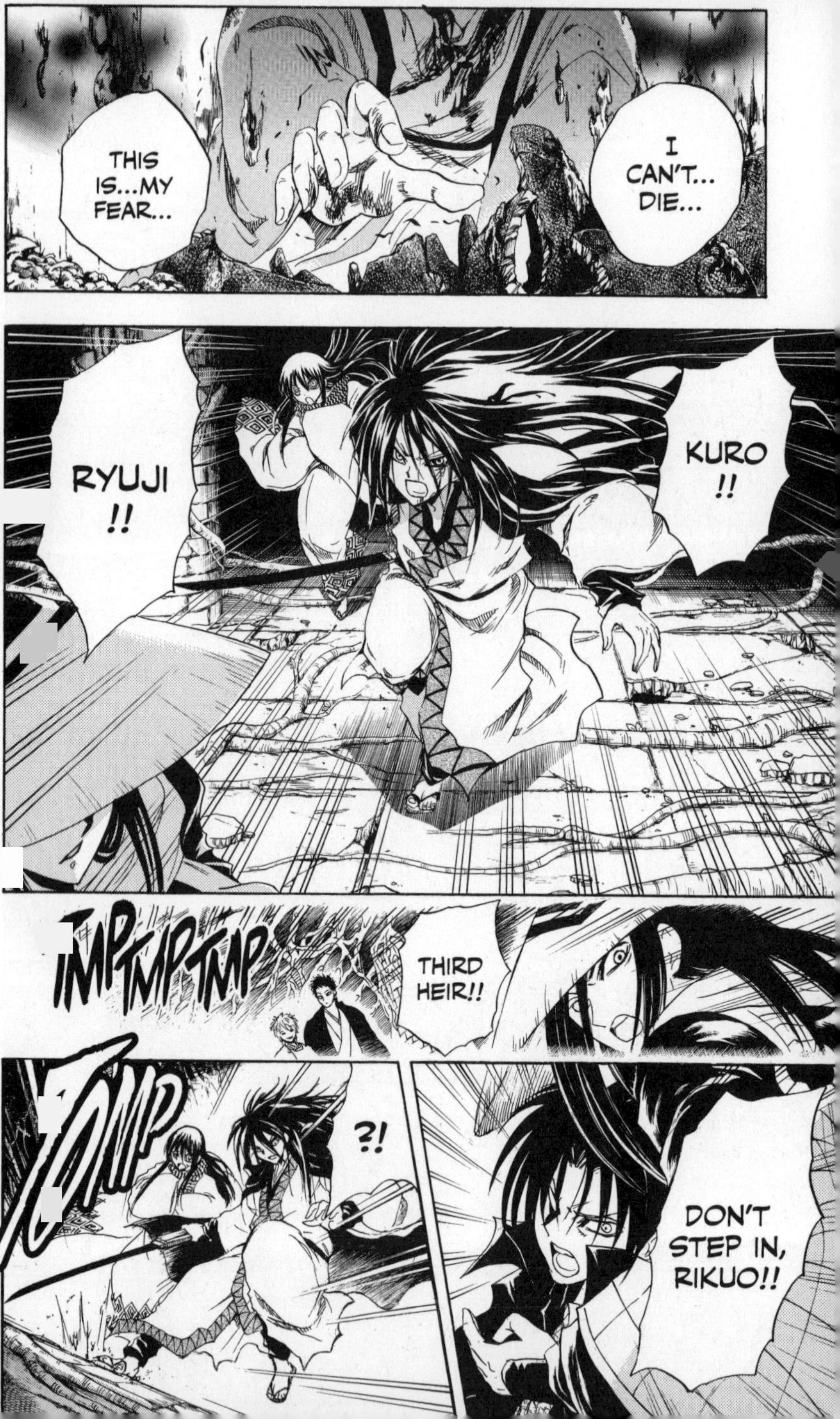
I CAN'T... DIE...
THIS IS...MY FEAR...
KURO!!
RYUJI!!
THIRD HEIR!!
TMP TMP TMP
DON'T STEP IN, RIKUO!!
?!
TMP

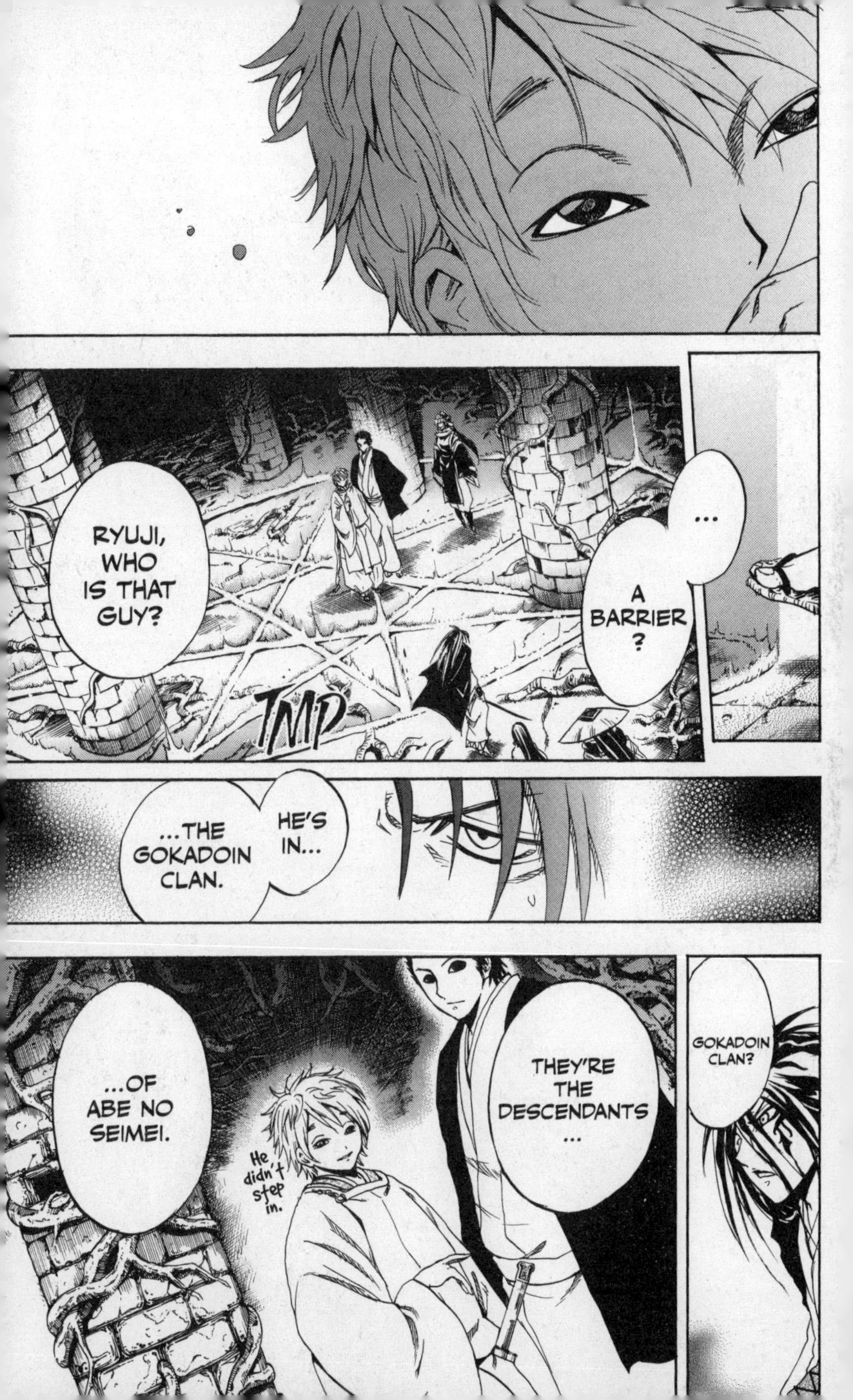
...
A BARRIER?
RYUJI, WHO IS THAT GUY?
TMP
HE'S IN...
...THE GOKADOIN CLAN.
GOKADOIN CLAN?
THEY'RE THE DESCENDANTS...
He didn't step in.
...OF ABE NO SEIMEI.

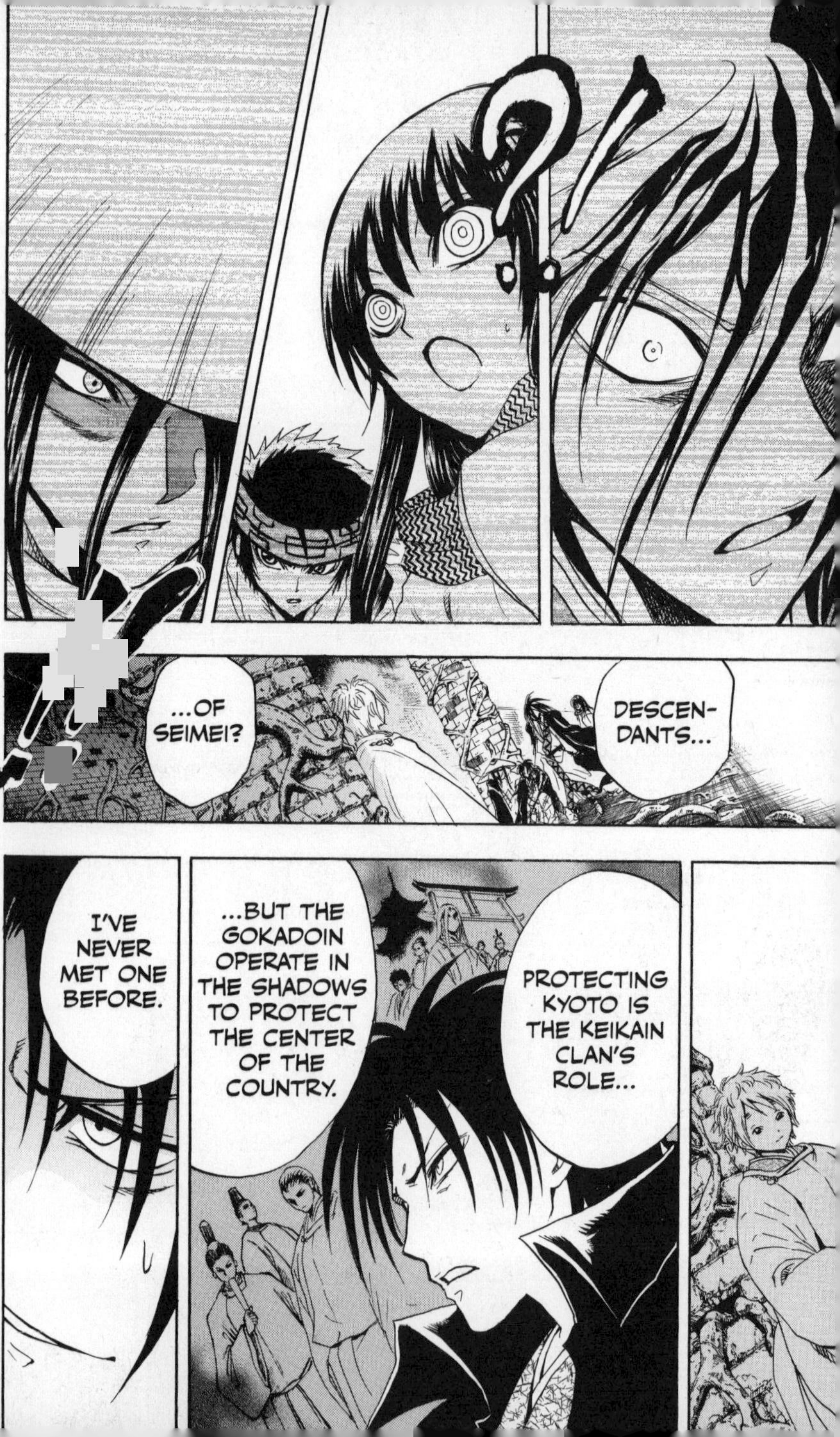
DESCEN-DANTS...
...OF SEIMEI?
PROTECTING KYOTO IS THE KEIKAIN CLAN'S ROLE...
...BUT THE GOKADOIN OPERATE IN THE SHADOWS TO PROTECT THE CENTER OF THE COUNTRY.
I'VE NEVER MET ONE BEFORE.

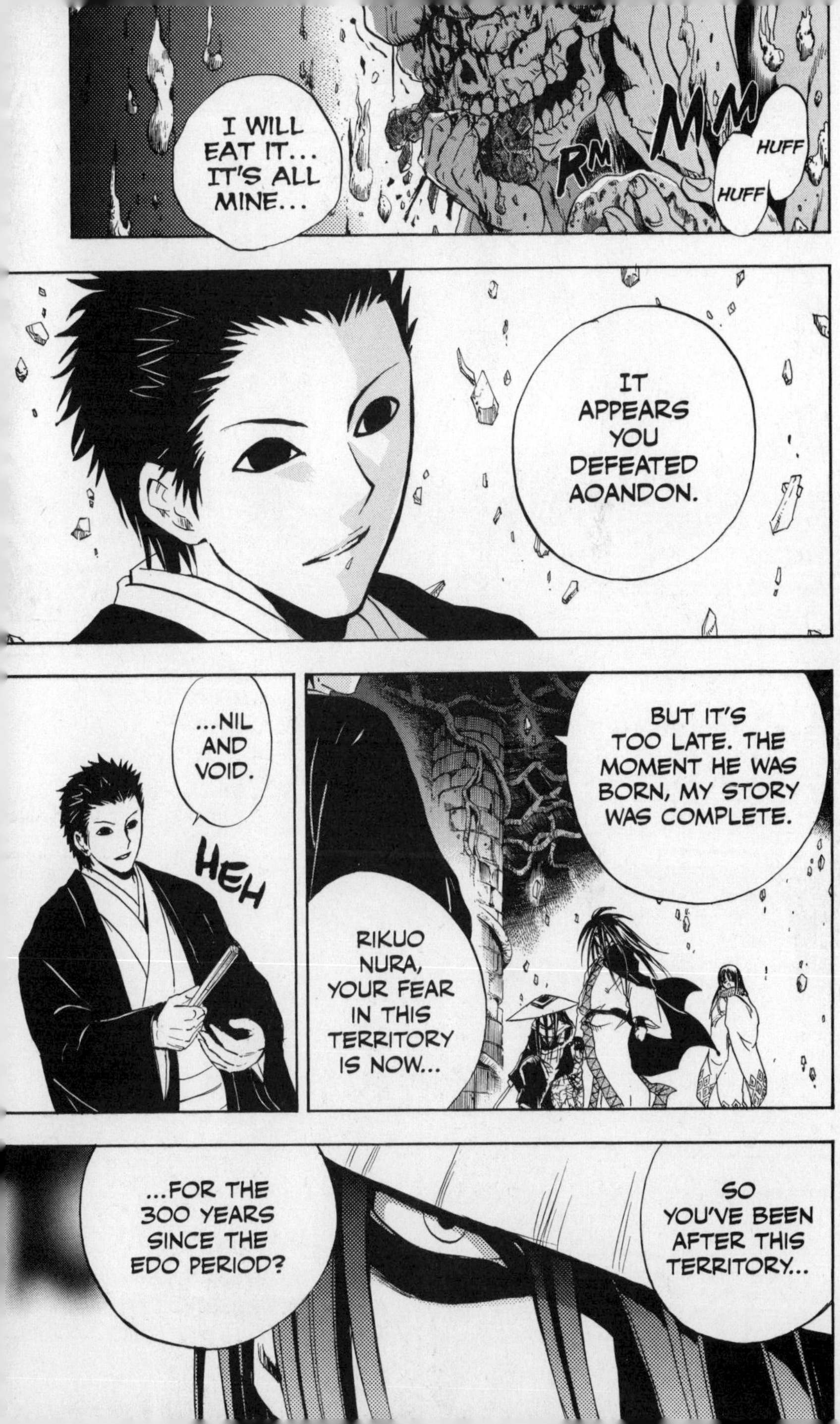
HUFF
HUFF
RMMM
I WILL EAT IT... IT'S ALL MINE...
IT APPEARS YOU DEFEATED AOANDON.
BUT IT'S TOO LATE. THE MOMENT HE WAS BORN, MY STORY WAS COMPLETE.
RIKUO NURA, YOUR FEAR IN THIS TERRITORY IS NOW...
...NIL AND VOID.
HEH
SO YOU'VE BEEN AFTER THIS TERRITORY...
...FOR THE 300 YEARS SINCE THE EDO PERIOD?

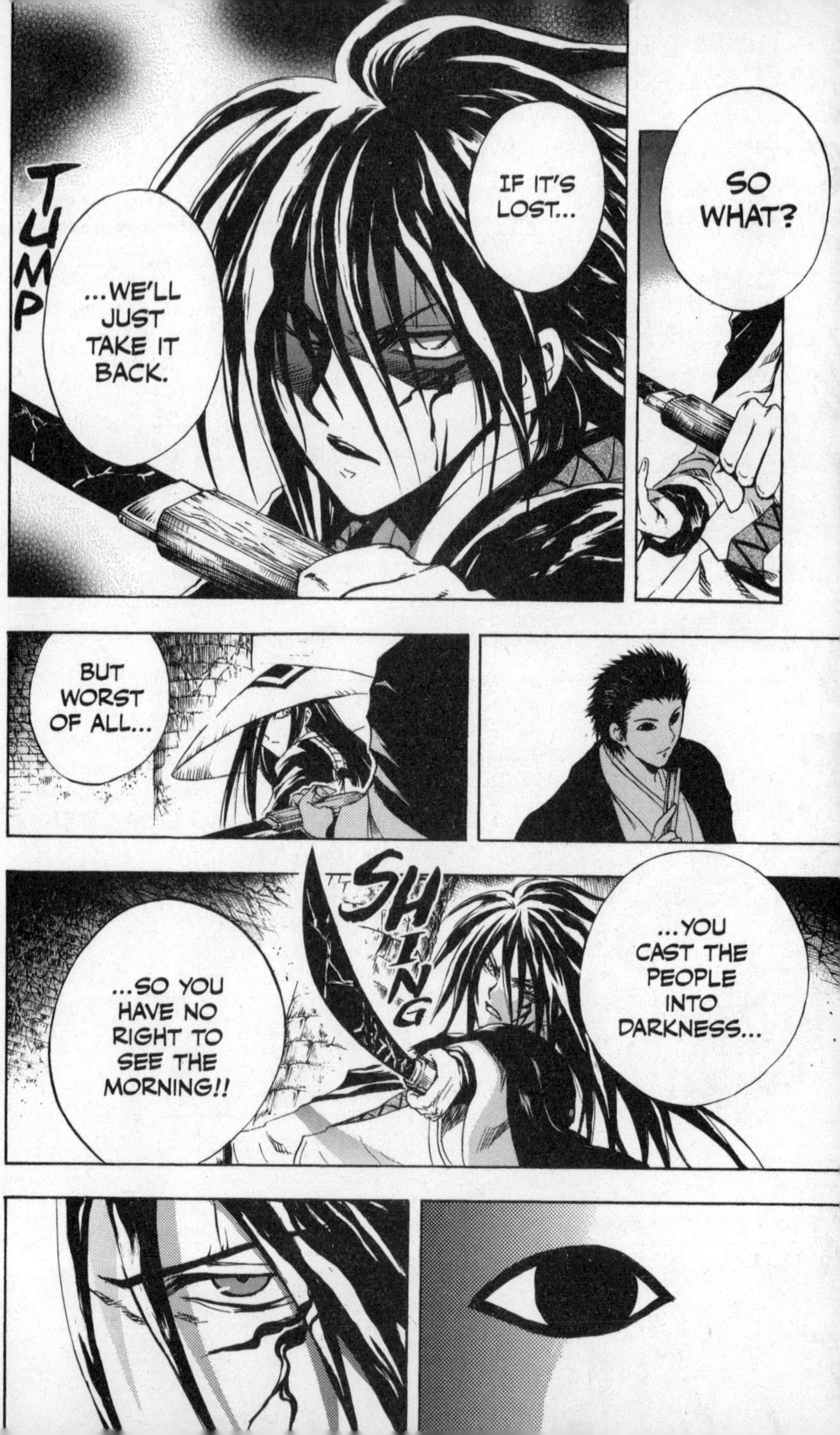
SO WHAT?
IF IT'S LOST...
...WE'LL JUST TAKE IT BACK.
TUMP
BUT WORST OF ALL...
...YOU CAST THE PEOPLE INTO DARKNESS...
SHING
...SO YOU HAVE NO RIGHT TO SEE THE MORNING!!

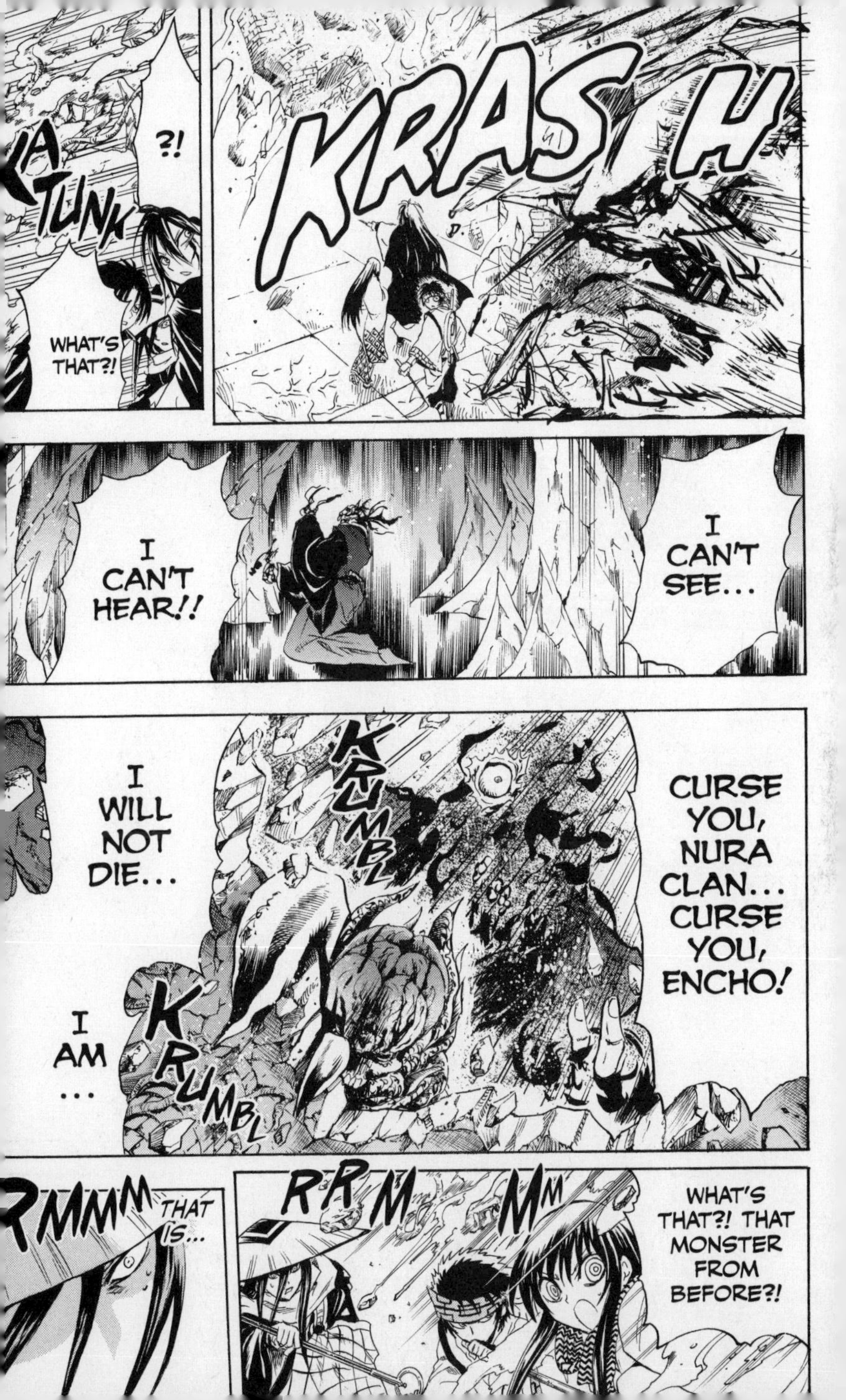
KRASH
?!
KA TUNK
WHAT'S THAT?!
I CAN'T SEE...
I CAN'T HEAR!!
CURSE YOU, NURA CLAN... CURSE YOU, ENCHO!
KRUMBL
I WILL NOT DIE...
KRUMBL
I AM ...
RRMMM
WHAT'S THAT?! THAT MONSTER FROM BEFORE?!
RMMM
THAT IS...

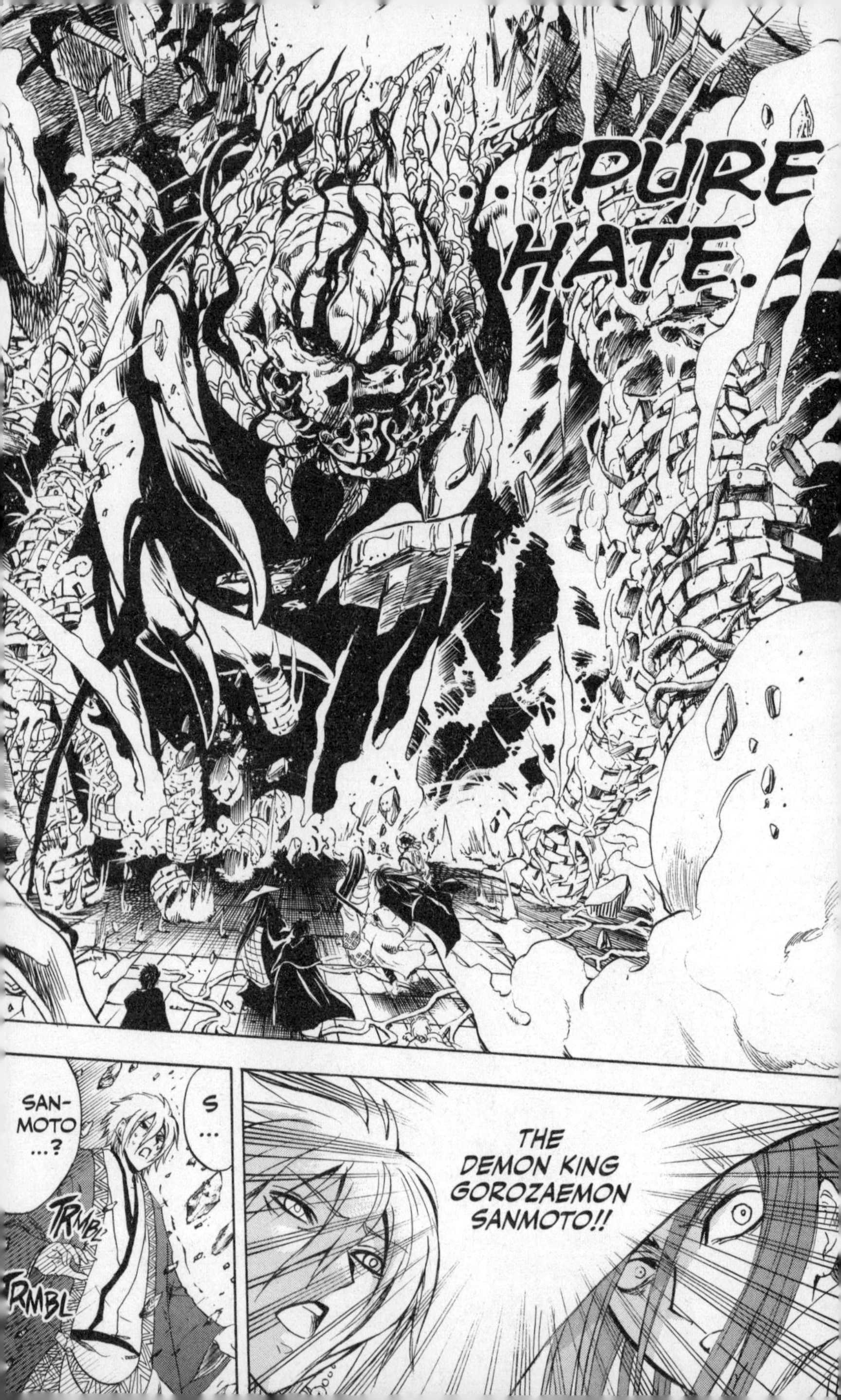
...PURE HATE.
THE DEMON KING GOROZAEMON SANMOTO!!
S...
SAN-MOTO...?
TRMBL
TRMBL

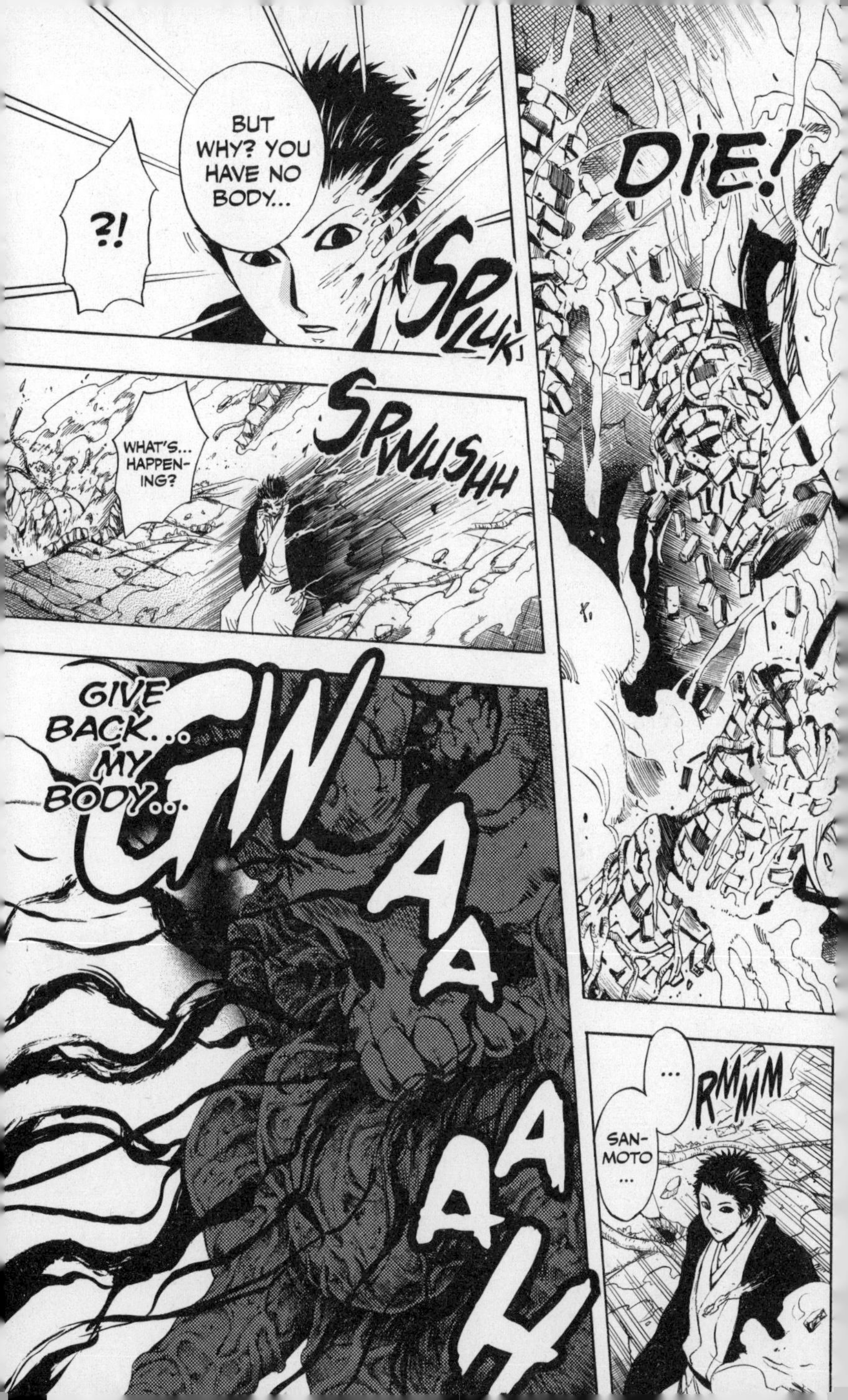
DIE!
BUT WHY? YOU HAVE NO BODY...
?!
SPLUK
WHAT'S... HAPPEN-ING?
SPWUSHH
...
RMMM
SAN-MOTO ...
GIVE BACK... MY BODY...
UWAAAAH

NURA: RISE OF THE YOKAI CLAN

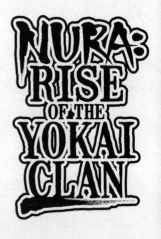

Act 183: Pure Hate

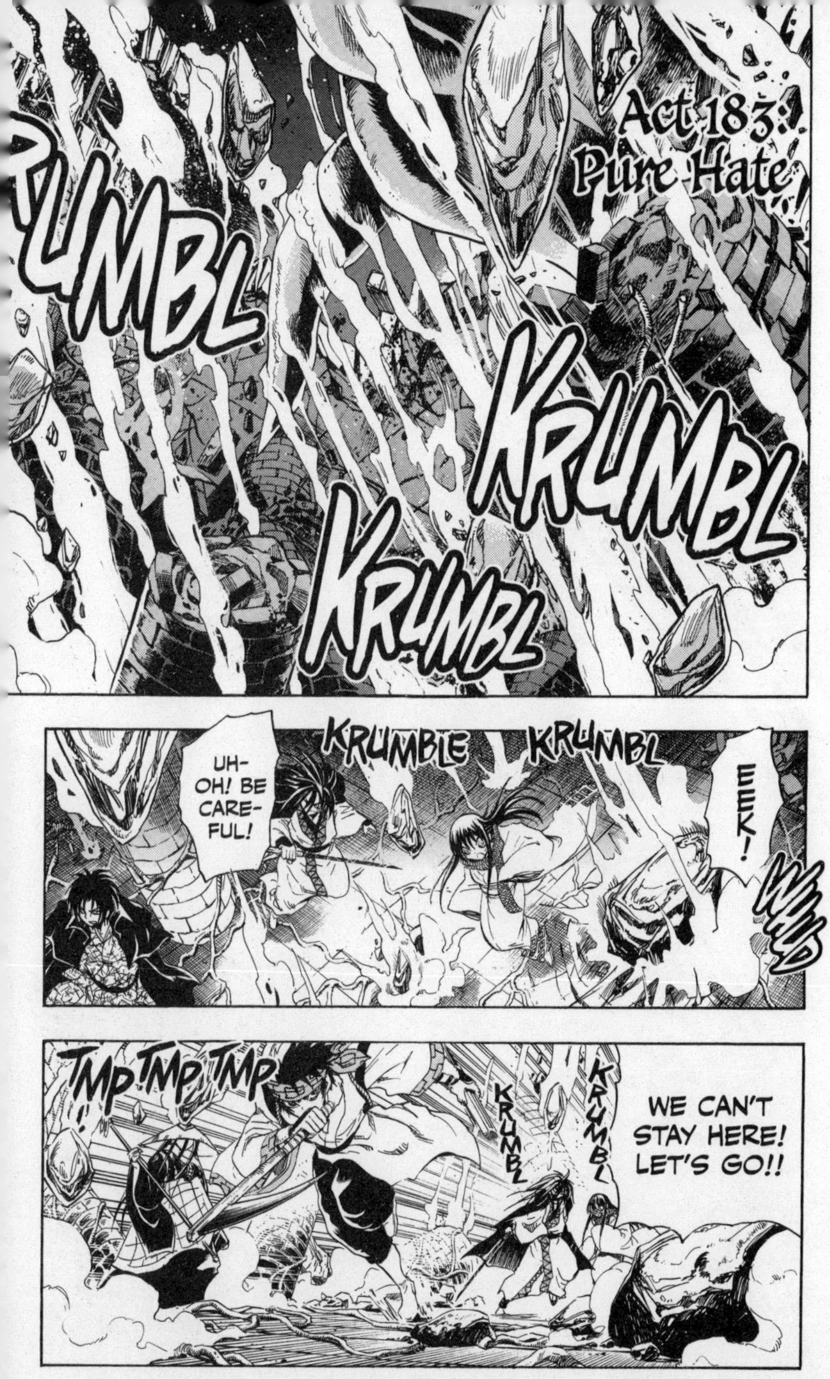
RUMBL
KRUMBL
KRUMBL
EEK!
WHUD
KRUMBL
KRUMBLE
UH-OH! BE CAREFUL!
WE CAN'T STAY HERE! LET'S GO!!
KRUMBL
KRUMBL
TMP TMP TMP

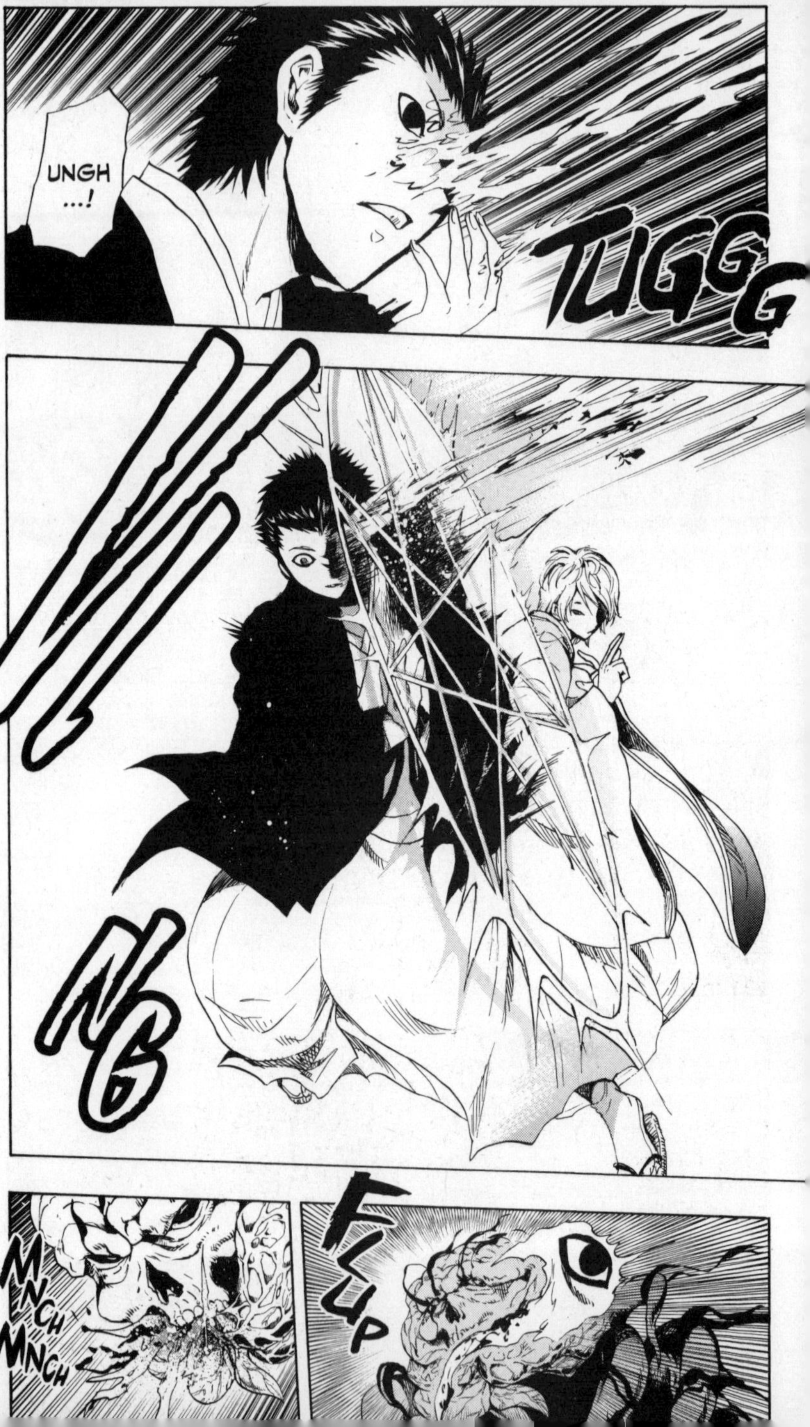
UNGH ...!
TUGGG
NNG
FLUP
MNCH MNCH

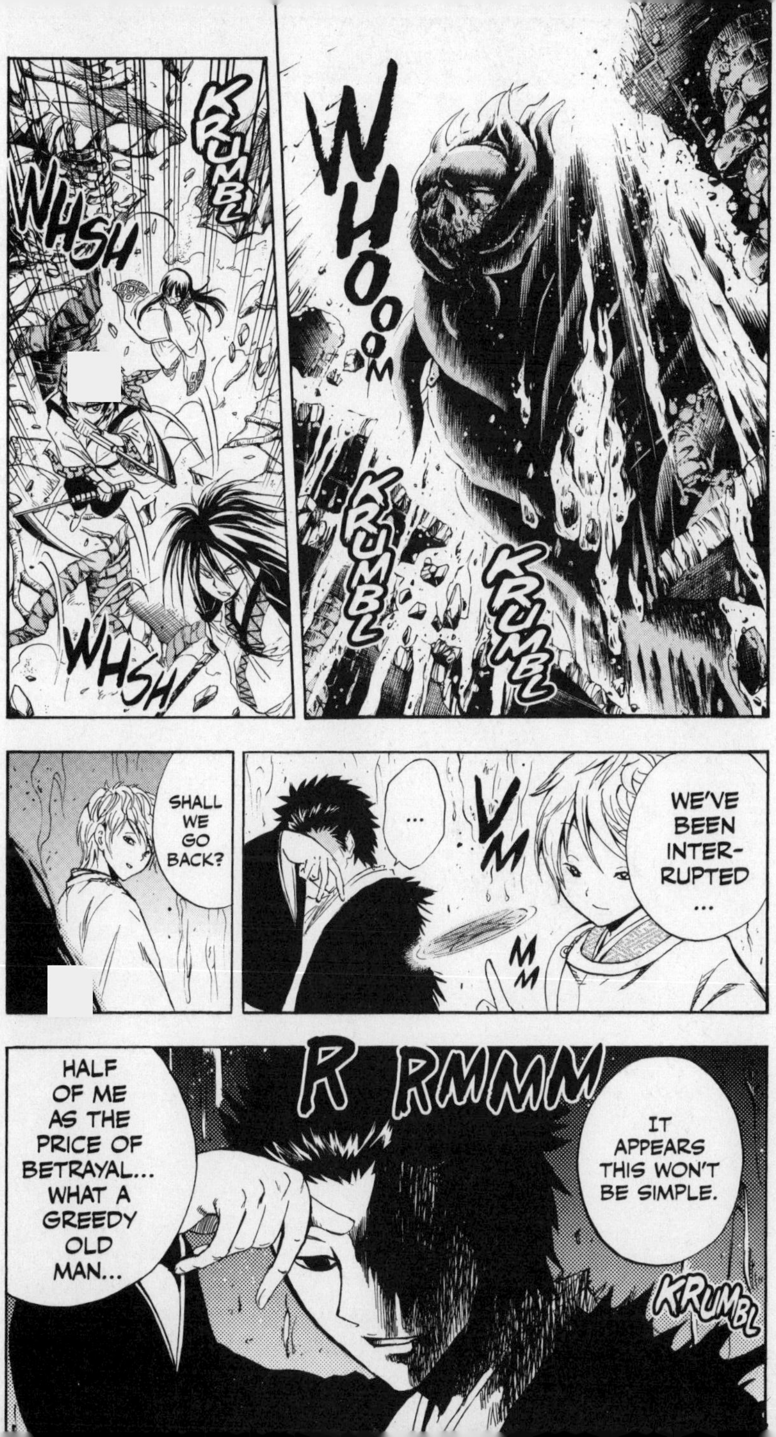
WHOOOOM
KRUMBL
KRUMBL
KRUMBL
WHSH
WHSH
WE'VE BEEN INTER-RUPTED ...
VM
MM
...
SHALL WE GO BACK?
R RMMM
IT APPEARS THIS WON'T BE SIMPLE.
HALF OF ME AS THE PRICE OF BETRAYAL... WHAT A GREEDY OLD MAN...
KRUMBL

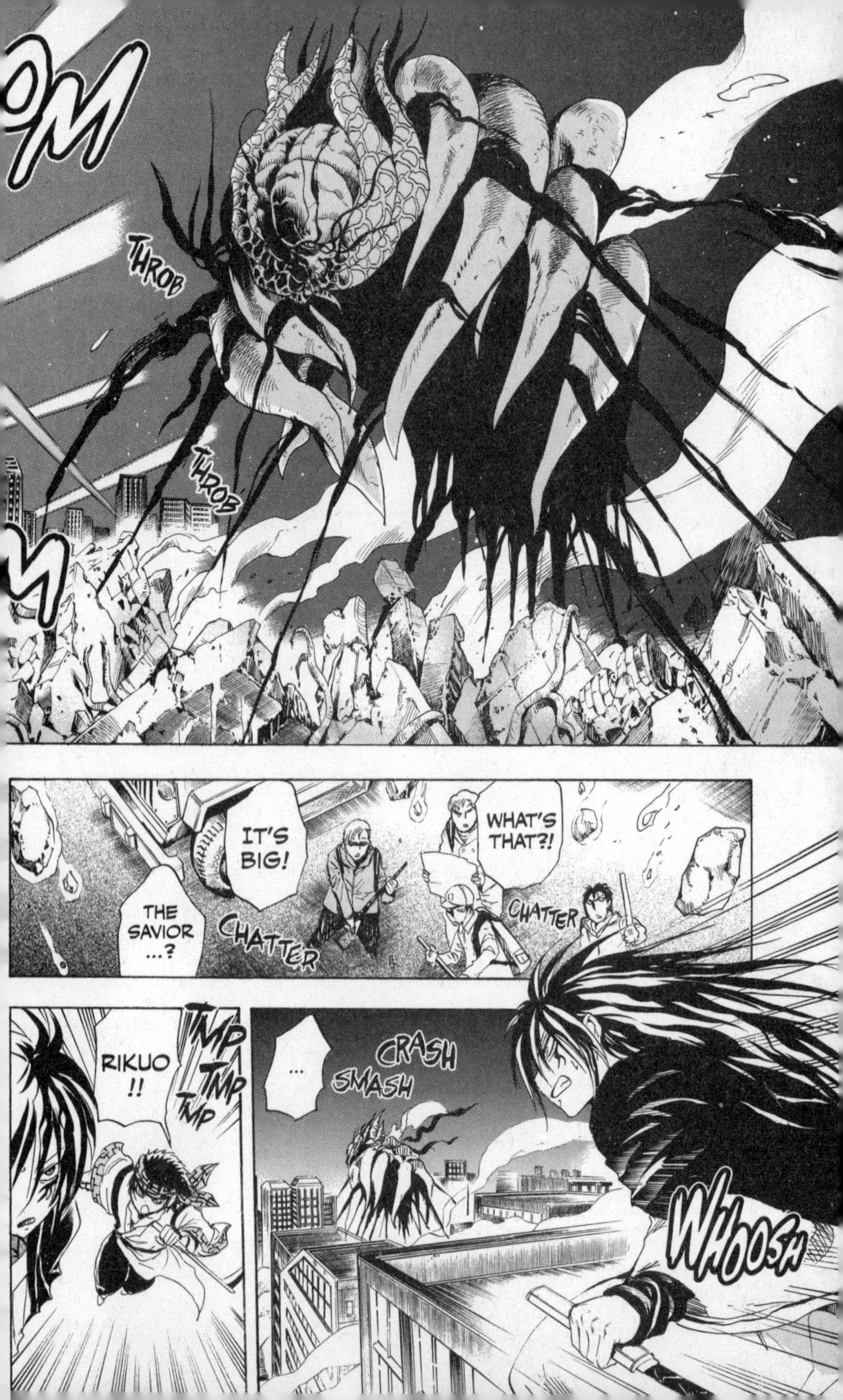
THROB
THROB
WHAT'S THAT?!
CHATTER
IT'S BIG!
THE SAVIOR ...?
CHATTER
...
CRASH
SMASH
WHOOSH
RIKUO !!
TMP
TMP
TMP

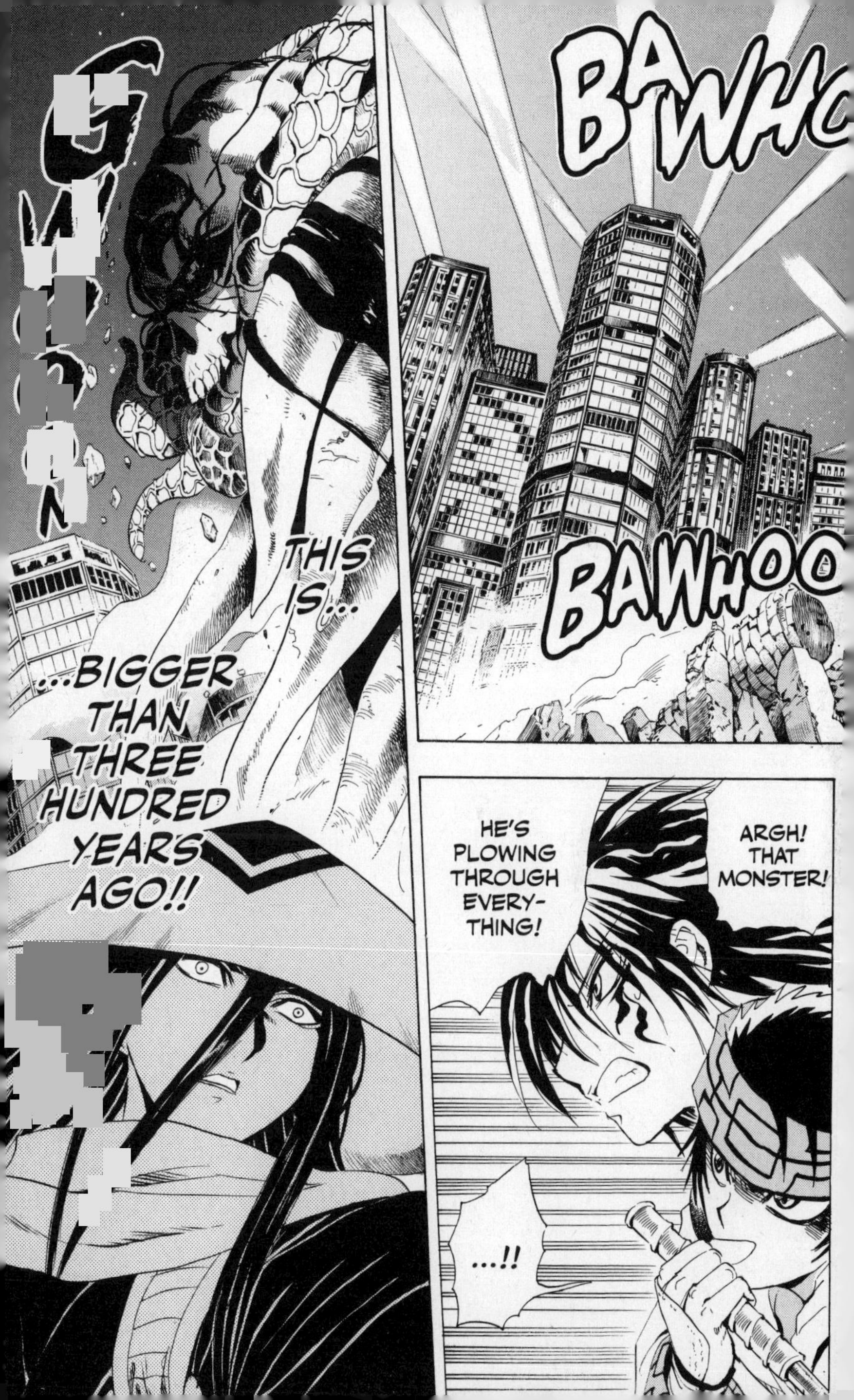
BAWHO
BAWHOO
ARGH! THAT MONSTER!
HE'S PLOWING THROUGH EVERY-THING!
...!!
THIS IS...
...BIGGER THAN THREE HUNDRED YEARS AGO!!

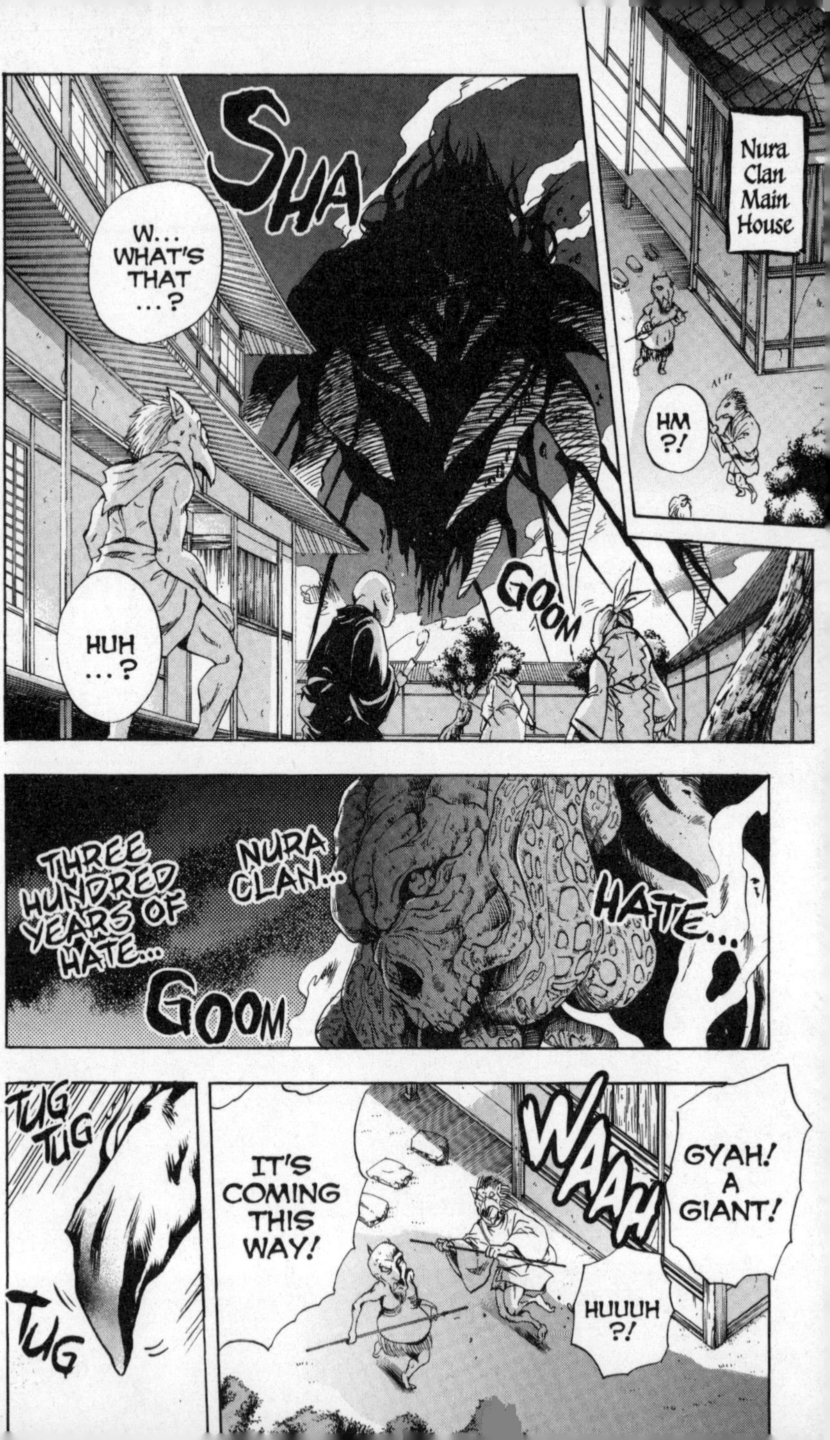
Nura Clan Main House
HM ?!
SHA
W... WHAT'S THAT ...?
GOOM
HUH ...?
HATE...
NURA CLAN...
THREE HUNDRED YEARS OF HATE...
GOOM
GYAH! A GIANT!
WAAH
IT'S COMING THIS WAY!
HUUUH ?!
TUG TUG
TUG

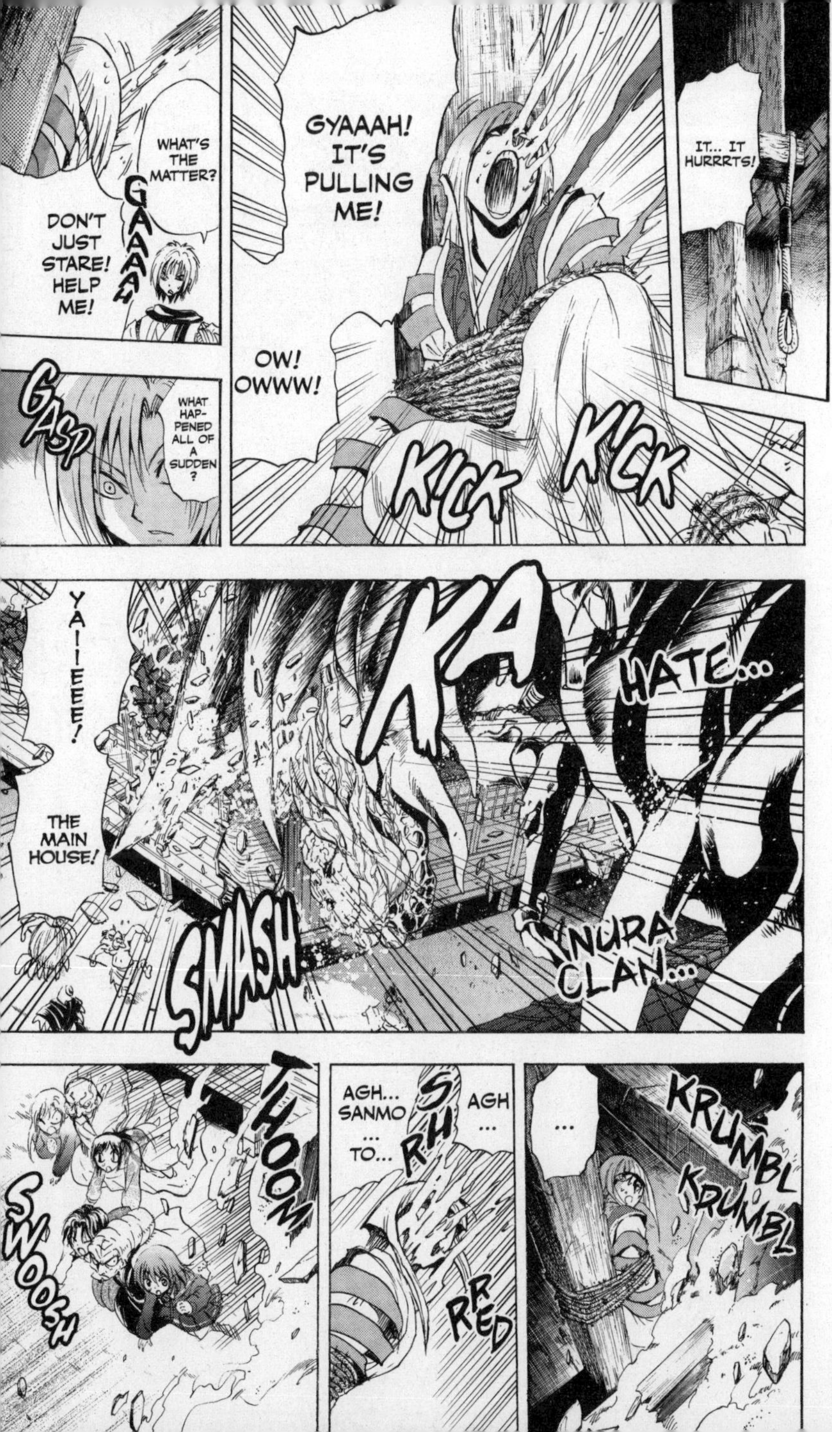
IT... IT HURRRTS!
GYAAAH! IT'S PULLING ME!
OW! OWWW!
KICK
KICK
WHAT'S THE MATTER?
GAAAAH
DON'T JUST STARE! HELP ME!
GASP
WHAT HAP-PENED ALL OF A SUDDEN?
KA
HATE...
NURA CLAN...
SMASH
YAIIEEE!
THE MAIN HOUSE!
...
KRUMBL
KRUMBL
AGH ...
SHRH
AGH... SANMO ... TO...
RRED
THOOOM
SWOOSH

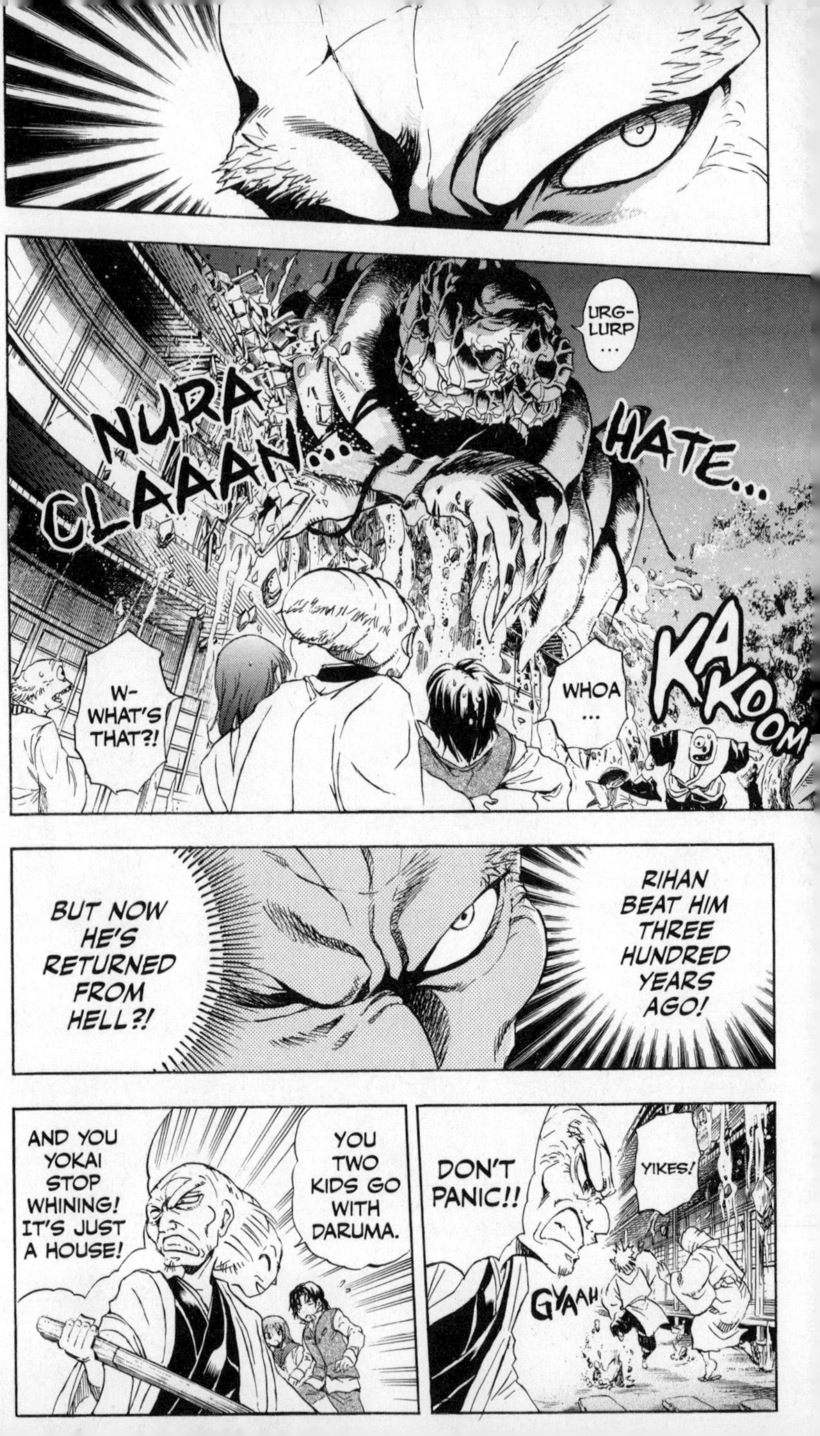
URG-LURP ...
HATE...
NURA CLAAAN...
KA KOOM
WHOA ...
W-WHAT'S THAT?!
RIHAN BEAT HIM THREE HUNDRED YEARS AGO!
BUT NOW HE'S RETURNED FROM HELL?!
YIKES!
DON'T PANIC!!
GYAAH
YOU TWO KIDS GO WITH DARUMA.
AND YOU YOKAI STOP WHINING! IT'S JUST A HOUSE!

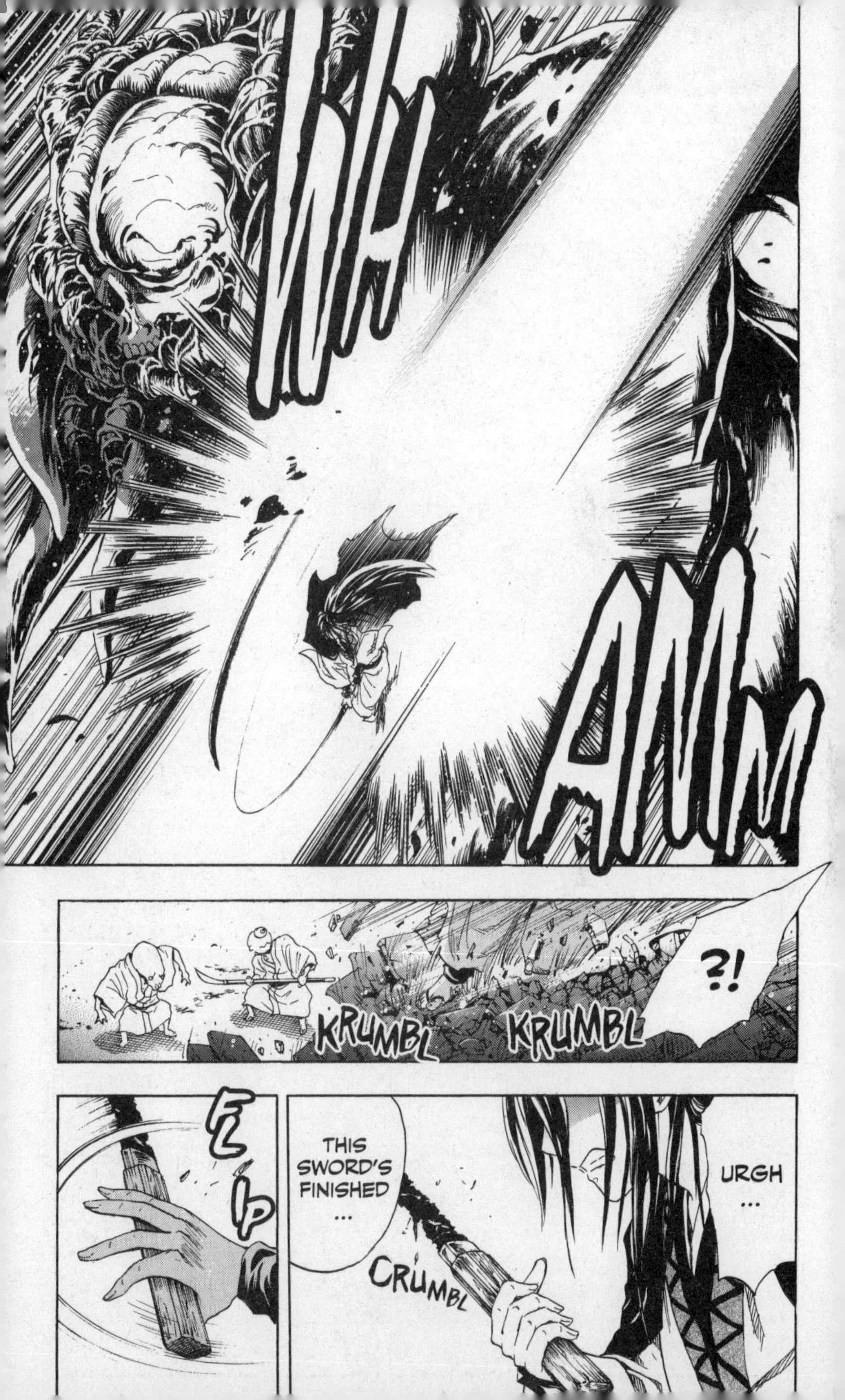
WHAMM
?!
KRUMBL
KRUMBL
URGH ...
THIS SWORD'S FINISHED ...
CRUMBL
FLIP

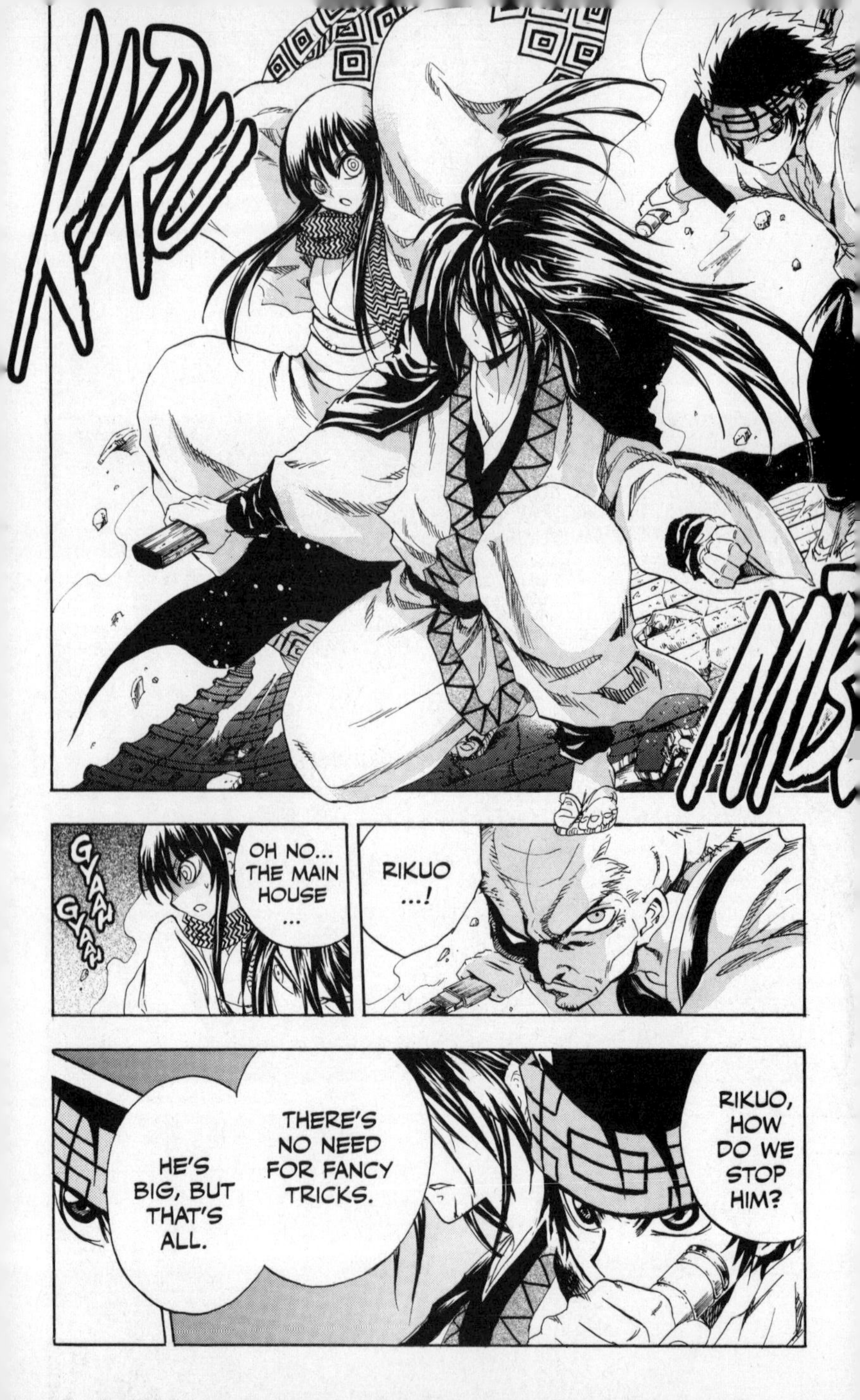
RIKUO ...!
OH NO... THE MAIN HOUSE ...
GYAAH GYAAH
RIKUO, HOW DO WE STOP HIM?
THERE'S NO NEED FOR FANCY TRICKS.
HE'S BIG, BUT THAT'S ALL.

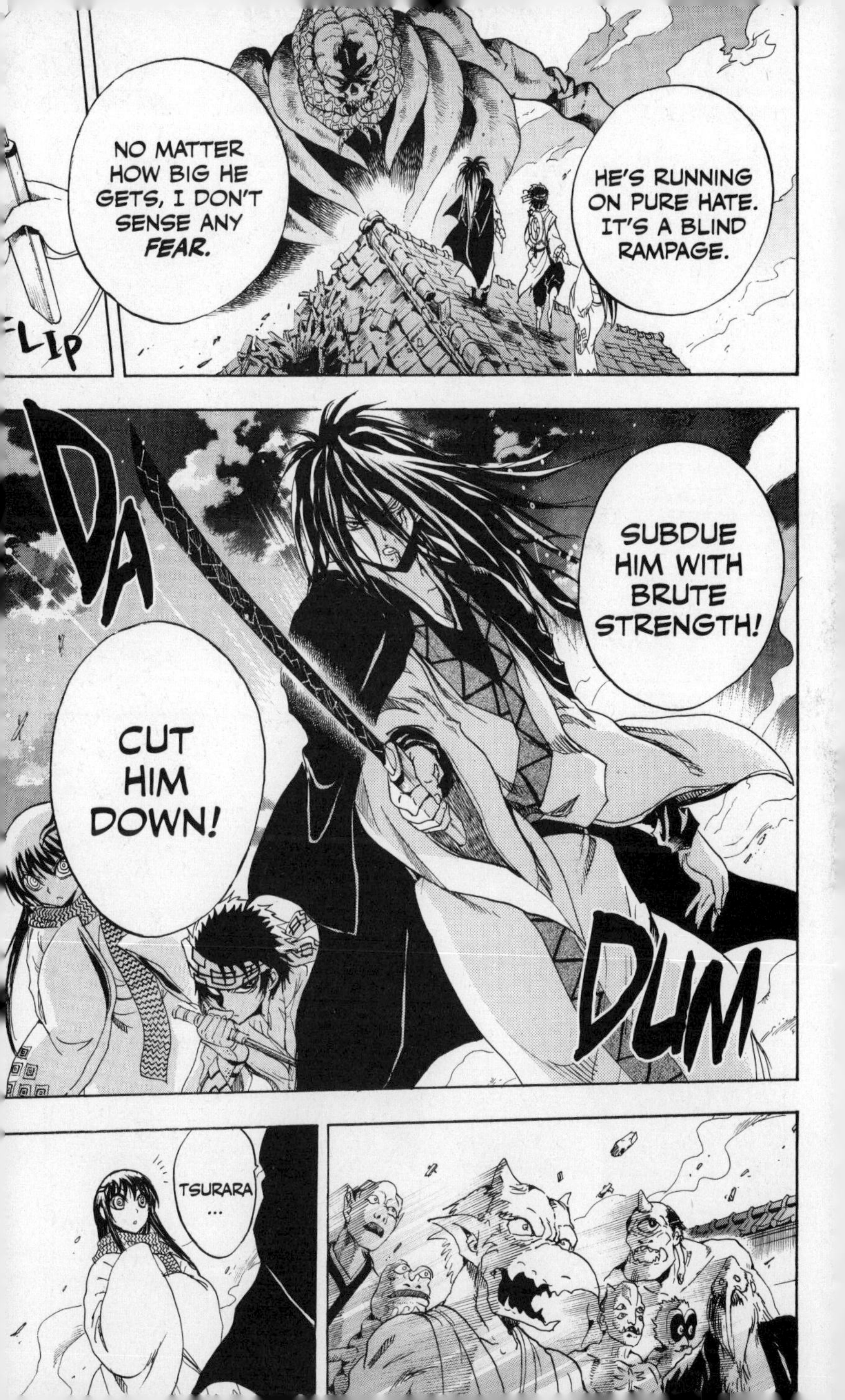
HE'S RUNNING ON PURE HATE. IT'S A BLIND RAMPAGE.
NO MATTER HOW BIG HE GETS, I DON'T SENSE ANY *FEAR.*
LIP
SUBDUE HIM WITH BRUTE STRENGTH!
DA
CUT HIM DOWN!
DUM
TSURARA ...

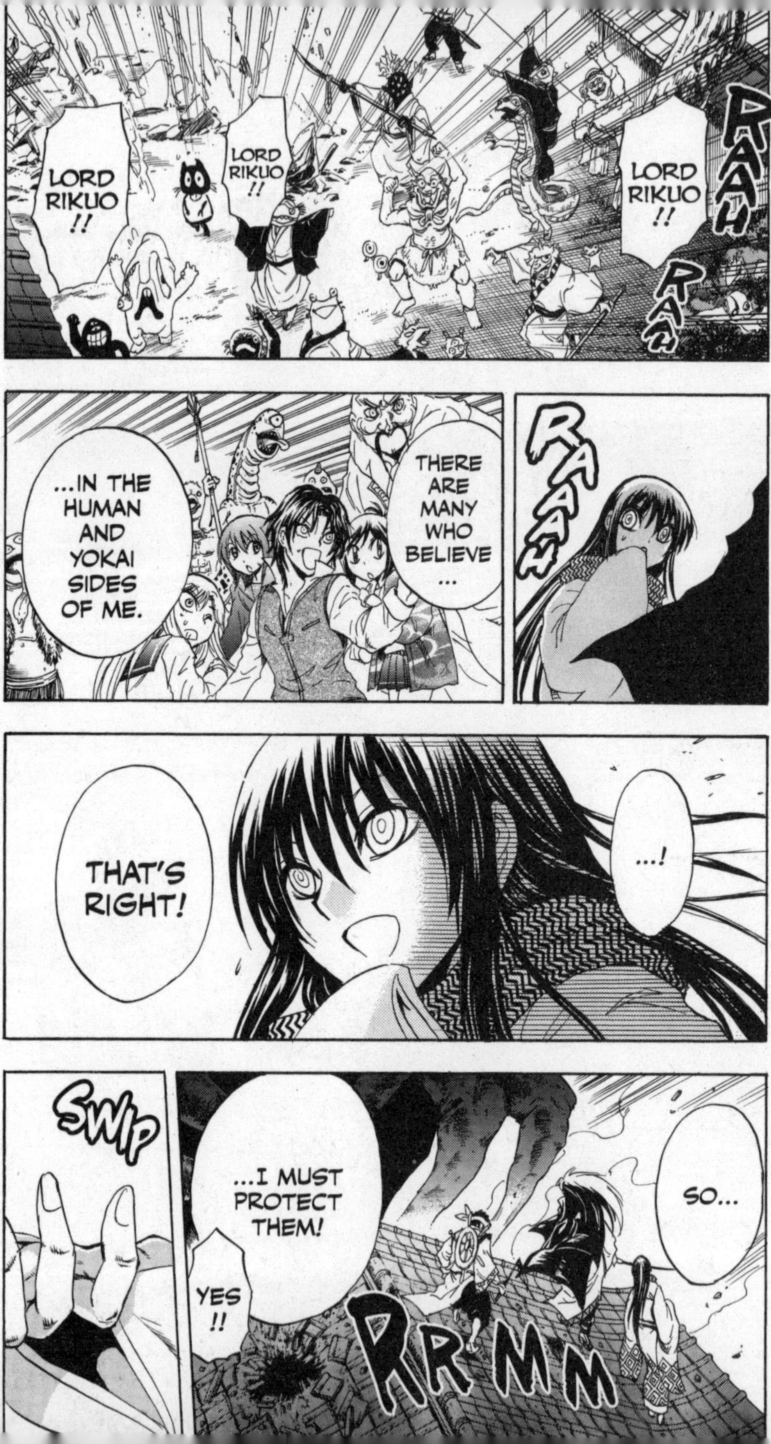
RAAH
RAAH
LORD RIKUO !!
LORD RIKUO !!
LORD RIKUO !!
RAAAH
THERE ARE MANY WHO BELIEVE ...
...IN THE HUMAN AND YOKAI SIDES OF ME.
...!
THAT'S RIGHT!
SO...
RRMM
...I MUST PROTECT THEM!
YES !!
SWIP

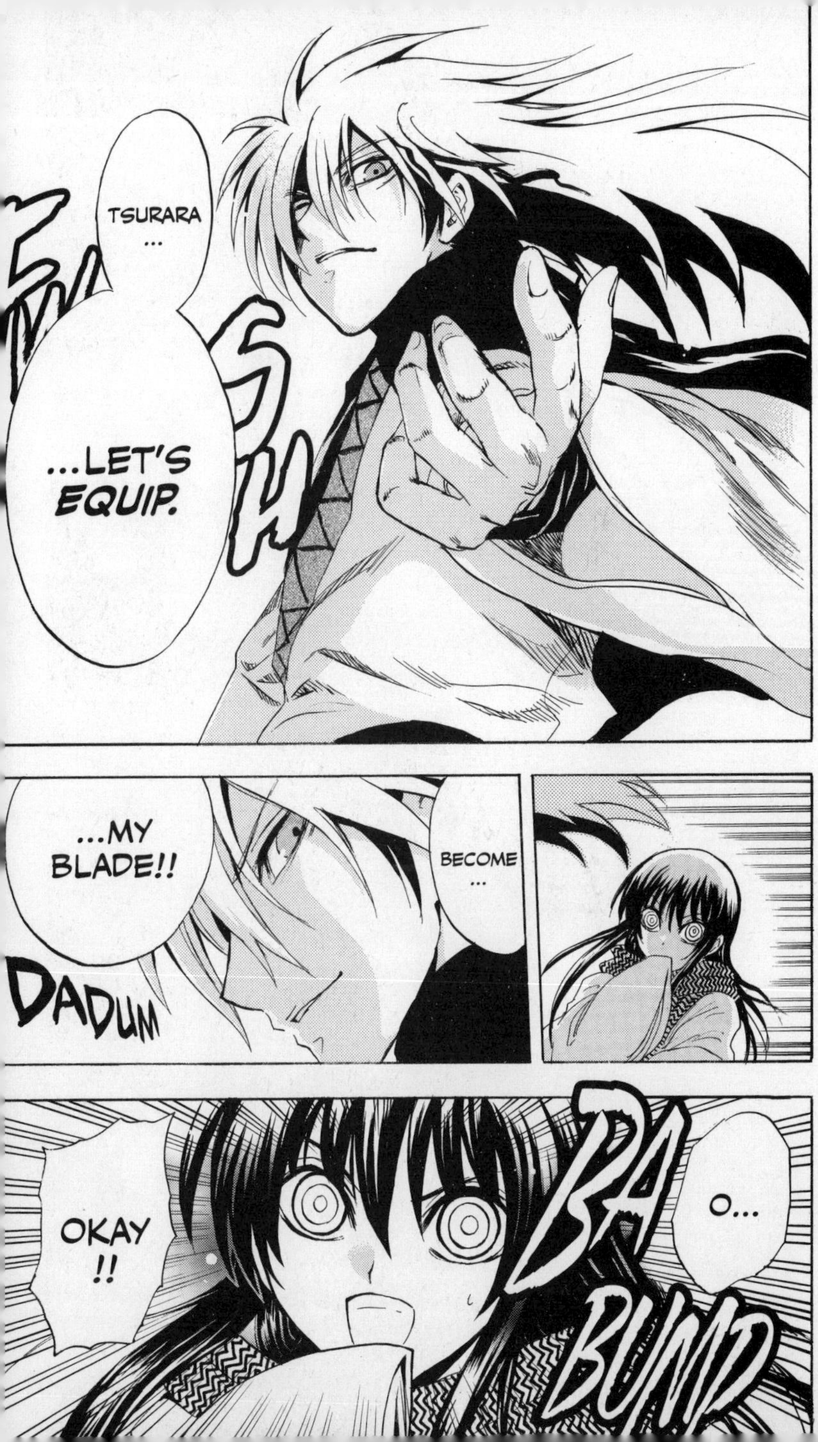
TSURARA ...
...LET'S EQUIP.
BECOME ...
...MY BLADE!!
DADUM
BA BUMP
O...
OKAY !!

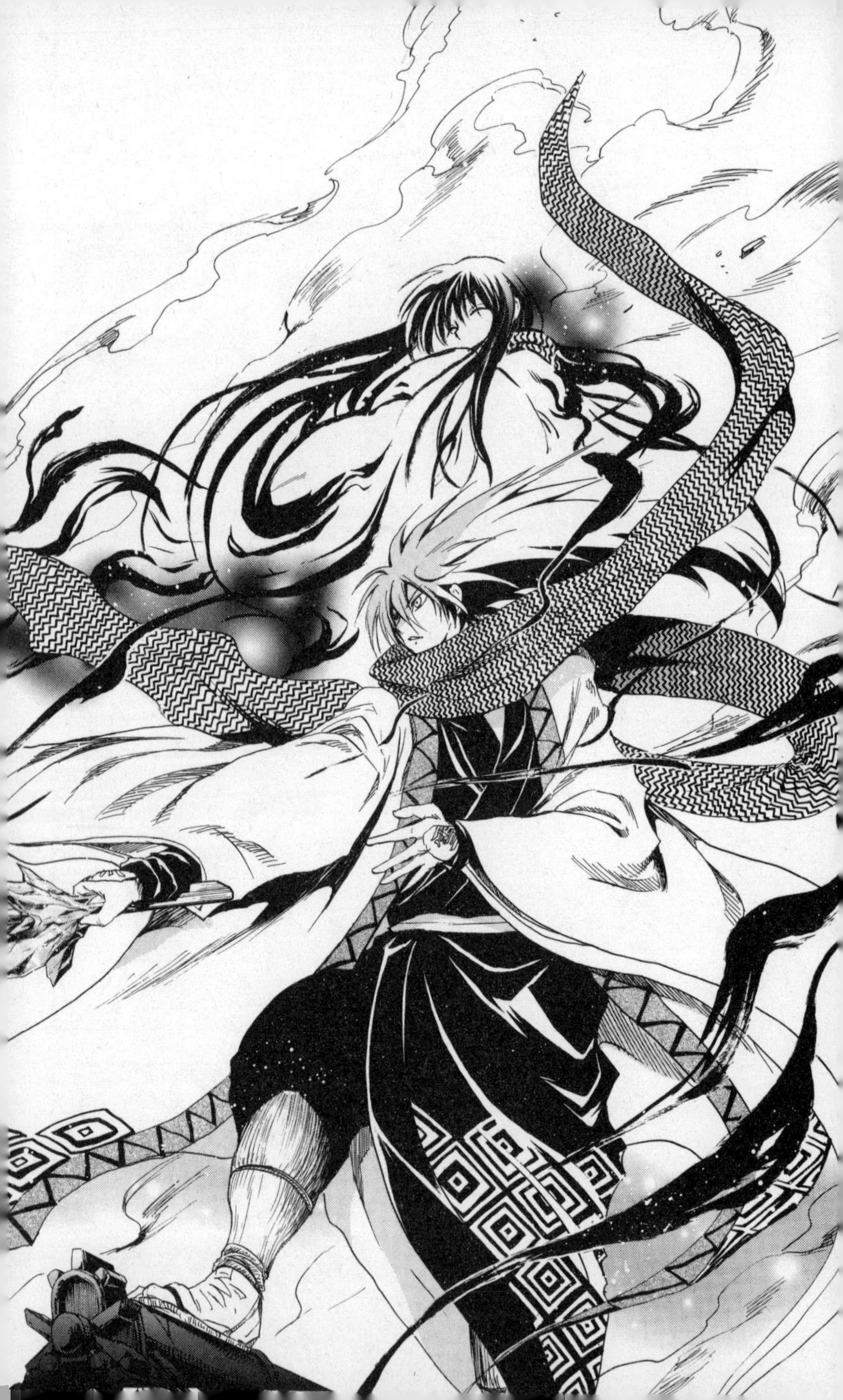

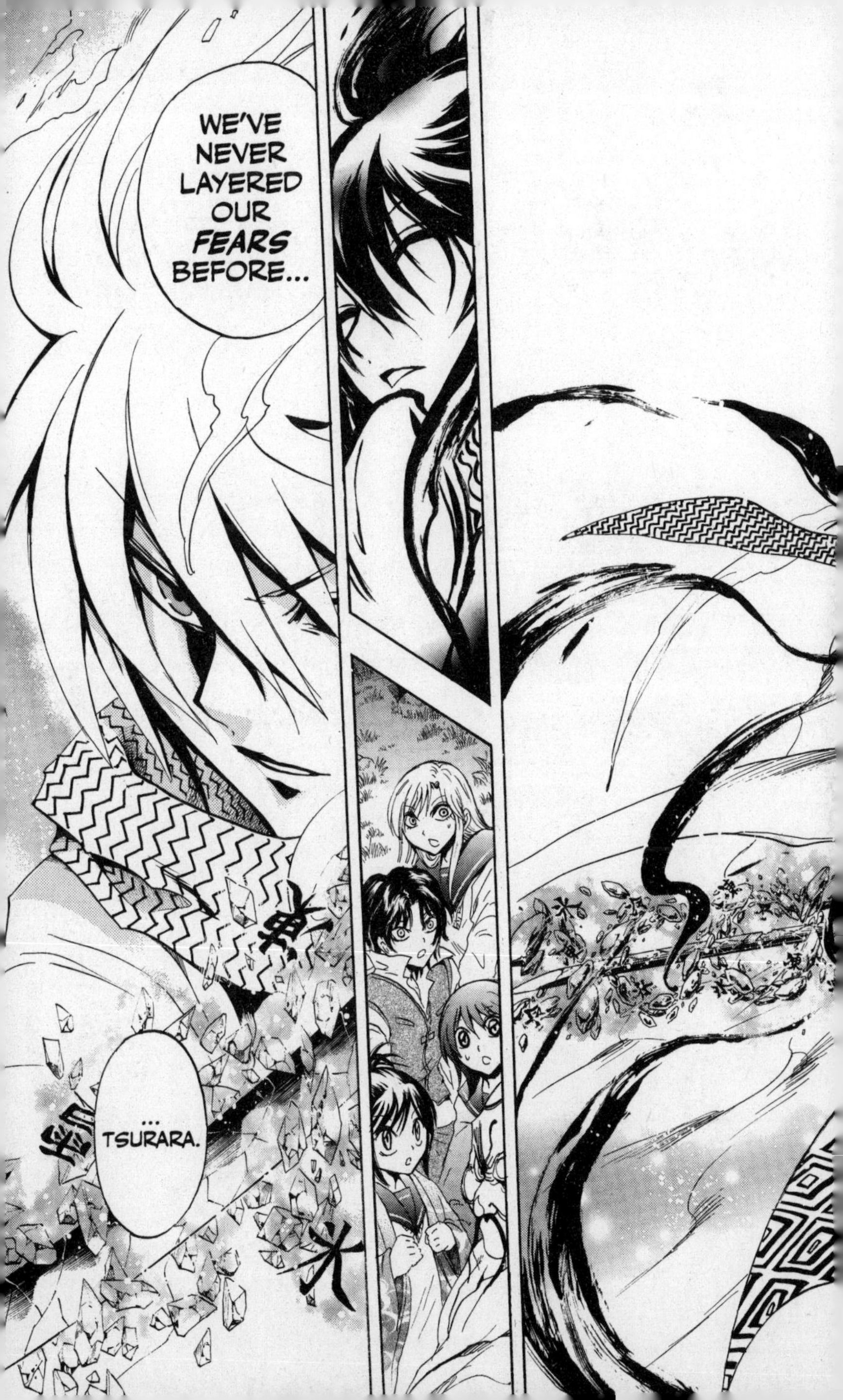
WE'VE NEVER LAYERED OUR FEARS BEFORE...
...TSURARA.

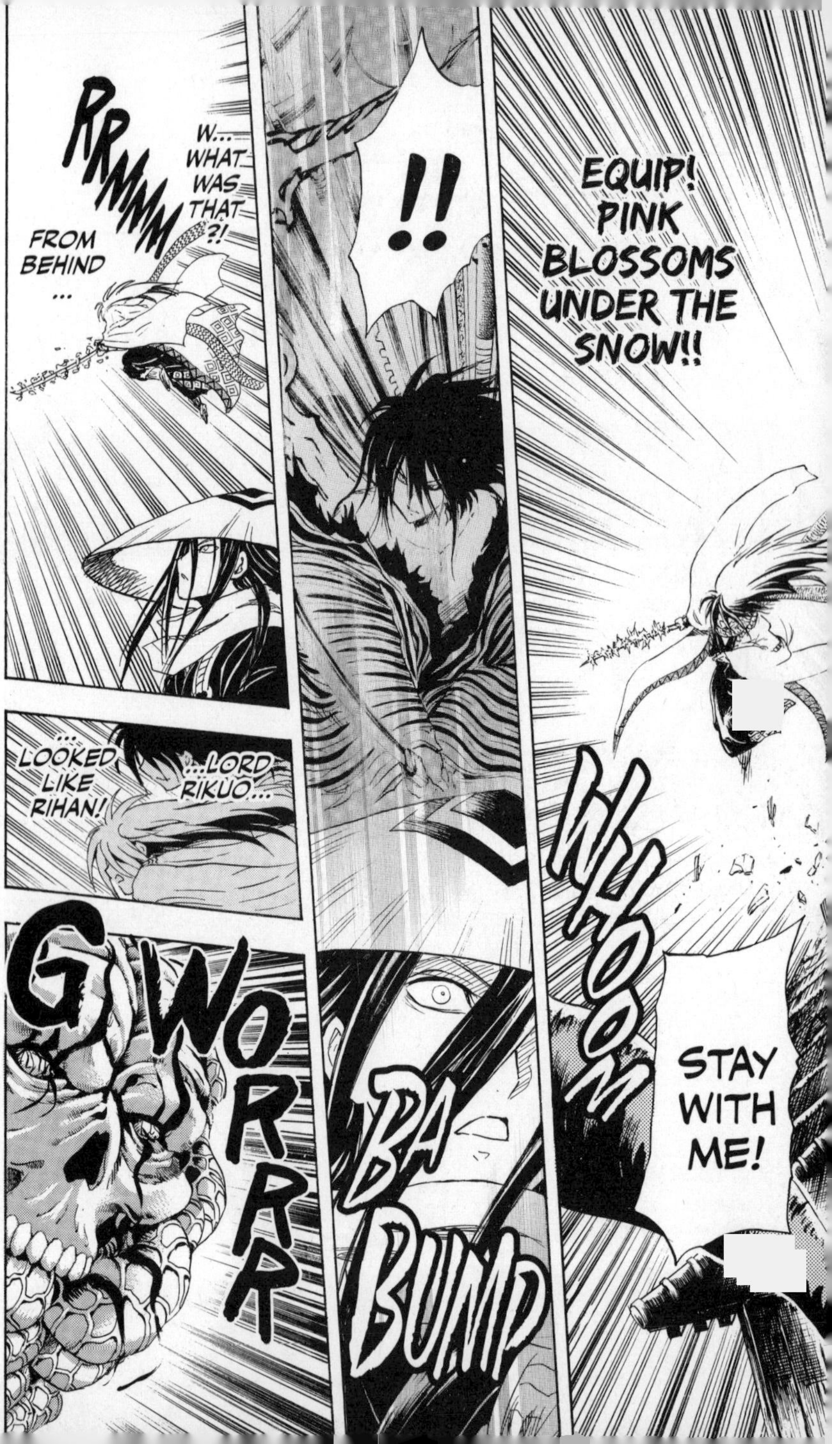
EQUIP! PINK BLOSSOMS UNDER THE SNOW!!
WHOOOM
STAY WITH ME!
!!
BA BUMP
W... WHAT WAS THAT?!
RRMMMM
FROM BEHIND ...
...LORD RIKUO...
...LOOKED LIKE RIHAN!
GWORRR

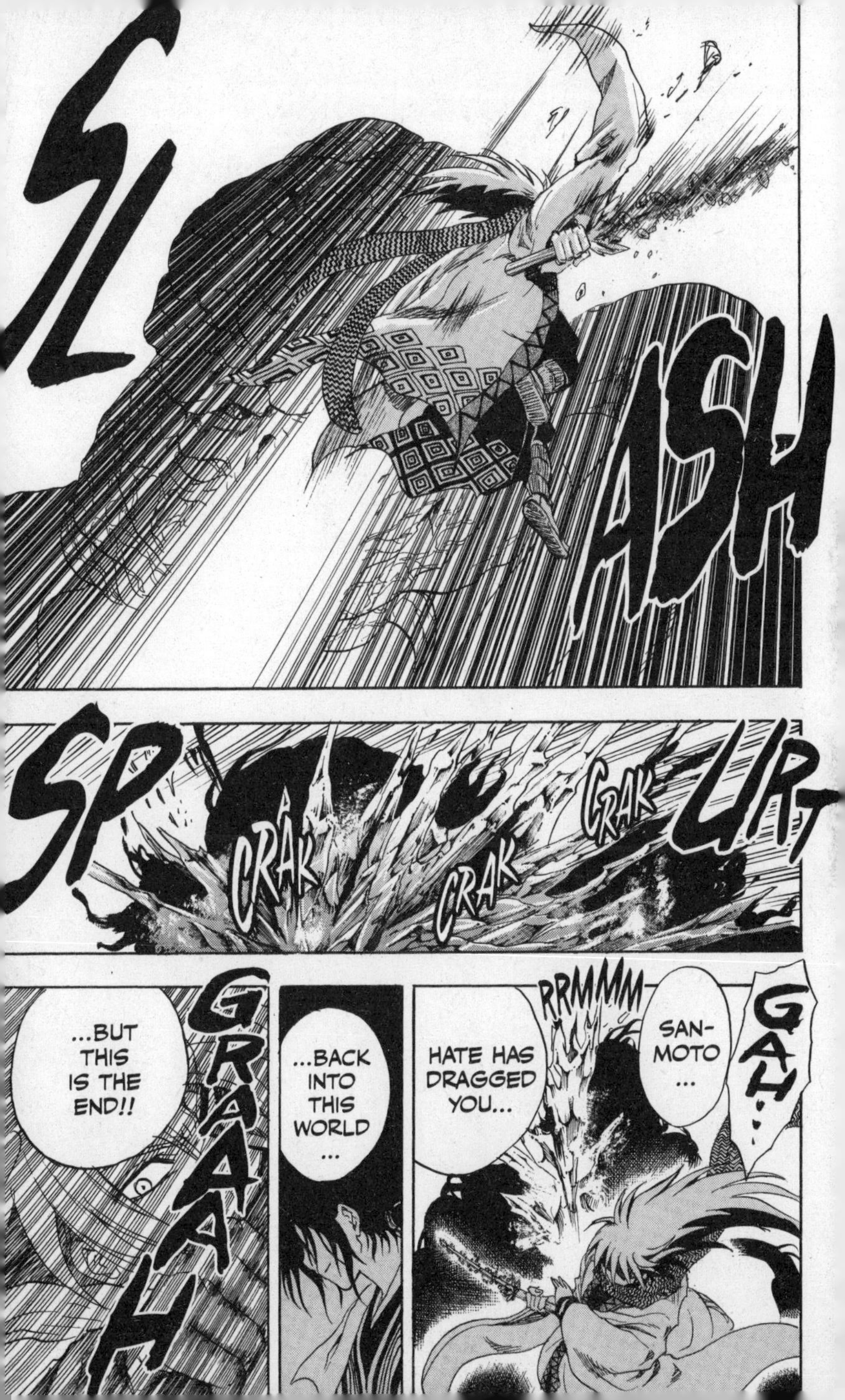
SLASH
SPURT
CRAK
CRAK
CRAK
GAH...
SAN-MOTO...
RRMMM
HATE HAS DRAGGED YOU...
...BACK INTO THIS WORLD...
GRAAAH
...BUT THIS IS THE END!!

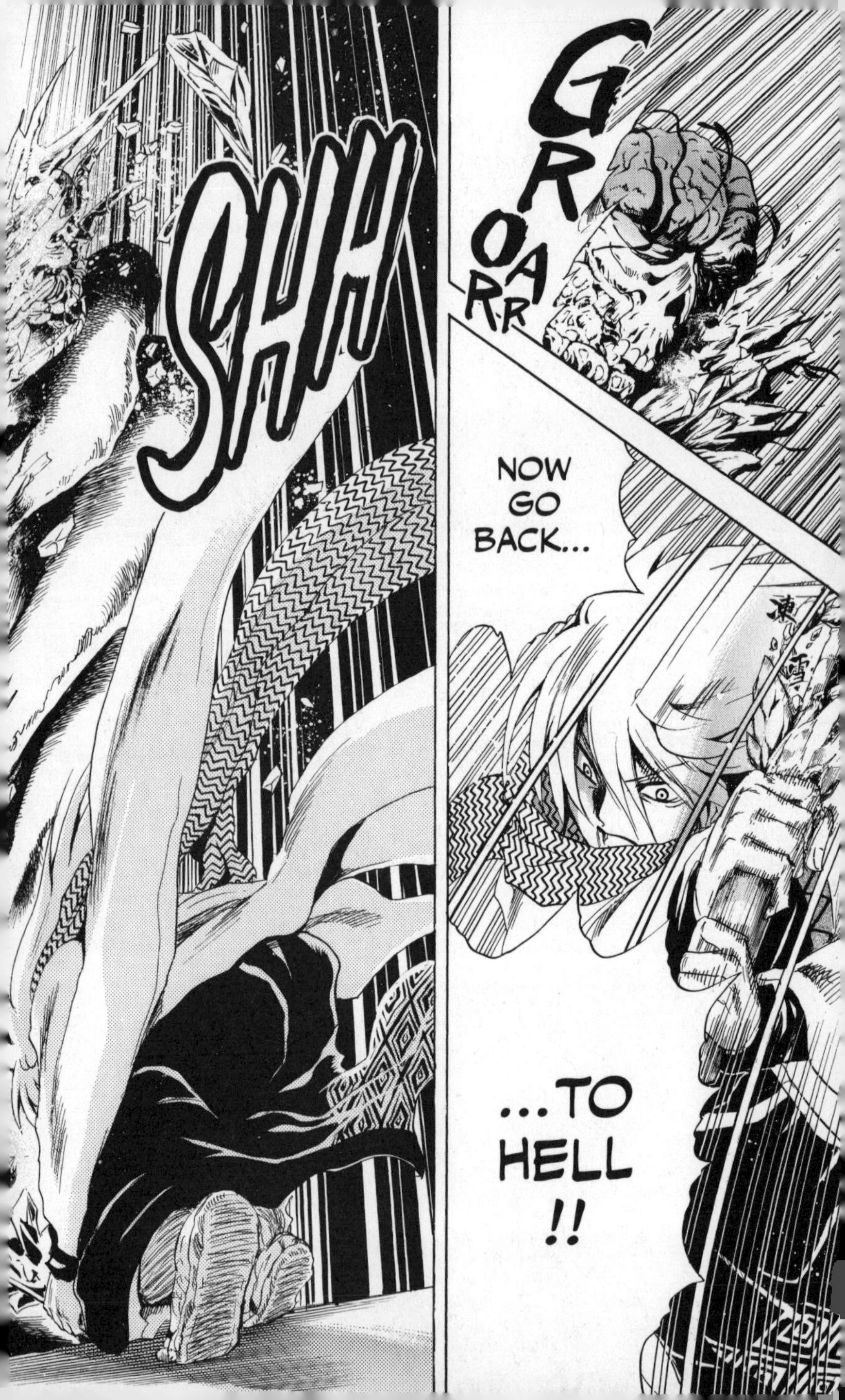
GROARRR
NOW GO BACK...
...TO HELL!!
SHH

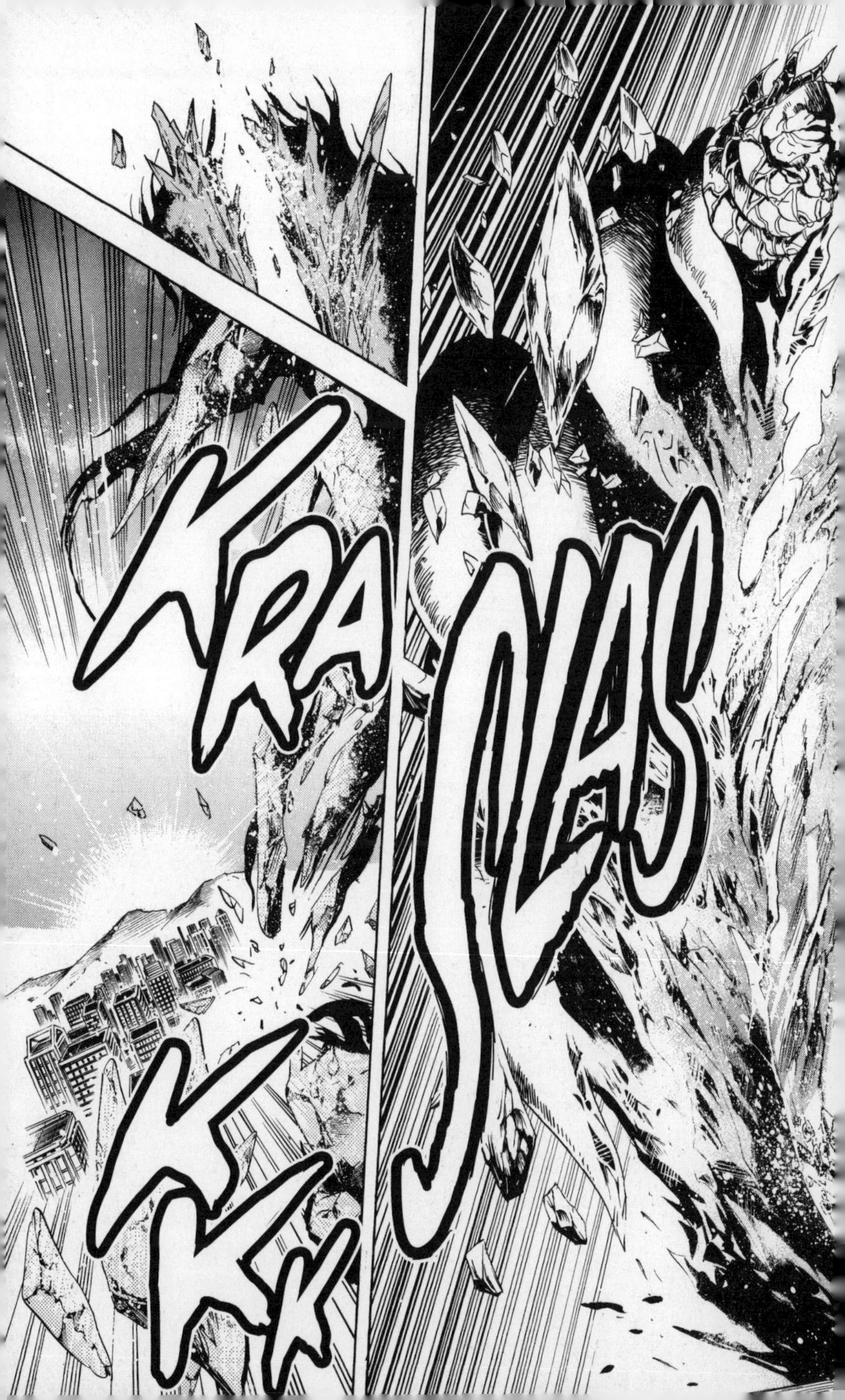
KRA

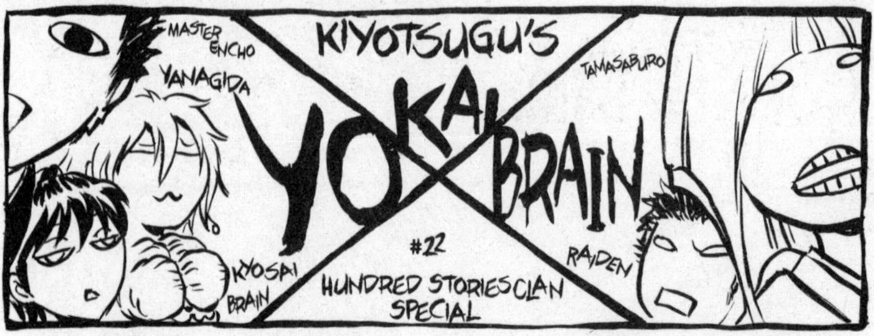
KIYOTSUGU'S
YOKAI
BRAIN
#22
HUNDRED STORIES CLAN SPECIAL
MASTER ENCHO
YANAGIDA
KYOSAI
BRAIN
TAMASABURO
RAIDEN

Q: DID DEFEATING HAGOROMO-GITSUNE REMOVE THE CURSE OF EARLY DEATH FROM THE KEIKAIN CLAN? *-SHO, KANAGAWA PREFECTURE*

RYUJI: HOW COULD WE KNOW THAT SO SOON?! MAYBE WE'LL KNOW IN 20 OR 30 YEARS OR SO.

Q: THIS IS A QUESTION FOR YURA! WHY IS HER UNIFORM SKIRT SO LONG? *-MINMIN, AOYAMA PREFECTURE*

YURA: HM? I THOUGHT IT WAS NORMAL. MAYBE EVERYONE ELSE'S IS TOO SHORT?

MAMIRU: YURA ISN'T WRONG. HER SKIRT'S JUST FINE.

Q: THIS IS FOR YURA-CHAN! I'M GOING TO KYOTO SOON. I'D LIKE TO MEET YOU, SO TELL ME WHERE THE KEIKAIN CLAN MAIN HOUSE IS. *-KOUA, OSAKA PREFECTURE*

YURA: IN KEIKAIN TOWN!! WATCH OUT FOR YOKAI!

Q: THIS QUESTION IS FOR KUROTABO! DO THE BLACK WEAPONS HIDDEN IN YOUR ROBE EVER STAB YOU? DO THEY HURT? AND...I LIKE YOU. *-YAMAINU, SAITAMA PREFECTURE*

KUROTABO: NO, THEY DO NOT. BECAUSE THEY DO NOT APPEAR UNLESS I SAY "HYAH!" AND...THANK YOU.

Q: I HAVE SOME QUESTIONS FOR TAMAZUKI FROM SHIKOKU! HOW OLD ARE YOU? ARE YOUR ANIMAL EARS REAL? AND HAVEN'T YOU GIVEN YOUR DOG A NAME? PLEASE, TELL ME! *-KOKOA, KANAGAWA PREFECTURE*

TAMAZUKI: I'M FAIRLY YOUNG AS FAR AS YOKAI GO. I'M NOT QUITE AS YOUNG AS RIKUO, BUT WE AREN'T FAR APART EITHER. THE EARS ARE REAL. ARE YOU WORRIED ABOUT THAT? MY DOG? MY DOG IS JUST MY DOG.

Q: WHY DID TAMASABURO ALREADY HAVE KUBINASHI'S SKIN THE FIRST TIME THEY MET? *-ANKU, SHIZUOKA PREFECTURE*

TAMASABURO: I COULD GET ALL KINDS OF INFORMATION ON KUBINASHI, SO IT WAS EASY TO MAKE HIS SKIN. BUT I DIDN'T GET IT FIRSTHAND, SO I THOUGHT SOMEONE CLOSE TO HIM MIGHT NOTICE.

Q: CAN TAMASABURO'S DISGUISES FOOL EVEN HIS FELLOW LEADERS? *-SOTENGARYUKI, NAGANO PREFECTURE*

TAMASABURO: I THINK SO. THE NURA CLAN HASN'T EVEN NOTICED MITSUME-YAZURA YET.

〈MULTIPLE QUESTIONS FOR THE HUNDRED STORIES CLAN〉 *-HEITARO, HOKKAIDO*

Q: THIS QUESTION'S FOR MASTER ARTIST KYOSAI!! WHEN YOU MADE THE SUBWAY GIRL, HOW LONG DID YOU MAKE YANAGIDA WAIT?

KYOSAI: I REDID IT SEVERAL TIMES, SO QUITE A WHILE. BUT THAT PICTURE TURNED OUT GREAT.

Q: KYOSAI HAS NEVER IDENTIFIED HIMSELF AS SANMOTO'S "ARMS," BUT IS HE?

KYOSAI: I'M NOT INTERESTED IN THAT.

Q: WHAT DO YOU DO WHEN YOU'RE NOT IN THE RIGHT MOOD?

KYOSAI: LAY ABOUT.

Q: DOES YANAGIDA USE THE INTERNET?

YANAGIDA: YEAH. A LOT.

Q: HOW DO YOU USUALLY COLLECT SCARY STORIES? IS IT EVER DANGEROUS?

YANAGIDA: EVERY DAY IS A GREAT ADVENTURE.

Q: DOES MASTER ENCHO HAVE PUPILS (EITHER HUMAN OR YOKAI)?

ENCHO: I HAVE HUMANS, TOO. BECAUSE I HAVE LOTS OF FANS AT SEIATEI. EVERYONE DID A GOOD JOB SPREADING MY SCARY STORIES AND RUMORS.

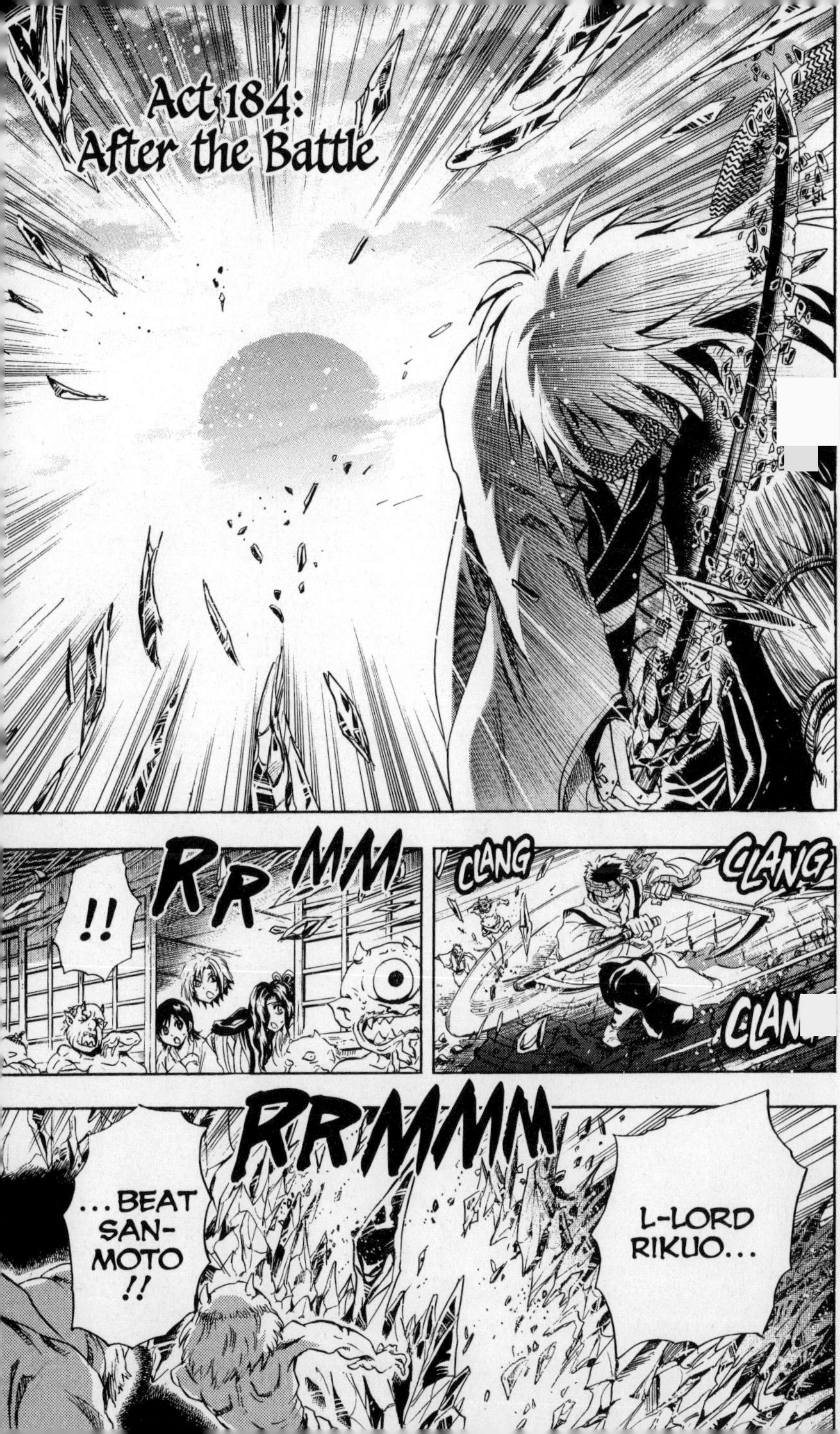
Act 184:
After the Battle
CLANG
CLANG
CLAN
RR MM
!!
RRMMM
L-LORD RIKUO...
...BEAT SAN-MOTO!!

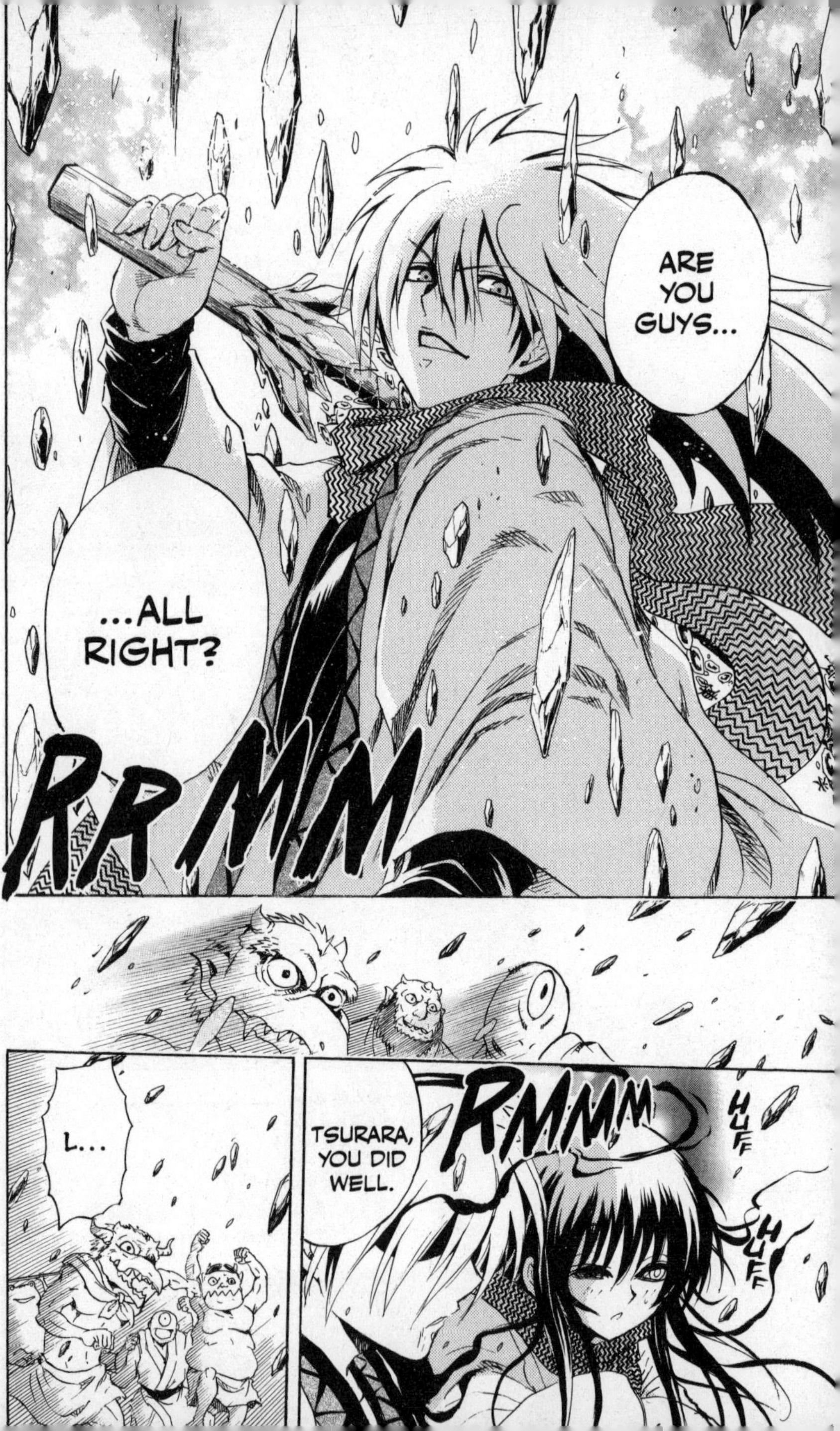
ARE YOU GUYS...
...ALL RIGHT?
RR MM
HUFF
RMMM
TSURARA, YOU DID WELL.
HUFF
I...

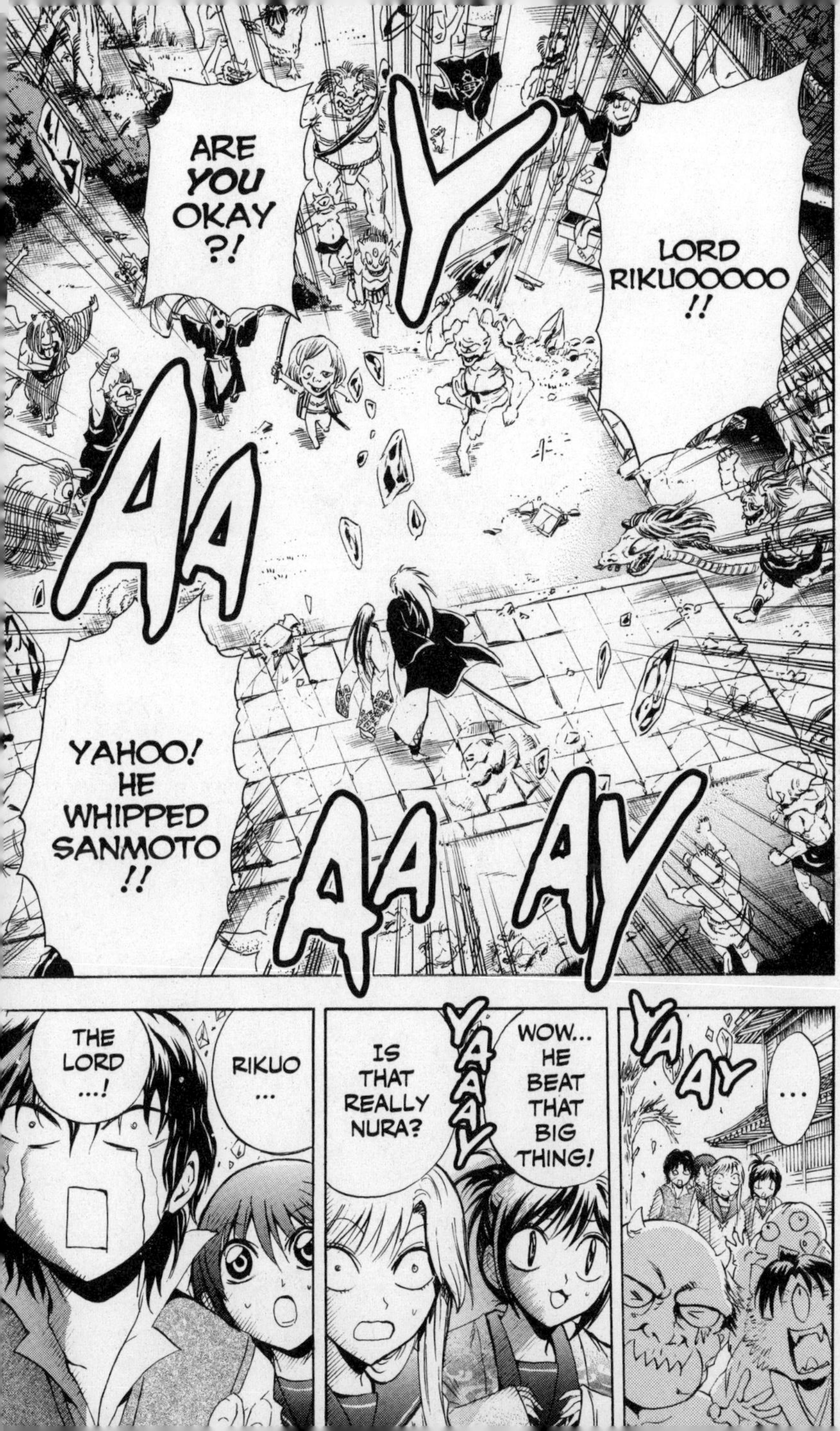
LORD RIKUOOOOO!!
ARE YOU OKAY?!
YAAAAAY
YAHOO! HE WHIPPED SANMOTO!!
YAAY
...
WOW... HE BEAT THAT BIG THING!
YAAAAY
IS THAT REALLY NURA?
RIKUO ...
THE LORD ...!

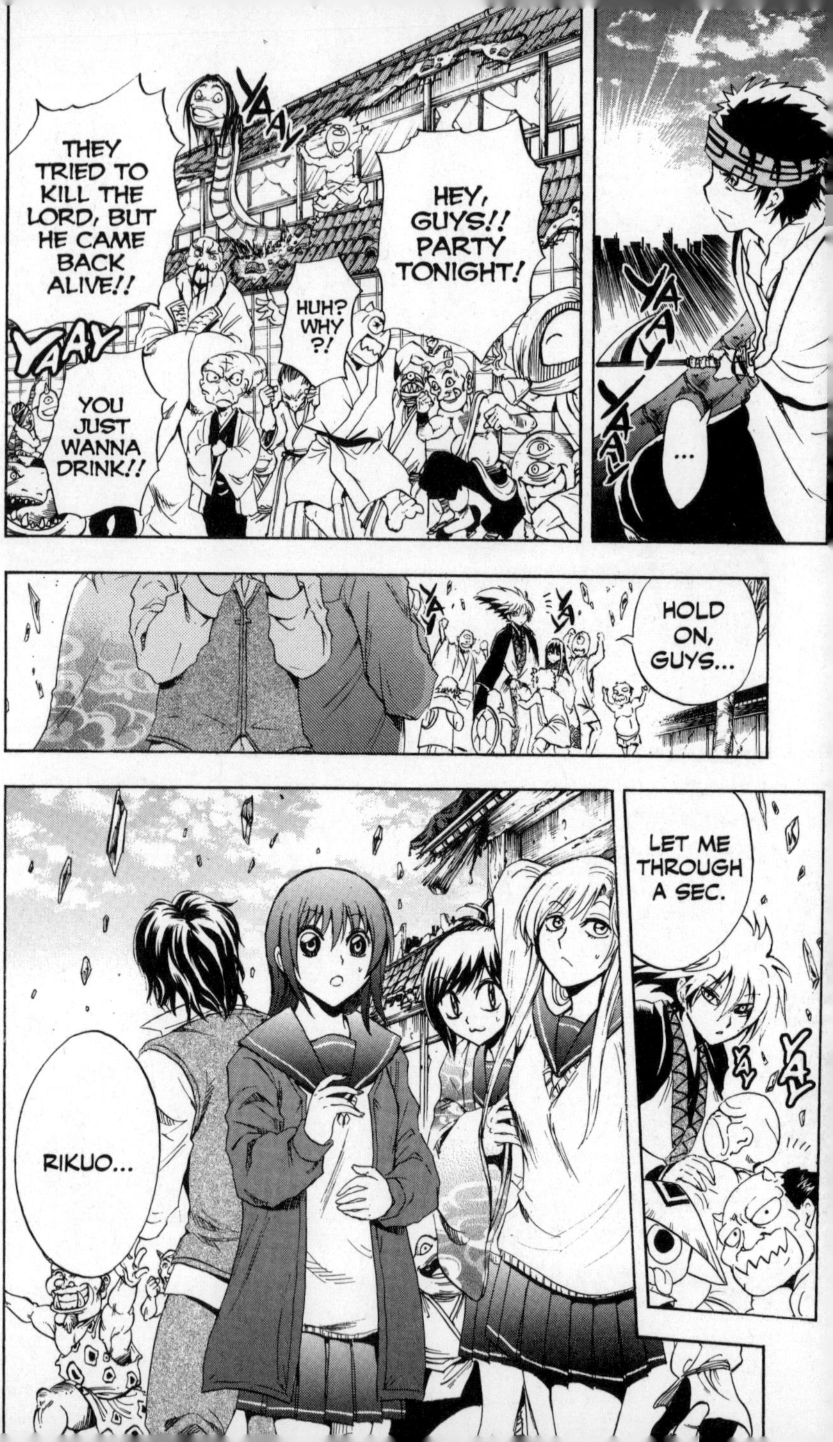
YAAY
YAAY
...
HEY, GUYS!! PARTY TONIGHT!
YAAY
THEY TRIED TO KILL THE LORD, BUT HE CAME BACK ALIVE!!
HUH? WHY?!
YAAY
YOU JUST WANNA DRINK!!
HOLD ON, GUYS...
YA
YA
LET ME THROUGH A SEC.
YA
YA
RIKUO...

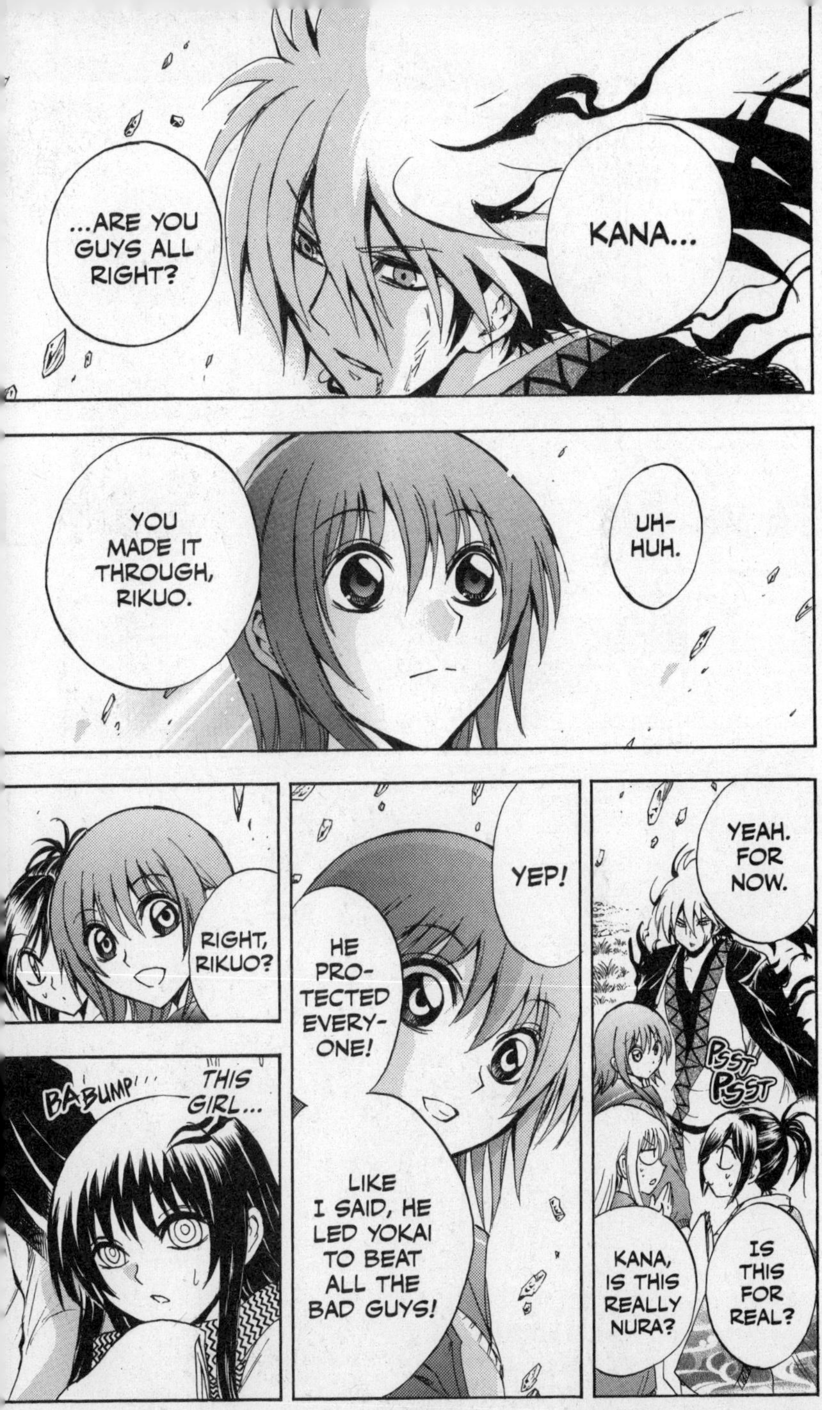
KANA...
...ARE YOU GUYS ALL RIGHT?
UH-HUH.
YOU MADE IT THROUGH, RIKUO.
YEAH. FOR NOW.
PSST PSST
IS THIS FOR REAL?
KANA, IS THIS REALLY NURA?
YEP!
HE PROTECTED EVERYONE!
LIKE I SAID, HE LED YOKAI TO BEAT ALL THE BAD GUYS!
RIGHT, RIKUO?
BABUMP
THIS GIRL...

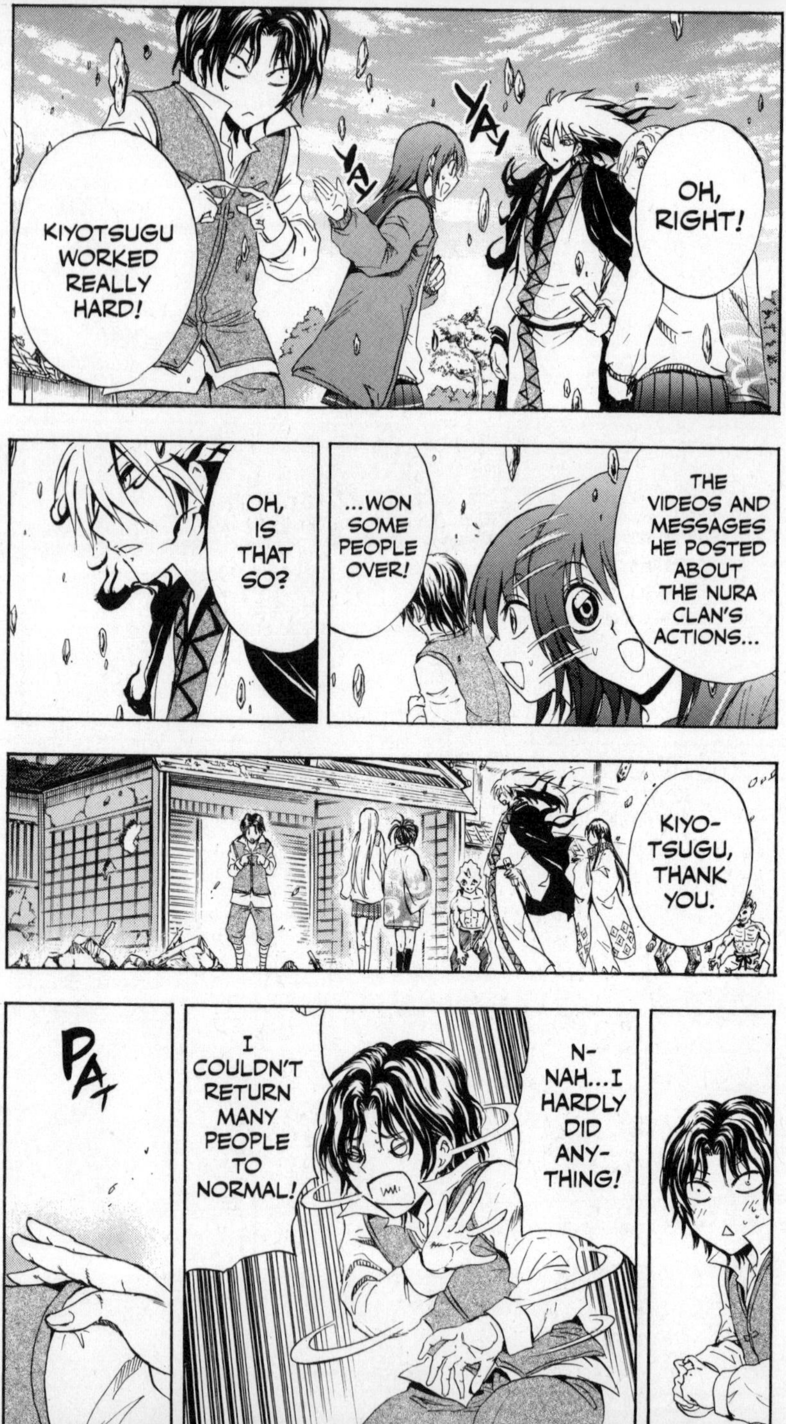
OH, RIGHT!
YAY
YAY
KIYOTSUGU WORKED REALLY HARD!
THE VIDEOS AND MESSAGES HE POSTED ABOUT THE NURA CLAN'S ACTIONS...
...WON SOME PEOPLE OVER!
OH, IS THAT SO?
KIYO-TSUGU, THANK YOU.
N-NAH...I HARDLY DID ANY-THING!
I COULDN'T RETURN MANY PEOPLE TO NORMAL!
PAT

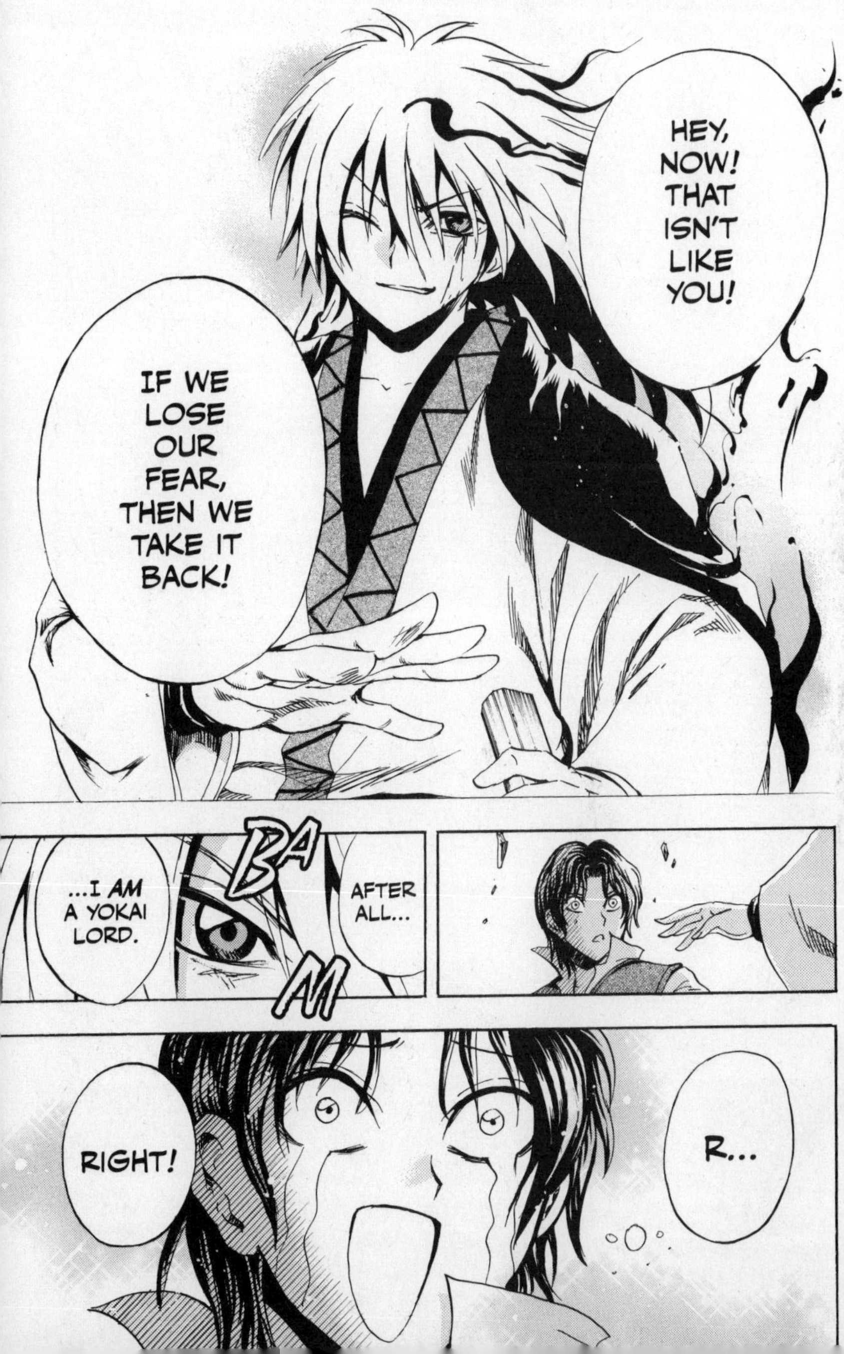
HEY, NOW! THAT ISN'T LIKE YOU!
IF WE LOSE OUR FEAR, THEN WE TAKE IT BACK!
AFTER ALL...
...I AM A YOKAI LORD.
BAM
R...
RIGHT!

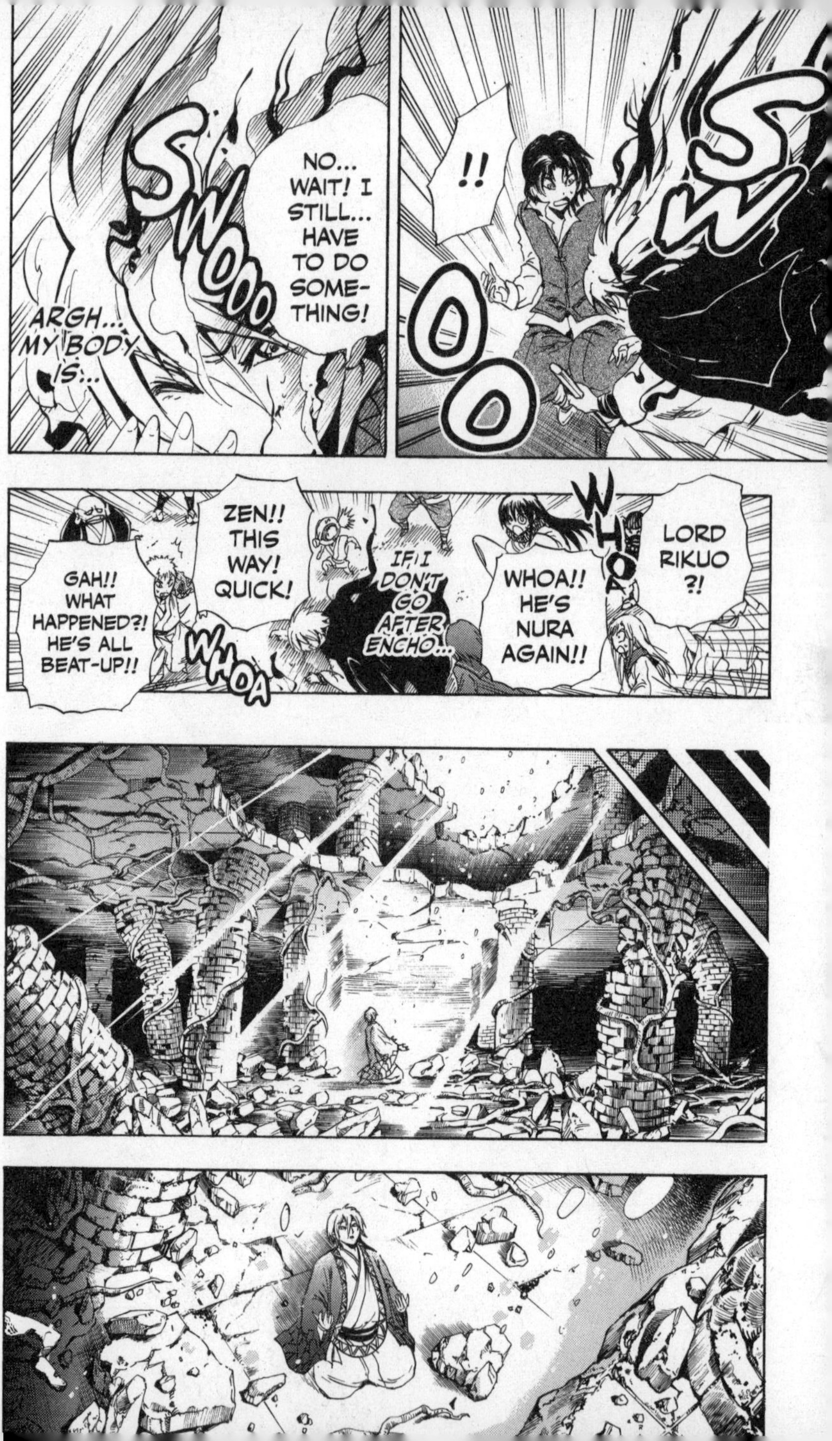
!!
SWOO
NO... WAIT! I STILL... HAVE TO DO SOME-THING!
SWOOO
ARGH... MY BODY IS...
LORD RIKUO ?!
WHOA
WHOA!! HE'S NURA AGAIN!!
IF I DON'T GO AFTER ENCHO...
ZEN!! THIS WAY! QUICK!
WHOA
GAH!! WHAT HAPPENED?! HE'S ALL BEAT-UP!!

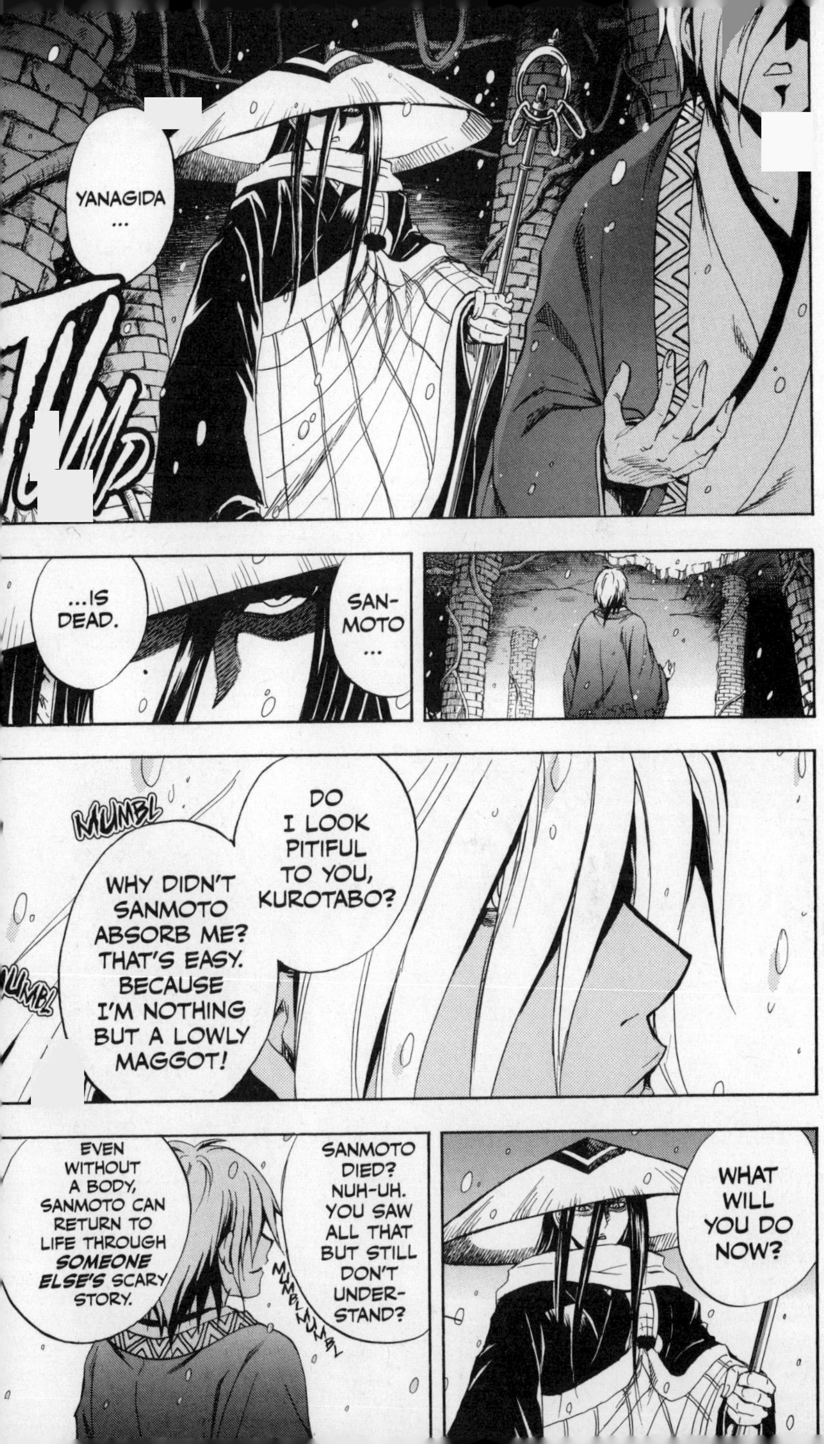
YANAGIDA ...
SAN-MOTO ...
...IS DEAD.
DO I LOOK PITIFUL TO YOU, KUROTABO?
MUMBL
WHY DIDN'T SANMOTO ABSORB ME? THAT'S EASY. BECAUSE I'M NOTHING BUT A LOWLY MAGGOT!
MUMBL
WHAT WILL YOU DO NOW?
SANMOTO DIED? NUH-UH. YOU SAW ALL THAT BUT STILL DON'T UNDER-STAND?
MUMBLMUMBL
EVEN WITHOUT A BODY, SANMOTO CAN RETURN TO LIFE THROUGH ***SOMEONE ELSE'S*** SCARY STORY.

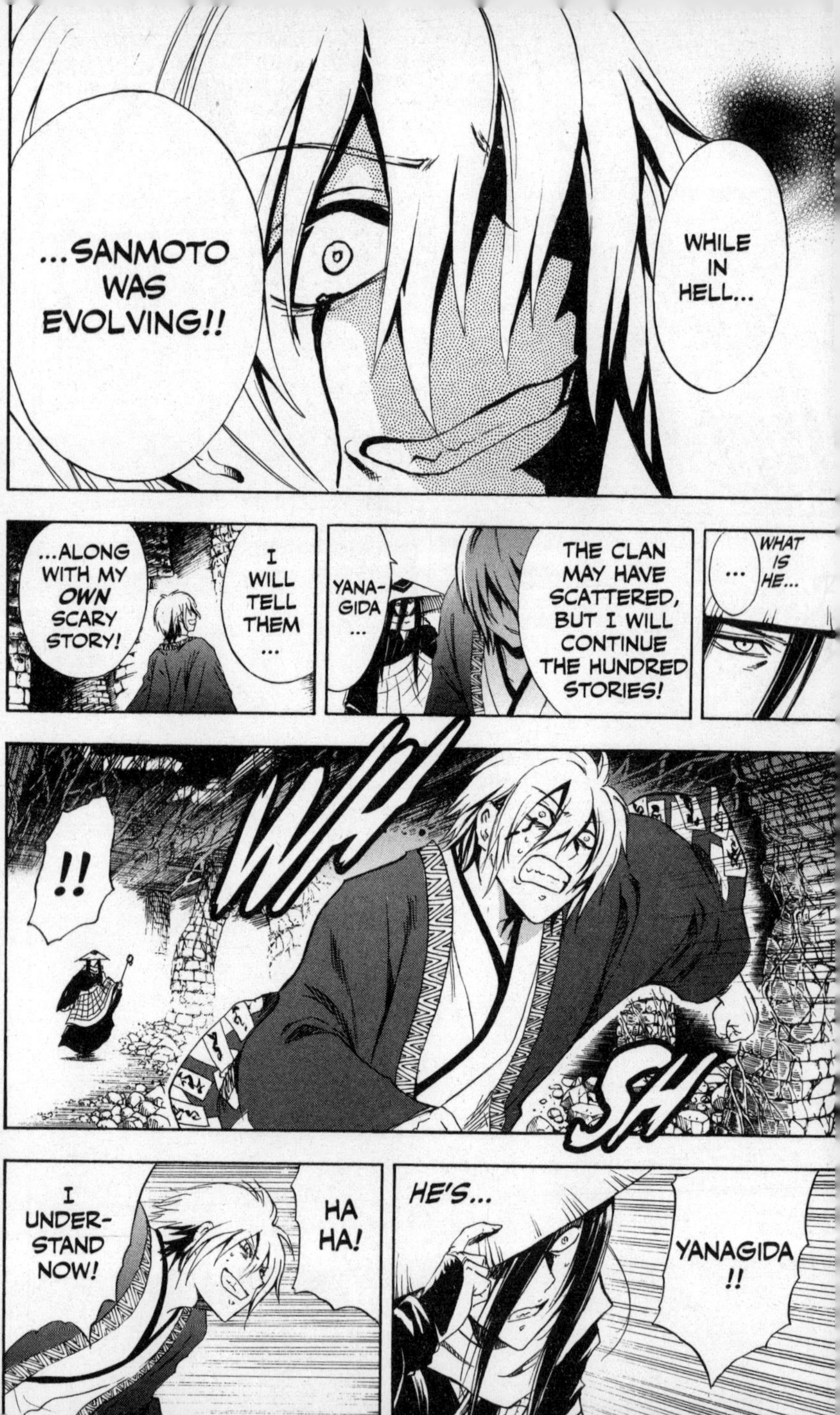
WHILE IN HELL...
...SANMOTO WAS EVOLVING!!
WHAT IS HE...
...
THE CLAN MAY HAVE SCATTERED, BUT I WILL CONTINUE THE HUNDRED STORIES!
YANAGIDA...
I WILL TELL THEM...
...ALONG WITH MY *OWN* SCARY STORY!
WH
SH
!!
YANAGIDA!!
HE'S...
HA HA!
I UNDER-STAND NOW!

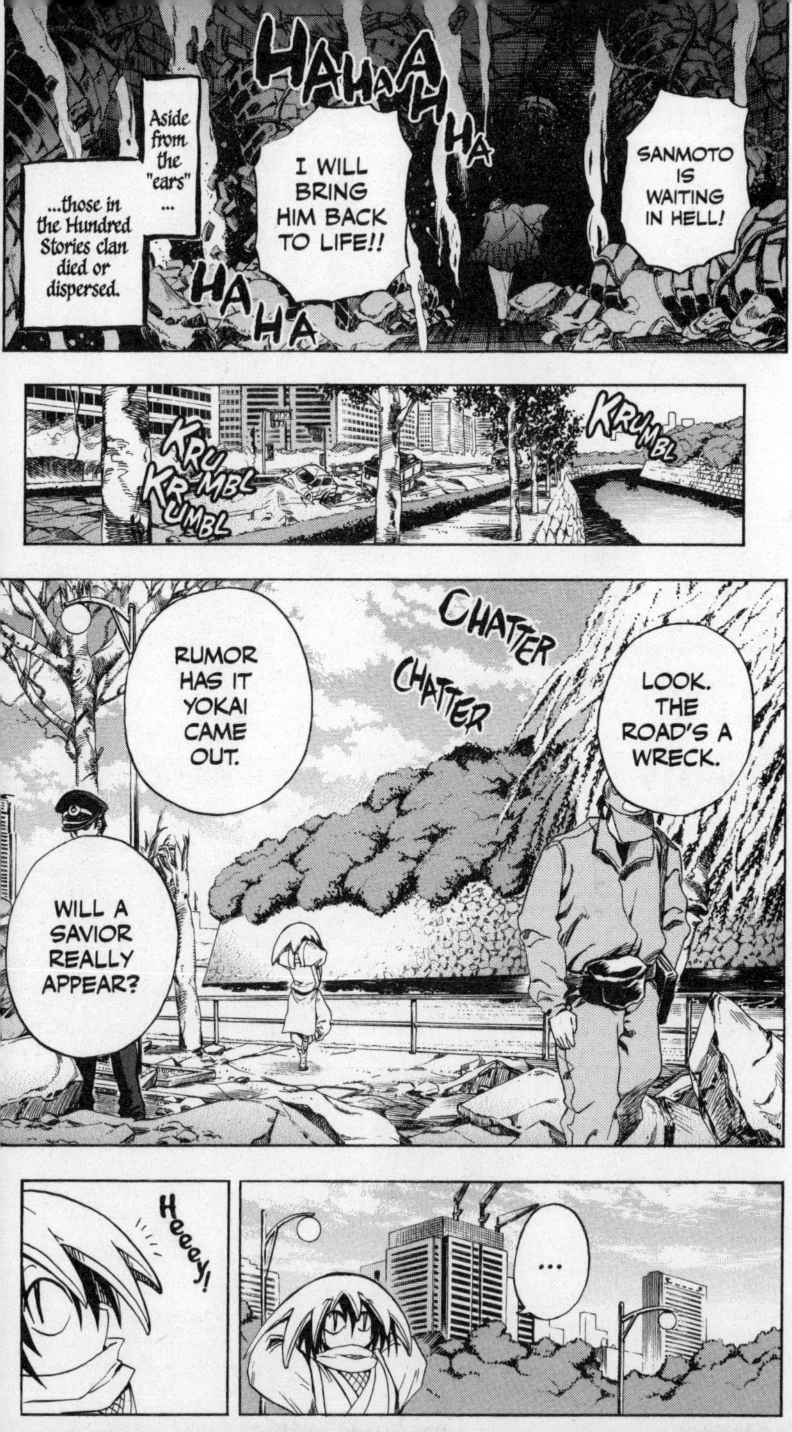
SANMOTO IS WAITING IN HELL!
HAHAHAHA
I WILL BRING HIM BACK TO LIFE!!
Aside from the "ears"...
...those in the Hundred Stories clan died or dispersed.
HA HA
KRUMBL
KRUMBL
KRUMBL
CHATTER
LOOK. THE ROAD'S A WRECK.
CHATTER
RUMOR HAS IT YOKAI CAME OUT.
WILL A SAVIOR REALLY APPEAR?
...
Heeey!

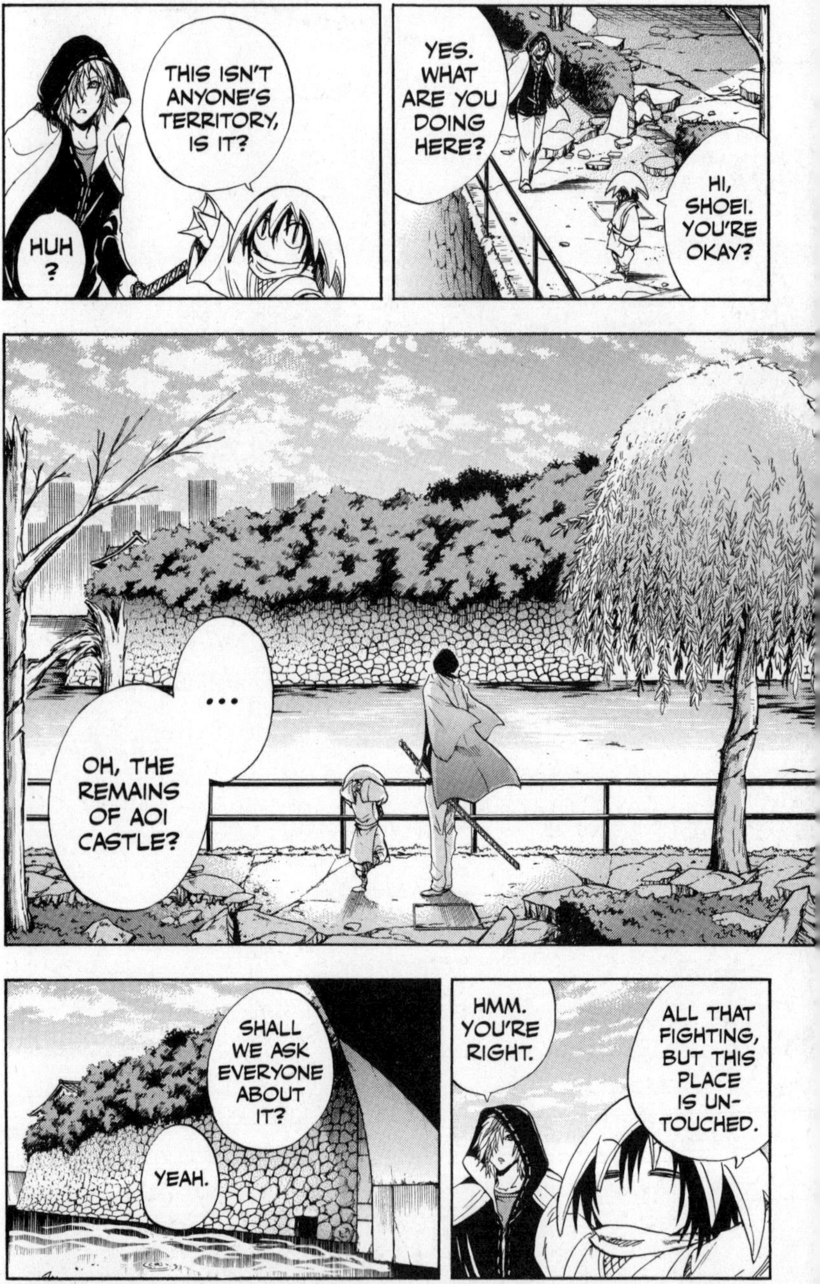
HI, SHOEI. YOU'RE OKAY?
YES. WHAT ARE YOU DOING HERE?
THIS ISN'T ANYONE'S TERRITORY, IS IT?
HUH?
...
OH, THE REMAINS OF AOI CASTLE?
ALL THAT FIGHTING, BUT THIS PLACE IS UNTOUCHED.
HMM. YOU'RE RIGHT.
SHALL WE ASK EVERYONE ABOUT IT?
YEAH.

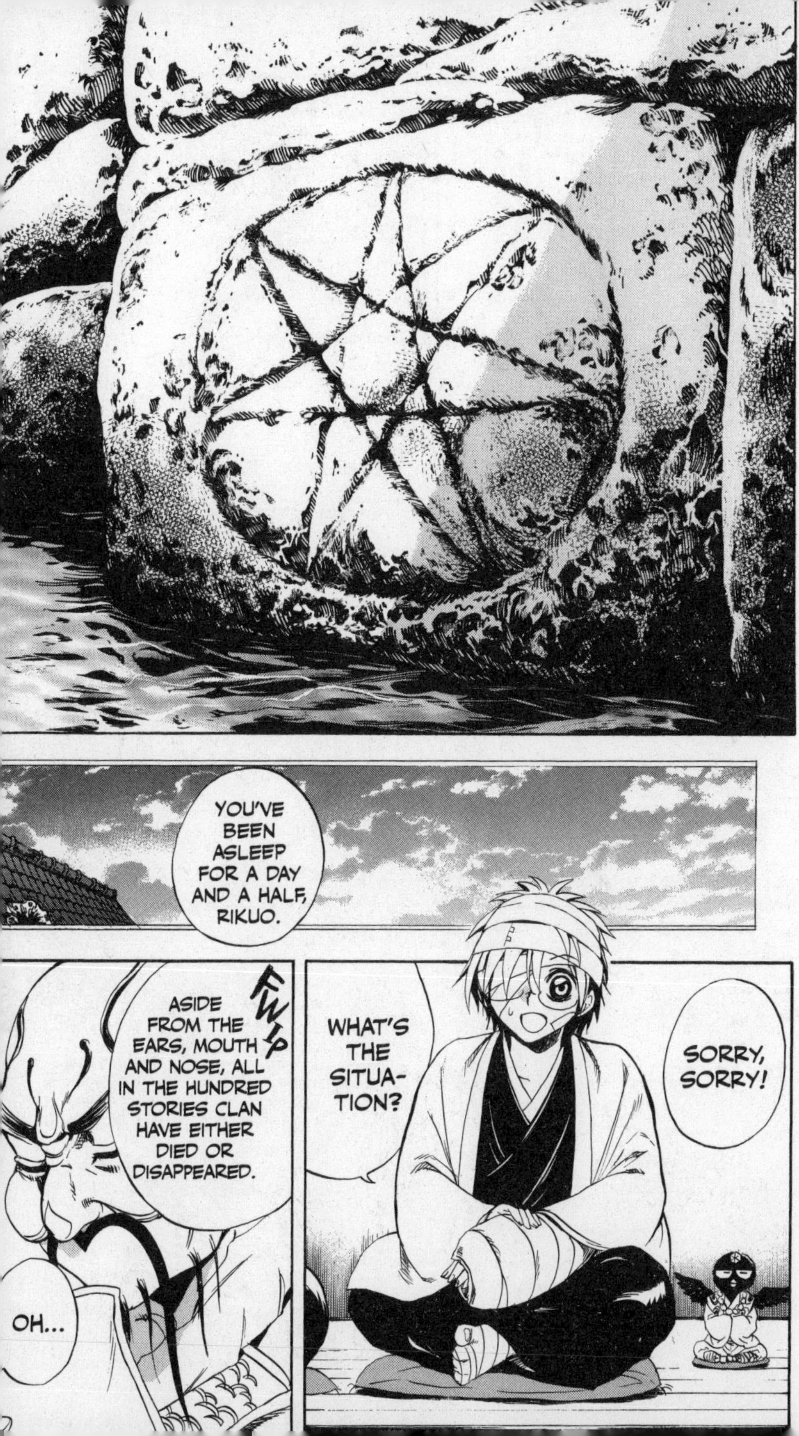
YOU'VE BEEN ASLEEP FOR A DAY AND A HALF, RIKUO.
SORRY, SORRY!
WHAT'S THE SITUA-TION?
FWIP
ASIDE FROM THE EARS, MOUTH AND NOSE, ALL IN THE HUNDRED STORIES CLAN HAVE EITHER DIED OR DISAPPEARED.
OH...

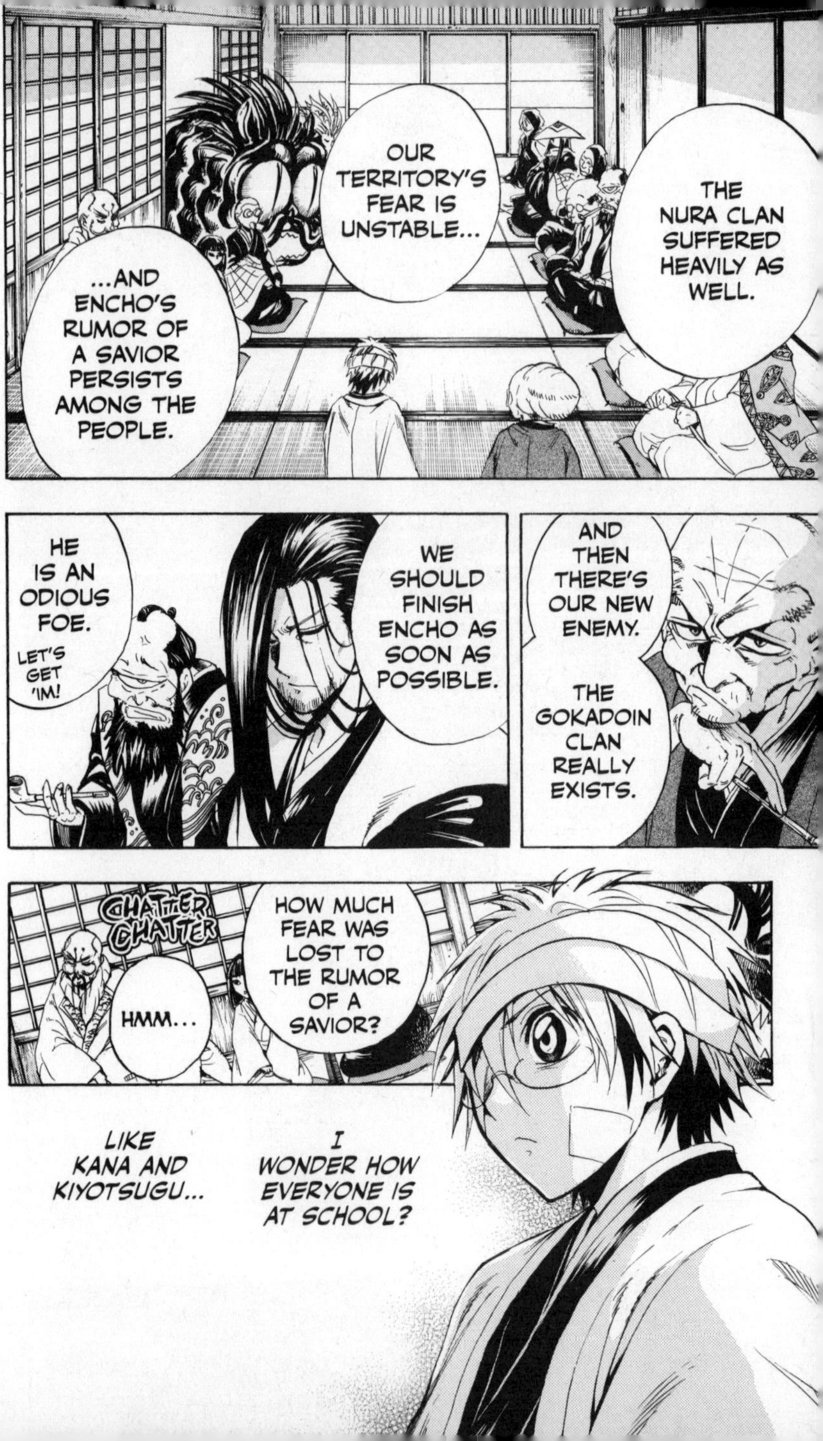
THE NURA CLAN SUFFERED HEAVILY AS WELL.
OUR TERRITORY'S FEAR IS UNSTABLE...
...AND ENCHO'S RUMOR OF A SAVIOR PERSISTS AMONG THE PEOPLE.
AND THEN THERE'S OUR NEW ENEMY.
THE GOKADOIN CLAN REALLY EXISTS.
WE SHOULD FINISH ENCHO AS SOON AS POSSIBLE.
HE IS AN ODIOUS FOE.
LET'S GET 'IM!
HOW MUCH FEAR WAS LOST TO THE RUMOR OF A SAVIOR?
CHATTER CHATTER
HMM...
I WONDER HOW EVERYONE IS AT SCHOOL?
LIKE KANA AND KIYOTSUGU...

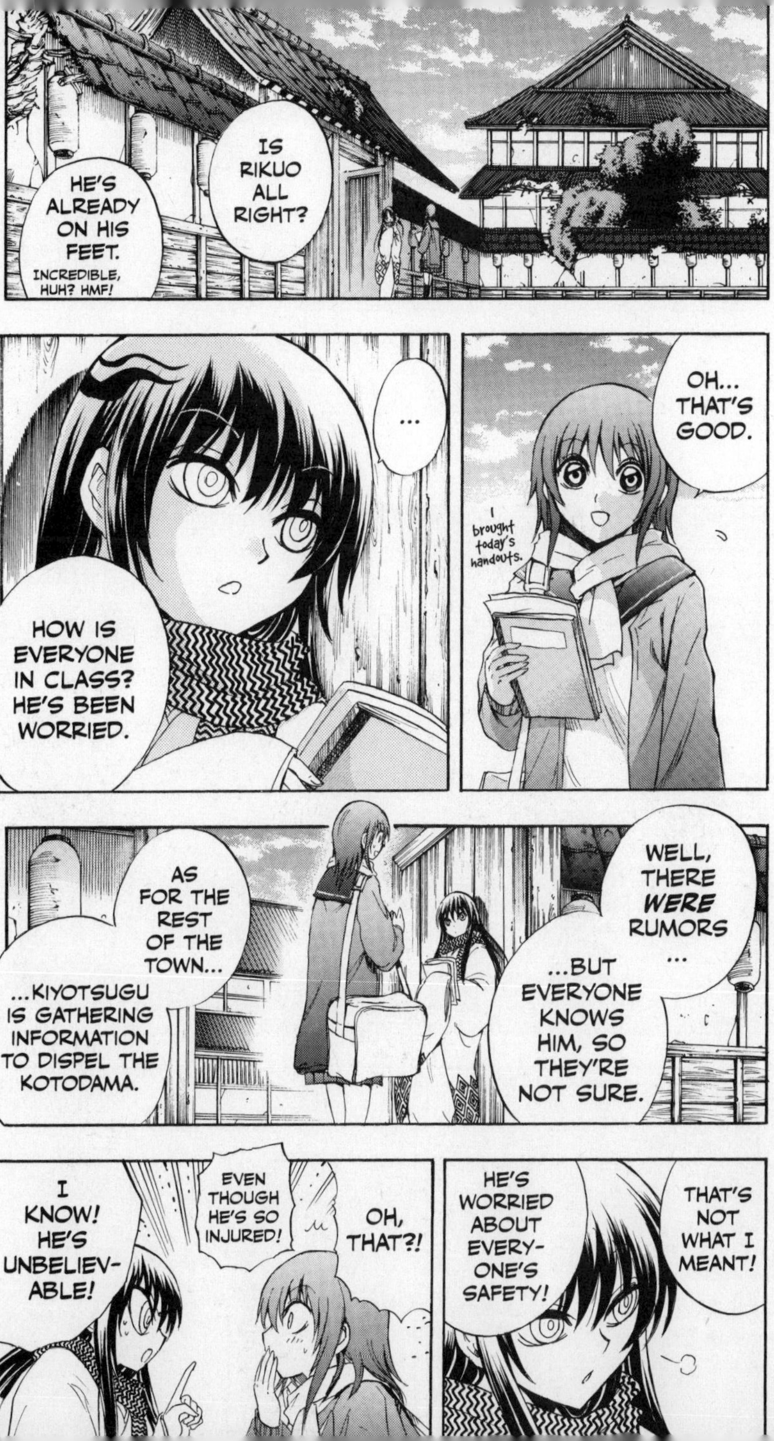
IS RIKUO ALL RIGHT?
HE'S ALREADY ON HIS FEET.
INCREDIBLE, HUH? HMF!
OH... THAT'S GOOD.
I brought today's handouts.
...
HOW IS EVERYONE IN CLASS? HE'S BEEN WORRIED.
WELL, THERE *WERE* RUMORS...
...BUT EVERYONE KNOWS HIM, SO THEY'RE NOT SURE.
AS FOR THE REST OF THE TOWN...
...KIYOTSUGU IS GATHERING INFORMATION TO DISPEL THE KOTODAMA.
THAT'S NOT WHAT I MEANT!
HE'S WORRIED ABOUT EVERYONE'S SAFETY!
OH, THAT?!
EVEN THOUGH HE'S SO INJURED!
I KNOW! HE'S UNBELIEVABLE!

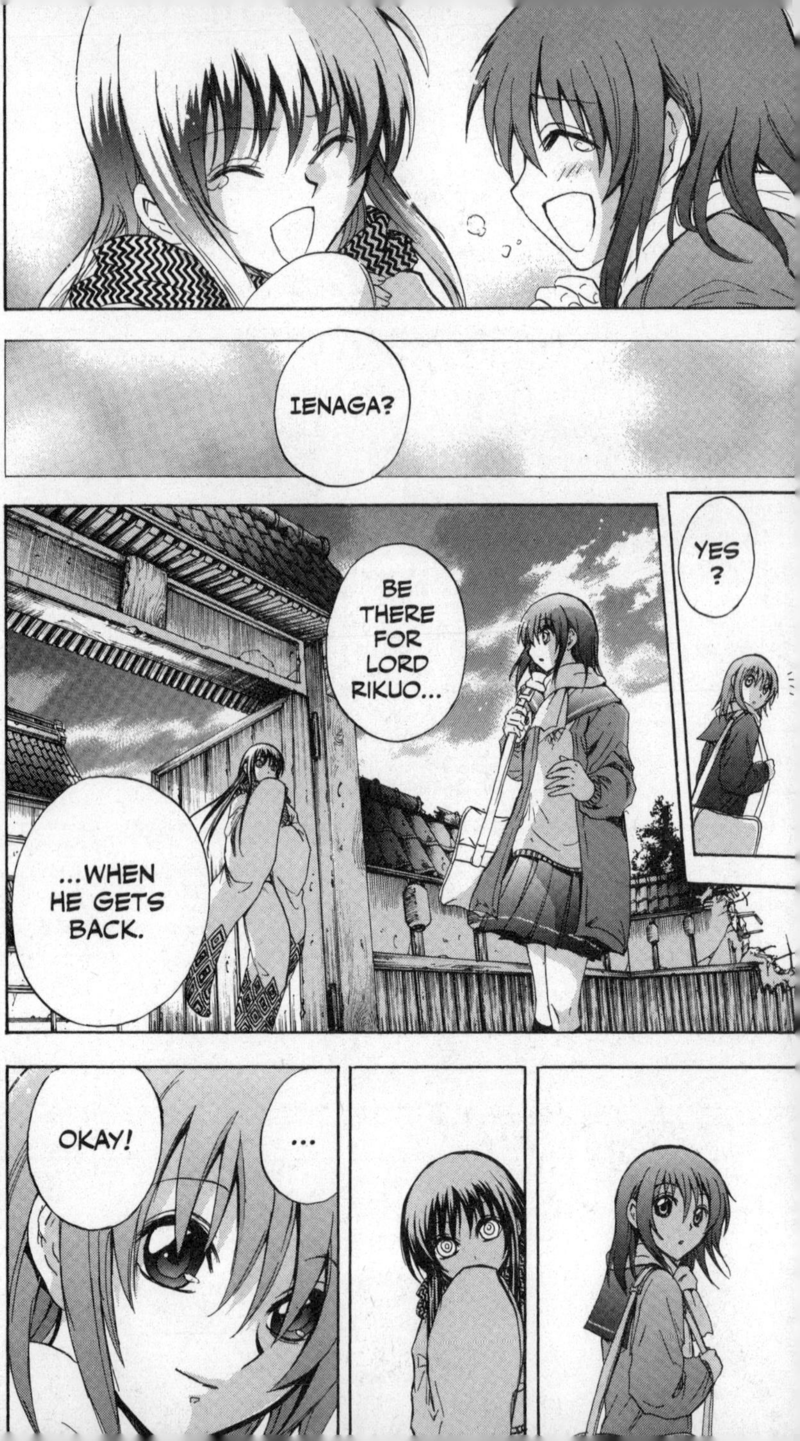
IENAGA?
YES?
BE THERE FOR LORD RIKUO...
...WHEN HE GETS BACK.
...
OKAY!

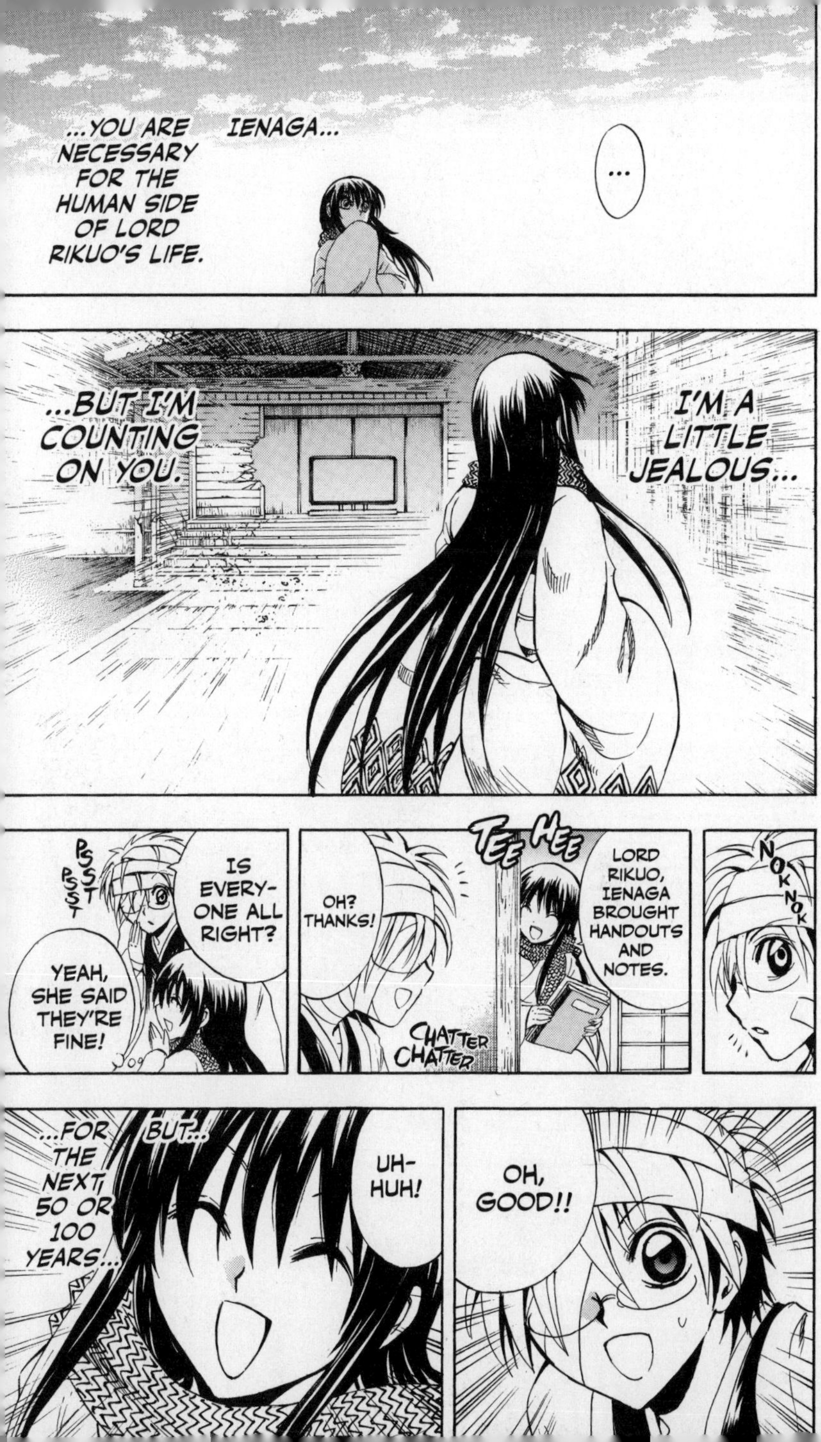
...
IENAGA...
...YOU ARE NECESSARY FOR THE HUMAN SIDE OF LORD RIKUO'S LIFE.
I'M A LITTLE JEALOUS...
...BUT I'M COUNTING ON YOU.
NOK NOK
TEE HEE
LORD RIKUO, IENAGA BROUGHT HANDOUTS AND NOTES.
OH? THANKS!
CHATTER CHATTER
IS EVERY-ONE ALL RIGHT?
PSST PSST
YEAH, SHE SAID THEY'RE FINE!
OH, GOOD!!
UH-HUH!
BUT...
...FOR THE NEXT 50 OR 100 YEARS...

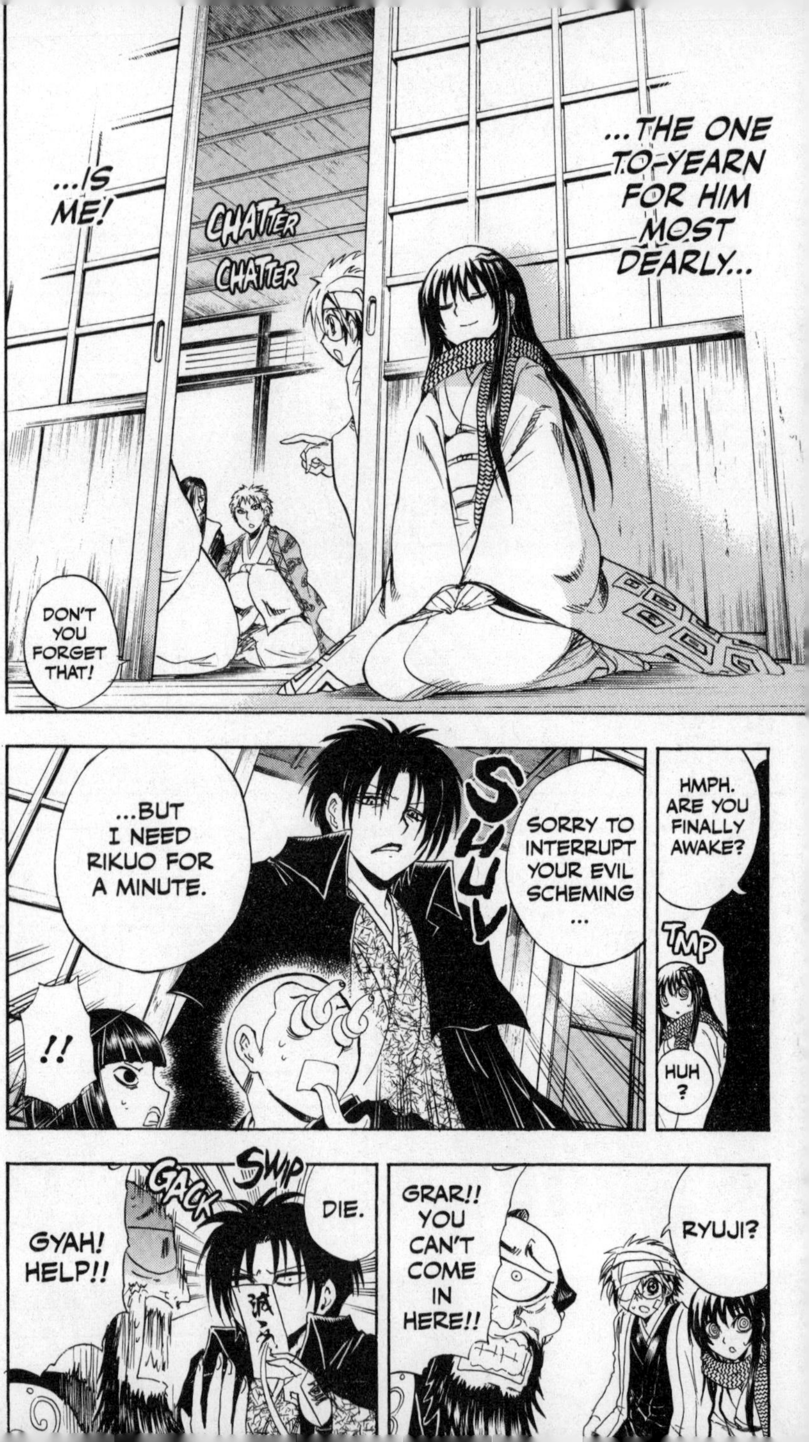
...THE ONE TO YEARN FOR HIM MOST DEARLY...
CHATTER CHATTER
...IS ME!
DON'T YOU FORGET THAT!
HMPH. ARE YOU FINALLY AWAKE?
TMP
HUH?
SHUU
SORRY TO INTERRUPT YOUR EVIL SCHEMING...
...BUT I NEED RIKUO FOR A MINUTE.
!!
RYUJI?
GRAR!! YOU CAN'T COME IN HERE!!
SWIP
DIE.
GACK
GYAH! HELP!!

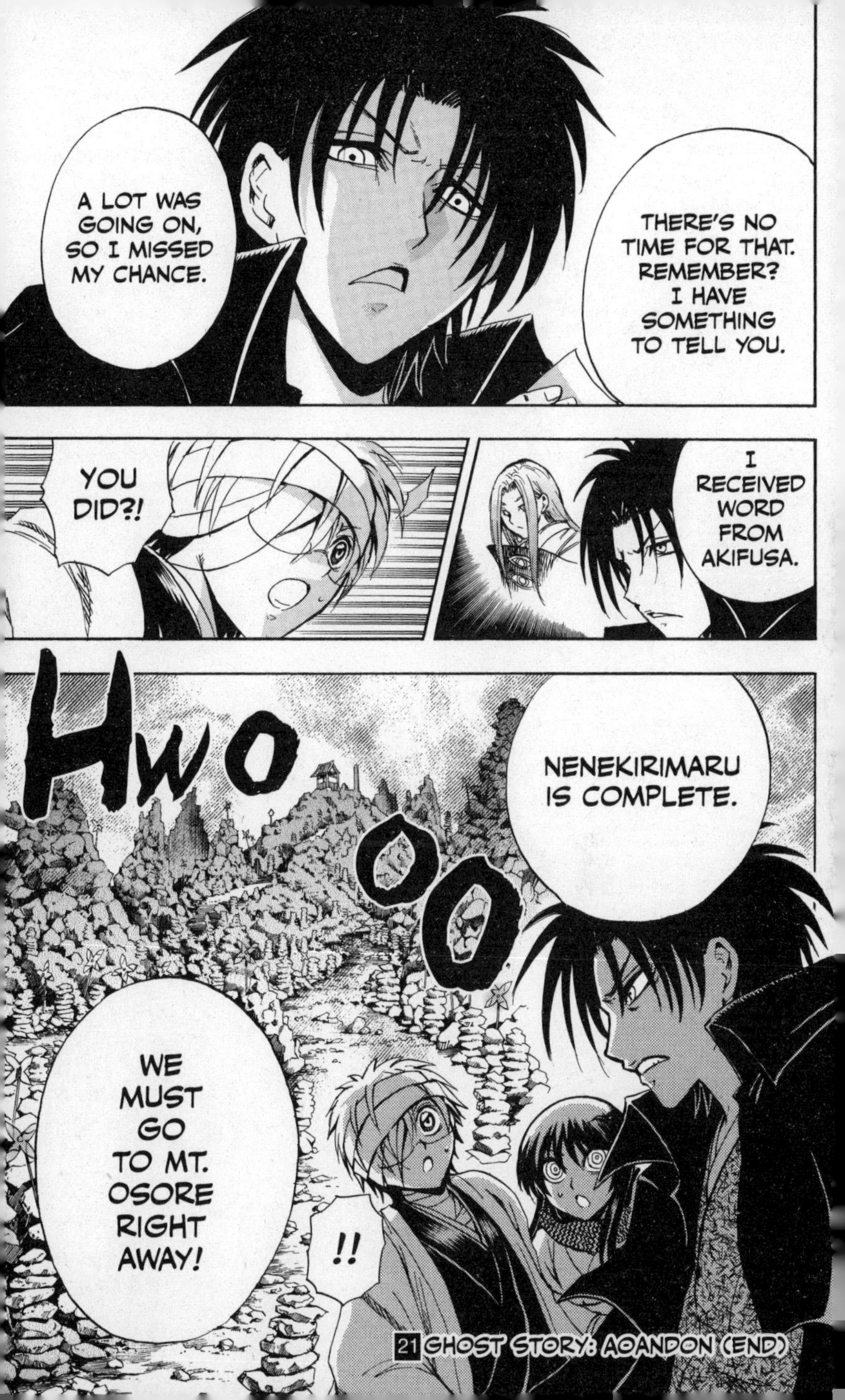
THERE'S NO TIME FOR THAT. REMEMBER? I HAVE SOMETHING TO TELL YOU.
A LOT WAS GOING ON, SO I MISSED MY CHANCE.
I RECEIVED WORD FROM AKIFUSA.
YOU DID?!
NENEKIRIMARU IS COMPLETE.
HWOOO
WE MUST GO TO MT. OSORE RIGHT AWAY!
!!
21 GHOST STORY: AOANDON (END)

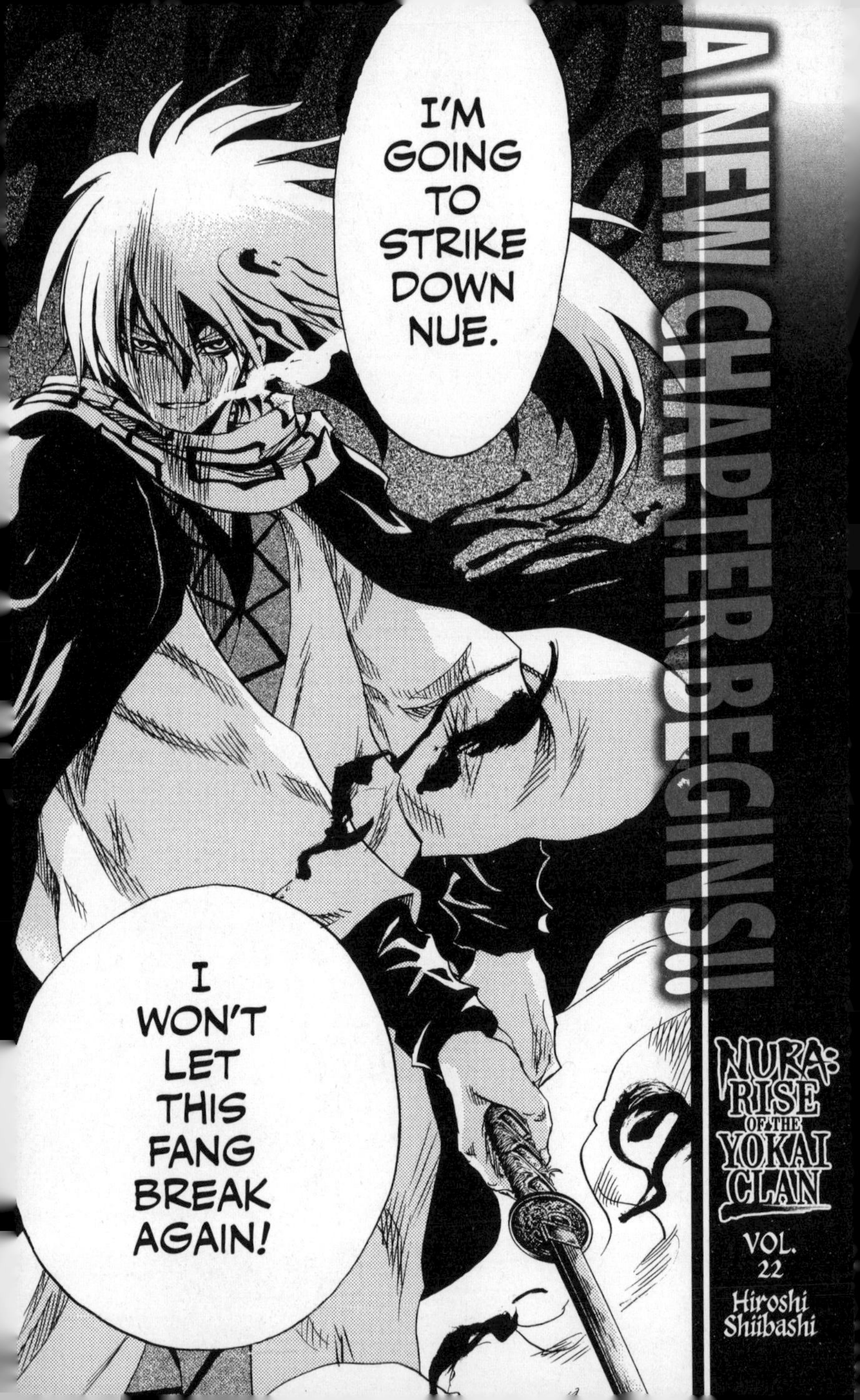
A NEW CHAPTER BEGINS!!
NURA: RISE OF THE YOKAI CLAN
VOL. 22
Hiroshi Shiibashi
I'M GOING TO STRIKE DOWN NUE.
I WON'T LET THIS FANG BREAK AGAIN!

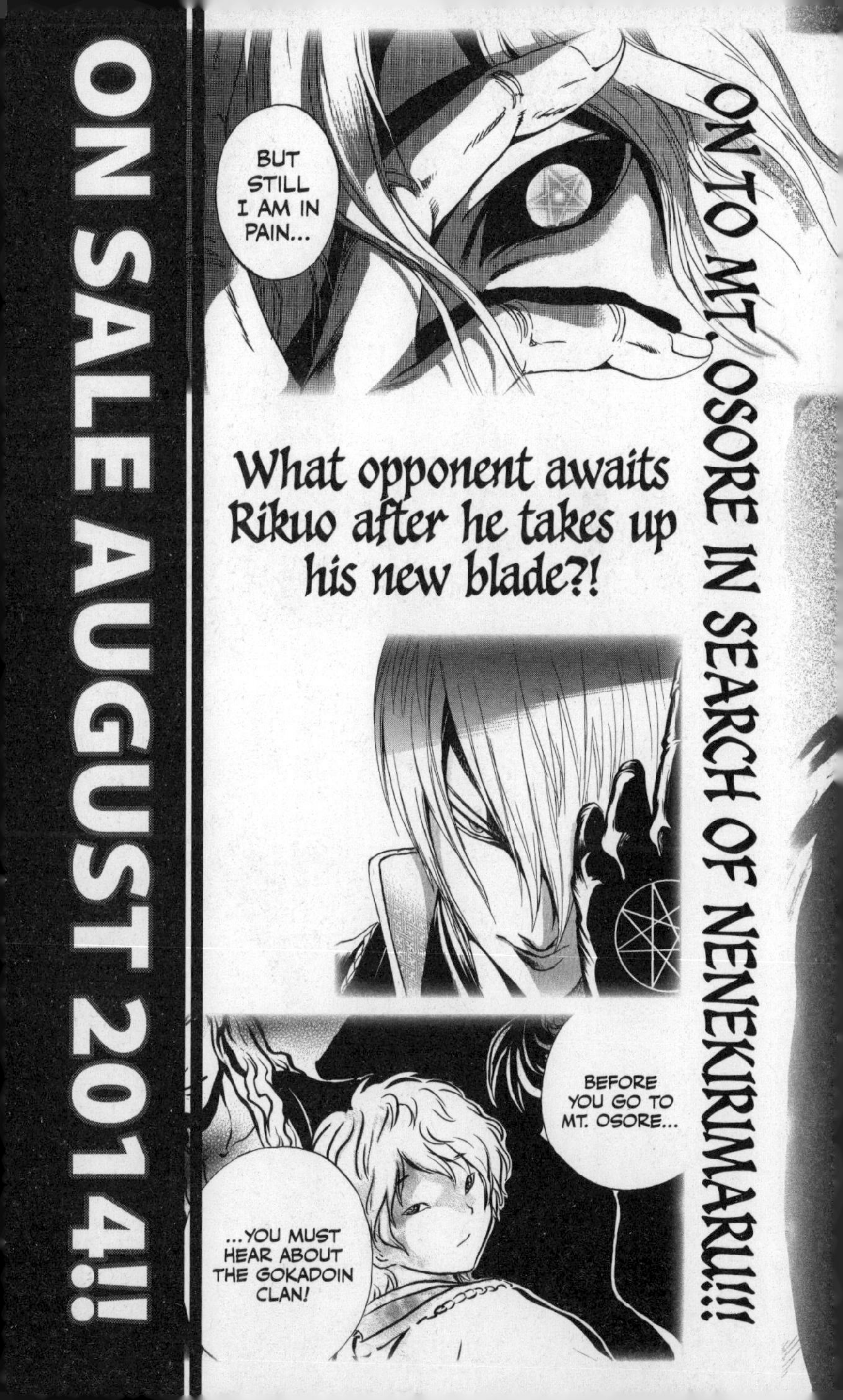
ON TO MT. OSORE IN SEARCH OF NENEKIRIMARU!!!
BUT STILL I AM IN PAIN...
What opponent awaits Rikuo after he takes up his new blade?!
BEFORE YOU GO TO MT. OSORE...
...YOU MUST HEAR ABOUT THE GOKADOIN CLAN!
ON SALE AUGUST 2014!!

BONUS STORY KANA IENAGA VS THE SHOPLIFTING G-MAN

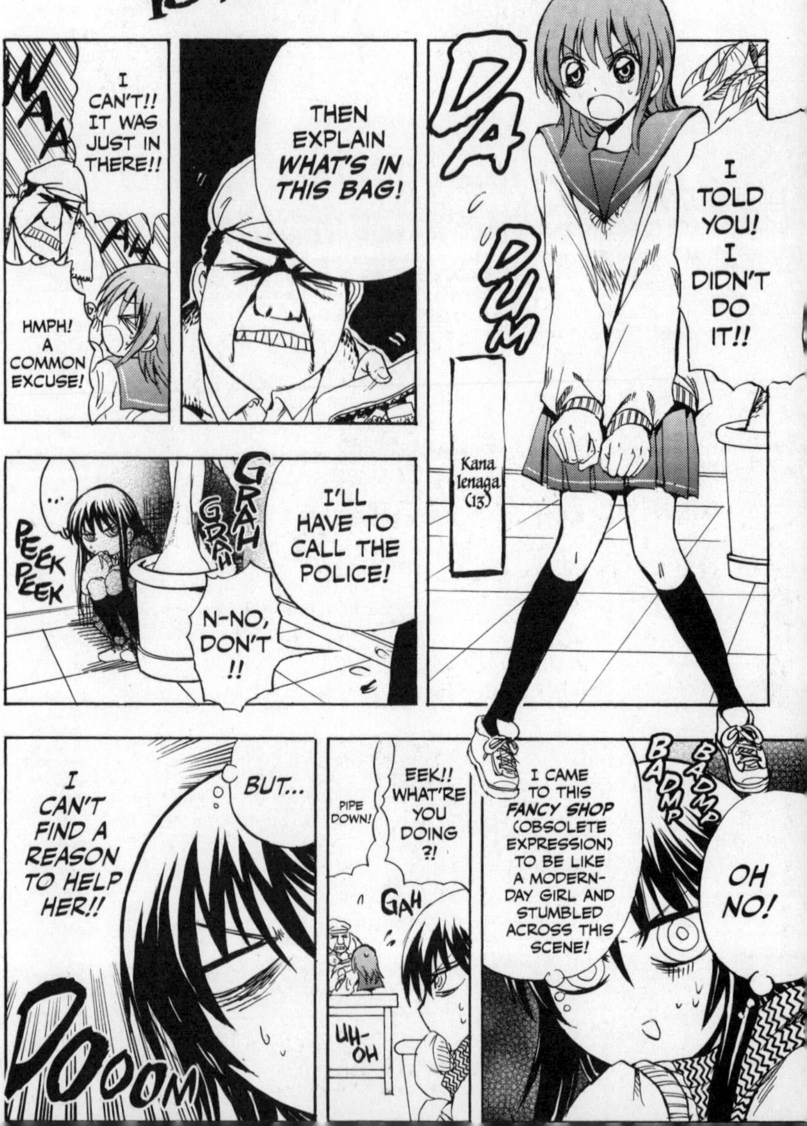
DA
DUM
I TOLD YOU! I DIDN'T DO IT!!
Kana Ienaga (13)
THEN EXPLAIN WHAT'S IN THIS BAG!
I CAN'T!! IT WAS JUST IN THERE!!
WAA
AA
HMPH! A COMMON EXCUSE!
GRAH
GRAH
I'LL HAVE TO CALL THE POLICE!
N-NO, DON'T!!
...
PEEK PEEK
BADMP
BADMP
OH NO!
I CAME TO THIS FANCY SHOP (OBSOLETE EXPRESSION) TO BE LIKE A MODERN-DAY GIRL AND STUMBLED ACROSS THIS SCENE!
EEK!! WHAT'RE YOU DOING?!
PIPE DOWN!
GAH
UH-OH
BUT...
I CAN'T FIND A REASON TO HELP HER!!
DOOOOM

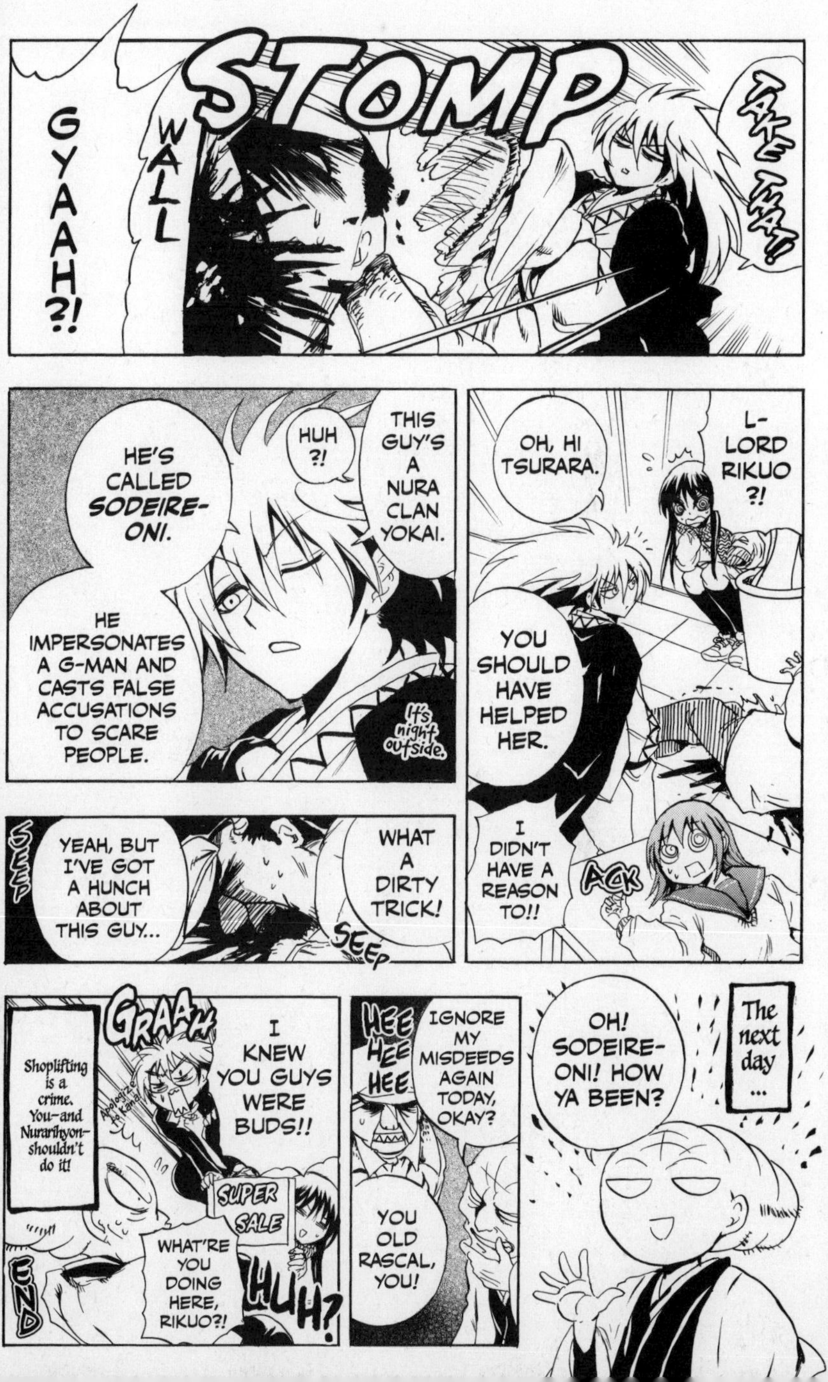
TAKE THAT!
STOMP
WALL
GYAAAH?!
L-LORD RIKUO?!
OH, HI TSURARA.
YOU SHOULD HAVE HELPED HER.
I DIDN'T HAVE A REASON TO!!
ACK
THIS GUY'S A NURA CLAN YOKAI.
HUH?!
HE'S CALLED SODEIRE-ONI.
HE IMPERSONATES A G-MAN AND CASTS FALSE ACCUSATIONS TO SCARE PEOPLE.
It's night outside.
WHAT A DIRTY TRICK!
YEAH, BUT I'VE GOT A HUNCH ABOUT THIS GUY...
SEEP
SEEP
The next day...
OH! SODEIRE-ONI! HOW YA BEEN?
IGNORE MY MISDEEDS AGAIN TODAY, OKAY?
HEE HEE HEE
YOU OLD RASCAL, YOU!
GRAAAH
I KNEW YOU GUYS WERE BUDS!!
Apologize to Kana!
SUPER SALE
WHAT'RE YOU DOING HERE, RIKUO?!
HUH?
Shoplifting is a crime. You—and Nurarihyon—shouldn't do it!
END

A Spring Storm of Image Changes, Final Chapter
~New Encounters~

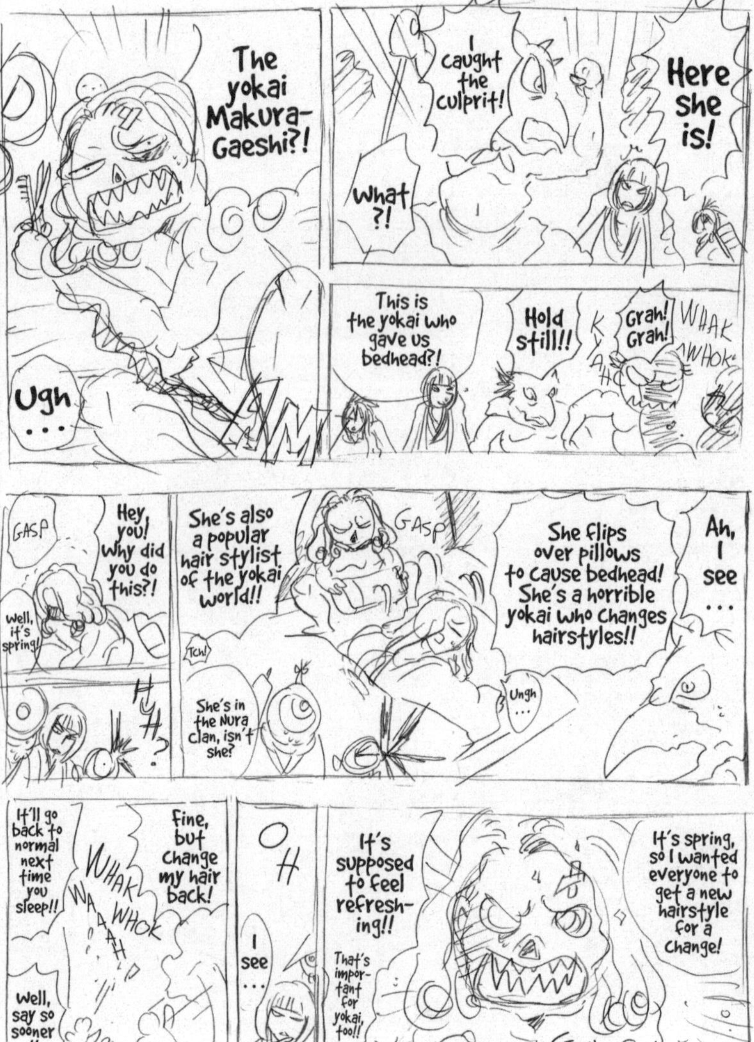
Here she is!
I caught the culprit!
What?!
Grah! Grah!
WHAK WHOK
KYAAHH
Hold still!!
This is the yokai who gave us bedhead?!
The yokai Makura-Gaeshi?!
Ugh...
Ah, I see...
She flips over pillows to cause bedhead! She's a horrible yokai who changes hairstyles!!
Ungh...
GASP
She's also a popular hair stylist of the yokai world!!
Tch!
She's in the Nura clan, isn't she?
Hey, you! Why did you do this?!
GASP
Well, it's spring!
HUH?
It's spring, so I wanted everyone to get a new hairstyle for a change!
GRAH
It's supposed to feel refreshing!!
That's important for yokai, too!!
I see...
OH
Fine, but change my hair back!
WHAK WHOK
WAAAH
It'll go back to normal next time you sleep!!
Well, say so sooner!!

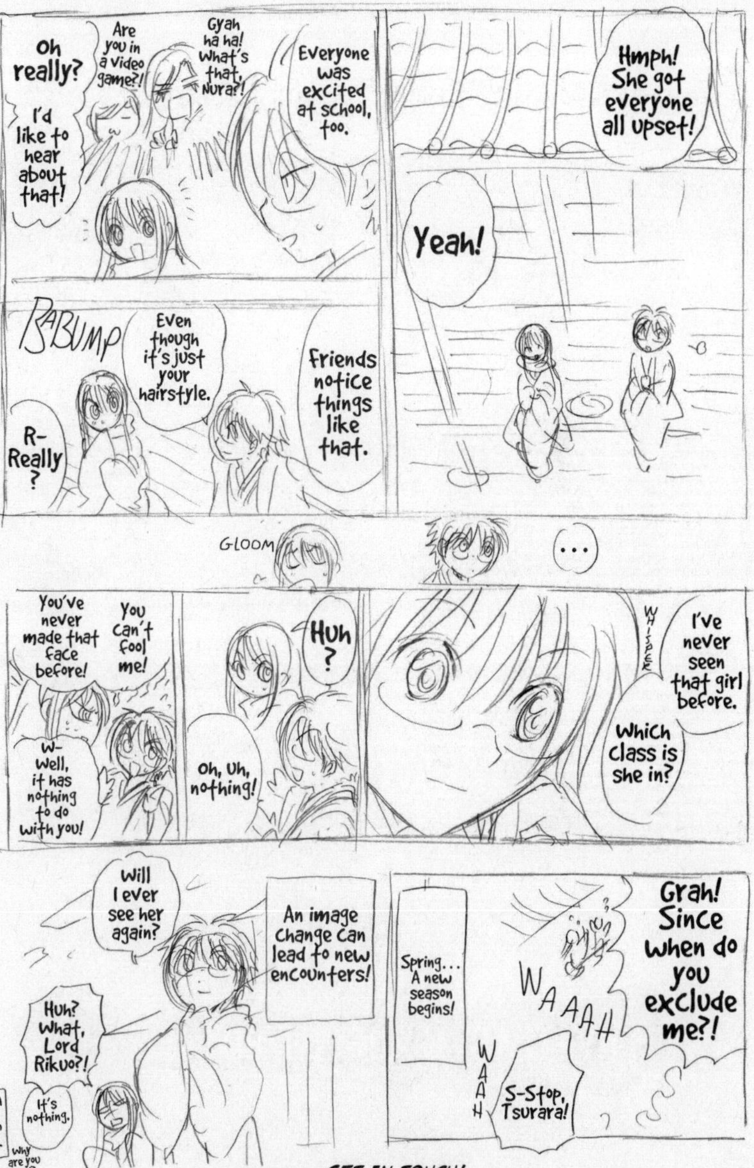
Hmph! She got everyone all upset!
Yeah!
Everyone was excited at school, too.
Gyah ha ha! What's that, Nura?!
Are you in a video game?!
Oh really?
I'd like to hear about that!
Friends notice things like that.
Even though it's just your hairstyle.
BABUMP
R-Really?
...
GLOOM
WHISPER
I've never seen that girl before.
Which class is she in?
Huh?
Oh, uh, nothing!
You can't fool me!
You've never made that face before!
W-Well, it has nothing to do with you!
Grah! Since when do you exclude me?!
WAAAH
WAAH
S-Stop, Tsurara!
Spring... A new season begins!
An image change can lead to new encounters!
Will I ever see her again?
Huh? What, Lord Rikuo?!
It's nothing.
The End.
Why are you mad?

GET IN TOUCH!

MAILING ADDRESS: NURA EDITOR
VIZ MEDIA
P.O. BOX 77010
SAN FRANCISCO, CA 94107

PLEASE INCLUDE YOUR NAME, AGE, ADDRESS AND PHONE NUMBER IN THE LETTER. IF YOU DO NOT WANT TO INCLUDE YOUR NAME, PLEASE USE A HANDLE OR NICKNAME. LETTERS AND ILLUSTRATIONS MAILED TO US WILL BE STORED FOR A CERTAIN PERIOD, THEN DISCARDED. IF YOU WISH TO KEEP A COPY, PLEASE MAKE ONE YOURSELF BEFORE MAILING IT IN. IF YOU'D LIKE TO HAVE YOUR NAME AND ADDRESS REMAIN ANONYMOUS, PLEASE INDICATE THAT IN YOUR LETTER.

IN THE NEXT VOLUME...
PURIFICATION

The battle against Nue heats up as Rikuo and members of the opposing clans move to Mt. Osore, a holy mountain where spirits of the dead are called into battle. Will a reforged Nenekirimaru, the renowned yokai-killing blade, work to defeat the legions of the undead?

AVAILABLE AUGUST 2014!